# Degrees of Empire

## NONCITIZEN STUDENTS AND THE MAKING OF US HIGHER EDUCATION

*Abigail Boggs*

FORDHAM UNIVERSITY PRESS  NEW YORK  2027

A portion of the introduction appeared as "Noncitizen Student," in *University Keywords*, ed. Andy Hines (Johns Hopkins University Press, 2025). Reprinted by permission of Johns Hopkins University Press.

Portions of Chapter 1 appeared as "Educational Pasts, Enduring Colonial Presents: Indigenous Student Conscripts and the Foundation of the US University," in *History of the Present* 12, no. 2 (2023). Reprinted by permission of Duke University Press.



Fordham University Press also publishes its books in a variety of electronic formats. Some content that appears in print may not be available in electronic books.

Visit us online at www.fordhampress.com.

For EU safety/GPSR concerns: Mare Nostrum Group B.V, Doelen 72, 4831 GR Breda, The Netherlands, gpsr@mare-nostrum.co.uk

Library of Congress Cataloging-in-Publication Data available online at https://catalog.loc.gov.

Printed in the United States of America

29 28 27 5 4 3 2 1

First edition

## Contents

## Preface

### *On Present Conditions: Trump's Promises and the Noncitizen Student*

In the opening weeks of Donald Trump's second presidential term, a surprising figure seemed to be centrally in the administration's crosshairs: the noncitizen student. When Trump returned to the White House on January 20, 2025, he quickly signed a barrage of twenty-six Orwellian Executive Orders (EO) on matters ranging from a regressive and scientifically inaccurate definition of how bodies are sexed to an effort to end diversity, equity, and inclusion policies, and an unconstitutional retraction of birthright citizenship.[1] Making good on his campaign promises, Executive Order 14161, "Protecting the United States from Foreign Terrorists and Other National Security and Public Safety Threats," set out a program to "protect Americans" through a "vigilant" visa-issuance process to identify persons who "bear hostile attitudes" toward the United States and its "citizens, culture, government, institutions, or founding principles" or "support designated foreign terrorists and other threats to our national security" "before their admission."[2] This is to be accomplished, according to the EO, by vetting and screening all potential visitors as well as those already present in the country, with a focus on "aliens coming from regions or nations with identified risks." The order goes on to make specific reference to two sections of the Immigration and Nationality Act that spell out "classes of aliens ineligible for visas or admission" based on criminalized acts or "security and related grounds," including "terrorist activities" and activities that "the Secretary of State has reasonable ground to believe would have potentially serious adverse foreign policy consequences for the United States." Moving beyond individuals granted visas, section (e) of the order calls for the "devotion of adequate resources to identify and take appropriate action for offenses described in 8 U.S.C. 1451," which prescribes the legal terms for the "revocation of naturalization."

Nine days later, as the onslaught of EOs continued, the White House published Executive Order 14188, "Additional Measures to Combat Anti-Semitism." This EO makes explicit the subtext of 14161, tethering its concern regarding monitoring students directly to supposed efforts to "hold to account the perpetrators of unlawful anti-Semitic harassment and violence" and reinvigorating an EO from Trump's first administration that folded the International Holocaust Remembrance Alliance's definition conflating anti-Semitism with critiques of Israel into the legal interpretation of Title VI of the Civil Rights Act of 1964.[3] As various commentators noted at the time, the choice to release this as order "14188" was a clear dog whistle belying any genuine commitment to anti-Semitism, given the number 14's reference to a popular white supremacist slogan and 88's use as a code "Heil Hitler."[4] A press release from the President's Alliance on Higher Education and Immigration, a nonpartisan, nonprofit organization composed of over 550 US college and university presidents, opines that the executive order "does not make immediate changes to existing law and policies."[5] Instead, it directs the attorney general and the secretaries of state, education, and homeland security to produce "recommendations for familiarizing institutions of higher education with the grounds for inadmissibility" so that they may "monitor for and report activities by alien students and staff."[6] As such, despite its inflammatory language targeting "pro-jihadist protests," on a fundamental level, the EO reiterates standing law that, as the President's Alliance writes, "mandates that student visa holders in the U.S. face potential deportation if they engage in criminal activity." Given the lack of clarity regarding how the EO would be implemented, the President's Alliance simply committed to monitoring developments.

Many political commentators and higher education experts expressed surprise at the targeted attack on noncitizen students these EOs promised and the offensive they presaged both on students and on the universities that host them. Yet, these executive orders are consistent with tactics employed, albeit less successfully, during the first Trump administration, the increasingly authoritarian rhetoric Trump used on the campaign trail from 2023 to 2024, and the cynical partisan strategies laid out in the Heritage Foundation's *Project 2025*, which proved to be the roadmap for the administration's political onslaught against higher education.

In mid-October 2023, then-former president and presidential candidate Donald Trump revived and intensified his well-rehearsed anti-immigrant rhetoric. As Israel Defense Forces rapidly expanded their aggressive onslaught on Gaza in the destructive first stage of their genocidal campaign of retribution and expropriation, Trump turned his sights on noncitizen students protesting in solidarity with the Palestinian people, whom he called "pro-Hamas protestors." Specifically, he threatened to "revoke the visas of foreign students who are 'antisemitic'" through "strong ideological screening."[7] Under his second administration, he vowed to impose an increasingly broad scope of elimination: "if you want to abolish the state of Israel, you're disqualified, if you support Hamas or the ideology behind Hamas, you're disqualified, and if you're a communist, Marxist, or fascist, you are disqualified."

In the spring, as student protestors galvanized to erect protest encampments across over 170 campuses globally, Trump's threats continued and the violent repression of student activists escalated on campuses from coast to coast.[8] On April 18, Columbia University President Minouche Shafik allowed the New York City Police Department onto campus for the first time since 1968. On April 30, NYPD arrested over one hundred protestors who participated in the occupation of a central campus building, which they renamed Hind Hall.[9] As part of the same operation, the NYPD also raided the encampment at the City College, working in close coordination with CUNY's "peace officer" force.[10] Just hours later, mobs of counterprotesters attacked the UCLA encampment with projectiles, bludgeons, and chemical sprays, while officers from the Los Angeles Police Department stood witness for hours before intervening.[11] In May, Trump's stump speech regularly included promises to deport students and assertions that when he returns to office, "we will not allow our colleges to be taken over by violent radicals."[12] "If you come here from another country," he continued, "and try to bring jihadism or anti-Americanism or antisemitism to campuses, we will immediately deport you."[13] In the swirl of accelerating protests and an increasingly aggressive crackdown on students and campuses tacitly allowed and frequently endorsed by Democratic politicians and avowedly progressive university administrators and boards of trustees, Trump's pronouncements were broadly acknowledged but rarely entertained as real threats to students, let alone to the institutions where they study.

Still, Republican politicians joined Trump's call. On May 9, 2024, Florida Senator Marco Rubio, who, in retrospect, may have been auditioning for his future role as secretary of state in Trump's second term, released a statement reporting that he had sent a letter to the US Department of Homeland Security Secretary Alejandro Mayorkas and Secretary of State Antony Blinken calling for the immediate revocation of visas for student protestors.[14] Invoking the government's responsibility and capacity to "track and monitor" both schools and the nonimmigrants who attend them through the Student and Exchange Visitor Program (SEVP) portal, he explains that people "in the country who espouse views in support of foreign terrorist organizations are in violation of their visa." Defying university or police orders "in favor of acting on pro-terrorist views" should, therefore, in his estimation, result in their "immediate expulsion from their host institution and our generous country."[15] Rubio presses on the responsibilities of colleges and universities to comply with federal requirements to report any student facing "disciplinary actions, termination and arrest," a reminder that failure to do so could result in the termination of the institution's ability to host future students.

Interestingly, however, before calling for the deportation of "non-compliant students," Rubio opens his missive with a more diplomatic message, acknowledging the long history of noncitizen students in the United States and the importance of their recruitment and education as a diplomatic tool. "For more than two centuries," Rubio remarks, "international students have attended American colleges and universities." He continues:

> They have learned, alongside Americans, the importance of the United States' culture and democratic system—and have brought those important ideals back to their home countries. The international study programs have served as an important diplomacy model, and will continue to do so. What cannot be tolerated, however, is for international students to violate the terms of their visa, and, especially, U.S. law.

Here, Rubio stresses the often unacknowledged but vital history of the presence of noncitizen students on US campuses, painting an unusually long historical imagination of this relationship and US colleges and universities more broadly. He also attends to the significant domestic and international roles noncitizen students have long played through their participation "alongside" US students in cultural and democratic education within the nation-state and their crucial role in exporting US frameworks abroad.

Just two weeks later, Trump also attenuated his hardline anti-noncitizen student rhetoric. On a podcast on May 20, 2024, he promised a Silicon Valley investor to address the desire to be able to "import the best and brightest around the world to America." This would be accomplished, Trump said, by granting a green card "automatically, as part of your diploma" to every noncitizen graduate of a US college, including two-year institutions.[16] The Trump campaign "walked back" the comment and reiterated the promise of an "aggressive vetting process" but left the door open to applying such a green card policy to the "most skilled graduates who can make significant contributions to America." Within a month, Elon Musk, the world's wealthiest man who was raised in apartheid South Africa and who had himself come to the United States on a student visa—the terms of which he violated by dropping out of school to start a company—threw the weight of his immense fortune behind Trump's campaign.[17]

While Trump's various declarations may feel new in their explicit, threatening tone, they are part of an architecture of recruitment and regulation targeting noncitizen students developed and employed by the US state over the last, as Rubio acknowledges, two centuries. When considered through the long history of this system's emergence and consolidation, what appear to be contradictions in Trump and his cadre's threats and promises to noncitizen students and the various stakeholders concerned with their presence in the United States are better understood as a calibrated, differentiated, and effective system for the conditional and temporally restricted incorporation of select noncitizen students enforced through the threat of deportation. Contextualizing this constellation of events as such opens the central questions with which this book is concerned: How to think and know the university, the state, and capital, their interests and their entanglements with each other, by reading them through their long-standing mutual investment in the recruitment, education, and management of nonwhite noncitizen students? And, how can approaching the study of US higher education through a history of the experiences of noncitizen students and the policies and politics that shape them provide new openings for what we do in and through these institutions in the present?

Even asking such questions troubles several prevalent and often contradicting doxa about US higher education—that it is an instrument of the state organized around the education and reproduction of the national citizenry, a tool and an iteration of corporate capital, a benevolent and neutral structure of opportunity and social uplift, or the font of liberal, radical, and/or leftist organizing and thought. Each story of the university and its purpose holds weight because it is backed by deeply ingrained discourses that register across popular, cultural, and political spaces. And, each can be bolstered by looking at policies directed at, stories told about, and the lived experiences of noncitizen students from specific and limited angles. But, thinking across the different uses of the university through the figure and figuration of the noncitizen student in an expansive, materialist, and historized way paints a far more nuanced and troubling picture of the interests, collaborations, conflicts, contradictions, and negotiations between the university, the state, and capital and their changes over time. Looking at this history from the perspective of the first months of the second Trump administration has, unfortunately, made its consequences for students and the institutions that host them all too clear. It also should allow those of us who remain concerned about and involved in the university to develop more strategic relationships with the institutions we relate to and help constitute.

Every empire . . . tells itself and the world that it is unlike all other empires, that its mission is not to plunder and control but to educate and liberate.

—EDWARD SAID, "BLIND IMPERIAL ARROGANCE,"
*LOS ANGELES TIMES*, JULY 20, 2003

# Introduction

## *Noncitizen Students and US Higher Education: A Genealogy of Empire*

This book provides a history of the underlying conditions of contemporary US higher education, surfacing the otherwise obscured entanglements and discrepancies of universities, the state, and capital as they emerge in the figure and figuration of noncitizen students.[1] It centers the noncitizen student in a reading of the university to, as Roderick Ferguson suggests, "re-know state and capital as interlocutors with rather than determinants of American university life."[2] Organizing such a study around the noncitizen student puts particular pressure on these relationships in that it necessarily denaturalizes the very categories of the university, the student, the state, capital, citizenship, race, and personhood through attention to the concrete historical processes of their creation, mutual constitution, recalibrations, and deployment.

Most accounts of noncitizen students in the United States start in the post–World War II era, centering on the Fulbright Program for international exchange. While I discuss Fulbright briefly in Chapter 6, this periodization fails to attend to how colleges and universities within what is now widely recognized as the United States have, since their inception in the British colonial period, wrestled with their status as settler colonial formations as they have sought to manage their relationships to students imagined as outside of their direct political community. This history of the present contends that the origins and operations of these institutions through to the late 1960s served a project of educating nonwhite noncitizen students to expel and export them as ambassadors for a specific set of logics, values, and technical capacities upon the completion of their education. In this way, they were to serve as "global agents" for what Thomas Jefferson imagined in the early nineteenth century as the United States' "empire of liberty."[3] The political conditions of the post–World War II era reconfigured this agenda as ideas about race morphed to meet the demand for a degree of inclusion and incorporation, and both university and immigration admissions policies became more formally open to nonwhite people, a shift discussed toward the end of this book. Even still, such inclusion was always predicated upon a set of requirements steeped in the differential valuation of ways of being and kinds of personhood aligned with American ideals of liberalism, capitalism, and whiteness. And, as the events of 2025 make clear, the fundamental logics of white settler liberalism remain prevalent in the most basic functioning of the US state, capital, and university system, marking the more racially inclusive moment of the late twentieth century as an aberration requiring its own analysis.[4]

The general meaning of the concept "noncitizen student" is in many ways self-explanatory. In scholarly, popular, and governmental texts, the students with whom this project is centrally concerned are often referred to as international or foreign students.[5] Rather than adopting this nomenclature, I use "noncitizen student" because of my central concern with how efforts to manage the lives of such students are organized around their relationship to the legal status of citizenship in ways that both valorize such a status and demonstrate its contingency. To write or think about the noncitizen student in the context of the US university is to consider the experiences and importance of students enrolled in US institutions of higher education who do not have the legal status of United States citizen and are, instead, present in the country on condition of acquiring and maintaining permission from the US state through the Student and Exchange Visitor Information System (SEVIS) and its primary form of documentation, the F student visa. As such, they do not have the legal and political rights of full membership in the community, including voting and holding public office, and can be subject to denial of entry and deportation by the state.[6] While the US Constitution formally extends protections such as due process and equal protection to "all persons," rather than just citizens, the challenges of gaining admission to the country and then the experiences of persistent monitoring and living under the threat of expulsion and future denial of entry mean that life in the United States is substantially restricted for students without US citizenship. The selective disregard of "due process" by the current US government makes this precarity even more material. These challenges are exacerbated for students racialized as nonwhite and those who have traveled from countries the US government considers threats to its security.[7]

In disciplines and fields such as American Studies, Asian American Studies, Latinx Studies, sociology, history, and immigration studies, scholars use the terms denizen, foreign-born person, alien, and noncitizen to mark the grouping of people who are in the United States without the status of citizenship.[8] A. Naomi Paik warns that the term noncitizen is imperfect in that it "defines a person by a status they lack and implicitly establishes citizenship as the norm."[9] I understand and appreciate this concern. Yet, tracing the convoluted and uneven history of how immigration law has conditioned the lives of students without US citizenship puts pressure on the certainty with which the category "citizen" itself is discussed, along with many of the analytical terms through which higher education, migration, and national politics are studied.[10] Understanding the processes and implications of the structured displacement of specific groups of people from what is presumed to be the "norm" of citizenship is a necessary aspect of contending with and contesting how such a status constrains the lives of myriad people it encompasses and the institutions, including the state and universities, with which they interact.

The term "noncitizen student" brings the study of higher education into conversation with the critical edges of immigration studies. And, importantly, such a framing stresses how the too often obscured and neglected experiences of noncitizen students, as well as institutional desire and need for them, fundamentally shape the history, practices, vulnerabilities, and politics of US universities and colleges. To study the US university with attention to noncitizen students requires grappling with the wide-ranging significance of the overlapping histories of higher education and immigration as tools of the state and capital in the international arena and in the very process of making and naturalizing the nation-state form.

The figure of the noncitizen student also highlights the fundamental contradictions that condition the importance of the status of citizen versus that of noncitizen. As scholars including Ferguson, Lisa Lowe, and Grace Kyungwon Hong argue, the relationship between the state and capital is organized around such a contradiction: the liberal state's expressed desire for a homogeneous citizenry to be treated equally and capital's desire for a heterogeneous, and thus differentially exploitable, workforce.[11] Yet, since the inception of the nation-state, there has been wide variability in how some citizens are substantively able to access and assume the existence of their rights as citizens, while others are denied any meaningful ability to make use of such rights. The real meaning of a person's status as citizen takes radically different forms across time, place, positionality, and relationship to the people and institutions responsible for allowing them to execute said rights. That is, the status of "citizen" offers few guarantees, especially for people whose ascribed racial, gendered, sexed, classed, and/or ability status allow the state and the people and systems that enact its policies to disqualify them from the entitlements the status of citizen confers through charges of criminality, dependency, or incapacity to self-govern.[12]

Nonetheless, for Lowe, Evelyn Nakano Glenn, and others, citizenship status itself has always been a crucial point of differentiation. There are different rights granted within the citizenry, but the starkest demarcation is between the citizen and the noncitizen. And, in many ways, the existence of and treatment of the noncitizen is precisely what enables the slippery slope of rights within the citizenry. Lowe is particularly concerned with how the Asian immigrant has surfaced as the paradigmatic figure for the "racialized and gendered *worker* alienated from citizenship."[13] It is not a coincidence, perhaps, that the majority of noncitizen students in the United States on visas to attend institutions of higher education are also from Asian countries. According to the Institute for International Education's 2024 *Open Doors Report*, 1,126,690 noncitizen students on visas were present in the United States during the 2023–2024 academic year. Of those, 805,238 students from countries in Asia constituted 71.5 percent of the noncitizen student population. India alone sent 331,602 students while China contributed 277,398, a significant decline from the country's all-time high in 2019 of 372,532.[14] Hong extends Lowe's argument, writing, "Asian migration to the United States is generated not only by the need for surplus labor within a domestic industrializing economy but also as residual effects of the United States' attempts to manage the pressures of a transnationalizing economy."[15] Despite efforts to present the university as domestically contained, the movement of noncitizen students makes clear that the university also shapes and is shaped by these pressures.

Noncitizen students, by definition, lack the rights of US citizens. They exist in a precarious position of exposure to the vicissitudes of immigration law, which permits a person to enter and remain in the country under specific and narrow conditions and leaves them vulnerable to the possibility of surveillance, scrutiny, detention, and deportation. Importantly, many noncitizen students are also workers in laboratories and classrooms—labor that is explicitly restricted by the terms of the student visa. At the same time, the status of noncitizen has been read as providing, at least for people with significant wealth, a flexible position—one allowing for freedom of movement across borders and spaces that can be augmented by a degree from a prestigious institution.[16] As the first months of Trump's second term demonstrate, the administrative architecture that has taken shape at the joint of the university and immigration policy places the noncitizen student in a position of unique opportunity *and* exposure as they are multiply recruited, registered, and tracked by the state and the university.

Many students who travel to US institutions for "the purposes of study" have been able to cross into the country with relative ease due to their status as white and because they travel from Western Europe or within the Western Hemisphere. For other students, however, the process can be much different. Policies meant to regulate the travel of noncitizen students have consistently targeted populations marked as racially and or culturally outside of the presumptive US norm of whiteness and Christianity, both for recruitment and for intense scrutiny or outright exclusion. In the late 1800s, this meant special scrutiny for Chinese would-be students; by the mid-twentieth century, Black students from the Caribbean and Africa; and since at least the 1970s, Arab and Muslim students. As such, this book addresses the specific importance of nonwhite noncitizen students to the US nation-state at different historical moments and the ways this has shaped their lives, the institutions they attend, and the policies the state imposed on both.

## Educate and Expel: Universities and Imperial Formation

What are the interrelated interests of capital and the state in nonwhite noncitizen students' movement and education, and how have their various agents in industry and philanthropy sought to further them? How might looking at the relationships of the state and capital to these students and the architecture of policy and funding built to manage them lay bare the entanglements of the state and capital with each other, their distinct interconnections with US universities, and the political, economic, and socially reproductive work institutions of higher education perform to the benefit of the United States as at once a governmental and an economic formation? What does doing so reveal about the function of borders for the United States' status as both a nation-state and an empire? And might such an approach enable a more robust, critical, and ideally generative understanding of the various investments of the state, capital, and US universities and colleges? Rather than collapsing the state and capital and assuming they use or work through the university toward the same ends, how can we disaggregate them? In doing so, what new insights might we gain, as participants in and critics of university life, that open onto new ways of being in and imagining different uses for the vast resources concentrated in these institutions?

*Degrees of Empire* grapples with these questions through a genealogical reading of universities, students, and knowledge, state, and economic formations from the initial founding of institutions of higher education in what became the United States through to the mid-1960s, tracking efforts to craft the country as a liberal settler nation-state and empire organized around (and organizing the idea of) whiteness. I trace how these institutions modulated to the terms of successive presents through the manipulation of two means of social reproduction operated in concert but rarely considered in parallel: higher education and immigration policy.[17] I refer to these as demographic levers, attentive to the emergence and application of statistical sciences of population management in and through the university from the late eighteenth century through to the present. Through the mid-1960s, institutions of higher education served the interests of the nation-state and its attendant empire through the temporary and conditional incorporation of nonwhite noncitizen students who were intended to leave the country after the completion of their education to function as ambassadors for US power and knowledge abroad. The goal was distinctly *not* to bring nonwhite people into the political community in any kind of lasting way—it was, instead, to educate and expel. It was only after 1964 that the modus operandi of this process shifted to allow for a more durational, though by no means expansive or unconditional, inclusion of a select few from among these students. While the opportunity to attain long-term permanent residency or even naturalized citizenship seems to provide some access to a more secure relationship with the nation-state and even membership in the political community, it provides no guarantee of security.

## The University, Empire, and Racial Capitalism

Taking the figure and figuration of the noncitizen student as the central object of analysis in a study of US higher education puts particular pressure on a fundamental conceit of the study of higher education and higher education institutions themselves—that the sector's primary purpose is, and always has been, the reproduction of an educated citizenry and labor force for a single nation-state from within its own population. As higher education historian Christopher Loss argues, during the Cold War, US policymakers invested in higher education as a global education strategy focused on the domestic sphere with the intention of cultivating "prosperous, civic-minded, psychologically adjusted democratic citizens worthy of special rights and privileges."[18] In an earlier era, he argues, "one of the major goals of the old-time denominational college, which dominated the nation's education landscape before the Civil War, was to train citizens for a life of public service in the new nation."[19] Tracing an even longer history of the contemporary university to the earliest era of British colonialism in the seventeenth century, Craig Steven Wilder illustrates that the work of these institutions was not just to support an existent empire, but to bring it into being through their function as "imperial instruments akin to armories and forts" and "as part of the colonial garrison with the specific responsibilities to train ministers and missionaries, convert Indigenous peoples and soften cultural resistance, and extend European rule over foreign nations."[20]

Since its publication in 2013, Wilder's work has been widely influential, pushing the field of higher education studies and higher education institutions themselves to contend with their pasts as they were fundamentally enabled through a mode of accumulation built on the labor and lives of enslaved people from Africa. However, less attention has been paid to Wilder's discussion of how the earliest colleges and universities in the United States—namely Harvard, William & Mary, and Dartmouth—secured both land and funding through the assertion of a mission to directly educate Indigenous students.[21] Wilder's recognition of this mission highlights how the university's work in producing and then reproducing the nation has aimed to assimilate noncitizens not only to the nation, but to the imperial project that undergirds it. Sandy Grande extends Wilder's argument with her theorization of the academy "as *an arm of the settler state*—a site where the logics of elimination, capital accumulation, and dispossession are reconstituted."[22] For instance, as discussed in Chapter 1, Harvard's Charter of 1650 required the school to "educate the English and Indian youth of this country in knowledge and godliness." Many scholars trace William & Mary's history to efforts as early as 1612 to found a university to take Indian children and "traine them up with gentlenesse, teach them our English tongue, and the principles of religion."[23] While few Indigenous students attended any of these institutions during the British colonial period, the histories Wilder surfaces show that the institutions themselves were both materially and epistemologically organized around the domination of Indigenous peoples and lands. Today, these efforts can be read as a central technique through which colonial forces attempted to implement assimilation as a mode of elimination. This eliminative mode fostered accumulation in two ways: through the dispossession of land and through the incorporation of Indigenous youth into British culture and knowledge systems.[24] The Harvard and William & Mary charters predate the founding of the United States, so the students were, of course, not "noncitizens." Still, they were definitively youth from polities other than that of their instructors and their benefactors. Their inclusion was unquestionably crucial to the founding missions, early funding, literal foundation-building, and fundamental knowledge of these institutions.

These cases make clear that people who do not belong to the governing polity most directly tied to educational institutions have never been wholly excluded from them. Just the opposite is true. "Foreign" students, or what I refer to here as noncitizen students, were central to the missions and actual function of many of the most prestigious higher education institutions in the United States from their very inception. That the student is not necessarily a citizen does not put into question the fact that institutions of higher education have long served the needs and interests of the empire, often underwritten with a Christian mission and in alignment with the development of capitalism. Rather, efforts to educate, convert, and "civilize" Indigenous students illustrate the deep history of students being selected and conditionally incorporated, whether that be through their education as potential future citizens, as future and current laborers, or as ambassadors-in-training who will, it is assumed, return to their homes and proselytize their communities in the ways of their educators.[25]

As Chapter 4 explores, by the mid-nineteenth century, new federal immigration laws and ideas about citizenship had emerged as the US economy and government reorganized after formal emancipation. Public, state-supported universities expanded significantly, tasked with developing knowledge projects to expand the means of capital accumulation and funded by the 1862 Morrill Land Grant Act, which distributed lands expropriated from tribal nations as "seed money for higher education."[26] While state and Christian boarding schools for Indigenous youth notoriously proliferated during this period, the new colleges and universities were generally not open to their enrollment. At the same time, exclusionary laws barring Chinese immigration through a broadly conceived ban on Chinese laborers included exemptions for categories of people of particular use for capital, including "merchants" and individuals traveling "for the purpose of study." As Madeline Hsu argues, this did not mean that would-be Chinese students crossed into the United States with ease. Rather, Chinese students were frequently detained and subjected to invasive medical exams and intense scrutiny of their travel documents.[27] That students remained technically exempt from the otherwise intensifying regime of racialized US immigration restrictions is a testament to the value governmental officials and industrial leaders saw in their education.

With a brief deviation in 1921, which anchors Part II, students have remained an exceptional category in US immigration through to the present. But the ways they are recruited, monitored, regulated, and policed have only intensified. Throughout the twentieth century and into the present, programs organized and funded by state, religious, and corporate philanthropic organizations made possible a pattern of recruitment of students from regions of the world otherwise excluded or severely restricted by US immigration law because students were imagined as "potential instruments of U.S. national power."[28] For instance, Part III considers how, from the late 1940s into the 1960s, programs recruited students from decolonizing countries in Africa and Asia that US forces saw as susceptible to communism. Such programs facilitated the US education and movement of former students including United

Nations Secretary-General Kofi Annan, the father of the United States' 44th president Barack Obama Sr., the parents of Vice President Kamala Harris, and prestigious university faculty such as Mahmood Mamdani and Gayatri Spivak, who is featured in the photo on the cover of this book, which was taken as part of a photo shoot for the 1963 *Newsweek* article upon which Part III and the conclusion are organized. Such students were in the middle of a "mini cold war for students" based on "the full realization that an international exchange of students can be an immense source of good will [*sic*] and propaganda."[29] By 1962, John W. Gardner of the Carnegie Corporation led a presidential commission that established the exchange of students as "a basic ingredient of the foreign relations of the U.S.," making clear that the interdependency of universities and the state exceeds the nation's borders and its population.[30]

## Educating Noncitizens for Empire: Universities and Imperial Thinking

*Degrees of Empire* works to account for the function of higher education in the United States' historical trajectory as a fractured empire, continuously under pressure and continuously in process. As Edward Said argued in 2003, the United States, like other empires organized around the conceits of liberalism and freedom, assures itself and "the world that it is unlike all other empires, that its mission is not to plunder and control but to educate and liberate."[31] Said wrote these words just months after the United States military invaded Iraq, as universities and scholarly production more broadly aligned themselves with the resurgent and expansionist nationalism demanded by the "War on Terror."

Only a few years earlier, however, to ask after the meaning of the university for the state and capital, there was a single text one had to engage with: Bill Readings's 1996 *The University in Ruins*. There, Readings polemically contends that because the historical raison d'être of the modern Western university has been tethered to "the national cultural mission," the post–Cold War decline of the nation-state has resulted in the university becoming a "different kind of institution, one no longer linked to the destiny of the nation-state by virtue of its role as producer, protector, and inculcator of an idea of national culture."[32] In forwarding this line of argument, Readings was in sync with work emerging from the critical, leftist edges of higher education studies by scholars such as Sheila Slaughter, Larry Leslie, and Gary Rhoades. Slaughter's now canonical collaborative work forwarded a thesis that "the restructuring of public education has paralleled" the economistic neoliberal turn in the state.[33] In arguing that capitalism had essentially triumphed over the nation-state form, Readings and Slaughter and her coauthors were part of a much larger theoretical wave that decried not just the end of the nation-state but also the effective end of history. Readings described this as a process of Americanization whereby "the generalized imposition of the rule of the cash-nexus" comes to replace "the notion of national-identity."[34] In other words, for these scholars, both the university and the state were subsumed by capitalist logics, desires, and modes of organizing the world.

During the same period, scholars in American Studies and adjacent fields were asking related questions about the status of the nation-state in the post–Cold War era, but their thinking was more historical and more encompassing of matters of culture, albeit read through and in relation to the economic and the material process of state-making. In the subtitle of her field-redirecting 1993 chapter "Left Alone with America," Amy Kaplan pointedly asks about "the absence of empire in the study of American culture." She does so to disrupt the "still resilient paradigm of American exceptionalism," spurring various lines of study often called transnational, postcolonial, or subaltern American Studies.[35] The resilience of the exceptionalist paradigm is predicated, in part, on the pervasive idea that the United States' revolutionary past somehow negates the existence of a coextensive imperial past, or the present or future possibility of empire-building, as well as the violences attendant to them all. It is also based on a presumption of the neutrality, benevolence, and universality of the American iteration of liberalism's theoretical vision and its claims to civilization and progress. Immigration and the university each figure centrally in narratives of this kind of America as "a nation of immigrants" and educational meritocracy. Yet, as this book argues, they often did so by working with and through each other in the service of a functionally, if not nominally, imperial vision of the United States.

As Said's statement above illustrates, in the aftermath of the events of September 11, 2001, the confidence with which the nation-state's power had been disavowed was roundly undone. Scholars in American Studies and those who work and think about the university became increasingly interested in the imperial and nationalistic function of the university as an arm of the state. For instance, Sunaina Maira and Piya Chatterjee write in the introduction to their edited collection *The Imperial University*, "the War on Terror and the post-9/11 culture wars made hypervisible the *persistent* role of higher education in shaping the discourses of nationalism, patriotism, citizenship, and democracy."[36] This research built on leading scholars of postcolonial thought, such as Said and Gayatri Spivak, whose insights were shaped by their own travel to the United States as students in the mid-century, regarding the imbrications of the university as a site of nationalist training and authoritative epistemological production. However, in Maira and Chatterjee's effort to recenter the nation-state and questions of nationalism, there is a tendency to collapse the pedagogies of nationhood, specifically the imperial nation, with the pedagogies of neoliberal capitalism, assuming an easy alignment between the two. Teasing out these distinctions was not their project, but in the current moment of resurgent and recalcitrant white ethnonationalism working in concert and conflict with capital, when questions of the role of the university and its future are as pressing as ever, it seems necessary to think through the continuities and discontinuities between state and capital interests in both universities and students. A central contention of this project is that one generative avenue for doing so is to think through the specific representations of and efforts to manage nonwhite noncitizen students.

If the burgeoning transnational, multicultural America of the 1990s gave urgency to Kaplan's argument, the resurgent and expanding "race realism" of white Christian ethnonationalism in the present requires expanding Maira and Chatterjee's insights to directly articulate the racial project that underwrites US empire today. As Moon-Ho Jung argues, "The United States was and is an empire. White supremacy has fueled and justified that empire, even as liberal claims to universal citizenship have obscured that history of violence."[37] In making this assertion, Jung is careful to mark that he means to disrupt rather than reproduce "a teleology that posits nation against empire."[38] This is evident, as he suggests, in none other than Thomas Jefferson's invocation of the United States as an "empire of liberty." Paul Kramer's writing on the articulated histories of empire and efforts to manage migration through both exclusion and exemption is especially crucial for this project. Empire, in his estimation, was not only made possible by race and racialist logics of difference, but "remade difference" in its various processes of instantiation and solidification.[39] Empire, that is, required and made possible innovative ways to calibrate and exercise hierarchies of humanity, especially in its use of immigration as a selective sieve.

Building on these analyses, this book explores the place of the university as a concrete entity and site of production for the constitutively racist and white supremacist imperial logics of conquest and possession. The production and modulation of racialized difference substantiates who can be recognized as a person, individual, and citizen. And the economic formations that emerge are both deeply imbricated with, and productive of, an assemblage of racial formations, gendered performances, naturalized sex categories, criteria for able-bodiedness, and assumptions of proper sexual desire in their organization and rationalization of daily life. The university plays a crucial role in this process.

As the institution claims a position of universal authority over the liberal arts of the humanities and scientific knowledge, it also develops, authorizes, and refines the knowledges that underwrite the state's organization and function.

Taking seriously these readings of the United States as an empire organized through ideas of American exceptionalism has several implications for the study of US higher education. Consider the nomenclature of the university and its direct etymological tie to the notion of universality, and its grounding curriculum, the liberal arts. The notion of US higher education's exceptionalism underwrites the idea that the colleges and universities are also neutral or benevolent in their work to gestate, authorize, and disseminate frameworks of thought, including the professed universality of liberal political theory and what Uday Mehta describes as "its systematic and sustained political exclusion of various groups and 'types' of people."[40] Indeed, this exclusion, in Mehta's reading of John Locke, is exercised in part through assessing different types of people according to "Measures of Civility" that can only be attained through "immersion in 'good Company,'" which provides an education initiating individuals into "the enormously significant specifications of time, place, and social status."[41] These systemic exclusions were a crucial component of the rise of the nation-state form as it relied on a restricted and rationalized popular sovereignty to demarcate a citizenry constitutive of and represented in state power. When read as an instrument for the making of the nation, the university can be seen as a technology for cultivating and conscripting the nation's population and for germinating and authorizing the knowledge necessary to secure and extend this project.[42] Such knowledge frequently came down to two primary and intertwined agendas. First, calculating the composition of the population, assessing the ideal composition and organization to meet the nation-state's leaders' primary goals, and planning ways to produce and reproduce such a state of being. This would include how a desired population could be produced and how to conceptually and physically manage resources, especially people and land. Hence, the early entry of both demography and engineering as central disciplines of the US university, as is discussed in Chapter 2.

Conventional thinking in higher education studies typically reads internationalization as the "strategies by which colleges and universities respond to globalization," which itself is taken to be a twentieth-century phenomenon.[43] At times, internationalization is given a more narrow periodization, as when Philip Altbach—the founding director of Boston College's Center for International Higher Education—and Hans de Wit deemed 1990 to 2015 "the era of higher education internationalization."[44] In response, Sharon Stein argues that while much of this work frames internationalization as "a neutral and inevitable response to contemporary patterns of globalization," critical scholars in education studies "increasingly problematize the overwhelmingly positive and depoliticized approaches to internationalization that tend to dominate in universities, and identify the continuation of enduring patterns of Eurocentric knowledge production, exploitative relationships, and inequitable access to resources."[45] Further still, she argues elsewhere for the need to account for the manifold ways the "inequities and injustices" of present-day universities are an extension of the deep foundational entanglement of these very institutions and the "logics, relations, and infrastructures of racial-colonial capitalism."[46] When Indigenous peoples' claims to sovereignty are taken as fact, it is necessary to grapple with how these foundational entanglements might themselves be thought of as something akin to an instance of internationalization at the very origins of higher education on the land currently claimed by the United States and how this "internationalization" was itself a process of nation-making in which the nation was secured within and through such relations.[47] As such, studies of higher education must contend with British colonial and other projects to educate Native youth as a foundational component of the history of US institutions of higher education and their fundamental internationalism as they facilitated and depended upon the movement of students across national borders and between sovereign polities for the purposes of study.

This project turns to Manu Karuka's reading of the United States "not as a national entity, but an imperial one, an international cartel that supplies a framework for coordination among major monopolist trusts."[48] Indeed, well before the mid-1960s, where this book concludes its historical arc, noncitizen students were primarily recruited to the United States, or British colonial education institutions, for their temporary presence and then eventual export, ideally with a glowing image of their educator's way of organizing life, locked into kinds of political and technical knowledge that would shape the economies of their home countries. This model is often thought of as one of diplomacy or foreign affairs, but it might more accurately be described as one of empire-building.[49] As such, their education figured into another key aspect of making and governing a nation-state: the production and management of borders as matters of geography and instances of often-militarized securitization. Geographically speaking, any student of US history and politics is aware that the borders of the US nation-state have never been static or as easy to locate and concretize as the drawing of maps and the building of walls would imply. This is evidenced by simply looking at the expanding map of territory claimed by the US government since its founding, or at the expansive array of US military installations around the world. Or at a map of US university outposts. The global reach of the United States as an entity is clearly drawn by a cartographic rendering of such institutions from the founding of the University of

Liberia in 1851, financed largely by the New York Colonization Society, to the American University of Beirut, initially chartered as the Syrian Protestant College in New York in 1863, through to New York University's current global network of campuses and centers on every continent except Antarctica.

## A Genealogy of Figures and Figurations

While there is much to be said about the implications of these questions for the contemporary university, this work is historically geared. It provides a history of our present conditions, tracing a genealogy of the relationship between institutions of higher education in what is now the political entity and territory of the United States from the early seventeenth century through to the mid-twentieth century. As Lisa Lowe describes, a genealogical approach refuses to take "given categories and concepts as fixed or constant," instead taking "as its work the inquiry into how those categories became established as given, and with what effects."[50] Each chapter dwells in a set of texts or stories that give form to the figure of the noncitizen student—at times with intention, and at others seemingly inadvertently—and then situates those texts in a broader historical context, synthesizing analyses of primary documents and more conventional historical readings of historical events, periods, and relationships, some more critical than others. Often, this means reading the figuration of students as historical characters told in the service of bolstering higher educational projects in the past and the present, from Caleb Cheeshateaumuck at Harvard in the 1660s, to the Catawba students held at William & Mary in the early 1700s, and Samson Occom's work with Eleazer Wheelock in the mid-eighteenth century, to ʻŌpūkahaʻia, often referred to as Henry Obookiah, at the Cornwall School (and at times by Yale), Wilbur Fisk Burns at Wesleyan, Yung Wing at Yale in the nineteenth century, and Nnamdi Azikiwe and Kwame Nkrumah at Lincoln University in the twentieth.[51] Throughout, I also consider how students are turned into the numerical figures of accounting and calculation required for the operation of demographic levers, turning to the ledgers the Brafferton Fund used to coordinate support for William & Mary, the census and quota charts of the late nineteenth and early twentieth centuries, and eventually the robust and influential International Student Census initiated by the Institute for International Education in the mid-twentieth century in partnership with the US Department of State.

I am primarily concerned with the formation of the categories, often within and through the work done on university campuses, that allow for the administration of lives lived in relation to the university, including shifting understandings of the citizen and the noncitizen and the student, and the ways logics of race, gender, religion, sex, sexuality, ability, and class come to shape them and take shape around them. Doing so entailed assembling an archive of thousands of governmental reports, statistical surveys, university documents, and popular press articles to be read alongside and through scholarly writing, particularly the work of critical historians of empire, race, power, and knowledge. The articulations, often autobiographical, of noncitizen students provide important historical evidence throughout—from Caleb Cheeshateaumuck's writings to Harvard's benefactors in the 1660s to the Cornwall School's publication of Henry ʻŌpūkahaʻia's memories as a fundraising tract in the 1810s, Yung Wing's reflections on his experiences as a student in the United States in the 1850s through to *Ghana: The Autobiography of Kwame Nkrumah*, a work that quite consciously collapses the nation-state and the individual, to interviews with students turned scholars, such as Gayatri Spivak. Reading each text for narrative and historical grounding and in their contradictions, placing each in the conjuncture in which it was produced and circulated, I take such writings as evidence and illustration, plumbing them, as Lowe suggests, for the "subjugated histories that inhabit" texts often taken to exemplify "individual rights and democratic freedoms."[52] As such, this work is both analytic and synthetic.

The stories told here do not attempt to provide an exhaustive compilation of the history of the noncitizen student and the colleges and universities in the United States. Instead, they reflect a constellation of flashpoints across and between the spheres of politics, economics, and culture. Following Michel Foucault's Nietzschean interest in the "will to knowledge," I take up the contention that "the instruments enabling us to analyze the will to knowledge will have to be made up and defined as we go along, according to the requirements and possibilities that are revealed by concrete studies."[53] This methodological approach enables what Foucault calls an "effective history" that "deals with events in terms of their most unique characteristics, their most acute manifestations" and, in the process, shows how "knowledge is not made for understanding; it is made for cutting."[54] This final phrase is usefully provocative in that it turns the work of study, research, and writing away from a search for singular origins and toward new ways of understanding the broader architecture of interests and relationships that condition the form and arrangement of the present. Following this impulse, I work outward from the concrete figure of the noncitizen student to locate this study at the interstices of university institutions, national imaginaries, state power, philanthropic organizations, and popular representations as they are crosshatched in and through each other.

This is, necessarily, not an exhaustive study of all of the different trajectories of student movement into and through the United States over this period.

There is a vast existing literature on specific institutions, historical periods, programs, and students. This book has a different project.[55] While the genealogical approach displaces a search for origins or even singular truths, it also provides a method of tracking discursive formations over "a vast accumulation of source material."[56] From within this vast accumulation, I pause in particular moments, or what Stuart Hall would call conjunctures and what Walter Benjamin's materialist approach to history describes as moments of crystallization, where a monad forms through which to observe "a constellation overflowing with tensions."[57] Each chapter takes up the figure and figuration of the noncitizen student in a given period of history and reads the ways the stories of the university, of immigration law, of the state, of capital, and their shared making of logics of personhood and difference take shape. As such, this project reflects what Lawrence Grossberg identifies as a basic premise of cultural studies' core method of conjunctural analysis—that its arguments will always be "partial and incomplete."[58] But this hopefully also opens the work to another aspect of this kind of thinking by inviting others to engage, critique, and extend some of the avenues of analysis it opens.

Throughout, this book works to implement the basic tenets of my collaborative work with Eli Meyerhoff, Zach Schwartz-Weinstein, and Nick Mitchell to theorize an abolitionist approach to the study of the US university.[59] Such an approach, we argue, highlights the "history and historicity of the university," making evident how universities exist "as complex terrains with many conflicting and intersecting modes of world-making," and, as this book argues more centrally, empire-making. Central to this approach is a consideration of how, as Mitchell and I argue, "there is no history of university that is not also a history of capital accumulation and capital expropriation."[60] To study the university in this way entails braiding the often-siloed histories of Indigenous dispossession, racial slavery, disciplinary formations, industrial innovation, diplomatic relations, racial logics, and state legal and political processes. The abolitionist mode of thinking we take up is deeply indebted to the Black radical tradition, Indigenous ways of knowing, and feminist thought, especially as they confront the foundational and enduring violences of masculinist settler racial capitalism while also struggling to think and build new kinds of relations and knowledge. When such an approach is applied to the study of the university, it is not an argument "for" or "against" the university as such. Instead, this book provides a genealogy of the university as a central technology of the United States' history, present, and potential future as empire, the work noncitizen students have done and are asked to do for its extension, and the ways these relations can open also onto empire's undoing.

## Outline of Book

The first section of the book, "Educate, Expropriate, and Export," looks to the earliest instances of higher education in what became the United States and their missionary-led projects for Indigenous education to consider their role in the cultivation of foundational ideas about and practices of what would become the university, Americanness, and whiteness. Such educational missions were organized around the dispossession of Indigenous lands, which underwrote the extraction of value through forced racial labor, and efforts to use education as a tool to export all nonwhite people from the domestic space. Through this export, Thomas Jefferson and other founding historical players imagined that racialized agents trained in liberalism's core logics of proprietary relationships to self, others, and land could, even or especially in their expulsion, function as instruments or even agents of an emergent form of US universalism. Chapter 1, "Native Students as 'Foreign Students' and the Foundation of the US University," looks to the histories of Harvard, William & Mary, and Dartmouth as key examples of such projects during the British colonial period. Chapter 2, "'Ridding America of these alien bodies' for the Empire of Liberty," turns to the pre–Civil War era and the American Board of Commissioners for Foreign Missions' Cornwall School for Native Youth. By the mid-nineteenth century, many colleges and universities, including newly founded historically Black institutions such as Lincoln University and small liberal arts colleges like Wesleyan University, where I currently teach, were educating students for the purpose of export.

Part II, "Empire's Educational Exemptions," contextualizes the exclusion of nonwhite noncitizen students enacted by the 1921 Emergency Quota Act, when students were briefly removed from what had been carved out as an exceptional category of inclusion within US immigration law. It turns to the post–Civil War era, and the attendant expansion of a federal administrative apparatus, organized in part around the development and expansion of institutions of higher education via the Morrill Land Grant Act of 1862 and the management of immigration, starting with the Anti-Coolie Act of the same year. These two efforts worked in tandem as tools for the management of land and other resources, the production of knowledge for the management of said resources and of a racially heterogeneous population, and the United States' relations with and ambitions toward other nation-states and empires—their territories, markets, and resources, human and otherwise. As the legal and infrastructural apparatus of immigration control took shape between the 1860s and 1920s, persons traveling for the purposes of study were granted special dispensation to move between polities, along with businessmen, ministers, and performers, since their exposure to and training in US-based ways of knowing was seen as beneficial to both the state and capital. Still, over the course of this period, Sinophobic anti-immigration organizers and politicians worked consistently to whittle down the meaning of the category student, eventually determining that the inclusion of students at all was simply, in the words of Congressman William Vaile, "too liberal."[61]

Chapter 3, "The Post-Emancipation University, Industry, Race, and International Politics," maps the expansion of US higher education after the Civil War, with a focus on the institutions funded by industrialists that incubated the race and population sciences of the time and underwrote the eugenic developmentalist international and immigration policy enacted by the US government. Chapter 4, "Open Doors, Yung Wing, and Immigration Law Before Exclusion," tracks the story of Yung Wing, the first Chinese student to graduate from a US university, the short-lived Chinese Education Mission, and the first efforts to restrict the movement of Chinese migrants into the United States. Chapter 5, "The Student Question in the Era of Exclusion," begins with the 1882 passage of the Chinese Restriction Act based on an argument that Chinese persons are a "distinct race" to trace iterative efforts to narrow the legal interpretations to effectively bar the entry of Chinese students into the country, culminating in the 1921 Emergency Quota Act.

Part III, "Education for a New Age of Empire," is organized around a close reading of a 1963 *Newsweek* magazine article entitled "Foreign Students: Diplomas and Diplomacy," which features the stories of noncitizen students from around the world, including the students on its cover and on the cover of this book, such as Mohammad Sa'aid and Gayatri Chakravorty, who is now much better known, especially within the academy, as Gayatri Chakravorty Spivak. Across two chapters, Part III situates the recruitment and education of nonwhite students from decolonizing polities in Asia and Africa as a key strategy through which both the US state and capital sought to reorganize racial logics and politics in the post–World War II era. As such, nonwhite noncitizen students were broadly understood as a key vector through which US empire could use the moment of decolonization to expand its reach. Chapter 6, "The State of the University and the University of the State After World War II," situates the post-1945 expansion of US governmental involvement in the recruitment of noncitizen students in relation to the rise of the Red Scare security state and the various legal mechanisms developed to manage the lives of noncitizens. Chapter 7, "The Lure of America: The Management of Difference and the 'African Student Problem,'" looks to how this history was fundamentally conditioned by a brief effort to use Black students from Africa as a tool to manage domestic race relations and international critiques of US anti-Blackness.

The book's conclusion, "The University Double Bind: The Imperial Model Minority and the Records We Keep," continues the thread from Part III through a sustained engagement with Gayatri Spivak's appearance in the *Newsweek* article as well as her relationship to and theorizations of the US university, through a discussion of the imperial model minority and the university double bind. Here, I reflect on a historical shift that occurred just on the outside of the period with which this book is concerned, when the terms of US citizenship and race were reorganized under neoliberalism in more nominally inclusive ways through the myth of the model minority and the Immigration and Nationality Act of 1965. At this moment, select noncitizen students, primarily, though not exclusively, those who would be categorized as Asian, increasingly came to shift the narrative from one of export after degree to conditional inclusion. This was possible, in part, because, as *Degrees of Empire* demonstrates, this version of incorporation into the university, the nation-state, and the empire had been rehearsed for several decades through the racial and global politics of the nonwhite noncitizen student.

# PART I

## *Educate, Expropriate, and Export*

In 2010, the Harvard Foundation "proudly unveiled" a portrait of Caleb Cheeshateaumuck, a member of the Wampanoag tribe and the only Native American student to graduate from the institution during the British colonial era. Cheeshateaumuck attended Harvard for four years and died shortly after his graduation in 1665. The director of the Harvard Foundation, S. Allen Counter, described the painting as part of a new initiative to commission portraits that "reflect the diversity of individuals who have served Harvard University for at least twenty-five years with distinction." He continued, the "addition of Cheeshateaumuck's portrait is especially significant because it speaks to Harvard's early establishment of the Harvard Indian College, and to its formal charter in 1650 for 'provisions that may conduce to the education of English & Indian youth of this Country in knowledge and godliness.'"[1] By incorporating his rather short-lived time at Harvard as tantamount to the twenty-five year service of others, Counter glosses over Cheeshateaumuck's relationship to the institution as student and the enduring impact of Harvard and its affiliates on the regional tribes. In so doing, he conscripts Cheeshateaumuck's memory in the service of illustrating a presumably benevolent historical relationship between Harvard and the Native peoples the institution's presence effectively displaced and attempted to negate.

Cheeshateaumuck's time at Harvard has come to be one of the best-known examples of the administrators of British colonial universities on the land now claimed by the United States enacting their oft-professed mission to bestow upon Indigenous peoples the "gift" of education and civilization. Institutional charters and tracts that functioned as fundraising materials from the seventeenth and eighteenth centuries articulate the ostensibly altruistic effort to spread Christian governance, values, literatures, and history to "heathen," "infidel" Natives—a mission that quite successfully garnered royal recognition, considerable land grants, and substantial donations. So trained, students were to absorb logics of individualism and property then return to their communities as exemplars of all that could be gained from British culture and Christian religious beliefs. The organization of and relationship to time—clock, calendrical, and world historical—were of particular importance to developing Puritan conceptions of education, personhood, and civilization in part because they organized new relationships to land as property that could be owned and foreclosed upon, a way of understanding that was in part imported from Europe and in part innovated as a new tactic of dispossession.[2] While most efforts to recruit and educate Indigenous students failed to achieve much success in terms of scale or duration, the imagined promise of such initiatives endowed settler colonists with the capital, authority, and land to establish and maintain several of what remain to this day the nation's most prestigious and well-resourced institutions of higher learning: Harvard, William & Mary, and Dartmouth.[3]

This project takes it as axiomatic that Indigenous peoples are sovereign political entities; as such, British colonial efforts to educate their youth were, by extension, explicitly counter-sovereign endeavors.[4] I make this assertion with an awareness that it can be misinterpreted as a simple reification of Western and white supremacist logics of statist power and structure. Following Indigenous scholars J. Kēhaulani Kauanui and Joanne Barker, I employ sovereignty as a "porous," embedded, and geographically and historically contingent term. In their theorizations, Indigenous sovereignty marks a set of embodied and relational dynamics prioritizing Indigenous self-determination. When read as such, British colonial efforts are counter-sovereign in that they were always structured, as Manu Karuka has argued, "in perpetual reaction to the prior and primary claims of Native people."[5]

Taking up this axiomatic, Part I expands the chronology and disrupts the geographic certitude through which "international education" and the history of US higher education have been discussed. Its central contention is somewhat straightforward: Colleges and universities in the British colonies and what became the pre-emancipation United States were founded and funded with the intention that they would function as a vital technology through which the nation-state, and white-Christian culture both before it and then through it, would reproduce and secure themselves, their possessions, and their futures. Tactically, this was to be accomplished through the assimilation, and at times temporary incorporation, of people, often youth, from polities understood as fundamentally other from their instructors and benefactors.[6] Assessments of the extent to which such visions materialized vary, but it is a historical fact that these institutions are rooted in colonial educational projects targeting Indigenous students. What it means to take the durational effects of this history on higher education in the present into account is less clear.

To fill the lacuna in existent studies of cross-polity education, Part I provides a genealogy of the ways colleges and universities attempted to operate in relationship to Native tribes as, to borrow Craig Steven Wilder's language, "a pillar of civilization" through which settlers consolidated, secured, and extended their power. I am not the first person to articulate this critique. However, previous scholarship that attends to this phenomenon, especially scholarship by Native writers, has been profoundly underappreciated, especially within higher education studies. In the late 1980s and early 1990s, for instance, Indigenous scholar of higher education Bobby Wright documented the multiple responses of Indigenous peoples to educational missions that "included genuine conversion, accommodation, intense theological debate and criticism, and finally violent opposition."[7] Yet, a failure to attend to this work and its implications in scholarly discussions of contemporary higher education has left intact a historical rendering of US universities that either entirely elides their role in the British colonial project or sanitizes it to the point of fictionalization. Reviving and extending Wright's reading of the role of Indigenous peoples in bringing about the failure of these projects disturbs reductive settler narratives by grappling with how the Indigenous people who attended or otherwise participated in these projects were not simply the pawns of colonial administrators but were instead, at least at times, willful participants with their own agendas. They were also, and quite consistently, agents of the projects' demise. Elevating this perspective works to trouble prevalent historical narratives that seek to disavow the present-day implications of this violent colonial legacy.[8]

Tracing these histories from Harvard to William & Mary to Dartmouth, Chapter 1, "Native Students as 'Foreign Students' and the Foundation of the US University," provides crucial insight into the development of a series of tactics of conditional, temporally delimited incorporation deployed against various Native peoples for the production, consolidation, and maintenance of the white settler state. The intention and manifestation of each iteration of "Indian education" was conditioned by the particular circumstances under which they took place, at times appearing to be guided by a Christian missionary impulse, at others more centrally by financial compulsion, eventually with a primary goal of cultivating something akin to soft power on behalf of a state-like formation. A desire to claim and control land as property underwrote each iteration. The architects of the various projects understood education and the work of the university as vital to shaping the future—to cultivating people, possessions, and relationships that could secure and extend the power and potential of white Christian culture and governance. Without exception, what was imagined by its supporters as a future-making project was predicated upon the cultural, social, and literal deaths of non-European students.

Chapter 2, "'Ridding America of these alien bodies' for the Empire of Liberty," covers the period between the 1810s and the 1860s, with particular attention to two institutions: the short-lived Cornwall School of Native Youth and Lincoln University. The history of these institutions, as well as the stories of and about noncitizen students that attended them from Hawai'i, the Cherokee Nation, and Liberia, is read in relation to Thomas Jefferson's advocacy for an empire of liberty and the expansion of a distinctly American form of higher education that first took shape under Jefferson's leadership at West Point. The sciences of engineering, demography, history, and race were especially important for this imperial project. The education and then expulsion of students who would otherwise be excluded from the status of United States citizen due to their racial identity or tribal affiliation served the goals of the empire of liberty. Through their education into white, liberal logics of personhood and property, they facilitated the distribution of such ways of thinking beyond American borders.

## Universities, Slavery, and Settler Colonialism

With Barack Obama—the country's first president of African descent, a Harvard alumnus, and the son of a noncitizen student from Kenya—in office, the 2010 diversity initiative that featured Cheeshateaumuck's portrait was part of a broader trend. In this period, US colleges and universities undertook self-studies of their institutional histories and their entanglements with and authorization of racial-colonial capitalism's exploits and violences. Scholars such as Davarian Baldwin trace the move toward statements about accountability and talk of reconciliation to 2003, when Brown University President Ruth J. Simmons, the first Black president of an Ivy League institution, appointed the Steering Committee on Slavery and Justice.[9]

Since 2003, a range of institutions have taken on similar projects, including Georgetown, Yale, William & Mary, and the University of Virginia-led consortium of over seventy-five schools named simply "Universities Studying Slavery." To varying degrees, such projects serve as a means by which university administrations seek to surface, contend with, and manage their historical reliance on and participation in economies organized around the enslavement of Black people and, generally to a lesser extent, the dispossession of Native land. As Vineeta Singh describes, this work has helped to foment important research through which scholars "address the color line as a central driving force in the history of U.S. higher education."[10] These efforts, often initiated by student and community protest, have done important work to resurrect long-buried histories and have brought about at least surface changes to campuses, including the removal of names of individuals who benefited directly from these systems, from buildings or colleges.[11] Yet, as Singh continues, that most such initiatives frequently use "the appellation 'project' (instead of center or institute) in their titles indexes an uneasy triangular relationship among an administration's desire to be absolved of past wrongdoings, historians' attempts to narrow the range of permissible lies an institution can tell about its own past, and the institution's inability to reckon with the scale of the oppression in which it has been complicit." In my work with Eli Meyerhoff, Zach Schwartz-Weinstein, and Nick Mitchell, I have argued that such initiatives often serve the institutional purpose of "owning" the past, acknowledging and incorporating past wrongs into institutional histories in order to effectively sequester them away and secure the goodness of the well-intentioned educational mission of the present.

It is not a coincidence, of course, that this surge in institutional confessionals arose just as a comparably robust body of scholarship in critical race and ethnic studies turned its eye upon colleges and universities. Such work is part of what Dylan Rodríguez identified in 2012 as the "thriving circuits of radical thought" that confronted "the academy's long historical complicities in racial/colonial genocide" and sought to "denaturalize and ultimately dismantle the conditions in which systems of massive violence are reproduced."[12] In this read, Rodríguez homes in on a central contradiction of the contemporary university as at once historically and persistently complicit in and responsible for racialized and colonial violence and also as a site through which disruptive scholarly and organizing work can and indeed has been made possible. As I have argued with Nick Mitchell, such disruptive work requires "undoing normative assumptions about the nature of higher education and the subjectivities that move through it" and attending to what we call "accumulation through education," or how education becomes a mechanism that enables particular regimes of expropriation.[13]

Wilder's 2013 *Ebony and Ivy* stands out as exemplary of such work. In his deep and capacious recounting of the stories of students and institutions from the colonial period to the mid-nineteenth century, Wilder illustrates how universities in what became recognized as the United States functioned as "imperial instruments akin to armories and forts, a part of the colonial garrison with the specific responsibilities to train ministers and missionaries, convert indigenous peoples and soften cultural resistance, and extend European rule over foreign nations."[14] Fundamentally undercutting pervasive narratives of northern and European innocence in histories of anti-Black racism and Indigenous dispossession, Wilder traces the travels of individual students from educational institutions in Massachusetts and Virginia to plantations in the South and to scientific laboratories in Europe. As the students moved, so too did the knowledge and logics they held, giving way to new scientific understandings of bodily difference that "justified expansionism and slavery" and the elimination of Indigenous peoples. Indeed, Wilder writes, "the rise of scientific racism—the attempt to discover the social destinies and identify the assumed divisions of human populations—required Americans."[15] In other words, universities in the so-called "new world" functioned materially and epistemologically to underwrite racial-colonial processes.

Even as many of the universities Wilder writes about cite his work as animating their projects of acknowledgment, in so doing, they often attend only to the specific and direct examples of university responsibility in slave economies: for instance, in the documented ownership or sale of people by the university or its funders. Rarely is there an effort to contend with Wilder's more substantive argument: That universities benefited from, provided the animating logic of, and continue to operate upon a material and epistemological foundation of dehumanization. And, as their names suggest, a focus on enslavement tends to eclipse a comparable reckoning with practices of colonial dispossession, often enacted, at least in part, under the banner of providing education to Indigenous students.

## The Indian College and the Settler University

In histories of US higher education, including Wilder's, and on the school's website, Harvard lays claim to being the "first college in the American colonies" with its founding in 1636.[16] William & Mary, which received its base funding and royal charter in 1693, is generally situated as the second such institution. William & Mary's "History & Traditions" website complicates the story a bit, however, by drawing attention to an earlier lineage, marking that "our original plans date back to 1618—decades before Harvard."[17] In fact, as early as 1612 settlers working with the Virginia Company of London produced tracts such as *The New Life of Virginia* that laid plans for colonists to take Indigenous children and "traine them up with gentlenesse, teach them our English tongue, and the principles of religion."[18] In 1619, this proposal was crafted into a law requiring jurisdictions to provide the means to educate "a certaine number of the natives Children." The "most apt in wit" were to be the first students of a proposed college. As in the plans for Harvard's students, they were to "return to their people and serve as missionaries in converting and educating others of the heathen race."[19] Other histories contend that the College of Henricus and the East India School of Virginia was founded in 1621 "for the training up of the Children of those Infidels," with thirty Natives enrolled as students in 1621.[20]

Despite these competing reads, the historical record is clear that from its earliest years, educating Indigenous youth was a core aspect of the Virginia Company's strategy for dispossession and control. By 1619, for instance, the company set aside ten thousand acres of land over which it claimed possession for a college and King James ordered the churches of England to take up a collection toward the same end. All such plans for the college were halted in 1622 after a coordinated attack on thirty-one English settlements by the Powhatan Confederacy. Private funds continued to flow toward a program of educating and converting Native youth, though it is unclear if one actually existed.[21] When William & Mary was officially granted its charter from the Crown in 1693, it was underwritten through the promise of ongoing funding from the Brafferton Estate, a trust created after the death of Sir Robert Boyle, a long-standing supporter of missionary educational projects, for the explicit purpose of educating Indigenous students in the British colonies.

Around 2010, William & Mary's effort to attend to its own history of enslavement took shape as the Lemon Project, an initiative named after a Black man enslaved by the university in the early 1800s.[22] Like many other projects in this vein, the Lemon Project splits the effort to engage in and account for histories of the enslavement of people of African descent from the coextensive history and processes of the dispossession of Indigenous land and the capture of Indigenous people. As its website attests, the project's goal is to "contribute to and encourage scholarship on the 328-year relationship between African Americans and W&M" and "continue and expand our leadership role in the growing national and international movement of colleges and universities studying their full histories as they relate to slavery and its legacies."[23]

In the case of William & Mary, this splitting is especially difficult to maintain in light of the fact that the school's first Indigenous students were the "purchased children of hostile tribes captured in war."[24] The university procured its first non-English students circa 1702 from the Catawba as part of a tributary system through which English colonists offered a degree of protection and land to specific tribes, at the time primarily coastal Algonquian speaking, in exchange for "tribute" in the form of beaver skins and enslaved members of nontributary tribes.[25] This fundamental fact, alongside the complicated practices of Black and Indigenous enslavement in Virginia during the seventeenth century, belies a simple binary rendering of enslavement and dispossession.[26]

As Justin Leroy argues, to understand how both settler colonialism and slavery function to justify extermination or elimination, it is necessary to understand their histories as coextensive, mutually constituting, and interlocking.[27] According to various historical records, all of the Indigenous students present on the William & Mary campus during the height of the institution's efforts to educate Native youth between 1702 and the 1730s were either captured in war or children of tributary tribes sent to the school as part of their treaty agreements with the English, often in the place of their established annual tribute of animal skins.[28] Wilder observes that the campus essentially functioned as a prison, holding the students hostage in order to secure "good behavior" from their tribes.[29]

## Institutional Reckoning and Indigenous Studies

In 2016, a new effort to account for William & Mary's history with Native tribes took shape in an exhibit at the campus's Muscarelle Museum of Art curated by Danielle Moretti-Langholtz and Buck Woodard, two cultural anthropologists who focus on Native Studies. As the extensive exhibition catalogue describes, "Building the Brafferton: The Founding, Funding and Legacy of America's Indian School" uses lenses of settler colonialism and political economy to intervene on past official histories and their focus on single events or figures.[30] The curators complicate narratives that reduced William & Mary's early efforts to "educate Western Indians" to a failure. Mirroring the contemporary discourse of institutions that support international education, they highlight the "accomplishments of Brafferton Indian alumni" and their "contributions to eighteenth-century diplomacy and the emerging American nation state."[31] In taking up such a position, they render the memory of this project legible and even desirable for institutional administrators and funders for whom such a story can secure, rather than disrupt, a narrative of progress and benevolent incorporation.

Importantly, however, Moretti-Langholtz and Woodard initiated and actualized the project with stakeholders other than university administrators and funders in mind as well. In her discussion of the legacy of the Brafferton Indian School, Moretti-Langholtz notes that the exhibition was in part inspired by a series of calls she received in 2001 from people she describes as "a representative of a Native community," "a member of a different indigenous community," and "yet another Native community member." According to Moretti-Langholtz, each person essentially made the same statement and asked the same question: "In the past, some of our young people attended the Indian School" and then "Can our young people come back as students now?"[32] The identities and experiences of the students who attended the school have been obscured in the historical record of ledgers and rosters, which reflects colonial administrators' primary concern with counting the 125 students who studied on campus in the eighteenth century. In his research, Woodard identifies the names and, where possible, the tribal affiliations and "the singular lives and extraordinary accomplishments" of twenty-seven Native students at William & Mary in the eighteenth century.[33] Using what he calls "strong circumstantial evidence" Woodard tracks the stories of several of the "Brafferton Students" who attended William & Mary between the 1720s and the 1770s, whom he describes as serving as interpreters, liaisons, and messengers between their communities and the Virginians.[34] Even as these stories are easily assimilable to a progressive institutional narrative, Moretti-Langholtz and Woodard also sought to enact broader institutional change through their research. For instance, the curators engaged Native stakeholders and formed "The Brafferton Legacy Group," composed of four William & Mary graduate students from Native communities with historical links to the Brafferton Indian School in the eighteenth century, and the institution hired two field archaeologists from the Pamunkey tribe.

Mirroring the way "circuits of radical thought" in critical race and ethnic studies both made possible and pushed against the rise of university projects investigating their histories in relationship to slavery, "Building the Brafferton" emerged in parallel to and, to its benefit, in engagement with a vibrant era in Native American and Indigenous Studies. Preliminary research for the exhibit was presented at the 2007 meeting of what would a year later formally become the Native American and Indigenous Studies Association (NAISA) and then again at the organization's second meeting in 2009.[35] As K. Tsianina Lomawaima, one of the members of the founding steering committee, articulated during a plenary panel at the first gathering, NAISA brings together scholars who share "a commitment to the fundamental concept of sovereignty; a privileging or centering of Native names, experiences, voices and narratives; and inclusive orientation that favors multiple, complicating, diverse perspectives over a monolithic 'one size or story fits all' approach; a commitment to the health, well-being and vigor of life in Indian country; responsiveness to the central issues and concerns of Native nations; a dedication to transform the institutional structures of the dominant society, such as school, colleges, and universities—however frustratingly slow and incremental that process can be."[36] As such, NAISA's charge supports work that responds to and moves beyond institutional statements of recognition and acknowledgment to center Indigenous perspectives that call for a material reckoning and decolonial projects of land back.[37] In leading with an insistence on sovereignty, NAISA aligns with Glen Coulthard's argument regarding "the limits of recognition-based politics for restructuring Indigenous-state relations, as it leaves intact the state's role as arbiter and therefore ultimately reproduces the very configurations of colonial power that Native peoples seek to transcend."[38]

As an exhibition and now as a catalogue, "Building the Brafferton" and the institutional practices that took shape around it seems to, at least in part, work to fulfill Lomawaima's and Coulthard's calls to "transform the institutional structure" of the university by moving beyond recognition to enact some substantive material change through the creation of new positions and the generation of knowledge about students that was previously undocumented in the official historical record. But, even in their laudable effort to provide a new framework and rich research, Moretti-Langholtz and Woodard shy away from more overtly political interventions, such as insisting on the sovereignty of the tribes in the region or any moves toward recognizing land claims. The processes and logics of education and dispossession that underwrote the founding of William & Mary are not merely historical facts to be observed and added to the historical record but are, instead, a constitutive and enduring aspect of the present. As Kevin Bruyneel explains, the issue is not actually "a lack of knowledge about the treatment of Indigenous peoples but a lack of acknowledgement that fundamental American liberal commitments to such institutions and beliefs as private property and liberal-individualism are created out of and built upon, in no small part, settler-colonial logic, practices, and structures."[39]

## Settler Colonialism and the Present University

Over the last twenty years, faculty, staff, and administrators at many colleges and universities in the United States have started to include land acknowledgments at the opening of public events. Too often, even in their enunciation of acknowledgment, university-based projects, especially as they fail to concretely affirm Native sovereignty and the call for land back, only further sediment the settler colonial project of elimination in the face of the continued existence, resistance, and persistence of Indigenous peoples.[40] Many universities, Harvard being something of an exception, claim a degree of innocence in Native dispossession because the institution came to occupy and make use of the land after the dispossession had occurred.[41] As such, land acknowledgments can recognize the "original inhabitants" or "historical stewards" of the land without directly implicating the institution or freighting its administrators with any actionable responsibilities. Such an alibi is less available to schools funded through the 1862 Morrill Land Grant Act, which "directly invested eastern states in the settlement, speculation, and securitization of federally claimed lands in the West as a means of generating capital for state colleges and enabled Western states to use colleges as a means of accumulating state capacity by mandating military training for college students."[42] The arc of this section of the book concludes in 1862, leaving a consideration of the post-emancipation university's engagement with noncitizen students and financial underwriting by the seizure of Native lands for Parts II and III.

What follows builds on interventions into fundamental questions of history, time, land, and sovereignty inspired by scholars associated with NAISA and the related field of settler colonial studies, including Lisa Brooks, J. Kēhaulani Kauanui, Patrick Wolfe, Jean M. O'Brien, Kevin Bruyneel, Colin Calloway, Khalil Johnson, David Chang, and others. Engaging their work as well as earlier scholarship on these histories, it registers and synthesizes existing archival records and historiographic understandings of university projects to selectively incorporate Indigenous peoples, often for the purpose of securing funding and land—and their repeated failures to do much else. The chapters surface these histories in order to flesh out the ways mere acknowledgment of past harms is inadequate to contend with or make any kind of amends for the ways the logics and practices of settler colonialism endure in their structuring of institutions of higher education and the knowledge they authorize.

# 1

# Native Students as "Foreign Students" and the Foundation of the US University

## Incorporation As/Toward Elimination

In insisting that educational projects directed, at least in name, toward the incorporation of Native students are a key aspect of the genealogy of US higher education, this chapter is grounded in four basic axiomatics. The first is the simple but necessary recognition of Native tribes as sovereign entities. As such, British colonial and other projects to educate Native youth are a foundational part of the history of what today is framed as international education: the movement of students across national borders or between sovereign polities for the purpose of study. The second is the basic and unassailable fact that histories of institutions of higher education are histories of dispossession and accumulation in part accomplished through the incorporation of people, land, and knowledge as a mode of elimination.[1] In other words, even as universities make futures, one of the futures they most frequently brought to visit upon students from other polities was premature death—be it by exposure to foreign illnesses, lack of care and inadequate sustenance, direct physical brutality, or experiences of displacement and depression. The third axiomatic is an affirmation of the need to grapple with the continuities between British colonial formations, processes, and logics of governing, those of the incipient nation-state, and the contemporary conditions and practices of educational institutions—these include the imposition of rigid conceptions of time, value, property, and personhood that enable and extend economies of exploitation and expropriation. And finally, the fourth is that while most canonical institutional histories suggest that projects centered on the education of Indigenous youth by settler institutions ended due to waning colonist interest, a more accurate reading of these histories must contend with the fact that most often such projects ended largely due to Indigenous peoples' active and pronounced refusal to participate—as, for example, when Mohegan scholar and minister Samson Occom eventually rejected the educational model enacted by his mentor Eleazar Wheelock.

The attempts at incorporation and assimilation explored in this chapter, both historical and present-day, exemplify key aspects of Patrick Wolfe's theory of settler colonialism. As he explains, the settler colonial project centers on an ongoing attempt to eliminate Native peoples with the primary goal of acquiring land. Wolfe penned what are now taken as two of the central precepts in settler colonial studies: that "invasion is a structure not an event" and that the endgame of invasion is "the elimination of the native."[2] As such, settler colonialism is an enduring process that sets out to "destroy to replace" both through explicit material and bodily violence and through more epistemic forms of violence that impose and cultivate logics, beliefs, and knowledges that condition understandings of the past, relationships to the present, and imaginations of the future. For Wolfe, assimilation, as one strategy of elimination, represents a "Faustian bargain": "have our settler world, but lose your Indigenous soul."[3] In other words, assimilation through training in the logic of liberal propriation and belief in the Christian faith, and the resulting dispossession of tribal land, offered a seemingly softer but no less effective route toward the attempted elimination of both the tribe and the Indian, itself "a kind of death."[4] In specific times and places, assimilation can be one of the most effective modes of elimination since, as Wolfe explains, "it does not involve such a disruptive affront to the rule of law that is ideologically central to the cohesion of settler society."[5] Even in cases where Native youth were forced into a status of "student," educative efforts toward assimilation have been rescripted as wholly nonviolent: a benevolent fulfillment of the white man's burden to civilize.

By the late nineteenth century, assimilation as elimination was the stated goal of advocates for Indigenous educational projects, such as Richard Pratt, who founded the now-notorious Carlisle boarding school for Indian youth in 1879. In 1892, Pratt famously made the connection between education, assimilation, and elimination explicit, arguing "that all the Indian there is in the race should be dead. Kill the Indian in him and save the man."[6] In his discussion of settler colonialism in the context of the United States, Wolfe is specifically interested in the federal government's post–Civil War efforts to manage Native tribes and expropriate native land through the "avalanche of assimilationist legislation" enacted during and after the Civil War.[7] Key among such legislation were the twinned Acts of 1862: the Morrill Land Grant Act, often lauded as the founding legislation of US higher education, and the Homestead Act.[8] Both of these acts secured the dispossession of Indigenous lands, transferring them directly to white settlers and to white settler-institutions, including Yale, Cornell, and what would become the broad swath of public state universities across the north and into the west. To this day, many of these institutions persist, in part, off the profits generated from the sale and exploitation of these lands.[9]

However, as is illustrated here, efforts to use education as a tool for incorporation and eradication long predate Pratt's deathly articulation, the formalization of US federal policy toward incorporation in the early nineteenth century, and even the formation of the nation-state itself in the late eighteenth century. The series of institutional histories explored in this chapter illustrates that in order to contend with the newly invoked and enacted powers of the federal government during and after the Civil War, it is necessary to first untangle a longer legacy of educational efforts that announce themselves as beneficent even as they often underwrote, enabled, and legitimized more directly violent eliminatory practices.

As Wolfe explains in a conversation with J. Kēhaulani Kauanui, "assimilation is held out as giving Natives the same opportunities as the White man," but "they won't actually get any of the advantages they were promised would be the fruits of the civilizing experience."[10] David Kazanjian has generatively theorized such assimilatory efforts as a process of "accumulation by possession," wherein settler accumulation is accomplished through the "imputation of codified modes of living, discrete values, and fictive conceptions of possession to the dispossessed."[11] Such a process, he continues, "entails endowing or investing the dispossessed, bestowing upon them, even conjuring in them a mode of being that aims to assume and, eventually, to consume them." In a similar vein, for Haunani-Kay Trask, racial-colonial power is often affected through occupations that "entrench foreign ways of life" in both land and people.[12] This can also be thought of as the double process of subjectification whereby a subject is both granted capacity to act and subjected to a given structure of power and knowledge. The mission statements and charters of the founding institutions of higher education in what would become the United States articulate and desire to do no less.

The following explores several case studies to trace a genealogy of the shifting modes and motivations that shaped a string of educational projects from the early seventeenth century through to the mid-eighteenth century. I begin by looking at how the initiation of higher education institutions in the Massachusetts Bay Colony and the Virginia Colony during the 1600s was predicated on their promise to English funders to indoctrinate the Indigenous tribes in their vicinity. I then mark a shift in the Virginia project in the 1740s toward education as soft diplomacy and look to a Northern example of such a project in Moors' Charity School, which morphed into Dartmouth College.

In each case, I'm cognizant that key to Kazanjian's theory of "accumulation by dispossession" is the attenuation he introduces with the language of "aims to." Its inclusion marks "accumulation by possession" as an effort rather than an accomplishment. As such, I am concerned with also tracing the "refiguration of those imputations by the possessed-dispossessed themselves." Most of the histories of the institutions discussed here feature an Indigenous student, whether it be Caleb Cheeshateaumuck at Harvard or Samson Occom at Dartmouth. Rather than simply accepting the presentation of each figure's story in conventional narratives as willful and desiring participants in the settler colonial project of education, I follow scholars critical of simple or transparent readings of the archive, including Lisa Brooks, Saidiya Hartman, and Avery Gordon, to look to the ways "performance and other modes of practice are determined by, exploit, and exceed the constraints of domination."[13] As such, the genealogy told here takes up the insights of recent scholarly work that provides more critical analysis of the archive to read the archive against the grain to see these figures as "producers and providers of knowledge and theory."[14] In *Our Beloved Kin*, Brooks, a scholar of Native American history in colonial New England, describes her methodology as "pursuing a decolonizing process of expanding the strategies through which we might do the work of history, which in the Abenaki language is called *ôjmowôgan*, a cyclical activity of recalling and relaying in which we are collectively engaged."[15] Inspired by Brooks, the stories told in this chapter work to "reverse the narrative of absence and reveal the persistence of Indigenous adaptation and survival."[16]

## Harvard and the Missionary Origins of the Colonial University

In 1636, a Puritan minister born in Southwark, England, established Harvard University as part of the Massachusetts Bay Colony. Harvard claims the title of the oldest university in the United States and was imagined by its first president, Henry Dunster, as "the Indian Oxford."[17] As Brooks documents, British settlers acquired formal access to the land upon which the university was located in 1639 through an agreement with the local Massachusett saunkskwa in return for a pledge to acknowledge her leadership and respect the subsistence rights of her community.[18] For the saunkskwa, the agreement represented the potential for protection and aid as epidemics took the lives of her kin, many of whom had formed relationships with settlers in the aftermath of one of the earliest settler-led genocides of an Indigenous tribe, what US historical records refer to as the Pequot War.[19] When the war ended with the signing of the Treaty of Hartford in 1638, many of the surviving Pequot people were made the chattels of enemy tribes, while others were declared the property of colonists and sold overseas to Britain or shipped south to the Caribbean.[20] During the war, Harvard faltered both in its finances and in its enrollments. Afterward, the institution found an initial foothold by recruiting British students from the very geographic region to which seventeen of the captive Pequots had been sent, initiating a cross-oceanic, if not quite international, pipeline of wealthy students to supplement its finances and enrollments through its relationship with the British slave-owning plantation class of the West Indies.[21]

Despite the influx of students and their tuitions, Harvard continued to struggle financially into the 1640s. To sustain itself, its leaders campaigned in England to raise funds, touting their efforts to bring the "poore Indians" out of their "hellish darkness."[22] In support of their case, they drew on a 1643 pamphlet entitled *New England's First Fruits.*[23] Brooks explains how the "tract promised and promoted the conversion of wild land and a wild people into a domesticated space and tamed population, which would gratefully serve the work of the Lord."[24] As such, it also laid out a basis for education as an incorporative strategy directed at both people and at land—missionary education as a way to bring "Native peoples and territories that surrounded them under the 'yoke' of colonial governance."[25] The promise and possibility of such a strategy was persuasive. After the text circulated in England, Harvard raised nearly £335; setting a standard that would be followed for the next century and a half, of this sum only £35 went toward efforts to educate Indian students while the balance was used to fund the college itself.[26] The education of students from the areas surrounding the new campus was thus established as not only a key component of the mission to spread Christianity but also, and perhaps more importantly, as a successful tact for funding universities in "the new world."

In 1649, the installation of an English Parliament aligned with the vision of the colonial Puritans provided a lifeline to the institution with the passage of "An Act for the Propagating of the Gospel." This act guaranteed Harvard ongoing monetary support to convert "the Heathen Natives of that Country" through the establishment of "Universities, Schools, and Nurseries of Literature settled for further instructing and civilizing them." As Brooks details, in addition to providing funding to Harvard, the act clearly delineated notions of nativity and foreignness, marked out the "country" as an uninhabited land mass, and, paradoxically, expounded on the current inhabitants' desperate need for Christianity.[27] The narrative of Harvard's capacity to fulfill such a mission was bolstered by the fact that Dunster, who remained president through to 1654, boarded two Native youth in his home at the time of its passage. In *Red Ink,* Drew Lopenzina discusses how Dunster continued to house the youth despite finding them to be "an hindrance" because doing so functioned as "a public relations gesture" and "the most effective manner of winning money from England for support of the college."[28] Though the historical record is inconsistent, there is some consensus that one of Dunster's boarders was Wawaus, son of Wampus, from an inland Nipmuc "praying town." In much historical and popular scholarship, Wawaus is referred to by what would come to be his English name, James the Printer.[29]

The Harvard charter, adopted by the Massachusetts Bay Colony a year later, further cemented the institution's commitment by declaring its mission to be "the education of the English and Indian youth of this country in knowledge and godliness."[30] This obligation was strengthened once again in 1655 when support from the Society for the Propagation of the Gospel in New England, which was also known as the New England Company, allowed for the construction of the Indian College, the campus's first brick building, designed to house twenty sons of Indian leaders who would be educated alongside the sons of English magistrates and clergy.[31] On its first floor, the college housed the colony's only printing press, upon which John Eliot worked with his apprentices Samuel Green and James the Printer to produce the Eliot Bible, a translation of the King James Bible into the Wôpanâak language.

In 1661, Harvard took its first steps toward fulfilling its mission to educate Native youth when two members of the Wampanoag enrolled: Joel Iacoomes, son of a "common man" Hiacoomes of Nunnepog, and Caleb Cheeshateaumuck, son of the sachem Cheeshateaumuck of Nobnocket.[32] Hiacoomes was one of the first Wampanoags to embrace Christianity through his exchanges with Thomas Mayhew, an English settler on the Wampanoag island of Noepe, which is now known as Martha's Vineyard. With Mayhew's encouragement, Hiacoomes learned to read and developed a syncretic analysis of Christianity and Wampanoag cosmology. Caleb's father Cheeschumuck "maintained his traditional leadership while weaving the 'emergent' religion into the fabric of his community."[33] Before their matriculation at Harvard, Joel Iaccomes and Caleb Cheeshateaumuck attended the Roxbury Grammar School and the Latin School in Cambridge, likely alongside Wawaus. At Roxbury, the students were educated in the Elizabethan tradition in both English and Latin and disciplined into English customs including a regimented, clock-regulated temporal system and, with it, a linear, progressive notion of historical time.[34]

In her necessarily attenuated reading of this history, Brooks complicates overdetermined narratives of British and Native relationships as unidirectional, arguing that in attending British colonial schools, the students extended a long-standing tradition whereby eastern Indigenous nations educated each other's sons as a way of enhancing alliances.[35] While settler narratives assume a binary between white, settler, British Christian ways of being and knowing and Native modes of doing the same, there is no reason to concretize such a reductive understanding, especially given that strategic practices of relationship building and preparation for leadership are well documented in several Indigenous nations. Given the first axiom of this chapter regarding the sovereignty of Indigenous tribes, these practices, too, can be understood as something akin to international education.

When Iacoomes and Cheeshateaumuck moved into the newly constructed Indian College at the center of the Harvard campus, they continued their formal scholarly and cultural educations. They extended their knowledge of English, Latin, and Greek and, like other Harvard students, were required to dress in gowns and cloaks when they left their dorm rooms and to keep "their grooming and comportment . . . consistent with English custom for learned men."[36] As part of their education, they were tasked with writing missives to the institution's benefactors to demonstrate their proficiency in the scholarly languages. One such letter, written by Cheeshateaumuck in 1663, is among the three surviving texts from the Indian College. In the letter to the "Honoratissimi Benefactores," the honored benefactors of the Indian College, Cheeshateaumuck expresses his gratitude to the patrons who, through their support, brought "blessings to us pagans."[37] Composed in Latin, Cheeshateaumuck's letter lauds "how powerful the force and virtue of education and of refined literature are in the transformation of the barbarians' nature."[38] He expresses his gratitude to the patrons along with his hope that he and the other Indian students will be "instruments to spread and propagate the gospel among our kin and neighbors." The letter was sent to Robert Boyle, an "armchair missionary" best known for his work as a chemist, who in 1662, had been appointed as the first governor of the Corporation for the Propagation of the Gospel in New England.

On the surface, Cheeshateaumuck's writing functioned to demonstrate the success of the educational mission as he emphasizes the power of literature and education to cultivate his status as a learned man. It is more than likely that his teachers encouraged him to write the letter with the specific goal of using it to persuade the benefactors to increase their financial support. In service to this project, the letter would display Cheeshateaumuck as a "tamed" Native, refined through his experiences and their generosity. This is the most straightforward reading of the text and its place in settler history.

However, Brooks and Lopenzina each offer persuasive counter-readings that complicate a simple rendering of Cheeshateaumuck as a tool of the campus leaders, one in which even Cheeshateaumuck's writing at the behest of campus administrators leaves a trace of critique and resistance, as per the third axiomatic of this chapter. Lopenzina argues that it is necessary to understand Cheeshateaumuck as consciously "performing a role, putting on a suit of clothes, so to speak, that he has learned to wear over a period of years."[39] Brooks proposes that Cheeshateaumuck's choice to frame his letter through a reading of the classical Greek myth of Orpheus can, and indeed should, be read as layered, at once fulfilling the benefactors' expectations and, simultaneously, flagging his own ambivalence about the missionary project. If Cheeshateaumuck's letter is taken at face value, he seems to tell the tale of Orpheus's successful transformation of the wild beings of the forest and even of himself. It is notable, however, that he omits the story's tragic conclusion when Orpheus looks back at Eurydice and loses her forever. As Brooks argues, Cheeshateaumuck likely used this writing as a tool, an instrument through which to "achieve a particular pragmatic goal, the continuance of his education."[40] Yet, his time at Harvard and in the company of settlers had indeed provided Cheeshateaumuck many reasons to look back and to question the efficacy of settler logics and efforts.

As the chapter's second axiomatic suggests, access to the "knowledge and godliness" of a Harvard education did not, as the institution's charter promised, bring the "poore Indians" out of what the colonizers derisively presented as their "hellish darkness." Rather, Cheeshateaumuck, Iacoomes, and the three other Native students who lived and studied, if briefly, at Harvard in the mid-1600s, lived rather harsh lives on the university's campus. Unlike the shared meals of locally harvested fish, game, and vegetables they would have had at home, meals at Harvard consisted of "a steady diet of beer and bread, with a midday 'dinner' of small portions of beef, lamb, or pork, sometimes accompanied by turnips or peas, and a similar 'supper,' a meat pie or hasty pudding."[41] Their lives were lived on the campus, organized almost exclusively around prayer and study, and regimented by the clock. Elezear and Benajmin Larnell, two of the students who studied at Harvard after Cheeshateaumuck and Iacoomes, both died before their graduation.[42] Moving to Cambridge meant new exposure to germs and viruses, though their deaths may also have been a result of malnutrition.[43] Before his graduation, Iacoomes was in a shipwreck on his return from visiting his family on Noepe. It is unclear if he died in the wreck or, if, as some histories suggest, he was "murdered by local Indians."[44] Caleb Cheeshateaumuck was the only graduate of the Indian College, receiving his degree in 1665. But he also was not able to experience the benefits or "fruits" of his education. Shortly after graduating, he died of consumption just a few miles from campus in Charlestown. Even after their deaths, Brooks contends, Cheeshateaumuck's and Iacoomes's time on the Harvard campus had a continuing impact on their kin who carried on their "intellectual and spiritual work."[45] In Noepe, the community maintained a critical but certainly interested engagement with Christian theology.

The Harvard Indian College closed in 1698, but the university continued to receive funds for missionary work among Indian tribes well into the eighteenth century. One source of these funds was the estate left by Sir Robert Boyle in 1693 to "Advance of Propagation of the Christian religion amongst Infidells," though, as is discussed below, only a small portion of the Boyle funds went to Harvard.[46] Bobby Wright describes the Harvard Indian College as the first among a string of such efforts that resulted in "lamentable failures." In its four-decade existence, the institution "enrolled only six natives and graduated one, who contributed nothing toward the hoped-for conversion since he died within a year of receiving his bachelor's degree."[47] After Elezear and Benjamin Larnell passed, Harvard's administrators continued to raise funds ostensibly for the education of local tribes, but they were primarily used to train white missionaries who were to spread the gospel.

## Education, Tribute, and Imperial Security at William & Mary

Like Harvard, the College of William & Mary was also founded, or at least funded, as a missionary effort to use education as a means to incorporate and manage Indigenous inhabitants of the land the institution occupied. The institution's administrators did not, however, share the Puritan religious vision, or perhaps alibi, of their counterparts in Massachusetts. Instead, reflecting the broader ethos of the Virginia Colony, they quite clearly understood their mission as one of financial exploitation and expansion. The education of Indigenous youth was a conscious strategic move to further their interests by securing the good behavior of their families and tribes.

According to Robert Beverley's 1705 *The History & Present State of Virginia*, the original concept of a college that had circulated in the 1610s was revived in the 1680s in hopes of providing education to colonists locally instead of sending them back to England, an expensive and inconvenient practice.[48] Commissary James Blair traveled to London from Virginia in the early 1690s with plans to gain an audience with King William III and Queen Mary II in hopes of securing a charter for the college and a vague charge from the Virginia General Assembly to obtain funding. The king and queen granted the charter along with an endowment for the college, rights to part of the export duties on furs and tobacco, and a grant of twenty thousand acres of land.[49] The College of William & Mary's founding charter stated "that the Church of Virginia may be furnished with a seminary of ministers of the gospel, that the youth may be piously educated in good letters and manners, and that the Christian faith may be propagated amongst the Western Indians." Thus, the college was, effectively, founded on the dispossessed lands of Native tribes, funded by these lands and proceeds from enslaved labor forced to work upon them, and intended to constitute a central component of the promulgation of Christianity among the local tribes.[50] As Krystlyn Marie Shefveland's documents in her history of Anglo-native Virginia, colonists attempted to bring taxes on Indian trade to finance the school and reapportioned land to make space for the college, "allotting twenty thousand acres of land from Pamunkey Neck and Blackwater Swamp from the Chikahominy."[51]

Blair's success in raising funds for the college built on earlier efforts by Harvard administrators and their use of Caleb Cheeshateaumuck's writing to cultivate Robert Boyle's missionary desires. Blair's trip took place shortly after Boyle had passed away and bequeathed the majority of his estate to "Advance of Propagation of the Christian religion amongst Infidells."[52] The administrators of his will purchased Brafferton, an estate in Yorkshire, creating the Brafferton Fund. The fund allocated the rents from the estate to fulfill Boyle's wishes. Annually, ninety pounds were to be distributed to the Society for the Propagation of the Gospel in New England, with forty-five pounds dedicated to Harvard's efforts, and the remaining sum, which turned out to be quite substantial, would go to the new College of William & Mary in support of its work educating Indigenous students. As in the chapter's third axiomatic regarding the continuities between British colonial formations and those of the incipient nation-state, the historical and material connections between Harvard and William & Mary triangulate through Boyle and his estate to demonstrate the ways logics, relationships, and material acquisitions accumulate and sediment over time. According to terms determined by the bishop of London and the Earl of Burlington, the Brafferton Fund's administrators, James Blair, who would serve as president from the institution's founding in 1693 until his death in 1743, and his successors would receive the necessary funds to provide room and board for "such Indian children as shall be hereafter brought unto the s[ai]d Colledg as also for buying or procureing such children."[53] The fund then promised fourteen pounds per year to support the students' education "till they are ready to receive orders and be thought sufficient to be sent abroad to preach and convert the Indians." To receive such funds, Indian students were to be placed under the direct supervision of the president, who was required to send a "regular census of Native students and reports on their progress."[54]

Even with funding from the Crown and the Brafferton Fund, the college struggled to recruit Indian students, no doubt due to animosities sown by the exploitative system of tribute established by treaty agreements between the English and the Powhatan Confederacy over the course of the seventeenth and eighteenth centuries. As Shefveland illustrates, a 1646 treaty ending the Tidewater Wars encapsulated all members of the Powhatan chiefdom under tributary status to the government of Virginia. This relationship undercut their sovereign claim to territory and "required hostage children from tributaries for placement in colonial homes."[55] The 1677 Articles of Peace at Middle Plantation that concluded Bacon's Rebellion reestablished both the tributary relations and trade agreements.

Kauanui incisively argues against what has become, at least within certain American Studies scholarship, a habitual romanticization of Bacon's Rebellion as a crucial historical moment of possibility, "when poor Africans and Europeans united to fight their common exploiters (the English elite)."[56] Critical race and leftist scholars frequently take this history as foundational to the creation of the racialized status of both whiteness and Blackness since it led to the creation of the Virginia Slave Codes of 1705, popularly understood as the moment that concretized the distinct legal relationship between Blackness and slavery. But, as Kauanui points out, all too often such histories fail to account for the fact that the alliances formed between Africans and Europeans were the result of a shared desire to eliminate Indigenous peoples they saw as thwarting their access to land. It is also necessary to mark that in both the aftermath of Bacon's Rebellion and the instantiation of the Virginia Slave Codes of 1705, both Black and Indigenous people were effectively rendered vulnerable to enslavement. For instance, Shefveland tracks a June 1676 law that stated that "all Indians taken in war were slaves for life."[57] An October 1705 act converted all enslaved people, whether African or Indigenous, into real estate and forbade Africans and Indians from holding public office in Virginia.[58]

These laws enabled the college to follow through on the Brafferton Fund's suggestion to buy or procure Indigenous children as students. According to the historian W. Stitt Robinson Jr., "the colony purchased children of hostile tribes captured in war, educating them with the income from the Boyle fund."[59] Francis Nicholson, who served as governor of Virginia from 1698 to 1705 "instructed Indian traders to procure children from several tribes on the periphery of the colony," purchasing Indian would-be students as slaves and then sending them to the college instead of to plantations.[60] Through these means, the college received its first four students by way of the Catawba tributary tribe sometime around 1702.[61] Very little is known about these students. But, the website for a ghost tour of the area surrounding William & Mary uses this historical fact to ground its tour of the building the Brafferton Fund eventually paid to construct in 1723. The site also makes one of the few direct connections between the type of education that took place at William & Mary and contemporary practices of international education, explaining how, "the College could not get any volunteers for their school until 1707, when six boys were taken as prisoners of war from a warring tribe and given to the colony as tribute. This first class stayed with local residents in town, much like a foreign exchange program." As the site explains, many of the students were "abused by their colonial guests, and died of disease."[62]

In 1710, Alexander Spotswood arrived in Virginia to serve as lieutenant governor with a keen interest in the college, which he saw as a potential tool to convert the Native peoples to Christianity and European concepts of property, personhood, and politics. Spotswood was aware that tributary tribes were quite reasonably concerned that the children they sent to the college would be sold into labor. To persuade tributaries that it was safe to send their children to William & Mary, he first worked to halt "the illicit Indian slave trade."[63] This effort was initially successful, and the Pamunkey sent several children to the school. When other tributaries remained reticent, he tried a different tactic, inserting a condition into the 1711 treaty negotiations whereby the tribe would send two of the "chief men's sons" and, in return, Spotswood would remit their annual tribute.[64] By the end of 1712, "there were hostages from all tributary Indians at the college," including the Meherrins, Chickahominy, Nottoways, and Nansemond. William & Mary entered a brief period of concertedly educating Native students, most between the ages of seven and fifteen.[65] Given the age of the students the college "recruited," however, it is more accurate to describe the schooling provided to them as preparatory rather than collegiate.[66]

While treaty agreements successfully populated William & Mary with Native students, pleasing the Boyle trustees, it also necessarily redirected Brafferton funds toward supporting the new students and away from the rest of the college, a development that frustrated Blair and his vision for the institution. Spotswood attempted to make up for this loss. He lobbied the Virginia Assembly for extra funds to cover the increased costs, arguing the funds were necessary since they would "save souls as well as give security."[67] In doing so, he made explicit a primary, though often submerged, component of the mission to educate Native students: providing for the security of borders through the education and, just as importantly, detention of tribal youth. When this state-focused effort failed, he turned back to the Anglican Society for the Propagation of the Gospel in Foreign Parts, emphasizing the missionary component of the school's project. When support was still not forthcoming, Spotswood's attentions turned away from such education-based projects and the active pursuit of educating Native students waned in the latter half of the 1710s.

Ironically, the lack of activity meant that monies from the Brafferton Fund accumulated in sufficient amounts to underwrite the construction of an Indian school building. As with Cheeshateaumuck and Iacoomes, the young students who continued their studies at William & Mary were both educated and enculturated in English norms of instruction, language, and dress. In her master's thesis on the history of the Brafferton School, Karen Stuart asserts that, as was the case with Indigenous Harvard students in the mid-seventeenth century, records show that "some died, others ran away, and none is known to have returned to his homeland as a Christian missionary."[68]

By the time the construction of the Brafferton building was complete in 1723 much about the project was in question. Two contemporaneous commentaries from 1724 capture the general concerns. The first is a book entitled *History of the Dividing Line* by William Byrd, a slave-owning planter notorious for recording his abuses of the people he enslaved in his diary. In it, Byrd writes of

> the bad Success Mr. Boyle's Charity has hitherto had towards converting any of these poor Heathens to Many children of our Neighboring Indians have been brought up in the College of William & Mary. They have been taught to read and write, and have been carefully Instructed in the Principles of the Christian Religion, till they came to be men. Yet after they returne'd home, instead of civilizeing and converting the rest, they have immediately Relapt into Infidelity and Babarism themselves.
>
> And some of them too have made the worst use of the Knowledge they acquir'd among the English, by employing it against their Benefactors. Besides, as they unhappily forget all the good they learn, and remember the Ill, they are apt to be more vicious and disorderly than the rest of their Countrymen.[69]

Reverend Hugh Jones, a "Mathematickal Professor" at William & Mary, also wrote about the college and its failures in relationship to Indian students in his 1724 *Present State of Virginia*. In a pattern similar to what had transpired at Harvard, Jones notes that the "abundance of the [Indian students] used to die, either thro' Sickness, change of Provision, and way of life; or as some will have it, often from want of proper Necessaries and due Care taken with them."[70] He goes on to observe that conversion efforts failed, in part because Indians "can live with less labour, and more pleasure and plenty, as Indians," even as he lamented a lack of attention to their "futurity."[71] Between the 1720s and 1740s, both interest in and activity at the Indian College waned, no doubt in part due to such assessments. For Blair, the decreased enrollment of Native students was desirable so long as just enough students enrolled to justify funding from the Brafferton Estate.

Between the 1740s and 1780s, William & Mary's educational projects shifted in response to political conditions. While the institution maintained missionary components and framing, its work took on new import as a means of expanding British soft power through relationships with tribes that occupied the boundary lines between British and French colonies. After Blair's passing in 1743, the Brafferton mission shifted in response to changing dynamics between British colonists who wished to expand their land holdings, local tribes, including Catawba and Cherokee, who resisted that expansion and sought more control over their trade, and increasing tensions between European powers, most notably the British and the French. The college emerged as one strategy for addressing these pressures, in part through recruiting Indigenous students who could go on to function as ambassadors to their tribes to extend English interests.

In the 1740s and 1750s, the Virginians held a series of treaty conferences and meetings with tribal leaders from the Six Nations Haudenosaunee Confederacy, composed of the Mohawk, Onondaga, Oneida, Cayuga, Seneca, and Tuscarora, in which they attempted to recruit students to expand their sphere of influence, but to little effect.[72] According to the minutes from the treaty meeting and also documented in a letter from Benjamin Franklin to Peter Collinson in 1753, tribal representatives refused various efforts to promote Indigenous education at William & Mary, another example of this chapter's fourth axiomatic; "it had been observed that for a long time after [students] returned to their Friends, they were absolutely good for nothing being neither acquainted with the true methods of deer killing, catching Beaver or surprising an enemy."[73] The representatives did, however, offer to host English children in Onondaga so they could be made "men" through an education in tribal ways. This offer asserts not only that the Onondaga no longer had an interest in what William & Mary had on offer, but that they were also quite aware that they had their own valuable knowledge to provide.

According to a roster of Brafferton students Buck Woodard includes in the Muscarelle Museum of Art exhibition catalogue, there was a resurgence in the enrollment of Indigenous students from the 1750s to the 1770s. Unsurprisingly, the students whose names he was able to trace in the archive are almost singularly the ones whose stories contravene a narrative of the failure of the "Brafferton Experiment." At times drawing on what he describes as "strong circumstantial evidence" triangulating "data from multiple sources and repositories," Woodard provides detailed accounts of seven Indigenous men who studied for varying periods of time at the Brafferton before going on to serve as interpreters, cultural brokers, and ambassadors between the British and their tribes: Robert Scholar (Nottoway), Thomas Step (Nottoway), Charles Murphy (Cherokee), John Montour (Delaware-Oneida), John Nettles (Catawba), Robert Mush (Pamunkey), and Henry Bawbee (Wyandot).[74] Woodard is careful to acknowledge that the experiences of these students differed significantly from others. For instance, in describing Murphy he remarks that he had a different experience from other Cherokee students who "did not like confinement, and in Course, no Inclination to Learning . . . they were too old . . . they co'd not be reconcil'd to their Books; they went away of their own accord with't leave."[75] The allegiance of the Cherokee first to the French and then to the British against the interests of Virginians and then nascent Americans throughout the eighteenth century suggests that the soft power inducements of education were especially ineffective in this instance.[76]

But, each of the students Woodard traces supports a reading of the Brafferton as a significant contribution to "American statecraft" and, as such, suggests the effectiveness of education as a settler colonial tactic.[77] Nettles, for instance, "grew up as Catawba, but his Williamsburg education molded and shaped him to be a person of different character than his tribesman."[78] While this led "his own people" to view "him with a measure of disdain," he also served important roles and, in 1801, wrote a petition to South Carolina to request education for the Catawba youth. Woodard takes this effort as "evidence that indigenous communities viewed the secular dimension of the Brafferton Indian School education as having value during a time of culture change and encroachment of settler society."[79] Robert Mush is discussed as a realization of British colonial goals to "convert, educate, and train indigenous ministers." In his post-Brafferton life, Mush was literate, fought in the military, attended church, paid taxes, and, as an important marker of his conversion, owned enslaved people.[80] Rather than reading Mush as a "celebration of colonialism," Woodard argues for a more individualistic understanding of Mush's story, contending that his "life experience should be considered in the context of time and place, noting his individual agency."[81]

## Moor's Charity School and the Failure of Assimilation

The turn toward using educational projects as a mode of incorporating Indigenous people into the British soft power project also took shape in northern institutions from the 1740s forward. Like William & Mary, such initiatives were underwritten by a combination of missionary beliefs and funding enlivened by the Great Awakening, even as they also functioned as a crucial component of efforts to recruit Native men to serve as agents of British interests among members of the Haudenosaunee Confederacy, including the Mohawk, Onondaga, Oneida, Cayuga, Seneca, and Tuscarora, many of whom had left the Virginia area in part due to the practices of the administrators at William & Mary. Dartmouth College and its origins in Moor's Indian Charity School is exemplary of this history. There is a robust body of historical scholarship on Dartmouth, Moor's, their founder Eleazar Wheelock, and his first Native pupil, Samson Occom. Colin Calloway's *The Indian History of an American Institution: Native Americans and Dartmouth* from 2010 is the most definitive of such histories, but other scholars, including Brooks and Craig Wilder, have also done substantial work to flesh out this history, especially in relationship to the question of dispossession and the extraction of labor from enslaved people.

As the story goes, in 1734, Eleazar Wheelock graduated from Yale University, acquired a license to preach, and purchased Fortune, a twenty-two-year-old Black man, for £245.[82] In 1735, he was ordained as the minister at the Second Congregational Church in Lebanon, Connecticut, opened a small school, and, soon after, obtained substantial farmland in the region. He also continued purchasing enslaved people, including Dinah, Ishmael, Sippy, and Peggy. When the Great Awakening swept New England in 1740, he traveled extensively to spread the revival, leading to concern within Connecticut's religious establishment that he had abandoned his own parish. As a result, he was denied his salary in 1743 for "regulating abuses and correcting disorders in ecclesiastical affairs."[83] To make up for his lost income, Wheelock began to house English boys to provide them with college preparation, in effect starting his own school, which was initially called the "Lattin School."[84]

Later that year, Samson Occom, a twenty-year-old member of the Mohegan Nation and member of the tribe's twelve-person governing council, joined the school with the intention of staying a short while to improve the literacy he had gained through self-study.[85] As with other figures featured in this genealogy, there are various narratives of what led Occom to seek out Wheelock and his tutelage. By some accounts, Occom, like Wheelock, had been taken up by the Great Awakening and, as the text widely discussed as his autobiography—one of the only such works thought to have been written by a Native person in the century—attests, at seventeen he turned to Christianity to understand "the Word of God" and share it with the Mohegan people.[86] It is also possible, as other scholars, including Brooks, argue persuasively, that Occom was motivated in large part by his increasing awareness of the importance of literacy and the law for Mohegan efforts to reclaim land lost through the legal machinations of English settlers.[87] In this way, Occom's interest in a Christian education was both about being integrated into and making use of capitalist logics of property that settlers used to justify Native dispossession.

Either way, once Occom arrived at the school, Wheelock saw his presence and abilities as an opportunity. He arranged for Occom to study at the school with financial support from the Boston commissioners of the Society for the Propagation of the Gospel in Foreign Parts, thus capitalizing on Occom's presence for financial gain most immediately. Occom proved himself to be an apt student, becoming proficient in Latin, Greek, and Hebrew in addition to his fluency in English over the four years he studied with Wheelock. After spending just over four years with Wheelock, Occom returned to Montauk and served as a schoolmaster and preacher to the Mohegan and Niantic peoples.[88] By 1756, he was ordained as a minister.

Inspired in part by what he saw as his successes with Occom and perhaps also by a growing sense of urgency for the British to assert influence on tribes in their vicinity with the start of the French and Indian War, Wheelock moved to expand his educational enterprise to recruit more Native students in the early 1750s.[89] James Axtell's 1982 chapter on "Dr. Wheelock's Little Red School" describes Wheelock's goal as twofold: "to save the Indians from themselves and to save the English from the Indians."[90] Axtell goes on to cite Wheelock's own words that clearly align with Pratt's 1890s articulation of the eliminatory project in Wheelock's desire to "cure the Natives . . . of their Savage Temper and 'purge all the Indian out' of his students."[91]

In 1754, two Indian boys from the Delaware Tribe traveled to the school at Wheelock's behest. Wheelock used their presence to raise funds from his neighbor, Colonel Joshua Moor, to "endow the fledgling school with several buildings and two acres of land."[92] So started "Moor's Indian Charity School." By 1761, Wheelock was teaching ten Indian students, and then between ninety and 140 more over the next eight years. According to Brooks, the majority of students came to Wheelock's school by way of Occom, including his brothers-in-law David and Jacob Fowler, as well as his cousin, and eventually his son, Aaron, and several other members of his tribe. Brooks argues that while the school was certainly part of "Wheelock's colonial experiment," for this group of Native students it also "provided a space of interaction" and enabled them to "utilize education for community empowerment."[93] One particular avenue through which interaction was enabled was Occom's successful effort to recruit approximately thirty students from Oneida and other Haudenosaunee nations during the 1760s, which enabled new relationships between coastal Algonquians and the Haudenosaunee Confederacy and made possible a shared understanding of their experiences of dispossession and strategies for resistance.[94]

As the number of Indigenous students grew, so too did Wheelock's complaints about the difficulty of his pursuit, betraying his animosities and prejudices against his pupils. In 1762, he sent a letter to George Whitefield complaining about challenges he faced, explaining that the students would "soon kill themselves with Eating and Sloth, if constant care were not exercised for them at least the first year."[95] As with past attempts by missionaries in Indian education, Wheelock marked his particular concern with the students' relation to time, complaining that they "used to live from Hand to Mouth (as we speak) and have no care for Futurity."[96] The school's curriculum reflected these concerns. According to Calloway, Wheelock "monitored his students, controlled their actions, and demanded that they reconceptualize their thoughts and deeds in terms of sin and damnation."[97] Wright describes how Wheelock took "much Pains to purge all *the Indian* out" of the students.[98] To instill a properly British or "civilized" sense of time and labor, he attempted to remove what he saw as "the deep prejudices, so universally in the minds of the Indians, against their Men's cultivating lands."[99] In so doing, he simultaneously worked to inculcate what he saw as the proper gendered relationships to work. While boys and men were sent to the fields, "Native girls were apprenticed to local women to learn 'the Female Part, as House-wives, Schoolmistresses, [and] Tayloresses' whereby they, as helpmates."[100] Whether Wheelock truly felt he was doing the Lord's work in assigning students to labor or simply exploiting them, he asserted his ability to enact strict punishment, writing in a letter to a friend in 1762, "I can correct & punish them as I please, and I find necessary, to humble them, and reform their manners."[101]

In their accounts of the school's history, Axtell, Wright, and Calloway each document that Wheelock's tendency to educate "with a heavy hand" did not go unnoticed.[102] Calloway describes how students and parents protested that pupils spent more time laboring on the land than they did studying and, as such, felt they were "exploited as cheap labor."[103] Wright attests that many students ran away, some successfully, while "a large number of them died."[104] For instance, according to Axtell, John Daniel, a Narragansett parent, wrote to Wheelock out of concern about his child's experiences at the school: "I alays tho't Your School was free to Natives; not to learn how to Farm it, but to advance Christian Knowledge, which wear the Chief motive that caus'd me to send my Son Charles to you . . . to work two Years to learn to Farm it, is what I don't consent to."[105] Axtell goes on to describe how, in 1768, Hezekiah Calvin, a Delaware Indian and schoolmaster at Moor's, left in protest over Wheelock's approach, widely publicizing his reason for leaving. In no uncertain terms, he accused Wheelock of using "the Indians very hard in keeping them to work, & not allowing them a proper Privelidge in the School."[106]

By the time Calvin circulated his missive, however, Wheelock was well on his way to actualizing a plan to move on from Moor's Charity School to a larger collegiate endeavor. As early as 1761, Wheelock wrote to General Jeffery Amherst about the possibility of opening a college. Amherst is the namesake of Amherst College, infamous for instigating the intentional distribution of blankets infected with smallpox to Ottawa Indians during their siege on Fort Pitt in 1763 and as part of his broader campaign to "effectually extirpate or remove that vermin."[107] In 1765, at the urging of Reverend Charles Jeffrey Smith, Wheelock sent George Whitefield and Occom to Europe "home a begging."[108] Throughout his year-long travels around England, Occom, the first Indian minister to visit London, delivered over three hundred sermons. One Minister wrote to Wheelock, describing Occom as "a Speciman of the beneifitt of ye school."[109] Before returning to Connecticut, Occom and Whitefield raised over £12,000, "the largest amount collected through direct solicitation by any American institution in the colonial era."[110] With this windfall in hand, Wheelock's vision for a college became a more concrete possibility. Since colleges expanded towns' economic potential, Wheelock was able to select from several offers of both land and capital, settling on Hanover, New Hampshire.

On December 13, 1769, New Hampshire Governor John Wentworth signed the charter for Dartmouth College. As with Harvard and William & Mary, the charter for Dartmouth College designed the institution's mission as "for the education & instruction of Youth of the Indian Tribes in this Land in reading, writing & all parts of Learning which shall appear necessary and expedient for civilizing and christianizing Children of Pagans as well as in all liberal Arts and Sciences."[111] According to Axtell, Wheelock added "and also of English Youth and any others" almost "as if an afterthought."[112] As Calloway documents, in August of 1770, Wheelock further asserted the college's standing when he gave public notice in regional newspapers that "My Indian charity school . . . is now become a body corporate and politic, under the name of DARTMOUTH COLLEGE." In the notice, he explained that the college would continue to support Moor's charity school for the education of Indian youth, but that the college would be for English youth as missionaries. As with other such institutions before it, Dartmouth was built by the labor of the people Wheelock enslaved. When he traveled to Hanover, he brought at least eight enslaved Black people: Brister, Exeter, Chloe, Caesar, Lavinia, Archelaus, Peggy, and a young child.[113]

The exact reasoning for Wheelock's turn away from Indian education is not entirely clear. Calloway contends that he lost interest and, in his poor health, he had "become increasingly frustrated by the cultural resistance and resilience of his Indian students."[114] Wilder suggests that both Wheelock and the trustees of William & Mary turned from the cause of educating Native youth because "tensions between England and the colonies extinguished British funding."[115] It is as important, however, not to frame the shift in the project singularly through Wheelock's own actions but also through the actions of the students, parents, and tribes he tried to recruit. By the time Dartmouth opened, Calvin's experiences at Moor's charity school had circulated along with stories from other former students and parents. In 1768, after one Oneida student nearly bled to death after he was "taken with Vomiting Blood," another died, and a third had to be "raised from the Gates of Death," Oneida parents withdrew their children.[116] In 1772, the Onondaga council added their rejection to the list of tribes refusing Wheelock's invitation in large part because of what they understood as Wheelock's "*manner* of teaching Indian[s]" which entailed "for every little mistake tak[ing] up a club & flog them."[117] The Tuscarora also sent word that they "had determined to have no English schools among them."[118]

In retrospect, perhaps one of the most damning accounts of Wheelock's failure to make good on his promises was penned in 1771 by Occom. Wheelock's one-time poster student was driven to express his frustrations, writing:

> I am very Jealous instead of your Semenary Becoming alma Mater, she will be to alba [white] mater to Suckle the Tawnees, for She is already aDorn'd up too much like the Popish Virgin Mary. . . . In So Saying I Speak the general Sentiment of Indians and English too in these parts . . . I verily thought once that your Institution was Inteded Purely for the poor Indians and with this thought I Cheerfully Ventur'd my Body & Soul, left my Country my poor young Family all my friend and Relations, to sail over the Boisterous Sea to England, to help forward your School, Hoping, that it may be a lasting Benefit to my poor Tawnee Breathren, With this View I went a Volunteer—I was quite Willing to become a Gazing Stock, Yea Even a Laughing Stock, in Strange Countries to Promote your Cause. . . . But when we got Home behold all the glory had declared and now I am afraid, we shall be Deem'd as Liars and Deceivers in Europe, unless you gather Indians quickly to your College, in great Numbers.[119]

Here, Occom calls Wheelock out for the bait and switch he had entangled him in. Occom had seen his journey to Europe as a righteous one that would extend educational possibilities to Indigenous peoples only to have Wheelock use the funds he raised to educate only white men.

As Axtell recounts in a talk in the late 1970s, "popular legend and collegial folklore tell us that Dartmouth was hewn out of the New Hampshire forest as an 'Indian college' to convert the natives to Christianity and civilization."[120] However, a more accurate interpretation of this history reveals that Dartmouth itself was never an "Indian College" but, instead, the very idea of an "Indian College" functioned as a marketing tactic through which Wheelock was able to amass the support, both financial and political, necessary to open a school to educate white would-be missionaries. The reason behind the change was both that Wheelock's desires shifted, in part because of his lack of success at educating Indians, but also, and importantly, because Native peoples themselves were not willing to participate in his schooling venture.

# 2

# "Ridding America of these alien bodies" for the Empire of Liberty

In 1856, nineteen-year-old Wilbur Fisk Burns traveled from Liberia to Middletown, Connecticut to study at a small Methodist liberal arts college, Wesleyan University. His father, Francis Burns was part of an early wave of free Black people who emigrated from the United States to the colony of Liberia in 1834. Backed by the US government and grounded in the writings of Thomas Jefferson, Liberia was founded in 1822, primarily through the efforts of the American Colonization Society (ACS). The ACS articulated its mission as twofold: to spread Christianity to the African continent and to resolve the contradictions of the United States' claim to universal equality and its subjugation of human beings racialized as Black and enslaved as property.[1]

For Jefferson, it was clear as early as 1779 that the equality of men professed at the founding of the new nation-state could not stand alongside the enslavement of people of African descent. But, in his mind, it was also the case that "the two races, equally free, cannot live in the same government." His proposed solution, which he articulated during debates in the Virginia House of Delegates in 1779 and then again in his 1821 *Autobiography*, was a "process of emancipation" necessarily connected to one of "deportation."[2] As David Kazanjian explains, Jefferson desired both the "racial purification of a domestic space and the exercise of imperial power over a foreign space."[3] In other words, colonization's secondary objective of resolving the nation's founding contradiction through its whitening was to be accomplished by removing or deporting all people of African descent from the United States and sending them to settle elsewhere as "global agents of

American universality."[4] At the same time, the expulsion of Black people from the American domestic sphere served to codify people racialized as white and those racialized as Black as "members of distinct, calculable populations that could be manipulated like numbers on a ledger or statistics on a census table," the latter of which was just emerging as a dominant academic style of thought in the early 1800s. Deporting US-educated people had the added benefit of expanding the territorial footprint of American ideologies of the nation-state and capital. As such, Liberia was one front in Jefferson's "empire of liberty."[5]

Born free in Albany, New York, in 1809, Francis Burns was indentured to a Methodist farmer when he was four. After falling ill at a young age, he was sent to school and eventually licensed to be a preacher.[6] He traveled with Reverend John Seys to Liberia as a missionary teacher, was ordained deacon, and was elected the first missionary bishop of the Methodist Episcopal Church in Africa two years after his son traveled to Connecticut. Burns understood that the "salvation" of Africa required the missionary project and believed that "Christianity, in order to preserve its vitality among any people, requires expansion, and *we* must spread or die."[7] In these articulations, Burns illustrates his fulsome embrace of the colonizationist belief that his education in the United States and then his "return" to Africa were, in fact, providential. In so doing, he was a model of the kind of global African or, more precisely, global African American Jefferson envisioned. Given Burn's deep commitment to Methodism, it is perhaps not surprising that his son shares the name of a prominent Methodist thinker and ACS member of his time, Willbur Fisk, the first president of Wesleyan.

Wilbur Fisk Burns was not the first Black student to attend Wesleyan, but he was the first to receive a degree. Charles Ray, a US-born student of African descent, attended the university briefly in 1832, the year after its founding, but was forced off campus by white students from both the North and the South who opposed his presence. Charles H. Gardner enrolled in 1855 but moved to Liberia without graduating in his senior year.[8] When Burns received his diploma in 1860, "there was a slight demonstration in the audience, but whether it was designed to express approbation for the graduation of colored student or otherwise, it would be impossible to say."[9] When the younger Burns returned to Liberia from his studies, the country was thirteen years into its declared independence. Still, the US government had yet to recognize this status.[10] This would occur two years later, in 1862, a crucial moment for US policy and for US higher education on many fronts.

After completing his studies, Burns returned to Liberia where he practiced law, "engaged in cultivating sugar-cane and coffee," and had a short career as the comptroller and surveyor-in-chief of the republic before he died in "1864 or 5" in Monrovia, or possibly 1869 in Sierra Leone.[11] As Figure 3 illustrates, the inscription in the Wesleyan alumni record is notably uncertain and revised. In other words, in the four to nine years he lived following his graduation and return to Liberia, Burns participated in several of the key forms of colonial economy and governance: the extractive practices of sugar and coffee production and the professional work of financial and geographic management, modeling a new era of global African Americanness with an increasing allegiance to capital rather than to Christ.

This chapter situates Burns's story in a broader history of US higher education and noncitizen students from the 1810s to the early 1860s to track the various uses education was imagined to serve the emergent nation-state and its imperial pursuits. Studies of US higher education often move quickly over the antebellum period, relegating it to a prehistory of the mid-nineteenth-century land-grant university or the late nineteenth-century rise of the research university.[12] Studies of international or noncitizen students at these institutions almost universally begin in 1847 with the travel of Yung Wing, the first Chinese student to enroll in a US university, Yale.[13] As Chapter 1 contends, grappling with the imperial present of US higher education requires a longer historical trajectory that accounts for the foundationally international and nation-state-making practices and relationships that constituted the logics, funding, and epistemologies of higher education institutions in the United States during the British colonial era.

Here, the story moves forward historically and expands geographically. I begin by examining how national leaders, with a focus on Thomas Jefferson, imagined colleges and universities would function as demographic tools for producing, reproducing, building, and managing the emergent nation-state. Given that for much of this period the project of higher education was focused on the cultivation of a white citizenry, I then turn to the satellite project of the Cornwall School for Native Youth, an institution founded by graduates of Williams College and Yale for the explicit purpose of educating, civilizing, and exporting "heathen youth" who traveled through the United States, beginning in 1816 with a student from Hawai'i and culminating in the 1820s with the education of two of the central players in the Cherokee Nation's removal. The end of the chapter returns to higher education and the founding of Lincoln University in the 1850s as an institution committed to educating students of African descent with the explicit purpose that they would contribute to the civilization and religious education of the African continent. The stories of

Figure 1. Portrait of Wilbur Fisk Burns. Wesleyan University class albums and autograph books. Special Collections & Archives, Wesleyan University. Courtesy of Special Collections & Archives, Wesleyan University.

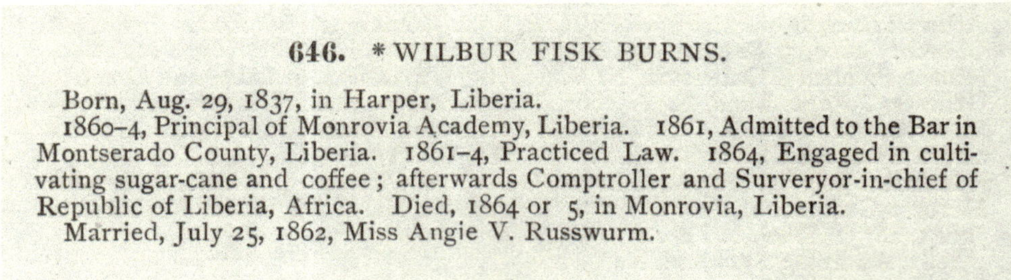

646. * WILBUR FISK BURNS.

Born, Aug. 29, 1837, in Harper, Liberia.
1860–4, Principal of Monrovia Academy, Liberia. 1861, Admitted to the Bar in Montserado County, Liberia. 1861–4, Practiced Law. 1864, Engaged in cultivating sugar-cane and coffee; afterwards Comptroller and Surveryor-in-chief of Republic of Liberia, Africa. Died, 1864 or 5, in Monrovia, Liberia.
Married, July 25, 1862, Miss Angie V. Russwurm.

Figure 2. Wilbur Fisk Burns's entry in the Wesleyan University Alumni Record from 1881–1883. *Alumni Record of Wesleyan University, Third Edition 1881–1883* (Lockwood & Brainard Company, 1883). Courtesy of Special Collections & Archives, Wesleyan University.

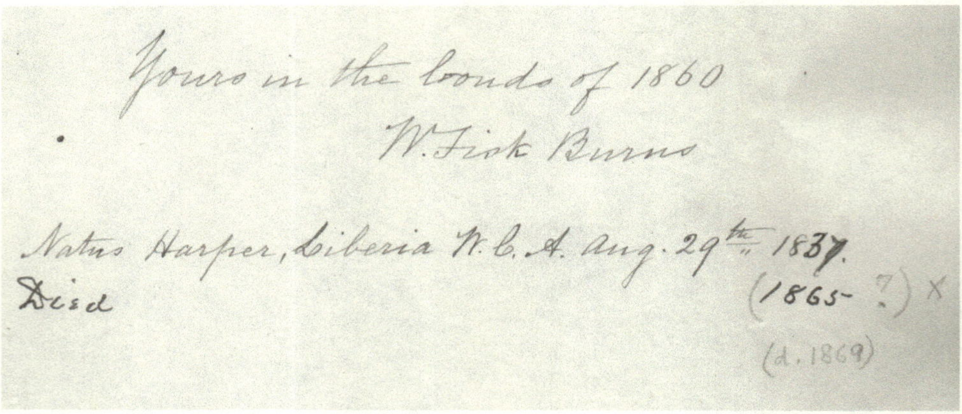


Figure 3. Wilbur Fisk Burns's signature in W. H Wardell's class autograph book. "Willbur Fisk Burns, W. H. Wardell—"A" (1860). Wesleyan University class albums and autograph books. Courtesy of Special Collections & Archives, Wesleyan University.

Burns and the Hawaiian and Cherokee students educated in Cornwall, Connecticut, in the early decades of the nineteenth century, and the work of Lincoln University, flesh out the overlapping and inter-implicated histories of colonialism, slavery, and US universities and the ways they surface a settler colonial and imperial project that spans continents and centuries.

## Post-Revolutionary Higher Education and White Nationhood

After the Revolution, the newly American educators were no longer motivated to pursue the education of Indigenous youth as part of a strategy to access funding from English armchair missionaries or as a benevolent project of civilization that authorized dispossession. Where facially incorporative logics had once prevailed, an agenda of removal took hold. Many of the most influential people who forwarded educational initiatives in the late eighteenth and early nineteenth centuries, Jefferson central among them, understood their work as part of an effort to shape the complexion of America as an emergent white nation-state, a "land of the future" ordained by destiny where naturalization was foundationally restricted to "free white people."[14] To meet this destiny, Benjamin Rush argued in 1786, "the new country required an educational system equal to the task of self-governance."[15] Despite, or perhaps because of, his education at the University of Edinburgh, Rush and his contemporaries, including George Washington, worried that the lack of higher educational institutions in the new country meant that American students would have to seek their education in Europe, "where they were in danger of absorbing anti-republican principles with the very air they breathed."[16] In 1785, Jefferson wrote to John Banister, lamenting that "an American coming to Europe for education loses in his knowledge, in his morals, in his health, in his habits, and in his happiness."[17] In other words, they believed that the sanctity and reproduction of the nation-state's founding philosophies and commitments required that future leaders be educated domestically. Over the next decades, this vision of education as a mode of reproduction and accumulation expanded its geographic footprint and ambitions.

In the two decades after the Revolutionary War, nineteen new colleges were formed, tripling the number of higher education institutions in the country. By the 1860s, another 220 campuses covered the eastern half of the country's extending map.[18] With very few exceptions, these institutions exclusively educated white men, though, true to Jefferson's ideals, the student body was drawn from both the wealthy and those of less means.[19] Many of the new institutions were the direct product of state and federal prerogatives, such as the Northwest Ordinances of 1785 and 1787, which variously dispossessed land from Indigenous peoples and "allocated a million acres of land in Ohio with the provision that a township would be set aside for the purposes of establishing an institution of higher education."[20] Despite the 1819 Dartmouth College ruling, which definitively established the status of private colleges and universities as corporate bodies protected from the will of the state, during this era many private institutions, including Harvard, Yale, and William & Mary, "accepted more state representation on their respective governing boards."[21] "Characterized by their openness as well as their empiricism," students and legislators "agreed that the new colleges should teach courses of value here in this world, not in the next, and should aim to turn out responsible and useful citizens."[22] This articulation marks a distinct move away from religious education and toward a model of education in the service of the nominally secular state. Importantly, however, the new frames of thinking most useful to the state, such as demography and political economy, were not themselves wholly distinct from religious ideas. Rather, as David Blaney has argued, "economic thought retains a theological structure . . . adapting or reconstituting theological principles in the form of a natural theology grounded in a mechanical universe."[23]

Thomas Jefferson is a key figure in this history. A Virginian and an alumnus of William & Mary, he understood education as essential to the cultivation of a self-governing citizenry.[24] One of his key projects during the Revolutionary War in 1779 was to reorganize his alma mater, eliminating the Indian School and adding faculty in fine arts and the law.[25] Jefferson is often lauded for his commitment to a broad-based democracy, albeit one predicated on what Uday Mehta might describe as certain "anthropological minimums" of education and race.[26] For Jefferson, education rendered individuals "worthy to receive, and able to guard the sacred deposit of the rights and liberties of their fellow citizens."[27] The racial parameters of this "worthiness" are evidenced in his staunch belief, referenced above, regarding the impossibility of white and Black people cohabitating in shared governance.[28]

While Jefferson initially rejected calls for a national university, due to his commitment to Republicanism, and efforts to form a military academy, because of his concerns about a professional army, during his presidency, he oversaw the founding of the United States Military Academy at West Point. In drafting and signing the 1802 Military Peace Establishment Act, Jefferson carved out a way to dismiss from the army many Federalists with whom he had strong disagreements while, simultaneously, creating West Point as a training academy for the kind of republican officers he preferred.[29] As Stephen Ambrose describes in his canonical history of West Point, "[w]hen Jefferson assumed the Presidency in 1801, he was eager to found a national institution that would eliminate the classics, add the sciences, and produce graduates who could use their knowledge for the benefit of society."[30] The broad push for a military academy provided the best chance to actualize this vision: "sectionalists opposed to a national university might be persuaded to support a national military academy, while the scholastics would be more willing to accept an empiricist academy than they would an empiricist university."[31]

Jefferson had long "shared with others a sense of embarrassment and uneasiness over the nation's deficiency of knowledge in engineering and other useful sciences," a perception that came into focus when he advised a friend that to study engineering his son would have to travel to France.[32] West Point, and through it the consolidation of an Army Core of Engineers, was an opportunity to correct this issue. The institution was to be led by a chief engineer and the students' training was to emphasize science.[33] The first faculty were a graduate of Harvard and an "acting professor of natural and experimental philosophy" who had taught at Yale.[34] Rather than the curriculums of Latin and Greek and religion, cadets studied French and math, learning to survey the landscape around West Point. Though it took a number of years, by the 1820s and under the leadership of the "Father of the Military Academy," Colonel Sylvanus Thayer, West Point adopted a course of study, method of discipline, and system for sorting students by merit that has remained consistent ever since.[35] An 1807 Dartmouth graduate, Thayer attended West Point, joined the corps, and then served in the War of 1812.[36] After receiving further training in France, Thayer became superintendent in 1817 intent on shaping the academy into a "national scientific institution" with a focus on civil engineering, fulfilling Jefferson's vision.[37] Cadets received training in design and construction of basic infrastructure, including roads, railroads, harbors, forts, and tunnels. In 1824, Congress passed the General Survey Act and the Rivers and Harbors Act, the US Supreme Court established federal authority over interstate commerce, and President James Monroe assigned responsibility for such projects to the Corps of Engineers. In this role, the corps took on the central task of literal empire-building.

While West Point allowed Jefferson to make good on his belief in the value and importance of scientific study and education to build the new nation's infrastructure, the emergent field of political economy was fundamental to his thinking on the management, or engineering, of the nation's demographic composition. When US students traveled to Western Europe in the late eighteenth and early nineteenth centuries to study, the academy was on the cusp of what Ian Hacking has called the "avalanche of printed numbers," an "era of enthusiasm" for statistical analysis, "the hallmark of the modern state" or the "science of the state." This new way of knowing and calculating the world emerged as a valid science, despite significant concern within the academic community about its lack of merit and objectivity.[38] As Michel Foucault argues, only with this "science" could new forms of government "rationalize the exercise of power, precisely in terms of the knowledge acquired through statistics."[39] Linda Gordon describes how the field "helped remove population from the area of ineluctable natural events to an area that seemed open to human manipulation."[40] Matters of birth, death, and the qualitative makeup of a nation-state's citizenry were no longer understood as a given; instead, the practices of governance could work to shape the conditions and creation of life.

Jefferson studied this work, extending particular praise to the work of Thomas Malthus, a British Liberal economist, specifically the 1803 second edition of his canonical *Essay on the Principle of Population.*[41] Malthus departed from more optimistic writers in that he understood the dynamics of population as a "natural phenomenon," casting doubt on utopian strands of thought and supporting conservative assumptions that poverty and human suffering were inherent to human existence, rather than the effect of structurally produced inequity in the distribution of resources. As he writes, "the power of population is indefinitely greater than the power in the earth to produce subsistence for man."[42] Jefferson was persuaded by Malthus's "pro-agrarian, laissez-faire teaching" but wary of some of his more pessimistic perspectives, believing them ill-suited to the United States, given its expansive territory, especially after the Louisiana Purchase in 1803.[43] A friend of Jefferson's recalls a conversation with him in which he suggested that "a well regulated System of gradual colonization might prove an effectual remedy, without adding to the inevitable mass of human misery."[44]

Jefferson's engagement with Malthus reinforced his early belief in deportation as a mode of managing the racial future of the country. By 1800, the world politics of the trade in subjugated humans was reconfiguring rapidly. In the 1790s, Haitians revolted against French colonial rule and abolitionist organizers in Britain agitated for the end of trade in enslaved people. In the aftermath of the American Revolution, the British established a settlement in Sierra Leone, initially for Black people who had been loyal to the Crown in the former colony but eventually as part of an effort to manage and remove impoverished Black people from London as well.[45] During this same period in the United States, free men of color like Paul Cuffe advocated for their rights, exposing "the new nation's hypocritical white settler colonial rule over people of color," and both enslaved and formerly enslaved Black people made demands either through occupying land abandoned by the British or through organized rebellions, such as Gabriel's Rebellion in 1800, which stoked white fears. In response, between 1800 and 1816, the Virginia legislature met no less than five times to "consider the peril" as the Black population of Virginia doubled from 15,000 to 30,000 in a decade. Fueled by "the anxiety felt by the white people of the state," James Monroe, the governor of Virginia, asked Jefferson to grant their governor treaty-making power to establish a "place in Africa or elsewhere for the colonization of free Negros."[46]

The emerging field of political economy and its modes for calculating populations and projecting their future growth fueled these fears, and the push for deportation, but the political process of establishing the colony of Liberia would take another two decades. The colony eventually established by the American Colonization Society in 1822 was the concrete outcome of this history. Kazanjian argues that the process of Liberia's founding clearly enacted at least part of Jefferson's efforts to execute a policy "of calculating the number of black Americans in the United States, paying for the emancipation of those held in slavery, and funding the exportation and resettlement of all black Americans outside the territorial boundaries of the United States" in order to "emancipate all Americans from slavery and realize equality in its most universal sense."[47] As Kazanjian reads these efforts, Jefferson's goals were twofold, "racial purification of a domestic space and the exercise of imperial power over a foreign space."[48] However, the colonization of Liberia for the purpose of deporting free Black people from the United States was not an isolated project. The imperial vision behind Liberia also took shape in educational institutions in the United States, albeit not in the exclusive white enclaves of colleges and universities. Instead, other experimental schools took the helm in efforts to educate, cultivate, and export nonwhite would-be agents of America and its religious and political beliefs to outposts abroad.

Wilbur Fisk was among the many college administrators drawn to the ACS project. For Fisk, colonization represented a reasonable compromise between the growing movement to abolish slavery and the status quo of widespread enslavement of people of African descent throughout the southern United States. Craig Steven Wilder goes so far as to argue that the "ACS was born on campus." "It was," he continues, "conceived from the collision between enthusiastic Christianity and the rigid racial definitions that governed social and political thought in the United States."[49] Indeed, the establishment of the ACS and its plans to export Black people were, in part, an outcome of growing concern on various northern campuses regarding the morality of chattel slavery and the concomitant decline in slaveholding by faculty and administrators in the early nineteenth century. But, since abolishing the practice and economy of slavery was, in the eyes of many northern white people, simply a political and economic impossibility, removal was the only reasonable solution. Shortly after becoming president of Wesleyan in 1834, for instance, Fisk referred to abolitionist strategies and efforts as "moral quackery," arguing that "public sentiment was abundantly better before abolitionists touched it."[50] Fisk's position reflected a broader sentiment among college and university leaders who had come to recognize the immorality and injustice of slavery but could not envision a multiracial American future.[51] The turn to colonization and repatriation was a solution for what were increasingly conceived of as "demographic concerns" for which, Wilder explains, "White Americans had already made ethnic cleansing a preferred solution to their self-constructed racial dilemmas" as evidenced by the various uses of "coercion, violence, cycles of debt and deceit to reduce Native territories . . . and displace Indians who stood in the path of white migrations and the expansion of plantation slavery."[52] As the story of the Cherokee Nation discussed below illustrates, such tactics were still very much in practice in the 1830s.

## Missionary Education and the Export of Civilization

While colleges and universities abandoned the project of educating people increasingly classified as "nonwhite" after the Revolution, the movement of resources, goods, and knowledge required by capitalism's growth also entailed the transit of many different kinds of people from many different sorts of places—sailors on merchant boats from around the world, formally enslaved people seeking life in Northern states, and Indigenous people subjected to "documentary genocide" through their erasure in census records and dominant narratives.[53] And the lack of clear systems for regulating borders, to say nothing of the combined ineffectiveness of and violence of such systems when they did come to be, further ensured that these people traveled through cities and campuses as visitors and laborers, and inhabited them as denizens. For many people, the presence of these "others," individuals denied the rights of citizenship or even personhood, was one more inconvenient mark on the facade of universal rights. Others took their presence as an opportunity—a chance to cultivate a body of ambassadors for a global, Christian American future.

In 1810, a group of recent graduates from Williams College, including Samuel Mills Jr., founded the American Board of Commissioners for Foreign Missions (ABCFM).[54] As the board's name suggests, its founding objective was "to effect, in the person of its members, a mission or missions to the heathen." Moved by the Protestant revival of the time, often referred to as the Second Great Awakening, and a founding belief that "the millennium would commence in America," this group of young white men had a distinct ambition to spread the faith "to *all nations*" and, in the process, "effect an entire moral revolution in the whole human race."[55] For the graduates, a key strategy for doing so was to found institutions "for the education of heathen youth." For Christians who, in line with Jefferson, were as troubled by the continuation or spread of an economy based in the enslavement of Black people as they were by any vision of something akin to a multiracial society, such a mission emerged as a convenient strategy to manage and eliminate through deportation nonwhite people who would otherwise make claims upon the young nation-state.

On October 29, 1816, representatives of the ABCFM drafted a charter for a school to be located in Cornwall, Connecticut, a small, remote town they saw as an "ideal society" and "wished to see replicated across the American countryside and around the world."[56] Unlike Harvard, William & Mary, and Moor's Charity School in the British colonial period, the Cornwall School was distinctly not imagined as a school for young Indigenous people who lived in its proximity. Rather, building on the ABCFM's vision of an American-led global missionary project, an 1816 issue of *The Panoplist, and Missionary Magazine* describes that the school would be a training ground for "those heathen youth, who, from time to time, are found in our country, with a view to employ them in civilizing and Christianizing the different nations to which they belong."[57] The plan for Cornwall built on the long-established history of educational projects designed "for the training up of the Children of those Infidels" to, as historian Karen Sánchez-Eppler describes, export American beliefs while at the same time "ridding America of these alien bodies."[58] In line with Jefferson's thinking, such an approach had two benefits. First, it was a strategic maneuver. Members of the board believed that employing "Natives" as the primary agents of missionary work would remove a "great obstacle" to missionary work in "heathen nations": the prejudice of local inhabitants against "more enlightened brethren."[59] Second, since it was a program of inculcation and distribution rather than one of incorporation, it mapped onto the emerging racial logics of the early 1800s.[60] Sánchez-Eppler explains that the school "less resembled other mission schools than it presaged the development of new educational institutions within the United States that over the next two decades would offer to exchange education for colonization, teaching nonwhite students on the condition of their departure from the United States."[61] The goal was simple: Temporarily and conditionally including racial others in order to export American beliefs and a faith in the idea of America as the site of world-historical progress while, at the same time, shaping the demographic of the country to align with white supremacist visions. This practice set an enduring legacy.

The Cornwall School's 1816 constitution and a set of other publications commissioned by the school and the ABCFM in the mid- to late-1810s, most notably *Narrative of Five Youths from the Sandwich Islands Now Receiving Education in this Country* and *The Memoirs of Henry Obookiah*, conjure an evocative mythology of the school's founding. According to the constitution, the Foreign Mission was initially inspired to start the school by the presence of several young men from a place they called "Owhyhee" who, influenced by "curiosity, and other various motives leave their country and directed by the providence of God, are conveyed to this land of gospel light."[62] More specifically, the school's founders were moved by the efforts of several members of the Yale campus to educate a "dark-skinned youth"—ʻŌpūkahaʻia—who would come to take the name Henry Obookiah upon his conversion to Christianity.[63] The story goes as follows: Two boys in their mid-teens, ʻŌpūkahaʻia and Hopu, joined a merchant ship in Hawaiʻi in 1808, befriending Russell

Hubbard, "a son of Gen. H. of New Haven [and] . . . a member of Yale College," having graduated in 1806.[64] On their journey to New York, Hubbard began teaching ʻŌpūkahaʻia some basics of English and Protestantism. After they arrived in New York in April of 1809, ʻŌpūkahaʻia and Hopu traveled to New Haven with the ship's captain. One afternoon ʻŌpūkahaʻia stood outside "the door to one of the colleges . . . weeping." When asked why he was crying, he bemoaned his lack of education and said, "No one gave me learning."[65] Edwin W. Dwight, a cousin of Timothy Dwight, Yale's president at the time, heard his plea, took him in, and inaugurated his education.

This lore has been reproduced across a range of texts in the intervening decades, including a 1926 study of the town of Cornwall, a 1978 article on the school by John Andrew, and the article cited above by Sánchez-Eppler. Here, I draw on each of these texts but rely centrally on John Demos's 2014 telling of this tale in *The Heathen School: A Story of Hope and Betrayal in the Age of the Early Republic*, the most extensive study of the school to date. I also turn to David Chang's critical intervention in the literature on this history. In his 2016 *The World and All the Things Upon It: Native Hawaiian Geographies of Exploration*, Chang argues that from the ABCFM's 1810s publications to more recent historical writings by American scholars such as Demos, the story of the Foreign Mission School has consistently done "violence to Hawaiian history, perverting it to serve the purposes of Americans who sought to create a missionary enterprise in Hawaiʻi."[66] While Demos "does much to understand ʻŌpūkahaʻia as a Kanaka," Chang argues, he still "undercuts that effort by portraying an adult man as an infantilized 'restless' teenager and using him as a player in a metaphor for the making of the United States."[67] This is in part due to an inaccuracy in the first ABCFM publication suggesting ʻŌpūkahaʻia was born in 1792 rather than 1787, which made him a man of nearly twenty when he boarded the American boat. I return to Chang's important critique of the dominant narrative of Cornwall, but first attend to the narrative as it circulates.

According to Demos and the ABCFM publications, through Dwight, ʻŌpūkahaʻia befriended Samuel Mills Jr., a graduate resident in theology at Yale. Mills had come to Yale with the explicit intention of expanding the project he had begun at Williams to initiate missions to educate "heathens" in foreign lands. Over the next four years, ʻŌpūkahaʻia's and Mills's lives ran in significant parallel and proximity. ʻŌpūkahaʻia learned and labored in various homes and schools across Connecticut, Massachusetts, and New Hampshire, staying most frequently with Mills and his family. In 1810, Mills was actively engaged in the founding of the ABCFM, and ʻŌpūkahaʻia's presence in New England, and even more specifically in his home, served as evidence of the potential of such a project.

ʻŌpūkahaʻia's time in these homes was less grandiose. Demos explains the pattern that emerged: "lodging, board, and 'learning' received, with labor given in return—a straight-up exchange."[68] Farm work was not simply a way of repaying any debts he accrued but was also imagined by his benefactors as part of the substance of his education since ʻŌpūkahaʻia planned to import this learning to his homeland as well. The documentation of his time also suggests that ʻŌpūkahaʻia was uniquely suited to the social demands of life as a visitor. For instance, Samuel Mills Sr. commented on his ability to meld himself to his environs and, at times, turn this skill toward humorous ends; "There was something unusual in regard to Obookiah. His attention to what passed before him, and his talent at imitation, were singular."[69] This capacity for imitation echoes postcolonial critic Homi Bhabha's famous discussion of mimicry as an "*ironic* compromise," the fundamentally ambivalent "desire for a reformed, recognizable Other, *as a subject of difference that is almost the same, but not quite*."[70]

Between 1810 and 1814, ʻŌpūkahaʻia moved between local ministries, supported in part by a grant from the ABCFM "for the purposes of defraying the necessary expenses of Henry's education."[71] These educative efforts culminated in ʻŌpūkahaʻia's request for baptism, at which point Demos describes him as shifting "from proselytized to proselytizer," animating his own story of conversion from "heathen" to "civilized" to challenge white New Englanders to embrace Christianity. According to Demos, after his baptism, ʻŌpūkahaʻia wanted to speak to the parishioners to ask them, "what they all waiting for?—they live in Gospel land—hear all about salvation—God ready—Christ ready—all ready—why they don't come follow Christ."[72] While he did not speak that day, over the next two years, he lived with various ministers in Connecticut. He participated in "social religious meetings," where he assisted in recruiting persons he perceived as "destitute of grace." Through such efforts and an expanding set of correspondence, ʻŌpūkahaʻia developed a public profile of significance. Perhaps in part inspired by the potential power of his exhortations and a growing awareness that he was just one of several Hawaiian youths in the region pursuing both education and faith, in November of 1815, the board voted to take ʻŌpūkahaʻia under its patronage, and on December 26, 1815, they established "a Fund for the purpose, especially, of educating heathen children and youth."[73]

As news of the fund spread, financial support began to accumulate. Less than a year later, in August 1816, three trustees, Charles Prentise, James Harvey, and James Morris, wrote to the board of their interest in forming a school that would "successively receive youths and educate them from all parts of the world."[74] Anticipating the industrial education that would supplant Christian education in the classical languages and the Bible by the end of the century, the founders described a curriculum through which students would be "inured to habits of industry and regularity" and taught "the art of government and subordination."[75] They went on to boast of their confidence that the school would be a "powerful auxiliary" to the board's existing fundraising.[76] On October 29, 1816, the board concretized their commitment by adopting incipient measures "for the establishment of a Foreign Mission School" and settled on Cornwall as the school's location, at least in part because the people of Cornwall "gave an academy building, 40 feet by 20, and other property, amounting to about $1,200."[77] According to minutes from the meeting, the students, "heathen youth" in their language, would be educated such that "they may be qualified to become missionaries, schoolmasters, interpreters, physicians, or surgeons, among heathen nations, and to communicate such information in agriculture and the arts, as shall tend to promote Christianity and civilization."[78]

In the final months of 1816, "the Agents appointed to establish a school for heathen Youth" published *Narrative of Five Youths from the Sandwich Islands, Now Receiving Education in this Country* to capitalize on public excitement regarding the idea of a school to train "foreign" students.[79] As Demos explains, the publication was "perfectly timed to catch a rising wave of public interest in 'heathens' abroad (as opposed to nearby American Indians, among whom the results of missionary work so far had proved disappointing)."[80] The authors were not subtle in their mission: Theirs was unequivocally a fundraising effort as they implored their readers in hopes that the "liberality of the public" would be "commensurate with the importance of the object."[81] The publication goes on to tell a sad story of "Henry Obookiah," an orphan boy who emerged from a "tragical scene" in which his entire family was "butchered" to be found years later weeping on the steps of Yale and have the good fortune to receive the kindness of the college's president.[82]

In part thanks to the circulation of the manuscript, the board's fundraising nearly tripled from the year it was published to the school's opening in 1817, going from twelve thousand to thirty thousand dollars.[83] Throughout the fundraising efforts, ʻŌpūkahaʻia was employed as proof that "heathens" were not "a race of idiots." Instead, as Reverend Nathan Perkins wrote in a letter to Dwight, his "talent, as well as piety, carried conviction to many that the Heathen had souls as well as we, and were capable of being enlightened and christianized."[84] Notably, the *Narrative of Five Youths* is, as its title suggests, a compilation of stories of several young men who traveled from Hawaiʻi to New England and received some education: Thomas Hopu, who had initially traveled to the United States with ʻŌpūkahaʻia, William Tennnooe, John Honoree, and George "Prince" Tamoree.[85] However, as the tale relayed here so far reflects, ʻŌpūkahaʻia, or Henry Obookiah as the books consistently refer to him, was the protagonist and primary exemplar of the promise and possibility of the board's educative mission.

The Cornwall School opened in May of 1817 to much fanfare. *The Hartford Courant's* announcement states that they "rejoice to learn that in this state there is . . . a Seminary for the education of heathen youth, at which there are twelve of this description from different countries."[86] The ranks comprised seven students from Hawai'i, two from India, one member of the Abenaki, and two white men from Connecticut and Massachusetts who wished to become missionaries overseas. As had been the case with 'Ōpūkaha'ia's previous instruction, the students took classes in English grammar, geography, and math, attended church, and labored on the school's agricultural property. Each May, the school hosted a public exhibition during which the students could demonstrate all that they had learned, which served, not incidentally, as excellent fundraising opportunities. One of the most telling records of these events is from a dictation taken from Mrs. Eunice (Wadsworth) Taylor by her daughter describing a presentation or pageant of students intended to display their civilizational accomplishment. Taylor describes how "The students spoke on stage, first in their own tongue, and then in our language. . . . The Indian pupils so genteel and graceful on the stage that the white pupils appeared uncouth beside them."[87] The students, in other words, were able to exemplify their education in ways that exceeded their white counterparts.

There are competing historical accounts, but it is clear that the school's enrollments expanded both numerically and in their geographic reach. According to a 1926 history of Cornwall, by the next year, the school's roster had expanded to include one Abenaki, two Choctaw and four Cherokee tribal members, two students each from China, Malaya, and the Marquesas Islands, one Bengali student, one student described as "Hindu," three "Americans," and several Hawaiian students. It was also a year of some tragedy for the institution.[88]

In January of 1818, 'Ōpūkaha'ia fell ill. By February 17, he had passed. Given his status as the figurehead of the school, 'Ōpūkaha'ia's passing could have created something of a crisis for the project's supporters. But, as Demos describes, alongside genuine feelings of loss, "the school had gained something—a martyr whose life (and death) might be useful in promoting its interests."[89] In telling the story of 'Ōpūkaha'ia's death, Demos includes a lengthy selection from one recounting of his passing. It concludes with a remembrance from Dwight that one of 'Ōpūkaha'ia's final statements was that "he came to this country to teach Christians how to die." As Chang observes, 'Ōpūkaha'ia's death as a result of being exposed to illnesses to which he "had no inherited immunity" was far from anomalous, but the extent to which his writing was used as a major tool for "the movement to send American missionaries overseas" was certainly unique.[90]

The story of 'Ōpūkaha'ia's passing was incorporated into the larger mythology of the school. Lyman Beecher, father of the abolitionist author Harriet Beecher Stowe and the minister in Litchfield, Connecticut, delivered the eulogy in which he traced the trajectory of 'Ōpūkaha'ia's life. As Demos paraphrases, Beecher began with 'Ōpūkaha'ia's "escape from 'the deep darkness of Owhyhee,' his arrival in 'this land of light,' the subsequent 'renovation of his heart,' and the final ascent of 'his immaculate spirit' to Heaven."[91] But his passing would have greater implications as "his death will give notoriety to this institution . . . and give it an interest in the prayers and charities of thousands."[92] Edwin Dwight seized the opportunity by turning 'Ōpūkaha'ia's collected writings into a book to be sold to further animate the missionary project. *The Memoirs of Henry Obookiah* was published in September 1818 and was a massive success. With as many as one hundred thousand copies in circulation, it was considered "the year's almanac. Ministers preached on it. Sunday School teachers read aloud from it, and young ladies sobbed over it."[93] As the book's circulation increased, so too did the school's fundraising sources.

Chang explains that in the documentation of his experiences that eventually circulated as his memories, 'Ōpūkaha'ia understood that he was writing for an early nineteenth-century American audience and fulfilled what he expected they wanted: A tale that emphasized his transformation in New England into a Christian. This made it easier for Americans to read their fantasies into his life with little explanation of his life in Hawai'i and of his travels to the Aleutians and China; the real 'Ōpūkaha'ia became an imaginary Henry Obookiah, a blank slate for constructing stories of the glorious possibility of American Christian evangelization.[94]

The misapprehension, repeatedly reproduced in the texts Chang critiques, originates in the error in dates by which Dwight marked 'Ōpūkaha'ia's birth. As such, Change argues, he "was not a child but a man, and not an ignorant savage but a learned kahuna who continued to seek more strengthening learning overseas."[95] Chang tells 'Ōpūkaha'ia's story as part of his larger work that centers Kānaka Maoli travel and knowledge production in the nineteenth century. For Chang, 'Ōpūkaha'ia's travel and life played a crucial role in this history and "spurred missionary action."[96] This action would have massive consequences quite quickly. By the 1830s and 1840s, the incursion of Christian missionaries led Hawaiian elites to institute "norms of private property, as well as heteropatriarchal understandings of home and family."[97]

'Ōpūkaha'ia's presence defined the first years of the Cornwall School and a deeply Christian and Christianizing vision of education for the purposes of export. It is telling, for instance, that the students of this period were so effective in their inhabitation of this incipient version of Americanness that white students appeared "uncouth" by comparison. And that ʻŌpūkahaʻia's story, albeit based on a fundamental inaccuracy, is one of such a successful transformation that any ambivalence he might have held regarding the project in which he played such a central character is wholly obscured in the historical record. But his was only the first chapter in the story of the Cornwall School, which is itself but a small part of the longer history of educational projects organized around and for the export of racial others and American ideas as part of the development of an overseas empire. The next chapter of the Cornwall story continued this project but shifted its focus toward settler colonial projects in North America, specifically the Cherokee Nation, their dispossession, and removal.

## Cherokee Removal and the Limits of Incorporation

Despite, and in many ways because of, ʻŌpūkahaʻia's death and the institution's animation of it as a fundraising tool, the Cornwall School flourished over the next several years. Nine of the original twelve students continued on, and eight new students arrived the following winter and spring from China, Germany, Pennsylvania, Tahiti, Australia, India, and elsewhere. While the global reach of the institution remained, the board also saw a new opportunity emerging in the education of Indigenous students from what they identified as the American Southeast, particularly from the Choctaws, Creeks, and Cherokees. To capture this audience, they had opened the Brainerd School near present-day Chattanooga, Tennessee. Between the fall and winter of 1818, nine students, seven Cherokees and two Choctaws, traveled to Cornwall. This new wave of students was decidedly different from the school's previous students: younger, wealthier, and often from politically prominent families who, in some cases, owned substantial plantations and enslaved Black laborers. In addition to family wealth, Edward Starr documents that in 1819, the school received $400 from the federal government to cover the cost of educating Indigenous students and another $238 to cover their travel.[98]

Other fundraising tactics also emerged during this era. One capitalized on the perception that students should Anglicize their names as part of their assimilation process. Rather than taking on generic names or names of their choosing, however, some students would take on English names of benefactors. For instance, a widow pledged $100 to fund a "suitable subject" who would take her deceased husband's name in return for a gift.[99] One of the students who participated in this process, if in a slightly less direct manner than others, was Gallegina Uwati, who is often also referred to as Buck Watie, the son of a leading family in Cherokee politics. His father, Uwatie, was a Christian convert and had married a woman of European and Cherokee ancestry, Susanna Reese. Gallegina Uwati was born around 1802, though some record suggests 1804, in Oothcaloga, a region of Cherokee country known for its "single-family homesteads," a mark that the community there had shifted away from Cherokee models of relating to land held in common and toward an ownership-based relationship to land as private property.[100] In 1818, he was recruited to Cornwall. On his journey from Georgia to Connecticut, he was introduced to Elias Boudinot, then the president of the American Bible Society, previously a congressman from New Jersey, and for nearly forty years a trustee of the College of New Jersey, which would eventually become Princeton University. Gallegina Uwati asked Boudinot if he could use his name, and Boudinot agreed. The newly designated Cherokee Elias Boudinot and his cousin Skahtlelohskee, who also used the name John Ridge and whose father, Major John Ridge, was a Cherokee leader, arrived in Cornwall toward the end of 1818. Their time in Cornwall would have decisive effects on the school's future and, arguably, the Cherokee Nation. Both were part of a generation of Cherokees who, by the 1810s, had chosen to strategically participate in various aspects of American political and cultural life, including availing themselves of missionary offers of educational opportunities.[101]

Between 1818 and 1823, the Cornwall School appeared to flourish. Students continued to learn, to labor in the fields, and to participate in exhibitions of their supposed transformation. Though some critiques of the project percolated, the school and its supporters continued to assert its success. As one advocate attested in *The Religious Intelligencer,* "The experiment has been tried, and has proved successful. Heathen youth can be civilized, and instructed, and prepared for extensive usefulness among their countrymen within a limited period and at comparatively small expense."[102] Based on such assessments, there was a push to install a new building and extend the project.

However, the school was not without significant issues. Internal administrators, including Reverend Herman Daggett, who took over as principal from Dwight in 1818, expressed significant concern regarding many students' failures to gain basic facility with the English language.[103] His fretfulness was so great that he recommended a remedial program of homestays with "respectable Christian families" for students "unacquainted with English." There was also significant discontent and even distress among the students. The board's records describe one student from New Zealand as "extremely nervous and almost insane" and a Cherokee as "so discontented & homesick that he made very little progress in his study." Another Cherokee student "manifests a suspicious & gloomy disposition, which renders him unhappy & unpleasant" and "The same scholar sometimes exhibited 'a considerable degree of mental derangement.'"[104] At times, there were also disputes between students, manifesting in physical violence and, once, even a stabbing. One Chippewa student wrote to the principal about the harassment he experienced at the hands of his classmates and his fear that "very soon I must be kill [*sic*] here if I say here any longer."[105] Finally, students also experienced significant health issues, ranging from consumption, dysentery, and colds to far more significant illnesses that resulted, in some cases, in death.[106] But none of this led to the 1826 shuttering of the school's doors.

While a student at Cornwall, John Ridge, the Cherokee scholar who arrived at Cornwall with his cousin in 1818, fell ill. To receive regular treatment, he stayed in Dr. Samuel Gold's home and often received care from Sarah Northrup, a fourteen-year-old white girl born and raised in Cornwall. Much to the dismay of the board, over the course of time, the two developed a romantic relationship that they both described as love. As Gregory Smithers describes in his history of Cherokee migration and diaspora, given the fear among white Americans regarding "the future complexion of the American population" and discussions of racial "amalgamation," the pair created significant distress for the white residents of Cornwall and the Cornwall School's administration.[107]

When their feelings were revealed, Northrup's parents sent her away for several months, and the board voted to send Ridge home. He went, but after touring the South raising funds for the missionary project and publishing tracts against racial prejudice, he returned to Cornwall and married Northrup on January 27, 1824. Many members of their closest community accepted the newlyweds, but the broader population did not. Local papers reported on the outrage that arose in neighboring towns, including reports that "fifty men had assigned an instrument in writing, promising to . . . go in a body to Cornwall, and not return till they had entirely demolished the building in which the school was kept."[108] The couple left Cornwall to return to the Cherokee Nation, but not before Ridge was nearly lynched. In their aftermath, the fury built, some of it accusing the school itself of having a mission "to break down all objections of *colour*, and make our daughters become nursing mothers to a race of mulattoes."[109] In response, the Cornwall School assumed what Demos describes as "a studiously defensive pose."[110] They had the dual agenda of avoiding any responsibility for the union and denying accusations that there were other such relationships and, of lesser priority, avoiding wholly alienating the Cherokees. Their top priority was clear, however: preserve the school's reputation and, with it, the flow of donations. Almost immediately, these goals became unattainable, and contributions to the school's coffers declined. It did not help that the broader popularity of missionary projects among both the Cherokee and white communities was already deteriorating.

In a final blow against the school's self-defense, in June of 1824, news of a second engagement between a Cornwall student, Elias Boudinot, Ridge's cousin, and Harriet Gold, a local white woman, began to circulate. Word of the relationship reached the board through Gold's brother-in-law. After attempting to dissuade Gold from the marriage, the board took action to protect itself from further critique by including a statement on the relationship in its annual report. There, they wrote:

> We feel ourselves bound to say, that after the unequivocal disapprobation of such connections, expressed by the Agents, and by the Christian public universally; we regard the conduct of those who have been engaged in or accessary [*sic*] to this transaction, as criminal; as offering an insult to the known feelings of the Christian community; and as sporting with the sacred interests of this charitable institution.[111]

The local community also made its disapproval known. On June 22, a collection of people, including one of Gold's brothers and several of her friends, gathered in an open space across from the school and burned effigies of Gold, Boudinot, and Lydia Northrup, Sarah Northrup's mother, who, by that point, had become the public scapegoat.

Over the course of 1824, donations to the school dropped precipitously from nearly $500 a quarter in 1823 to $60. The board suffered a nearly 30 percent loss as well.[112] By September 1824, the board entertained the possibility of shifting its relationship to the school. Rather than immediately disassociating, however, they implemented a new set of policies requiring the school to submit regular reports "of the progress and character of each pupil." They explained their continued support as such: "These strangers of different and distant climes and regions . . . [who] have a skin not colored like . . . [our] own. They have immortal souls; they have intellectual faculties, also, which . . . may be made eminently instrumental to the salvation of their pagan countrymen."[113]

But these sentiments were matched by statements hedging their more durational commitment to the project. For instance, according to their *Fifteenth Annual Report*, the board began to express a concern that some of the students "are not capable of rendering any essential service," though they acknowledge that at least some of the failure was the result not of the students' incapacities but, rather, of the fact that they were "treated in various respects, as though they were and must be inferior to ourselves." In many instances, the students felt "as though they were *mere shows*."[114] By October of 1825, Jeremiah Evarts, the secretary of the board and the person responsible for the day-to-day management of the school introduced the question of "whether it is practicable, in the majority of cases, to take ignorant & uncivilized boys, place them in a school by themselves, & have them educated so that they will become *men*, capable of taking an active part in human affairs."[115] By this point, the relationship between the school and the Cherokee had also suffered irreparable damage. After learning of the school administrators' accusation that his relationship to Gold was criminal and hearing about the burning of effigies, Boudinot wrote to Evarts that "the Cherokees will not send any youths to the school."[116] With this withdrawal and the deaths of two students from Hawai'i during the summer of 1826, the school's closure became imminent.[117]

While a student at Cornwall, Ridge had already initiated his work advocating for the Cherokee Nation in relation to the US government in a 1821 letter to President James Monroe, in which he supported Cherokee "improvement" toward the "privileges of civilization" through being "educated like the whites."[118] After he left Cornwall in 1824, he was part of a delegation sent to Washington, DC to defend the Cherokee Nation's territorial claims against the Georgian encroachment, and he returned in 1825 as part of the Cherokee National Council. By 1825, Boudinot was also a widely respected representative of the Cherokee Nation, traveling through New England and the mid-Atlantic speaking in support of the Cherokee cause. His most famous speech, from May 26, 1826, in Philadelphia and later published as "An Address to the Whites," was a defense of Cherokee land rights and a critique of white racism against the Cherokee.

Yet, even in making such arguments, Boudinot embraced a logic of civilization whereby he asserted that he was "not as [his] fathers were—broader means and nobler influences Have fallen upon me."[119] Smithers contends that in making this argument, "Boudinot's chronology was designed to counter the way Euroamericans racialized time by presenting Cherokees (and other Indigenous Americans) as stuck in a 'primitive' stage of development."[120] Though Boudinot's intention here may have been to assert Cherokee agency as historical actors, it is likely that white audiences took this sentiment as validation of the missionary project. Many scholars have perceived Boudinot as a tragic figure, split between his allegiance to "traditional" Cherokee culture and a "civilized" Euro-American one. In response, Smithers argues that his was a position of "political pragmatism" steeped in "an assertion of Cherokee social and cultural evolution, and a vision for the Cherokee future."[121] Between 1826 and 1828, Ridge and Boudinot were both part of several efforts to negotiate for the Cherokee Nation to retain their land east of the Mississippi. Their efforts took several forms, including a failed attempt to open a seminary and a far more successful effort to acquire a printing press, with which they started the first newspaper published by an Indian tribe, the *Cherokee Phoenix*. In 1827, the Cherokee Nation ratified a constitution largely modeled on the US Constitution. However, instead of garnering respect for the Cherokee Nation's sovereignty, the constitution provoked alarm in the white population of Georgia. As Patrick Wolfe argues, rather than serving as evidence of their civilization, "Cherokee's farms, plantations, slaves and written constitution all signified *permanence*" and thus also as "provocations to the officials and legislators of the state of Georgia."[122]

The 1828 election of Andrew Jackson ushered in a federal government unquestionably averse to any recognition of Indigenous sovereignty. After Jackson proposed legislative action to impose removal in 1829, Ridge was part of a delegation sent to DC to negotiate on behalf of the Cherokee Nation. Despite their protestations, Jackson signed the Indian Removal Act into law in 1830. Between the 1830 act, Chief Justice John Marshall's declaration of Indigenous peoples as "domestic dependent nations" in *Cherokee Nation v. State of Virginia*, and the Jackson administration's refusal to enforce an 1832 decision in *Worcester v. Georgia* that rejected Georgia's right to supersede federal authority over tribes, which should have been a win for the Cherokee Nation, Ridge came to doubt that removal could be successfully opposed. He shifted to a belief that "the only alternative to save his people from moral and physical death was to make the best terms they could with the government, and remove out of the limits of the States."[123]

Against a group of Cherokee staunchly anti-removal led by John Ross, the Cherokee Nation's Principal Chief, Ridge and Boudinot formed what would become known as the "Treaty Party." As Smithers argues, Ridge and Boudinot switched their tactic with full awareness of "how vile, violent, and bloodthirsty whites could become," knowledge they'd gained through their experiences in Cornwall.[124] In hopes of lessening the consequences of removal, they began negotiations with Jackson, with whom Ridge apparently became so close as to name his last child after, and eventually secured the Treaty of Echota in December of 1835. According to the treaty's terms, the Cherokee Nation would receive a large federal land grant in Arkansas and Oklahoma along with a payment of $4.5 million in exchange for their land east of the Mississippi.[125] As they signed, the members of the "Treaty Party" were well aware that in effectively selling communal Cherokee land, they were breaking a central directive of their constitution that mandated death as a punishment for doing so. It was widely assumed among Ross and his sympathizers that Ridge, Boudinot, and others received substantial payoffs for their support of the treaty.[126]

Ridge, Boudinot, and their families traveled West in October of 1836, two years before the federally enforced stage of removal in 1838 and 1839 pushed twelve to thirteen thousand Cherokee off of their homelands. While many US history books refer to the removal as the "Trail of Tears," Smithers instead surfaces one emigrant who recalled that the "trail of exiles was a trail of death."[127] As the Cherokees traveled West, completing the final stage of efforts to expel the Cherokee people and their national formation, they were subjected to freezing temperatures, starvation, and illness, resulting in nearly four thousand deaths. Before their arrival, Ridge and his family flourished as they capitalized on the moment and ran a general store that allowed them to profit from the material needs of others on the move. On June 22, 1839, however, this momentary success came to an end. Within hours of each other, John Ridge, his father Major John Ridge, and Boudinot were each murdered. The assailants' identities in each case are unknown, though it is generally assumed that they were associated with the Ross Party. In total, they numbered at least forty. Demos suggests that their weapons of choice—knives, hatchets, and a rifle—marked the potential of both Cherokee and white assassins.

There is a direct chain of events, lives, and logics from ʻŌpūkahaʻia's travel to and education in the United States, the founding of the Cornwall School, and the immensely tragic and violent acts committed by the United States government against the Cherokee people. From the records that are available, ʻŌpūkahaʻia, Ridge, and the other students at Cornwall attempted to navigate the circumstances in which they existed. For Ridge, this amounted to an effort to operate within white civilizational ideas both for himself and, ostensibly, for the Cherokee Nation. But the clear failure of such a strategy is apparent in the longer game of dispossession and expropriation. This was accomplished in part by the limited inclusion of a few who were educated in such a way that they would sell themselves and their people out. It is notable, however, that among the global diversity of students educated at Cornwall, none seem to have come from Africa.

## Education for Africa and Africans

On the very day in October 1816 that the ABCFM met to write the constitution for the Cornwall School, a group of religious leaders in Parsippany, New Jersey, announced the founding of a school to instruct "blacks as preachers and teachers." Unlike Cornwall, this school, known as "an African School," was not initially funded by colonizationists but, instead, by the free Black community of New Jersey. By 1818, however, the funds proved insufficient, and the project became more explicitly linked to colonization efforts. The school was to be a training ground to enable the spread of "the blessings of Christianity and civilization during the approaching period of the millennium" throughout Africa.[128] In alignment with the project of deportation and colonization, the school was designed as a project to educate young people of African descent already present in the United States in order to then export them "back to Africa" where they could spread both the Christian Gospel and the basic tenets of liberalism and capitalism as they were taking shape in the new nation. But the school continued to struggle. As a November 1825 issue of the *African Repository and Colonial Journal* reports, "efforts to obtain funds for the school in its present state have been vain," and it was necessary for the institution to rethink its model of education to commence "in early life."[129] Like the Cornwall School, the school in Parsippany was short-lived, closing in 1827 due to difficulties raising funds and recruiting students.[130] However, the school's closure did not undo a collective resolve that the success of the colonization efforts in Liberia required educated Black missionaries.

Jehudi Ashmun, chief agent of the Colonization Society, traveled to Liberia in June 1822, escorting a group of forty Africans who had been smuggled into Georgia in 1821, against the prohibition on the importation of enslaved people. A month after their arrival, Ashmun's wife died of a fever, as did many of the other people with whom he had traveled. Reflecting on his first year, he wrote to the board that his "health is nearly restored. I stand a monument of God's mercy, and behold the grave of fifteen white persons around me; all of whom have died since I landed."[131] Ashmun left the colony in 1824, but returned later in the year and remained until 1828, when illness drove him back to the United States. Over his five years in Liberia, Ashmun functioned as something of a director. He brokered treaties, organized food provision, and fought in battles. He died shortly upon his return, but was immortalized seven years later in a biography by Ralph Randolph Gurley, an agent of the ACS who had met Ashmun in his first year in Liberia.[132] Based on his experience of illness and loss, Ashmun was thoroughly convinced that white people were ill-suited for the climate of Liberia. Because of this, he was convinced that the only way to settle the new colony was to train Black missionaries in the United States.

Despite what the historian Horace Mann Bond describes as Ashmun's "mercurial" early life and "almost wasted career," Gurley's tale of his life was "a religious tract written also with the desire to 'sell' the cause of colonization to a pious and highly orthodox American community" rather than a "realistic and thereby revealing silhouette of a man."[133] The year after Ashmun's passing, Gurley met with other members of the colonization movement to found the African Education Society, with the objective of "preparing the destined emigrants, by a suitable training, for prosperity and usefulness in Africa . . .

without such preparation they were wholly unfit to stem the tide of barbarism, to exercise the difficult and hardly tenable functions of self-government, to become the leaders, teachers, and rulers of barbarous people, the enlightened citizens, the wise founders and supporters, for the rising nations of Africa."[134] The inspiration for this institution was none other than Jehudi Ashmun, lauded in the public *Appeal* from the African Education Society for his "intellectual and moral cultivation."[135]

It took another twenty-five years, but in 1854, John Miller Dickey, an alumnus of Milton Academy, Dickinson College, and the Princeton Seminary, established "an institution to be called the Ashmun Institute for the scientific, classical and theological education of colored youth of the male sex."[136] In an 1853 sermon, he presented his ideas for the institute to his congregation. Dickey explained how it would contribute to the colonization project—the repatriation or deportation of people of African descent. According to Bond, in so doing, he never gave "the slightest suggestion that the African or his American descendant suffered from any natural or permanent disability to be associated either with his origin, his color, his physical configuration, or his status in contemporary civilization." Essentially, his proposal was built around his understanding of "the African" as "truly a man."[137] In April, Pennsylvania Governor William Bigler, a former classmate of Dickey's at Dickinson, signed the bill granting the Ashmun Institute's charter. A month later, President Franklin Pierce signed the Kansas–Nebraska Act, illustrating that whatever Dickey's understanding of racial difference may have been, as a matter of law and politics, the status of Black people in America was decidedly in the hands of a public willing to expand unfree labor into new territories. The act also hastened the appropriation of land for settlers and the dispossession and removal of several Indigenous tribes, including the Caddo, Keechi, Waco, Delaware, Tonkawa, and Penateka Comanche.[138]

At the institute's inaugural gala in 1856, Cortlandt Van Rensselaer, a wealthy Yale graduate and the chief executive officer of the Presbyterian Board of Education, gave an address on the theme "God Glorified in Africa." His was a decidedly racialist perspective. The talk's central thesis was that "the African race in this country is to be the greatest instrumentality for signal displays of God's goodness, grace, and glory in Africa" and reflected the racial thinking of the era and his theological understanding of providence, the *"fixedness of color,"* and greatness of "God's plan, the best and true solution of African destiny . . . ; the wonderful plan of colonization."[139] But colonization itself was not sufficient on its own. Rather, according to Van Rensselaer, the Ashmun Institute itself was part of "God's design": "The Ashmun Institute stands like a nursing mother, appointed of God to watch her opportunity by the Nile of turbid and overflowing worldliness; and she longs to rescue some noble Africans from their bark of slime, and to train them for the statesmanship of great and growing Republic."[140] Here, Van Rensselaer provides a theological and civilizational rationalization of the practice of capture and enslavement as, in fact, salvific—arguing quite directly that the future redemption of the continent of Africa required the history of subjugation. The students trained at the institute would "return" to the continent to save it. When Van Rensselaer's address was printed, it included a footnote to the Supreme Court's decision in the Dred Scott case, also printed that week, which constitutionally enshrined the ineligibility of people of African descent for citizenship.[141]

Classes at the institute began on the first day of 1857 with just two students enrolled, both from the United States. In the fall, they were joined by a third, the child of immigrants to Liberia from Louisiana, whose presence showed some promise of fulfilling Dickey's vision. A reflection by an 1860 graduate, Christian A. Fleetwood, describes the ten students then in attendance: six from Pennsylvania, one each from Rhode Island and South Carolina, one from the "Spanish West Indies," and one from Liberia. Financing the institution was a struggle, especially with the start of the Civil War, which "emptied the classrooms." In an effort to attend to the institution's mission and manage the institution's finances, John Wayne Martin, an administrator at the school from 1861 to 1865, wrote to Edward Blyden, a Liberian official, to request financial support for a West Indian student he had hoped to enroll at the school.[142]

One peculiar aspect of Lincoln University was its relationship to manual labor. Indigenous students throughout the British colonial period and nonwhite students from around the world at Cornwall were expected to complete various agricultural and other upkeep labor around their schools. At Lincoln, however, students were to focus on their formal education. As Bond explains, "manual labor was never esteemed either as a discipline or as a useful training device for leaders."[143] This was a radical approach that would fall out of favor with alumni by the 1880s as trends in educational philosophy shifted in more pragmatic and industrial directions.

After the war, enrollment swelled as veterans and "recruits from the new schools for freedmen in the South poured into the institution."[144] A new president, Reverend Isaac Norton Rendall, took over leadership. On his first walk to campus in the position on April 15, 1865, he carried with him a newspaper reporting the assassination of President Abraham Lincoln the night before. Less than a year later, the school applied for a new charter "in honor of the illustrious patriot, statesman, and philanthropist, the loved and lamented Abraham Lincoln, who, when living, delighted to serve the long-oppressed and neglected people for whom this institution has provided, and who, in dying, sealed his devotion to an emancipated race."[145] The application goes on to explain the desire for the institution to "bear the worthy name of him who did so much to lift the crushing loads from the mind and the heart and the body and the manhood of the African": "Lincoln University is the nation's . . . pledge of universal and complete emancipation."[146] As the present-day institution attests on its website, Lincoln is "the nation's first degree-granting Historically Black College and University (HBCU)" and "educates and empowers students to lead their communities and change the world."[147] Under the new charter, Lincoln's board was also reconstituted. The chair of the board was Edwin Morgan, a senator from New York whose election Bond describes as a "token of the brief identification of the institution in that year of post-war jubilee with civil rights legislation and all it stood for" and as indexical of Dickey's move away from a strictly colonizationist mindset.[148] Despite this, the school's curriculum remained distinctly traditional and biblical under Rendall for whom "The Bible is a textbook through the whole course."[149]

After the war, the ratification of the Thirteenth, Fourteenth, and Fifteenth Amendments formally reshaped the legal relationships of people of African descent to the United States and with it the institution's imagined mission to facilitate the export of the United States' domestic Black population. In 1865, the Thirteenth Amendment abolished the enslavement of people of African descent; in 1868, the Fourteenth Amendment extended citizenship; and in 1869, the passage of the Fifteenth Amendment granted voting rights to Black men. As Saidiya Hartman argues convincingly, "the differences between slavery and freedom" were not "negligible" but the formal equality these amendments instantiated effectively enshrined a racialized form of subjugation under the terms of the "double bind of freedom": "being free to exchange one's labor and free of material resources."[150] Hartman describes this state as "burdened individuality" in which Black people were saddled both with an indebtedness to the nation-state that had spent blood and treasure to free them and with "the onerous responsibilities of freedom" even as they experienced "few of its entitlements."[151] This new state of being was enacted through the law and through other logics and techniques of governance, regulation, and discipline including the work of formal and informal education in institutions. Through these various means, Hartman reads the state and adjacent actors' efforts to transform previously enslaved people "into a rational, docile, and productive working class," an aspirational state of being understood to be adjacent to, if never the same as, whiteness.[152]

And the fictive indebtedness of the formerly enslaved extended still further. In alignment with Van Rensselaer's narrative of the providential and salvific promise of both capture and enslavement, post-emancipation texts published by the Freedmen's Bureau generated a remembrance of slavery itself as a paternalistic practice of training into personhood, a kind of educational gift that could, if properly appreciated, engender a form of responsible individuality "worthy of freedom."[153] Through this way of reimagining the violence of the past, Black people who attained the status of the individual through their performance of responsible personhood were situated as what Bayley Marquez describes as "a model of civilization . . . indebted to slavery as a civilizing force."[154] This logic took concrete form in the Freedmen's Bureau's education institution, the Hampton Institute, founded in 1868 by General Samuel C. Armstrong. Born and raised in Hawai'i, the child of American missionaries, Armstrong identified as Hawaiian but was committed to a white, Christian missionary worldview. He came to the United States in 1860 or 1861 and attended Williams College for two years before joining the Union Army. After the war, he joined the Freedmen's Bureau and founded the Hampton Institute as a school for Black students in 1872, collaborating with Richard Henry Pratt to add a program for Indigenous students from 1878 to 1923.[155]

Armstrong's approach to education differed dramatically from the more traditional missionary curriculum at Lincoln and other colleges and universities. His educational philosophy was deeply paternalistic toward nonwhite people, including native Hawaiians, the Indigenous peoples of North America, and Black Americans and Africans, whom he believed to suffer from innate deficiencies. As Armstrong wrote in his 1884 piece "Lessons from the Hawaiian Islands," to his mind, "The negro and the Polynesian have many striking similarities. Of both it is true that not mere ignorance, but deficiency in character is the chief difficulty, and that to build up that character is the true objective point of education."[156] Such an education, for Armstrong, required not only "an enlightened head and a changed heart" but "very largely on a routine of industrious habit. . . . Morality and industry generally go together, Especially in weak tropical races, idleness, like ignorance breeds vice."[157] Thus, rather than biblical or liberal studies, he saw labor and industrial knowledge as the most effective way to overcome these "inherent deficiencies" of nonwhite people.

Like many other white men of his era, Armstrong saw slavery as itself one of the most vital and impactful forms of education, writing in the 1880s that "Slavery brought coloured men into close contact with his white brother, training him in habits of work, giving him knowledge of the white man's language and religion." "Never," Armstrong continued, "in the history of civilization, has a great mass of barbarous people advanced so rapidly as have the Blacks on this continent." Here, Armstrong anticipates a core component of the relational logic of US racial dynamics wherein one subordinated group is lauded for its comparative advancements in civilization vis-à-vis other racialized peoples. This comparative frame was made especially clear in 1878 when Richard Henry Pratt, who would go on to found the infamous Carlisle Indian Boarding School, brought Indigenous prisoners of war to Hampton. Even as Black students were situated as model students for their Indigenous classmates, that this status was predicated in logics that justified slavery as a pedagogical project only further entrenches the fundamental anti-Blackness of this project.[158] At Hampton, Armstrong instantiated a curriculum that emphasized practical and industrial skills. In 1872, Booker T. Washington enrolled and would go on to be Armstrong's protege.

The expansion of this highly conditional form of inclusion in the liberal contract of citizenship was not restricted to current inhabitants of the United States. At a moment of mass migration, the laws governing citizenship were under significant pressure in several countries. In 1870, the British Parliament's Naturalization Act radically shifted British law by abdicating their claim to "perpetual allegiance" from British subjects.[159] In the United States, fears of "fraudulent practices" and "illegal voting" perpetuated by recent Irish immigrants to New York during the 1868 election led to a congressional effort to continue the centralization of government functions under federal control.[160] Congressional debates in 1869 and 1870 resulted in the expansion of US naturalization policy from the narrow language of the 1790 Naturalization Act, which restricted naturalization to "free white persons," to add the still limited but more inclusive language "and to aliens of African nativity and persons of African descent."[161] By some interpretations, H.R. 2201, the Naturalization Act of 1870, extended the work of the postwar reconstruction amendments to the domain of immigration policy. For others, including Moon-Ho Jung and Najia Aarim-Heriot, the act marked a retreat from a promise or even potential of racial equality through its exclusions of people of Asian and Indigenous descent.

Olanipekun Laosebikan argues that the process through which people of African descent were incorporated as naturalizable illustrates the broader dynamics of race, labor, and exclusion of this moment and fundamental to US logics of law and citizenship, questions I take up in more depth in Chapter 3. As he explains, Senator Charles Sumner first proposed an amendment to strike the word "white" from immigration records during congressional debates on immigration procedures in 1869. While his intention was to extend access to naturalization to Chinese immigrants, he framed his argument in regard to African immigrants in an effort to win support. Sumner's amendment failed, but in the last debates on the act, Senator Williard Warner of Alabama introduced an amendment to insert what became the final language, including people of African descent.[162] Laosebikan asserts that Warner's argument for the inclusion of Black immigrants positioned people of African descent as a "model" immigrant population "suitable to be juxtaposed against unwanted groups like the Chinese."[163] He goes on to suggest that this shift in law and rhetoric contributed to an important new frame for recruiting African students to schools like Lincoln. As the following chapters demonstrate, the deeply racist and xenophobic anti-Chinese arguments that allowed for the exclusion of nonwhite and non-Black people from US citizenship would also go on to have long-lasting implications.

In the late 1860s, several "Americ-Liberians," either US-born or the children of emigrants sent by the United States for their studies, came to the Lincoln campus. It was not until 1873, however, that a sizable class of ten Liberians traveled to Lincoln. The early 1870s were a time of significant financial turmoil for the country and the school. The depression had effectively "destroyed the fund-raising drive."[164] As Bond describes, "The boys came—and this proved Providential, likewise—at a time that was financially calamitous for the institution. It was the middle of the 'money panic' of 1873, and the new university was on the threshold of complete bankruptcy."[165] Reverend Edward Webb, the institution's financial agent and "promotor extraordinary," saw "the students themselves" as the "best promotional device."[166] When the students arrived in June of 1873, Webb orchestrated a publicity campaign to extract "every possible value" from their arrival:

> He had them photographed, unkempt and disheveled as they finished their thirty-five day journey, in the shabby clothes they brought with them; and then outfitted them in less outlandish garments and cut their hair. The party was duly presented at the Commencement of 1873. Several months later they were photographed again. The "before and after" portrait showing the civilizing effects of a Christian education at Lincoln University on former African tribesman was made into postcard sized promotion inserts for thousands of letters sent to churches, Sunday-schools and other prospective donors.[167]

These students, who Bond describes as "Lincoln University's meal ticket," were among a cohort of approximately sixty-eight African students who studied in the United States between 1870 and 1900. Of this group, thirty-two were from Liberia, the next largest group was seventeen students from South Africa, then eleven students from Sierra Leone.[168] There was a growing consensus that "converted and educated Africans would be more effective doing mission work among their own people than outsiders" and, reflecting a central tenant of the emerging school of scientific racism, that they were more likely to survive the "tropical climate."[169] Most of the African students attended white-sponsored schools that catered to Black students, like Lincoln. Through 1896, thirteen of the fifteen African students who came to Lincoln were from Liberia.

But, after 1896, it was another fifty years before another Liberian student attended Lincoln. When this occurred, it was under a very different set of conditions and a different kind of missionary project, one more infused by the spirit and power of corporatist and statist philanthropy. The reasons for the cessation are not entirely clear, but one factor was likely frustration among the African students with the depth of misunderstanding, misrepresentation, and flatly racist beliefs of white and Black Americans toward Africans and Africa. One Lincoln student told the *Washington Bee*, for instance, that he was shocked by the prejudice of "the American Negro public against their brethren" and their perception of Africa as "a barren waste, a hot bed of fevers" and "abject barbarism."[170] George Peabody, a Bassa prince in Liberia, extended his rebuke to the education on offer at Lincoln too, saying that African students were disappointed in their educations, which could have been sufficient for those "aspiring to second class citizenship in America," but was below the standards of "free men" whom he set distinctly against "freedmen."[171] Here, Peabody homes in on crucial discrepancies in the substance of the status of citizenship as experienced across racial lines. In 1896, the infamous *Plessy vs. Ferguson* decision clarified and cemented the legality of the second-class status by sanctioning the notion of "separate but equal."

Another likely factor was the significant changes underway in Liberia: The first was the establishment and growth of the College of Liberia in 1862, a project missionaries first proposed in 1850 as the first American collegiate institution with the specific purpose of educating Black students, albeit not on US soil. The second was a series of shifts in the life and educational philosophy of Edward Blyden, the Liberian official with whom Martin had corresponded about sending students and funds to Lincoln in the 1860s. Blyden was born on the island of St. Thomas in 1832 and immigrated to the United States in 1850 with plans to attend a theological college. However, when Rutgers Theological Seminary refused him admission due to his race, he moved to Liberia to attend a Presbyterian-backed high school. He would eventually be credited by both V. Y. Mudimbe and L. S. Senghor as "the father of negritude," and as having directly influenced the pan-Africanist ideologies of several twentieth-century leaders, a trajectory I discuss in further detail in Chapter 7. One change was Blyden's resignation from the Presbyterian Church and potential conversion to Islam in the mid-1880s, which likely contributed to his loss of interest in the missionary project.[172] But, perhaps more important, were a series of relationships he developed with educators in the United States. One especially important connection was Blyden's correspondence with Samuel C. Armstrong. In 1880, Armstrong reached out to Blyden about sending students from Liberia to Hampton through the ACS. As historian Kenneth King describes, Blyden's response illustrates his broad disillusionment with education abroad:

> As a rule without a single exception, those [Africans] who go abroad for their education return on stilts—altogether out of sympathy for their own people. They may be giants when they return, but they walk on their heads. The infants who have stayed at home are stronger than they for the purpose of the country.[173]

Armstrong responded with agreement that it is "generally unwise" for African students to be sent to America for their studies but that a Hampton education would be different and students "would go back to Africa right side up."[174]

In 1881, just a year after Blyden and Armstrong exchanged letters, Booker T. Washington was appointed the founding leader of a new school in Alabama built in the image of Hampton, Tuskegee Normal and Industrial Institute. As W.E.B. Du Bois would describe in his 1903 *Souls of Black Folk*, Washington rose to prominence as "the leader of not one race but two,—a compromiser between the South, the North, and the Negro."[175] As the promises of Reconstruction wilted and the violences of the double burden of freedom set upon the Black population of the United States, Washington articulated an accommodationist position that relinquished claims to political power, civil rights, and higher education. In their place, he proposed a program of "work and money" in hopes of cultivating a class of Black businessmen and property owners.[176] After becoming acquainted with Washington's work in 1894, Blyden wrote to him "expressing his agreement" that "the interests of both races will be served if the Nego will eschew politics and political aspirations" and turn instead to the "religious and industrial spheres" where "his possibilities are unlimited."[177] One place Blyden and Washington did disagree, however, was about the place of Black people in the United States. While Washington saw their future in America, Blyden remained committed to an eventual "exodus to Africa."[178]

The significance of the history of Africans educated at Lincoln in the nineteenth century is quite evident. Bond, for instance, describes how "the ancient reputation of Lincoln University, as the school intended to glorify God through the work of its graduates in Africa, attracted Nnamdi Azikiwe from Nigeria to enroll in 1929."[179] As is discussed in much greater detail in Chapter 7, Azikiwe would go on to be known as the father of Nigerian nationalism. Azikiwe is also credited with sending Kwame Nkrumah from the Gold Coast to study at Lincoln. Writing in 1976, Bond described their accomplishments as such:

> in the Centennial Year of John Miller Dickey's and Cortlandt Van Rensselaer's African-oriented institutions, two heads of emerging states, Prime Ministers—the chief elective officers of populations totaling twenty-five million, almost twice the number of persons of African descent in the United States—were graduates of Lincoln University. This was justification beyond the wildest hopes of any educational dreamer of this or any other time or country.

Somewhat oddly, Bond does not comment upon either Azikiwe or Nkrumah's critical relationship to the United States and its central values of liberalism and capitalism, let alone the nation-state's colonial and imperial practices.

It is difficult to overstate the role of universities in the expansion of these logics; as Dylan Rodríguez argues, "genocidal methodologies and logics have always constituted the *academically facilitated* inception of a hemispheric America."[180] Within this white supremacist settler mindset, a mindset embedded in and often emerging from the academic community, it was only logical that a similar solution of removal would be attempted for people of African descent. ACS advocates argued that the removal of this population would benefit Africa, by providing the continent with a population "*partially civilized and [C]hristianized*," while simultaneously being an advantage for "our blacks themselves," since they also "would be put in a better situation."[181] In this way, the Liberian colony was part of the increasingly international missionizing efforts of American Christians in the nineteenth century. Spanning the Hawaiian Islands, India, Palestine, and China, such initiatives presented US missionaries and the university with opportunities to build on their legacies of evangelism without requiring them to necessarily advocate, contribute to, or enable a less-white American future.

Wilbur Fisk Burns's legacy after his return to Liberia from Wesleyan is difficult to trace, perhaps because he lived for so few years after completing his studies or perhaps because his work as a lawyer, surveyor, and agricultural manager was simply rote for the colonial moment. The stories of Burns and the Indian students educated in Cornwall in the early decades of the nineteenth century are useful for fleshing out the overlapping and inter-implicated histories of colonialism, slavery, and US universities.[182] But theirs are rarely the stories told in the narrative of universities and noncitizen students in the United States. In too many cases, their premature deaths foreclosed their ability to make good on the supposed opportunity and potential their education in the

United States was promised to provide them and which they were to provide the nation-state and the institutions at which they were educated. Their stories are important, however, not for the work they do to recover or recuperate a forgotten past of these institutions, but rather, to borrow Lisa Lowe's language, because they help us to "comprehend the particular absences of the intimacies of four continents, to engage slavery, genocide, indenture, and liberalism, as a conjunction, as an actively acknowledged loss within the present."[183]

# PART II
## *Empire's Educational Exemptions*

According to the Institute for International Education's February 1922 Third Annual Report, "foreign students" attempting to enter the United States after the passage of the 1921 Emergency Quota Act experienced "considerable hardship."[1] All previous federal immigration laws, which had worked incrementally since 1862 to dramatically restrict immigration by people from China, Japan, and eventually what was called the "Asiatic Barred Zone" extending from Afghanistan to the Pacific, included special exemptions for several classes of travelers, including merchants, teachers, diplomats, clergy, and, of particular import for the history of the US university, students.[2] The 1921 Act instantiated a novel quantitative, nation-of-origin-based approach using statistical knowledge and geographic parameters to effectively restrict access to only immigrants from select countries, primarily Western European, with populations regarded as white in the dominant racial imagination of the US government and academe. The quotas in question, however, only applied to people who were eligible for citizenship—anyone deemed "ineligible to citizenship" could be denied entry. In 1870, the Naturalization Act expanded the 1790 restriction on who could naturalize to become a US citizen from only "free white persons" to include "aliens of African nativity and persons of African descent."[3] The Immigration Commissioner-General W. W. Husband explained to a *Boston Globe* reporter that the quota law would ensure "the blood of America" would continue to reflect "the fundamental stock of the people."[4]

The 1921 act retained general exemptions that permitted admission for "Government officials" and those traveling with them, and for aliens visiting the country temporarily as tourists for business or pleasure. It also provided special relief for "aliens" of a range of professions, including "actors, artists, lecturers, singers, nurses, ministers . . . professors for colleges" and others who were to be admitted even after the quota for their nationality had been exceeded. However, somewhat inexplicably, students were, for the first time, omitted from either class. When Representative Lester David Volk of New York inquired into the omission, Representative William Vaile, a staunch advocate of immigration restriction, explained that "you can not make the bill too liberal without entirely destroying the bill. We thought we were particularly liberal on this."[5] As Part II will illustrate, the definition of "student" had, in fact, been under the pressures of redefinition and reinterpretation for more than thirty years, with great consequence for US and global politics.

For Stephen P. Duggan, the Institute for International Education's (IIE) director and a professor of political science at City College of New York, this abrupt change to immigration policy for noncitizen students was deeply distressing. Just three years earlier, Duggan collaborated with Nicholas Murray Butler, president of Columbia University, and Elihu Root, a former secretary of state, to form the IIE.[6] With the support of grants from the Carnegie Endowment for International Peace, the Ford Foundation, and John D. Rockefeller, IIE's post–World War I internationalist mission set out to enable the United States to "secure a better understanding of foreign nations" and to enhance the ability of "foreign nations to obtain accurate knowledge of the United States, its people, institutions, culture."[7] But, the 1921 Immigration Act threatened this work. Because the law no longer included students as an exceptional category exempt from quota limits and other bars to immigration, a number of would-be student visitors from countries, colonies, and territories outside Western Europe and the Americas were detained for deportation when the established quota for their point of origin was reached or because immigration from their country of origin or for people of their racial designation was barred altogether. Without a guaranteed exemption for students, the new law threatened to effectively stem the travel of nonwhite students to the United States entirely, dramatically reducing IIE's capacity to build international understanding and, perhaps more importantly, broader efforts to exert American influence globally through the distribution of US-educated future leaders of industry and government. While IIE was no doubt aware that nonwhite students, and especially students read as Chinese, had long been subject to harassment and entrance denial at ports of entry under suspicion of being laborers rather than bona fide students, the formal omission of students as an exempt class in the 1921 law and news of the resulting detentions spurred Duggan to action. He made good on the recently formed institute's charge by contacting top immigration officials in DC and on Ellis Island.

As the IIE report explains, through negotiations with these officials, Duggan was able to establish an administrative process whereby "a foreign student complying in all other respects with the immigration law will be admitted . . . even though the quota of the country from which the student comes has been exceeded." To make the special conditions acceptable to immigration officials and to quell their concern that the travelers could be laborers rather than persons entering the country "solely for the purpose of study," students were additionally required to "give a bond in the penalty of $500 that he will leave the country within a year."[8] Notably, the phrasing in the report does not directly address students excluded for reasons other than their country's quota, but the way it was applied suggests that at least some immigration officials understood its terms to apply to immigrants ineligible for citizenship as well. Duggan also proposed the incorporation of new provisions for the next immigration law for "the protection of foreign students." According to these recommendations, at the end of every academic year, "alien students" would "be required to present to the immigration authorities a statement from the college or university in the United States in which he was studying, certifying that he has completed the year's work and that he intends to continue his studies in that institution the next year."[9] In other words, colleges and universities would be deputized as a de facto auxiliary enforcement and surveillance branch of the federal immigration regulation apparatus.

Part II expatiates the ambivalence of the US state toward the figure of the nonwhite noncitizen student during the sixty-year period between 1862 and 1924, when the nation-state developed its foundational policies regulating the movement of people across its borders and higher education reconfigured as a post-emancipation institution providing knowledge for the expanding state form and its corporate entanglements. The rather speedy reversal of the 1921 act's omission of students illustrates both the power of particular kinds of internationalists and the imagined importance of nonwhite noncitizen students to the project of securing US interests beyond the nation-state's borders. At the same time, the reversal was the occasion for the development of novel strategies to administer and regulate the presence of noncitizens in the country. This was possible because students continued to be seen as potential threats. This concern turned into a tactic for regulating the educational institutions in which they enrolled, institutions the US federal government at the time had little other power over. At the foundation of these concerns was a fear that would-be laborers would exploit the exception provided for students. As such, the position of student was constituted in distinct, if always incomplete, opposition to that of worker.

The temporary and conditional inclusion of Chinese and other students "ineligible for citizenship" initiates precisely the kind of limited inclusion most serviceable to the purposes of American imperial pursuits. It aligns with and extends Jefferson's vision for the cultivation of "global agents of American universality" discussed in Chapter 2 by making the pursuit of education function in support of a broader internationalist project of the white liberal, capitalist nation-state. The stories of the Chinese students discussed in Chapters 4 and 5 demonstrate how this endeavor served to proliferate the liberal, capitalist nation-state form itself. As Madeline Hsu has argued, the politics around noncitizen students also provides crucial insight into "the ideological and institutional foundations for how quickly Chinese transitioned from being racialized as an unwanted yellow peril to become welcomed model minorities within the space of one generation."[10] This history surfaces the central role of the politics of cross-border student movement in the process of defining and shaping relationships between nation-states in formation in the United States and in the world during the latter half of the nineteenth century and the earliest decades of the twentieth. All too often, the student and education more broadly are framed as marginal considerations. Tracing the history of this period through changes in the form, function, and funding of US universities and efforts to regulate and administer the migration of Chinese students to the United States reveals that they were anything but marginal.

Colleges and universities were not simply passive bystanders to the epistemic changes that shaped immigration law of the 1920s, which set crucial legal rationale and precedent for our present moment. They were, rather, central players in the development of the very knowledge formations that made such shifts possible. This was especially the case as institutions were increasingly funded by wealth accumulated through the extractive and expansionist practices of settler racial capitalism and fomented emergent sciences for the categorization of populations and the distribution of life chances. Understanding the contours and histories of late nineteenth- and early twentieth-century immigration law and US higher education necessitates contending with the stories told about non-European, noncitizen students who attended college and university in the United States. To this end, Part II situates the emergence of US law regulating the movement of students in the second half of the nineteenth century in relation to a genealogy of the university-generated statistical sciences of race and difference upon which such laws were based and stories told about and by Chinese students in the United States. While Part II is especially concerned with the eventual form of the 1921 Emergency Quota Act and the Immigration Act of 1924, it tracks a longer genealogy of the historical figures that made these acts possible, looking to the law as an example of the state's articulation of how and when it does and does not desire, and thus make possible, the presence of specific noncitizens. As such, Part II demarcates the stories, logics, and forms of knowledge that contributed to the law's eventual form and chronicles the narratives and discourses that emerged in response to it.

# 3

# The Post-Emancipation University, Industry, Race, and International Politics

With European institutions devastated after World War I and America rising in global prominence, by 1921, the United States had become the foremost destination for higher education. This was in part a result of the damage done to European institutions during the war, in part a product of concerted efforts by US internationalists to recruit students and scholars, and in part the culmination of a sixty-year remapping of US higher education in the service of the state and capital. After the Civil War, colleges and universities expanded rapidly and came to serve a central role in training a labor force and providing a knowledge base for the post-emancipation economy in which capital accumulation was accomplished through emerging technologies in agriculture, mining, and manufacturing. The tentacles of the slave economy ran deep throughout the US and world economies from the wealth held in captive people and their reproductive capacities to the violent expropriation of their labor for the cultivation of raw materials, to the distant and distinctly Northern sites of manufacture that transformed said materials into goods to be sold domestically and internationally, and the often also remote locales where food products like salt cod were produced to be shipped South as cheap food for enslaved people. Colleges and universities and the new knowledge they produced promised to generate the modernizing and civilizing technologies necessary to secure the next generation of capital accumulation.

The geographic expansion of higher education proceeded through the development of an administrative state operating on multiple fronts and the emergence and consolidation of new forms of industrial capital reliant on scientific advances. Domestically, this meant opportunistically seizing Indigenous lands and redistributing them as federal funding for educational institutions through the Morrill Land Grant Acts of 1862 and 1890.[1] The acts' stated purpose was to promote "the liberal and practical education of the industrial classes" and "such branches of learning as are related to agriculture and the mechanic arts," i.e., engineering.[2] The passage of the 1862 act was only possible during the Civil War because Congress was absent of the Southern representatives who had previously blocked federal land allocation to nonslaveholding populations. Richard Lewontin argues that the first research conducted by these institutions was intended to help develop "the replacement of southern by northern crop production," a mission clearly also conditioned by Southern secession.[3] As I have argued with Eli Meyerhoff, Nick Mitchell, and Zach Schwartz-Weinstein, land-grant institutions took up an explicit role in the "certification and subjectification of citizens for the state" and "anticipated the rising value of research especially in the fields of 'scientific' agriculture and mining technology [and] in the expansion of statistical thinking and the categorization of human differences."[4]

This chapter explains how this expansion also extended beyond continental borders as the US empire moved across oceans to encompass Hawai'i, the Philippines, and Puerto Rico, with universities serving as anchor points. The following sections provide a schematic overview of the transformations in US higher education between the 1860s and the early 1920s, changes that served as the backdrop against which the legal status of noncitizen came into formation. To this end, I am particularly concerned with the increasing prominence of business magnates in their founding and funding of institutions of higher education, the focus of these institutions in disciplines that dovetailed with the emergence of scientific racism and the development of the administrative state and its immigration apparatus, and where these both played out in the foreign policy world and in the professorial and political career of Woodrow Wilson.

## Capital and the Academy

Wealthy industrialists who saw universities as unique spaces for the development of new technologies began taking an interest, literally and figuratively, in higher education institutions in the decades before the Civil War. In 1847, the cotton textile manufacturer Abbott Lawrence made a donation of $50,000 to found the Lawrence Scientific School at Harvard, "motivated by his own frustrations locating qualified engineers and planners to build his mills and towns."[5] Stephen Van Rensselaer's chartering of the Rensselaer Polytechnical Institute in New York in 1824 is an even earlier example of the investments of the manufacturing elite in practical education.[6] In 1859, Peter Cooper, an iron industrialist, established the Cooper Union for the Advancement of Science and Art in New York. But, after the emancipation of the enslaved people upon whom the previous economy depended, wealthy philanthropists ensured that industry was at the center of higher education's buildout. A series of industrialists opened higher education institutions as their namesakes, starting with Ezra Cornell in 1865, and then Cornelius Vanderbilt in 1873, Johns Hopkins in 1876, Leland Stanford in 1885, Jonas Gilman Clark in 1887, and Andrew Carnegie in 1900. In 1890, John D. Rockefeller followed suit in function, if not in form, by providing the base funding for the University of Chicago.

Johns Hopkins, Clark, and the University of Chicago departed in significant ways from prior US institutions of higher education, importing the German-style structure and a focus on research as the production of knowledge through graduate education.[7] As Christopher Newfield describes, the post–Civil War moment inaugurated a "revolution" whereby the research university became "industry's indispensable adjunct."[8] Such adjunctification was necessary as industries too adapted to a post-slavery global economy of goods, people, and knowledge. Newfield goes on to explain that "the university supported economic development, which was largely the province of science and engineering, while simultaneously promoting self-development, which was the traditional province of the humanities."[9] University knowledge was essential beyond the industrial and infrastructural engineering of the postwar world. Social, political, and cultural worlds also required new frameworks for making sense of relationships between people and peoples, frameworks colleges and universities would cultivate, authorize, and distribute. Scientific scholarship worked to carve out and define the domain of selfhood and personhood, i.e., the population to which such concepts could even be applied and made accessible in substantive ways. As the number of universities expanded, so too did the fields they taught, notably in the social sciences. Thomas Leonard asserts that before the Civil War, "professional social science simply did not exist."[10] The academic discipline of economics, for instance, was established between 1880 and 1900, transforming into a proper scientific practice and bestowing on its practitioners in the university an array of kinds of authority.[11] As Clyde Barrow argues, these arrangements can be understood as exemplary of how higher education institutions were utilized by the consolidating capitalist class of the late nineteenth century to form and facilitate a corporatist accumulation regime.[12]

## Scientific Racism and Population Management

New disciplinary questions spoke to concerns that arose in the decades before the war, when movements for the end of slavery took two primary forms: those that called for the abolition of slavery and the instantiation of racial equality and others that, as discussed in Chapter 2, saw the end of slavery as inevitable but hoped to avoid a multiracial national future through the mass deportation of all people of African descent and the removal of Indigenous peoples to the American West. In response to moral and religious arguments against slavery, advocates for its continuation made their own arguments regarding the merits of the slave economy for the nation and for all people, what is referred to as the "slavery as positive good" perspective. Vice President John C. Calhoun's 1837 speech exemplifies this perspective:

> Never before has the black race of Central Africa, from the dawn of history to the present day, attained a condition so civilized and so improved, not only physically, but morally and intellectually. It came among us in a low, degraded, and savage condition, and in the course of a few generations it has grown up under the fostering care of our institutions, as reviled as they have been, to its present comparatively civilized condition. This, with the rapid increase of numbers, is conclusive proof of the general happiness of the race, in spite of all the exaggerated tales to the contrary.

Here, Calhoun depicts the history and condition of enslavement as a progressive, benevolent, and educative experience of collective uplift for Black people due to the supposed benefits of being exposed to white institutions and their attendant "civilization." Writing in 1859, James Lawrence Cabell, an intellectual descendant of Thomas Jefferson, professor of Anatomy, Physiology, and Surgery, and chair of the faculty at the University of Virginia, lent academic and scientific credence to Calhoun's proto-developmentalist ideas. In *The Testimony of Modern Science to the Unity of Mankind*, he promoted the "natural law" idea of fundamental differences between "varieties" of the human distinguished by anatomical traits "perpetuated by hereditary transmission," which held to a monogenistic theory consistent with biblical ideas whereby all human life descended from a common ancestor.[13]

The same year, Charles Darwin famously published *Origin of the Species*, a text widely understood to have spurred the evolutionist revolution. As Stephen Jay Gould argues, after the publication of *Origin*, "subsequent arguments for slavery, colonialism, racial differences, class structures, and sex roles would go forth primarily under the banner of science."[14] Colleges and universities were crucial sites for the effort to provide a scientific rationale for these various and mutually constituting modes of subjection. As biological sciences of race rapidly expanded within and beyond the university over the course of the next several decades, scholarship such as Darwin's and Cabell's morphed into developmentalist logics of racial difference and found a strong foothold in the minds of people who grasped onto racial inequality domestically, internationally, and, by the turn of the century, in spaces with statuses somewhere in between, including Hawai'i, Guam, Puerto Rico, and the Philippines. The scientific merit of evolutionist thought was bolstered by a second major trend in the human sciences, what Gould describes as "the allure of numbers, the faith that rigorous measurement could guarantee irrefutable precision, and might mark the transition between subjective speculation and a true science."[15] As he continues, "evolution and quantification formed an unholy alliance . . . their union forged the first powerful theory of 'scientific' racism."[16] The linkage between the two is perhaps not surprising given that Darwin was himself inspired by one of the foundational thinkers of population science, Thomas Malthus. Darwin turned to Malthus for two reasons. One was that building on the work of "a man of the cloth" obviated some of his concerns that his theory of evolution would be taken as an attack on Christian belief in creationism. Secondly, as Heather Remoff discusses, Malthus's work explained, in compelling and simple terms, a basic mechanism through which Darwin could elucidate his theory of natural selection, "in the fight over scarce resources, only the strong would survive and pass on their superior traits to their offspring."[17] However, Darwin departed from Malthus in his fundamental understanding of evolution, and in many ways history itself, as a process of progressive change over time.

In *Origin*, Darwin restricts his theorization of natural selection to the world outside of human life, only referencing the "human" five times throughout the text.[18] It was Darwin's cousin, Francis Galton, who infamously translated his work on evolution to the reproduction and management of human life, founding and extolling his findings under the label "eugenics." In so doing, Galton became a leading scholar in statistical thought and quantification, particularly after the publication of *Hereditary Genius* in 1869. Darwin's and Galton's work inspired scholars in the emerging social scientific fields of statistics and sociology, such as Francis Walker, the president of the Massachusetts Institute of Technology from 1881 until his death in 1897, and William Graham Sumner, a professor of political economy and the first scholar to teach a course in sociology at Yale. Sumner imported Herbert Spencer's extension of Darwin's thought and his thinking on "the survival of the fittest," which rationalized poverty and exploitation as natural and inevitable.[19] Walker brought the combined weight of Social Darwinist thought and statistical analysis to bear on social policy through his role as superintendent of the 1870 and 1880 censuses.[20] By the 1890s, he was a central member of the Immigration Restriction League based on his theory that the presence of "foreigners" slowed the natural birth rate of Americans.[21] As Mae Ngai demonstrates, "Walker's theory of the declining native birthrate and the census data upon which it was based became the foundation for the restrictionist claim that immigration threatened to overwhelm the American nation."[22] Over the course of the next three decades, this line of argument would underwrite the incremental development of increasingly restrictive immigration laws, culminating fittingly in the Quota Acts of 1921 and 1924.

## Frontier Expansion and Imperial Rule

The 1870s to the 1920s was also a period of intense economic instability and the remapping of American understandings of land and territory, national conundrums to which university knowledge proposed solutions or at least frameworks for understanding. Part of what conditioned and strengthened the immigration restrictionist's position in the 1890s was the declaration by Fredrick Jackson Turner, an 1891 history PhD from Johns Hopkins and professor at the University of Wisconsin, that the "American frontier" was closed. Turner studied at Johns Hopkins under Richard T. Ely, the founder of the American Economic Association in 1885 and a proponent of the social gospel, which preached a liberal Protestantism often aligned with eugenics that "pursued economic and social improvement through a scientifically informed mission of social redemption."[23]

Turner presented his "frontier thesis" at the 1893 meeting of the American Historical Society (AHA), opening his comments on the centrality of the frontier to "American development" with a discussion of the 1890 census. In doing so, he took inspiration from Walker's statistical cartography.[24] In addition to consistent references to demographic data, Turner draws, in no uncertain way, on evolutionary frameworks and biological rhetoric, referring, for instance, to the "vital forces" that call the "organs" that are governmental institutions "into life"; to the "germ theory of politics"; the "evolution" and "development" of institutions of the nation-state itself from primitive to civilized, seeing in the United States "the record of social evolution."[25] For Turner, the frontier was a space of "perennial rebirth," providing "its continuous touch with the simplicity of primitive society" that "strips off the garments of [European] civilization . . . puts him in the log cabin of the Cherokee and Iroquois." Indigenous peoples are figured as a step in the chain of human progress, rather than human themselves, and as a condition of the frontier and its wilds. Here, "in the crucible of the frontier the immigrants are Americanized, liberated, and fused into a mixed race," "a composite nationality for the American people."[26] In other words, transformed by the wilderness, a "new product that is American" emerges: a new and specifically American form of whiteness.[27] This new racial formation illustrates how encounters with and incorporation of the frontier or margin came to be understood as fundamental to the energizing and reinvigoration of an active and robust form of American citizenship.[28]

Throughout Turner's work, the triumph of settlers over the continent is rendered as simply a scientific fact of progress and thus predestined, whether by God or by nature. In his cogent work on the mutually constituting histories of Indigenous nations and Chinese workers, Manu Karuka argues that, for Turner, the expropriation of Indigenous lands "is facilitated by conceiving the territorial, legal, political, and economic unit of the settler 'nation' as the only rightful unit to govern collective life on the continent."[29] By reframing these events as part of the natural process of human progress, Turner grants a kind of license or even innocence to settlers, who acted as the agents of a larger historical force, and their descendants.[30] As Karuka continues, read through this logic, "The 'domestic' space of the United States, the 'nation's interior,' is governed on the principle of extraterritoriality, of legal impunity for colonizers and for their economic and political institutions."[31] But, as the discussion of the colonization of Liberia in the 1820s and the broader distribution of US-based missionary efforts in Chapter 2 illustrates, this understanding of the inevitable movement of progress and civilization had implications that had already taken root far beyond the continental United States. In January of 1893, seven months before Turner delivered his talk on the frontier at the AHA conference, US Minister of Foreign Affairs John L. Stevens led the unlawful overthrow of Queen Lili'uokalani, the sovereign monarch of the Hawaiian Kingdom. Five years later, the United States annexed Hawai'i and took colonial possession of the Philippines, Guam, and Puerto Rico.

Turner's contributions were just one component of the broader intellectual architecture of novel ways to manage the supposedly innate inequity between races domestically, which in turn helped rationalize the United States' turn to direct extra-continental expansion. Robert Vitalis argues that this new academic project can be traced to the founding of various academic associations starting in 1889 with the American Academy of Political and Social Science. This new field formation was called international relations, but had both inspiration and implications domestically. As Vitalis explains, it took up the primary question of "how to ensure the efficient political administration and race development of subject people, from the domestic dependencies and backward races at home to the complex race formation found in the new overseas territories and dependencies."[32] The scholars associated with the field, many of whom are still hailed as some of the most important forefathers of the discipline today, were "evolutionists to a man," their work securely committed to "notions of organic and innate differences among the 'races' of mankind."[33]

At its core, international relations built on evolutionary biology and other racial sciences to craft new theories of white racial superiority that could help guide strategies for governance. G. Stanley Hall's "recapitulation hypothesis" is a key example. Hall was a Williams undergraduate, Harvard psychology doctorate, Johns Hopkins faculty member, and the founding president of Clark University, where he served from 1889 until 1920. According to this theory, there is a single developmental progression of the individual over the course of their life from childhood to adulthood and a parallel developmental progress at the scale of races from savagery to barbarism to civilization.[34] This theory, as Gould argues, provided "an arsenal of racist arguments supplied by science to justify slavery and imperialism."[35] White people were the most advanced in this process, while nonwhite people existed on a spectrum. Because of this, it was the responsibility of white people to act benevolently toward racial others through the provision of instruction that could mitigate, if not overcome, the inherent differences between the races. Education served as a panacea, if not a cure, for developmental deficits.[36] The goal was to maintain racial separation while instilling in people elsewhere the basic abilities for civilizational development in alignment with the American imperial market agenda.

Domestically, the idea of inherent differences between races gained wide traction in the 1890s through the work of Booker T. Washington and his 1895 "Atlanta Compromise" speech. As the only Black speaker at the Cotton States and International Exposition that year, Washington articulated what would be his most famous reading of US racial dynamics, stating, "In all things purely social we can be as separate as the five fingers, and yet one as the hand in all things essential to mutual progress."[37] To enable this "mutual progress," Washington implored "those of the white race" to help and encourage his people through "education of the head, hand, and heart." Washington's conception of an appropriate education for Black people as distinctly industrial was the product of his training at the Hampton Institute and his work with the institute's founder Samuel C. Armstrong, who had come to his own understanding of education for nonwhite people during his education as the child of missionaries in Hawai'i and then, five years before Hall, at Williams College.[38] Washington's Atlanta speech cleared the way for the US Supreme Court cases of *Plessy v. Ferguson* and *United States v. Wong Kim Ark,* which legally formalized subordinated forms of citizenship. While the 1898 Wong case held that birthright citizenship extended to the US-born children of Chinese parents under the Fourteenth Amendment, *Plessy,* decided two years earlier in 1896, had already effectively bifurcated citizenship through the doctrine of "separate but equal," which "upheld the constitutionality of racial segregation."[39]

In 1901, the court seemed to extend its reasoning regarding such principles of hierarchy beyond the continent in what are called the "Insular cases." As Vitalis explains, this series of rulings established one set of rules for territories composed of so-called "civilized people" who would be formally incorporated into the United States through being granted, eventually, the status of statehood, and another set of rules to guide the governance of the "uncivilized people" of spaces who were to remain "unincorporated."[40] The court's decision rested largely on the work of Albert Lawrence Lowell, a "Harvard man" through and through from his bachelor's degree through to his JD and then as professor of government and finally president from 1909–1933.[41] Lowell's arguments for the differential treatment of unincorporated territories extended from his position that the "theory of universal political equality does not apply to tribal Indians, to Chinese or to negros [*sic*] under all conditions."[42] Thus, at the turn of the century, both the question of citizenship and territorial control were neatly organized by ideas about people and people's capacities for civilization and self-governance. There was much debate among politicians and scholars about how to classify different peoples and geographies, but there was a shared belief that they all needed some degree of American tutelage to move toward civilization. Their status as uncivilized was imagined not as the result of concrete incapacities but rather capacities in need of nurturance, guidance, and education that could be developed over time.

## Imperial Education and Benevolent Assimilation

From the 1890s into the first decade of the nineteenth century, the United States' imperial ambitions in Hawai'i, the Philippines, and Puerto Rico were implemented through educational projects, including the founding of US-backed universities.[43] Victor Bascara's work illustrates how "education was a central trope in turn-of-the-century U.S. imperial discourse."[44] As discussed in Chapter 2, US-based missionaries, like Armstrong's parents, had long been central to the formal education structure of Hawai'i and Hawaiian students studied in the United States at least since 'Ōpūkaha'ia met Edwin Dwight on the steps of Yale College in 1809. Because the Philippines, Guam, and Puerto Rico had been under Spanish rule before the United States took possession of them after the Spanish-American War, they did not have a history of US-based missionary presence. Even as Filipino nationalists fought for their independence, the United States began its educational incursion into the country, sending five hundred American teachers to Manila in August of 1901 as part of President William McKinley's project of "benevolent assimilation."

Malini Johar Schuller argues that "the Philippines was the largest educational project in the U.S. empire, with thousands of American teachers sent within the first decade of colonial rule."[45] Whether or not this project ranks as the largest such project depends on how one defines both empire and education, but without question, it was one of both scale and effect and notably one executed by the US government, rather than nonstate actors such as missionaries. General Douglas MacArthur himself requested the funds for education as "adjunct[s] to military operations, calculated to pacify the people and procure and expedite the restoration of tranquility." The teachers were drawn from the recent graduates of prestigious colleges and universities, including Yale, Harvard, Cornell, the University of Chicago, the University of California, and the University of Michigan.[46] At these institutions, the would-be teachers were schooled in the kinds of evolutionary thought discussed above, applied directly to the people of the Philippines by scholars and colonial administrators, including Dean Conant Worcester, a University of Michigan-trained zoologist who took his first expedition to the archipelago in 1887. In his 1899 book *The Philippine Islands and Their People*, Worcester describes Filipinos as "Negritos": "a wretched, sickly race, of almost dwarfish stature. . . . Mentally they stand at the bottom of the scale, and their experience seems to have proved them incapable of civilization."[47] Based on this kind of racist assessment and in consultation with Booker T. Washington, Fred W. Atkinson, a Harvard alumnus and the general superintendent of Public Instruction in the Philippines, believed that "the education of the masses here must be an agricultural and industrial one, after the pattern of our Tuskegee at home."[48] As Schuller contends, "schooling was intended as a form of control that could implement the aims of the colonial government and stave off demands for independence."

Despite his derisive assessment of the general capacities of the Filipino people, Worcester advised the Philippine commission to initiate a program to bring especially gifted students from the Philippines to study at US institutions. This recommendation was in line with a 1900 report from the Schurman Commission, which found that the best way to provide the "lessons of civilization" would be by sending students to spend several years in the United States. The proposal came to fruition in 1903 when the US Philippine Commission's Act 854 passed "An Act Providing for the Education of Filipino Students in the United States," which is now referred to as "The Pensionado Act."[49] The act instructed each school division to create a "list of students best qualified" for an education in the United States. The students had to be "students of the public schools and native of the Philippine

Islands, of good moral character, sound physical condition," and between the ages of sixteen and twenty-one. Another group of students would be selected by the civil governor, with half of them assigned to study "agriculture and the useful mechanical arts and sciences" and then assigned to another course of study. Upon their selection, students were to be "subjected to a thorough physical examination" and required to take an "Oath of allegiance to the Government of the United States" and sign a legal agreement that they attend their assigned institution for four years, "conform to all regulations, rules, and laws of said institution," and return to the Philippines to work for the government for a period equivalent to the time spent in the United States. In return for following these strictures, the government would arrange for the students' travel and "make all necessary arrangements for the entrance of such students into said institutions and for their care, protection, and welfare." All of the costs associated with the students' travel, education, and maintenance were to be paid by an appropriation of $72,000.[50] The first one hundred students were sent to the United States in 1903 to be given a preparatory year of high school education before being sent to colleges and universities across the country, though concentrated in the Midwest, particularly in Illinois, and the East Coast.

The Pensionado program both built on the existing precedent of largely missionary-led education of noncitizen students in the United States and innovated upon this history in that the United States government played the central role in the initiation, implementation, and funding. It was an explicitly imperialist effort to educate students from other polities in the United States and into American knowledge and culture in order to distribute both back to the students' homeland. However, while another hundred students were sent to the United States in 1903 and 1904, participation in the program declined in 1905. Teresa Bevis and Christopher J. Lucas suggest that the reasons for this decline were twofold. One was that the US-supported University of the Philippines was founded in 1908. The second was that the program's funding was significantly curtailed when the definition of the students it included was restricted to only apply to graduate students.[51] This second issue regarding the redefinition of the status of "student" aligns with similar changes in US law and policy implemented targeting students from China from the 1890s through to 1905. Indeed, another possible factor may have been a redirection of energies around the education of noncitizen students away from the Philippines and toward addressing the large-scale boycott of US products underway throughout the Chinese diaspora, led by students provoked in no insignificant part by the poor treatment of would-be Chinese students when they tried to enter the United States. Chapter 5 elaborates on this thread.

As the field of international relations continued to take shape over the first decades of the twentieth century, questions of race, difference, power, and empire remained at its center. In 1910, Hall, the president of Clark University, who popularized recapitulation theory, and George Hubbard Blakeslee, a historian, established the discipline's founding journal. The publication, first circulated as *The Journal of Race Development*, was renamed the *Journal of International Relations* in 1919, and then sold to the Council of Foreign Relations and renamed the now more familiar *Foreign Affairs*.[52] As the original title of this publication suggests, its fundamental concerns reflect Vitalis's characterization of the discipline of international studies as fundamentally organized around the "political administration and race development of subject peoples, from the domestic dependencies and backward races to the complex race formations found in the new overseas territories and dependencies." International relations, that is, was conceived of as a new field of study that could "marshal the country's burgeoning intellectual resources in support of the expanded empire."[53] This was the dominant state of thinking in US academic and political worlds regarding international politics at the outbreak of World War I, a war that begot a radical rearrangement in the world order. As Ngai describes, "the war simultaneously destabilized and entrenched nation-state boundaries, ushering in an interstate system based on Westphalian sovereignty, which sanctified the integrity of the territorial nation-state and the principle that no nation can interfere in the affairs of another."[54] At the time, Woodrow Wilson was president of the United States and his policies reflected his deep entrenchment in the logics and knowledge of university-based thought about racial hierarchy, progress, and governance.

## Woodrow Wilson and the Racial State

Woodrow Wilson was born in Virginia in 1856 and spent most of his early life in Augusta, Georgia, coming into consciousness as the Civil War raged around him. His father, a Presbyterian theologian, studied at the Princeton Theological School in New Jersey. During the war, he helped orchestrate the separation of the Southern Presbyterian Church from its Northern brethren.[55] Wilson and his son were unabashed supporters of the Confederacy and its attendant logics during the war and into Reconstruction, and the younger Wilson would retain his commitment to the Dunning school of history. In 1901, he famously wrote, for instance, of the "perilous state of affairs" created by "absolute emancipation" where a people "unpracticed in liberty, unschooled in self-control," "a host of dusky children untimely let out of school . . . were a danger to themselves as well as to those whom they had once served."[56] In 1875, Wilson traveled to Princeton, New Jersey, to start his second attempt at college, having left Davidson College the year before shortly after starting his studies. At the College of New Jersey, Wilson studied history and political philosophy. He then went to the University of Virginia Law School, but did not complete his degree.

In 1883, he began doctoral studies at Johns Hopkins, with Ely and alongside Turner, also in history and political science, with a focus in German. After he completed his PhD in 1886, he taught at Bryn Mawr from 1885 to 1888 before moving on to Wesleyan University, where he published his first major work, *The State*, a "comprehensive and theoretical treatment of political principles [that] draws heavily from his study of foreign systems and German writers."[57] Ronald Pestritto contends that this text already carries the clear marks of Wilson's most enduring understanding of race, history, and governance, particularly in his embrace of a Hegelian perspective on "stagnated nationalities" of people "who have not come into conflict with their superiors and consequently have not progressed beyond a primitive stage of development."[58] *The State* also reflects the influence of the Social Darwinist thinker Herbert Spencer on Wilson's interpretation of the world, though Wilson likely encountered him primarily through the work of the English essayist Walter Bagehot.[59] The Darwinian impulse of the project was so clear that it nearly cost him his next appointment—a coveted professorship at the College of New Jersey. According to Wilson biographer August Heckscher, "the conservative element" of the school's board of trustees was critical of Wilson's potential appointment because "in *The State* he had minimized the 'supernatural' element; there was too strong an emphasis on the Darwinian theory of evolution."[60] Wilson's supporters prevailed and were successful in securing him the appointment. Wilson returned to his alma mater as the chair of Jurisprudence and Political Economy.

Wilson taught at the College of New Jersey throughout the 1890s, speaking at the institution's 150th anniversary in 1896, which also served as an opportunity for its renaming as Princeton University. Wilson's oratory was titled "Princeton in the Nation's Service." The same year he attempted, though failed, to hire Frederick Jackson Turner, still riding the high of his vastly influential speech on the closing of the American frontier. In 1899, Wilson expressed concern about the United States' seizure of the Philippines but his organic and evolutionary theories of the state also brought a larger question forward: "Were the people of the islands . . . in a state of development ripe for freedom."[61] Heckscher continues, "Wilson was groping at this time for a coherent approach to foreign policy, one recognizing America's predestined world role, affirming its special mission, and adjusting its actions to particular conditions." Wilson was elevated to the Princeton presidency in 1902. He invited Booker T. Washington to campus for his inauguration and then spent his entire eight-year presidency working to ensure that the student body stayed as white as possible, even as peer institutions integrated, however insufficiently.[62] The same year he published *A History of the American People,* a survey of US history sympathetic to British perspectives and ensconced in the "Lost Cause" narrative of the Confederacy in which slavery was a benevolent practice and the Ku Klux Klan figures as a valiant protector of "the southern country from some of the ugliest hazards of a time of revolution."[63] In 1906, Wilson hired well-known eugenicist Edwin Conklin to chair the biology department: "A notorious proponent of eugenics and social Darwinism" praised by the American Philosophical Association and elected to the National Academy of Sciences. The Society for Developmental Biology still grants an award in his name each year.

Upon his ascendancy to the United States presidency in 1913, Wilson's commitments remained consistent. Much as he had maintained segregation on the Princeton campus, he empowered his cabinet, dominated exclusively by Southern segregationists, with the capacity to segregate the federal workforce.[64] During the Wilson administration, "Jim Crow became more widespread than ever before in the federal government."[65] Wilson aligned with the perspective articulated by some Black conservatives, including Washington, that segregation was actually beneficial for white and for Black people since keeping the races separate could "reduce friction until time could ameliorate the prejudice whites felt toward African Americans."[66] For instance, he paternalistically told a gathering of Black leaders in 1914 that "[s]egregation is not humiliating, but a benefit, and ought to be so regarded by you gentlemen."[67] Wilson's historical perspective was also clearly on display in the White House with his notorious 1915 screening of D. W. Griffith's *The Birth of a Nation,* also called *The Clansman.* While there is some disagreement among historians as to how fully Wilson endorsed Griffith's fundamentally white supremacist depiction of American history, that Wilson's historical scholarship shaped Griffith's worldview and the film itself is painfully clear. Griffith included interstitials quoting directly from Wilson's *The State*: "The white men were roused by a mere instinct of self-preservation . . . until at last there had sprung into existence a veritable empire of the South, to protect the Southern country."[68] The third quote Griffith highlighted provides important context for Wilson's broader philosophy on race and politics in his concern regarding the "determination" of Congress to bring about a "veritable overthrow of civilization in the South." Wilson's interpretation of the meaning and importance of determination would become one of his most enduring contributions to global political thought.

In canonical writing about the "Wilsonian Moment" at the end of World War I, Erez Manela documents Wilson's emergence on the world stage as "a champion of the right of all peoples to self-determination . . . the prophet of a new era in world affairs, one in which justice, rather than power, would be the central principle of international relations."[69] As was clear to many, however, Wilson's interpretation of "self-determination" was quite circumscriptive. For one, the concept itself was, as Richard Seymour argues, "purloined from Bolshevik discourse in an attempt to neutralise the latter's appeal."[70] In so doing, Wilson and his co-architects of the League of Nations twisted the idea of self-determination in the service of liberal, capitalist, white supremacist empire. Adom Getachew cogently contends that they enacted a "reassociation of ideas" that "recast self-determination as a racially differentiated principle . . . fully compatible with imperial rule."[71] In so doing, they turned the idea of self-determination toward counterrevolutionary ends through which even the inclusion of nonwhite countries functioned so as to consolidate racial inequity and only the most burdened forms of recognition. To come under the auspices of the League of Nations was not to enter into a horizontal set of relations with other political entities. Instead, it meant becoming part of a complex system of differentiated inclusion for self-governing states, dominions, colonies, and mandates organized according to a developmentalist worldview in which some peoples had progressed to be capable of self-rule, and others had yet to do so. For the two African member-states, Ethiopia and Liberia, this meant that inclusion "produced the conditions of their domination."[72] For former territories of the German and Ottoman Empires turned "mandates," such as Palestine, Lebanon, Syria, New Guinea, and others, their status marked them as having "latent capacity for self-rule . . . deferred . . . because of their backwardness."[73]

Wilson's developmentalist and racialist understanding of the world also structured his governance of the space between the domestic and the international—borders and the field of immigration regulation and restriction. During his campaign for the presidency in 1912, he wrote about his support for a policy to exclude Chinese and Japanese laborers based in his belief that "Oriental coolism will give us another race problem to solve."[74] However, Wilson's concerns went beyond worry about labor competition. Even more fundamentally, the presence of nonwhite people was, for Wilson, anathema to the creation of a "homogenous population" that would best serve the interests of the state and the white men he understood it to operate on behalf of. He was not, however, an unreserved restrictionist. For instance, he vetoed the 1917 Immigration Restriction Act based on his belief that "the literacy test violated the principle of equality of opportunity by excluding those who were denied an education."[75] Congress overrode Wilson's veto in 1916, notably enacting the first immigration law to restrict white, European immigration to the country.

Woodrow Wilson left office on March 4, 1921, two and a half months before the passage of the 1921 Emergency Quota Act. As discussed in the introduction to Part II, the 1921 act elaborated on established immigration bars to engulf much of the world in restrictions that effectively closed the border to immigrants who experts at the time deemed to be "undesirable." Henry Pratt Fairchild was one such expert. A professor of sociology at New York University, a founder of Planned Parenthood, and president of both the American Eugenics Society and the American Sociological Association, Fairchild penned a 1924 article in which he explained the intent of the immigration laws in no uncertain terms: they sought to "[weed] out certain undesirable elements on the basis of their personal qualities," which included national and regional origin, political beliefs, physical characteristics, and, perhaps most importantly, the likelihood that an individual would be "unproductive" and become a public charge, i.e., require state support.[76] As Thomas Leonard argues, from the 1880s on, immigration became the domain of an expanding administrative state that increasingly relied upon social scientific expertise, supposedly devoid of political investments, to guide the regulation of immigration and, through it, the composition of the nation-state's population.[77] In other words, immigration regulation employed the sciences of race and statistics to function as a demographic lever.

Marking the government's understanding that immigration was primarily a matter of labor and resource management in an era when the United States was working to craft a post-emancipation economy no longer fueled by the explicit exploitation of enslaved people of African descent, implementing these restrictive policies was entrusted to the Department of Treasury in 1882, which became the Department of Commerce and Labor in 1903, and then the Department of Labor in 1913.[78] The management of immigration was a political-economic issue of labor management. As Edward Valentine, a Republican congressman from Nebraska, succinctly captured in articulating his support for the 1882 Exclusion Act, "In order to protect our laboring classes, the gate must be closed."[79] Even as some scholars and politicians had collaborated over the decades to work toward the eventual restrictions of the 1921 and 1924 acts, there was also consistent debate about what form the restrictions should take and which potential immigrants should be deemed so undesirable, so dangerous to the nation's health, that they must be excluded.[80] As the next chapters demonstrate, they also met with significant pushback from advocates for more open immigration, specifically from supporters of international education from the ranks of the academy, the church, and industry.

# 4

# Open Doors, Yung Wing, and Immigration Law Before Exclusion

After the passage of the 1924 Johnson–Reed Immigration Act, which continued the conditional and temporally restricted inclusion of nonwhite students ineligible for citizenship, several internationalist organizations took it upon themselves to write reports and handbooks narrating the history and experiences of these students. The primary goal of such reports was to provide guidance for students and demonstrate the value and national importance of supporting noncitizen students during their studies in the United States.[1] Such organizations included the Committee on Friendly Relations Among Foreign Students (CFRFS), which was founded in 1911 by John R. Mott, a Cornell University graduate who helped to found the World Student Christian Federation in 1895 and served on the YMCA's International Committee. *The Foreign Student in America,* published under the auspices of the CFRFS in 1925, is a primary example of this genre to which contemporary scholars frequently turn as documentation of this era.[2]

Across its three hundred pages of reports from over twenty experts in the field of international education, *The Foreign Student in America* provides an account of the history and condition of the education of "foreign students" in the United States with a particular focus on the place of these students in American life and in relationship to the Christian Church. Presbyterian missionary Robert E. Speer's foreword to the volume frames the project through the concept of "opportunity": the opportunity that education in the United States offers students and the opportunity that educating students presents to US institutions. According to Speer, it was imperative for both the nation and, given the specific interests of the CFRFS, the church, to recognize this prospect to "send back each year to their many lands an army of ambassadors of good-will and helpful intercourses of international confidence, hope and peace."[3] Speer is careful to mark, however, that these efforts are not always successful. He reports that all of the students "came here full of confidence and hope," but despite this fact, "[m]any of them are going back disillusioned, some bitter, some sorrowful. Many of them received their first shock at the port of entry as they came in."

Mott's interest in Chinese students in particular was part of what Michael Hunt termed the "Open Door constituency" made up of "American businessmen, missionaries, and diplomats—with a common commitment to penetrating China and propagating at home a paternalistic vision . . . of defending and reforming China."[4] It was sparked in the early 1900s as concern grew that Chinese students' negative experiences navigating the United States immigration process and encountering racist prejudice in the country threatened to undermine the promise of international education. This included groups such as the foreign divisions of the Young Men's Christian Association (YMCA) and the national board of the Young Women's Christian Association (YWCA), and, by the 1920s, newly forming organizations, such as the Institute for International Education (IIE).[5] They shared a belief that the education of students from China was essential both for world peace and for the sustained power of the US economy—and educators were central to their work.[6] According to Mott, "the future of a nation lay in the youth, and nothing was more important than winning the students for the Christian cause."[7]

Mott worked closely with several wealthy industrialists with strong Christian commitments, including Andrew Carnegie, Cleveland Dodge, George Perkins, and others, leveraging them to support the cause of international education. As he wrote to Carnegie, "schools and universities are the strategic points."[8] And, in a separate letter, "If we influence on the right lines the ideas, spirit and practices of the men who are to become the legislators, statesmen, jurists, editors, authors, teachers, doctors, engineers and other leaders of thought and action, we determine the destiny of a nation of people."[9] In 1911, Mott drew on his various connections to form the CFRFS. Liping Bu argues, CFRFS marked the "beginning of a unique endeavor of American Christian groups to win the hearts of foreign future leaders to Christianity."[10] But it was also novel in its provision of secular support to facilitate students' access to basic counseling, educational information, and hospitality.[11]

In *The Foreign Student in America's* first chapter Henry H. King, the secretary of the international committee of the YMCA, provides a sweeping "Outline History of Student Migrations" from the Middle Ages through to the years just before the book's publication. The chapter's opening pages make the broad claim that "the university as an institution owes its origin to student migrations," paying homage to the importance of travel to German universities in the education of significant figures in US political and academic history, including Henry Wadsworth Longfellow, Benjamin Franklin, Edward Everett, and George Ticknor. When King shifts to the stories of students traveling to the United States, he relies heavily on a balance of statistical accounts and descriptive reports from the US Department of the Interior's Bureau of Education and IIE, periodicals such as *The Pan-American Magazine*, *The Student World*, and *The Outlook*, and the newly formed international organization, the League of Nations. This reduction of student lives to accounting and ledgers mirrors colonial archives that tallied bodies but failed to account for the more intimate lives of their subjects.[12]

According to the Bureau of Education's 1920–1921 report, 8,357 noncitizen students were in residence in the United States, with 1,443 students from China representing the largest portion of this group, followed by Canada and three territories under US possession—the Philippine Islands, "Porto Rico [*sic*]," and "Hawaii," which sent 957, 302, and 208 students respectively.[13] Looking at the accounting more regionally, King notes that there were "1,425 Latin-American students in academic residence in the USA during the year under review, 1,379 Europeans, and 2,506 Asiatics."[14] The number of students studying in the United States from Canada and Latin America can be explained by geographic proximity and a lack of immigration restrictions placed on movement within the Western Hemisphere. The presence of students from territories recently acquired by the United States can rightly be understood as a result of the explicit state efforts to use education as one spoke of imperialist efforts discussed above. The perhaps surprising fact that the largest proportion of students, representing over a sixth of the total, traveled from China, especially at the pinnacle of severe restrictions on immigration from what were then termed "Asiatic" countries, requires more explanation and historicization.

## Yung Wing and the Chinese Educational Mission

While the first Chinese students to travel to the United States for schooling came in the 1820s to attend the Cornwall School, discussed in Chapter 2, King's discussion and almost all that followed focus on Yung Wing, whom he describes as "the pioneer" of Chinese travel to the United States for higher education. Yung journeyed to the United States in 1847 and graduated from Yale in 1854.[15] He went on to initiate the Chinese Education Mission (CEM), "a movement which bore fruit in 1872 in the sending to America of thirty boys" with the support of the Peking government.[16] The CEM continued to send students to preparatory schools and colleges in New England until, in King's description, "a reactionary movement in China against this westernization of these picked Chinese youth led to the cutting off of the stipend, and the recall of all these students, who returned home almost in disgrace, so discriminated against that it was hardly possible for them to obtain employment vouchsafing them a livelihood."[17] At a later date, King continues, they were to be heard from—one as "the brains of the anti-opium crusade," another as president of the Board of Foreign Affairs of the Imperial Chinese Government; another as chief engineer of the Peking–Kalgan Railway, the first to be constructed entirely under Chinese survey and supervision; and others in other positions of the very highest importance in the life of the nation. Here King characterizes the termination of the CEM as the fault of Chinese officials feeling threatened by students acclimating to US culture while simultaneously suggesting that China still benefited in various fields from the training said students had received despite the officials' prejudice.

King's description of this history is replicated and then expanded upon in much contemporary scholarship on the education of noncitizen students at US institutions of higher education before World War II, perhaps most notably in Teresa Bevis and Christopher Lucas's *International Students in American Colleges and Universities: A History*. In this 2007 book, Bevis and Lucas trace the long history of international students in the United States holistically while leaving "it to others to interpret the full significance and meaning of the subject."[18] Their chapter on "Early American Colleges and Education Exchange" relies very little on statistical accounts of student travel before 1900, opting instead to tell the stories of individual students through direct reference to *The Foreign Student in America*.[19] Like King, Bevis and Lucas are especially focused on Yung and the CEM. According to Bevis and Lucas, Yung accompanied his missionary teacher, Reverend Samuel Brown, to Connecticut in 1847 to complete his high school education before matriculating at Yale in 1851. Yung was the first Chinese subject to attend higher education in the United States, and, as they mention parenthetically, was granted US citizenship in 1852.[20] Yung excelled at Yale, especially in English composition, but he was "regarded as something of a curiosity by his classmates, as he kept his topknot and wore a traditional Chinese tunic."[21] He graduated in 1854 and developed a plan with a classmate to initiate an education mission that would "ensure the rising generation of China would have opportunities for Western education."[22] Bevis and Lucas's story continues, documenting that when Yung returned to China after graduation, he discovered he had lost his fluency in Chinese. He returned to the United States during the Civil War and attempted to enlist, but the army turned him away because he was "not really American."[23]

Yung's plan came to fruition after the passage of the 1868 Burlingame Treaty, a bilateral agreement between the United States and China that effectively aligned the two as trade partners, forbade restrictions on immigration, and set forth an understanding regarding educational exchange wherein "Chinese subjects [enjoyed] all the privileges of the public educational institutions under the control of the government of the United States."[24] Yung found a supporter in Li Hongzhang, a Qing official who saw the education of Chinese students in the United States as an opportunity for modernization. The first group of CEM students arrived in 1872 during what Bevis and Lucas curiously characterize as a "time of tolerance toward minorities and immigrants." The students performed well academically, athletically, and socially. In 1874, ninety Chinese students were pursuing their studies in Connecticut. In 1875, Chen Lan-Pin joined the mission. He and Yung were officially named as China's first government representatives to the United States.

As Bevis and Lucas recount this history, by the mid- to late 1870s, the mission began to encounter problems following a visit from Chen Lan-Pin. Echoing King's description of the "reactionary movement in China against this westernization of picked Chinese youth," Bevis and Lucas describe Lan-Pin's displeasure with several aspects of the students' experience, most notably his fear that their studies in the United States were leading to a process of "Americanization" by which "the educational process was resulting in the alienation of young people from Chinese tradition and might create a cadre of 'westernized' scholars who could pose a threat to the Confucian elite."[25] According to these conventionally historical and Americanist texts, the Chinese government abandoned the mission in 1881 due to concerns about the ineffectiveness of the project and because of the growth of anti-Chinese agitation. Both President Ulysses S. Grant and the president of Yale University, Noah Porter, appealed to Qing leaders to reconsider their decision, but to no avail. When the mission ended, only two students had completed their degrees.

True to the modernization mission, the two students graduated from the Sheffield Scientific School at Yale, which had been named after Joseph Sheffield, a railroad magnate. Bevis and Lucas repeat King's report on the eventual successes of the returned students. Unlike King, they also track Yung's life through his death, documenting his return to the United States after publicly supporting the progressive movement against the Manchu-led Qing Dynasty in the final years of the nineteenth century. Marking his continued commitment to Yale, Bevis and Lucas note that upon his death, Yung donated his collection of Chinese texts to Yale, providing the basis for the Sterling East Asian book collection. Yale includes Yung's portrait in its University Center. The authors conclude their review of Yung's story with a quote from his autobiography, published in 1909, the year of his death: "Before the close of my last year in college I had already sketched out what I should do. I was determined that the rising generation of China should enjoy the same educational advantages I had enjoyed; that through western education China might be regenerated, become enlightened and powerful."[26] In punctuating their recounting of Yung's place in the history of international education with this quote, Bevis and Lucas cement Yung's position as an avatar or model of the desire for and promise of education in the United States for the noncitizen student and their home country.

Yung's story has received a great deal of attention of late, including Liel Leibovitz and Matthew Miller's 2011 *Fortunate Sons: The 120 Chinese Boys Who Came to America, Went to School, and Revolutionized an Ancient Civilization*; Weili Ye's 2001 *Seeking Modernity in China's Name*; Edward J. M. Rhoads's 2011 *Stepping Forth Into the World: The Chinese Educational Mission to the United States, 1872–81*; and, most generatively for this project, Madeline Y. Hsu's 2015 *The Good Immigrants: How the Yellow Peril Became the Model Minority*.[27] In their discussion of the CEM, King and Bevis and Lucas neglect to provide important historical context regarding the motivation of Chinese officials and the impact of the increasingly Sinophobic atmosphere in the United States, and particularly in federal law, on their decision to conclude the project. It is important, also, to consider how Yung's narrative features within recent Chinese nationalist histories, where historian of World Christianity Lian Xi argues Yung and the mission students have been "rediscovered" as "patriotic heroes of modern times." Yung in particular is held up for his "tireless efforts to introduce to China Western statecraft and other fruits of Western civilization—from contract laws and modern mines to railroads and national banking" and the project more broadly is understood as foundational to the emergence of China as a modern state.[28]

## Race, Labor, and the Making of Chinese Exclusion

During his time at Yale, Yung was able to naturalize as a US citizen, in part because, in 1852, processes for naturalization were quite decentralized, administered by local city courts rather than the federal government.[29] A decade later, the grounds upon which Yung was able to "adopt" America as his country would become fundamentally less secure. The shift initiated in California, bonded by, among others, Leland Stanford, a railroad magnate, the governor of California from 1862–1863, and US senator from 1885–1893, who used wealth acquired through the United States' settler and imperial expansion to found Stanford University in 1885. In his inaugural gubernatorial speech in

January of 1862, Stanford extolled the importance of discouraging the "settlement among us of an inferior race . . . by every legitimate means" and the need to "check immigration." According to Stanford, "the presence of numbers among us of a degraded and distinct people must exercise deleterious influence upon the superior race."[30] Unironically, the degradation of these "distinct people" in California was largely in the service of expanding the very infrastructure from which Stanford himself profited, especially when he became president of the Central Pacific Railroad during his short stint as governor.[31] Just five weeks after Stanford's speech, the US Congress passed "An Act to Prohibit the 'Coolie Trade' by American Citizens in American Vessels." According to the act, a "coolie" was an individual "disposed of, or sold, or transferred, for any term of years or for any time whatever, as servants or apprentices, or to be held to service or labor."[32] As such, according to US law, coolie status was associated with "indenture, a status marked in time, distinct from slavery."[33] While this act proved unenforceable because of its imprecise definition of coolie, its legacy was enduring.[34] In April of 1862, the California state legislature passed its own "Anti-Coolie Act," which instituted a tax on Chinese workers. As Manu Karuka argues, contrary to the federal law's assignment of coolie to a particular labor condition, "'coolie,' in the logic of the California law, meant 'Chinese,' a racial status, not a debt and labor structure."[35] I largely agree with Karuka's reading of this law but also see questions of racial status as deeply entangled with and even constituted by questions of wealth, debt, and labor.

According to Hsu, in much US history scholarship, the federal Chinese labor law of 1862 is described as an effort to forestall efforts by Southern planters who sought to replace enslaved people of African descent with "pliant Chinese coolies during the Civil War."[36] As such, to "vote for Chinese exclusion was cast as a vote against slavery."[37] Drawing on Moon-Ho Jung's work on the racial formation of the "Chinese coolie," Hsu reads this 1862 law as marking the "ideological linkages between African slavery and Chinese contract workers that conflated the significant differences between the two labor systems."[38] Also building on Jung, Lisa Lowe extends this point in her argument that the "Chinese contract laborer occupied a liminal, ambiguous intermediary position throughout the nineteenth century, brought to the Americas to supplement, replace, and obscure the labor previously performed by slaves, yet to be differentially distinguished from them."[39] In Jung's original writing, however, he makes an even broader argument regarding the significance of the 1862 law, contending that "the act of outlawing 'coolies' racialized 'immigrants' as decidedly white and European in American culture, negating the legal space afforded to 'free voluntary' Chinese migrants."[40] To be Chinese in this logic was to be definitionally unfree and not an immigrant. The first effort by the federal government to regulate immigration was therefore also, as Jung argues, "the last slave trade law," through which the racialization of Chinese migrants was secured.[41] Importantly, Tao Leigh Goffe argues, the coolie was imagined as a temporary worker. He—and the Chinese migrant laborer was almost assumed to be a he—would labor for approximately five years before returning home.[42] As such, it set a precedent for providing and prescribing temporary access to the country as a tactic for managing the presence of people deemed to be desirable in specific, temporary, and limited ways. The particular ramifications for students will become evident moving forward.

From these initial efforts to regulate the cross-border movement of people from China forward, the domain of immigration policy was decidedly entangled with efforts to define personhood along race and class lines. Well beyond the border, immigration laws served to regulate the lives and working conditions of laborers upon whom capital depended. In this way, "race was a calculus of profit maximization," and the state and federal "anti-coolie" laws were a primary mechanism for its concretization.[43] In March 1870, just a year after the completion of the first transcontinental railroad, which transformed California "from an overseas to a continental possession," the state's senate passed an act "to Prevent the Importation of Chinese Criminals and to Prevent the Establishment of Coolie Slavery."[44] The act required any "Chinese or Mongolian, born either in the Empire of China or Japan" or in any of the adjacent islands to obtain a permit from the commissioner of immigration. According to Karuka, with this permit, "a forerunner of the visa, the state, itself, would now manage the importation, selection, and oversight of labor, a sea change that continues unabated to the present."[45] The 1870 Naturalization Act's bar to Chinese immigration passed just months later.

## Educational Modernization and Imperial Strategy

While the US and California governments were passing Sinophobic laws and Darwinian conceptions of race stratification concretized through Francis Galton and other scholars in the first years after the Civil War and emancipation, Yung Wing was in China attempting to cultivate support for his educational mission. After his 1855 return, Yung spent seventeen years advocating for this project, waiting for support from government officials interested in modernization. In 1870, Yung was called to Tianjin to help with negotiations in the aftermath of an attack on Christian missionaries, itself a response to incursions by the United States, Britain, and France into the region following an 1858 treaty that opened the city as a trading port. Yung took the opportunity to pitch his idea to Zeng Guofan and Li Hongzhang, representatives of the Qing state.[46]

As Hsu explains, the Qing government's primary intention for the CEM was to enroll Chinese students in West Point or the Naval Academy so that they could return to China and contribute to "self-strengthening projects" using their newly acquired expertise in Western technological specialties.[47] When Yung attained support for the educational mission in 1870, it was made clear that the enterprise was not meant to "signal openness to Western civilization." Instead, it was part of a "calculated policy," which had been in process for thirty years, to "master the superior techniques of the barbarians," the very techniques employed to force the Treaty of Tianjin upon China in 1858, "in order to bring the barbarians under control."[48] The 1870 act's exclusion of Chinese persons from naturalization and the various anti-Chinese laborer laws would seem to suggest that the US government would not have been open to their enrollment in these institutions. However, the terms of the 1868 Burlingame Treaty reflect the conflicting interests of the US state in relationship to China and Chinese people and gave Chinese officials good reason to assume this would be allowed. According to the treaty, Chinese subjects visiting the United States were to "enjoy the same privileges, immunities or exemptions in respect to travel or residence as may there be enjoyed by the citizens or subjects of the most favored nations" and "all the privileges of the public educational institutions under the control of the government of the United States."

When the CEM began in 1872, most of the students were quite young and engaged in studies to prepare them for collegiate experiences. Yung was also involved in other projects as an unofficial and then official representative of the Qing government in the world. For instance, his biography includes a short chapter on his "Investigation of the Coolie Traffic in Peru" in 1873. A short trip to China in the spring of 1873 "for the sole purpose of introducing the Gatling gun" overlapped with a visit from a Peruvian commissioner attempting to make a treaty with China to expand the "importation of coolie labor into Peru."[49] The viceroy asked Yung to confer with the Peruvian representative, at which point Yung reflected upon the "facts and horrors of the coolie traffic."[50] The viceroy then commissioned Yung to travel to Peru to report back, which he did in a matter of months. He sent a written report along with "two dozen photographs of Chinese coolies, showing how their backs had been lacerated and torn, scarred and disfigured by the lash."[51] Yung reports in his biography that "since our reports on the actual conditions of Chinese coolies in Cuba and Peru were made, no more coolies have been allowed to leave China for those countries. The traffic had received its death blow."[52] According to Edmund H. Worthy Jr., a historian writing in 1965, Yung's advocacy on behalf of Chinese laborers continued into the late 1870s when he worked to sway political opinion against more restrictive immigration policies.[53]

But Yung's efforts to stop the passage of such laws were, in the end, unsuccessful. In fact, the US government failed to abide by the Burlingame agreement in several ways. Yung explains that by the time a cohort of the CEM students were far enough along in their studies for him to put forward their applications to the State Department for admission to West Point or the Naval Academy in 1876, the "spirit of Kearnyism and Sandlotism" had overtaken the country.[54] Yung continues, "The race prejudice against the Chinese was so rampant and rank" that his inquiry was summarily dismissed with "cold indifference and scornful hauteur." The Burlingame Treaty was "trampled under foot unceremoniously and wantonly." With the denial of Chinese students' entrance to the military academies, the closure of the CEM was a foregone conclusion. Weili Ye's account of this history aligns with Yung's. According to her, Chinese officials decided to end the program in part because of their concerns about students adopting American lifestyles, as King and Bevis and Lucas submit, but also because of "the rise of anti-Chinese sentiments and actions in America at the time," which "led the U.S. government to back off from their earlier agreement to let the Chinese students enter American military academies."[55]

## The Page Act and Administrative Exclusion

Somewhat confusingly, stories about the CEM rarely consider the 1875 Page Act as an important component of this story, perhaps because the act pried open the possibility of immigration restriction by targeting "convicts, prostitutes, and involuntary Oriental laborers." The Page Act is broadly discussed as the first law to successfully implement restrictive immigration at the federal level. It used moralistic social arguments about sexuality, race, and class to circumvent the US–China agreement on immigration put into place via the Burlingame Treaty.[56] In her review of the significance of the Page Act, Kerry Abrams situates the law historically within a "cultural crisis over the regulation of sexuality and marriage" that was used as "a means of achieving regulatory ends that are otherwise prohibited."[57] That is, rather than radically reconfiguring previous laws to restrict the "free migration and emigration" of Chinese citizens, the Page Act targeted people presumed to be moral threats to the nation-state, effectively enabling the administrative review of all Chinese immigrants and building on the 1862 effort to prohibit the entrance of Chinese laborers. As legal scholar Leti Volpp explains, the legislation required that all immigrants from China, Japan, or "any Oriental country" be cleared by the consul general and thus put into place a procedural requirement that, in effect, denied entrance to all Chinese laborers, most Chinese immigrants, and many would-be immigrants from countries deemed "Oriental." Admission required proving that the immigrant was not entering the country for "lewd and immoral purposes," a deceptively broad and subjective category.[58] As such, the Page Act instantiated what would become a long tradition of utilizing underspecified, overtly moralistic language infused with and productive of naturalized valuations of racial difference, proper gender performances, class norms, and sexual mores to rationalize immigration policies.[59] Its purpose was, simply put, to dramatically curtail the entrance of members of a racialized class through administrative means and, in so doing, to constitute that very class.

However, the administrative limits of the Page Act failed to satisfy white nativist advocates of restriction, and in 1880 the US government renegotiated the 1868 Burlingame Treaty, which had affirmed "the mutual advantage of free migration," to allow for more expansive and explicit immigration restrictions.[60] After extensive talks between Chinese commissioners and the US government, represented by James Burrill Angell, the president of the University of Michigan, the Angell Treaty was ratified by the Senate in May of 1881. It granted the US government the capacity to "regulate, limit, or suspend" the travel of Chinese laborers to the United States.[61] Article I states the United States' right to regulate immigration but "not absolutely prohibit it" and that this right "shall apply only to Chinese who may go to the United States as laborers, other classes not being included in the limitation." Article II enumerates that those "proceeding to the United States as teachers, students, merchants or from curiosity, together with their body and household servants, and Chinese laborers who are now in the United States shall be allowed to go and come of their own free will and accord."[62] The Qing representatives understood the list of exemptions as simply examples of the kinds of persons and professions that could demonstrate that an entrant was not a laborer. Many US immigration officials came to apply the law in the opposite way, seeing in the list of exemptions a set of categories that could be narrowed over time so as to make exclusion complete. Their central concern from this point moving forward became how they could redefine the distinction between laborers and non-laborers—a decidedly unscientific distinction drawn most often through assessments of class. Functionally, this meant continuously limiting the categories of student and merchant so as to exclude as many would-be Chinese immigrants as possible.

## The End of the Chinese Educational Mission

Conservative pressure on Li Hongzhang, the Chinese official with oversight of the CEM, eventually prevailed, undoubtedly bolstered by the terms of the

Angell Treaty. In July of 1881 a dispatch from the imperial court formally ended the CEM and the students were ordered to return to China. Before the recall, the students had, at least according to Thomas La Fargue's 1942 telling of their story, understood their task as "leading China out of a morass of an effete Confucianism onto the firm ground of Western science and technology."[63] Even with the abrupt cessation of the mission, the students still expected an enthusiastic welcome. Instead, they were met with what La Fargue describes as a "rude reception." Wong Kai-Kah, a returning student, wrote to his American host mother to describe "the shabby treatment" the students "received at the hands of [their] paternal government," which included being exposed to "[c]rowds of coolies, wheel-barrow, and jinrickshaw men . . . shouting, gesticulating and quarreling for business."[64] The students were then held for four days in a place too "vile" for a "Western imagination" to "conceive," before being summoned before the highest official in Shanghai to prostrate themselves. In a 1913 piece published in *The Journal of Race Development*, Tsao Yun-Hsang, a Chinese student who received his AB from Yale in 1911, writes that upon their return the students "were despised, suspected and watched by the officers of the Manchu government." They were "left to shift for themselves for the government had no use for such 'semi-foreigners.'"[65]

As I discuss further in the next chapter, this was not the end of the story for Yung Wing, for the students who had participated in the CEM, or for the broader project of educating Chinese students at US institutions. It was, however, the end of this phase. When the Chinese government's decision to end the CEM in 1881 is placed in the historical context of the Page Act and the Angell Treaty, Bevis and Lucas's contention that the Westernization of Chinese students was the sole reason the mission ended is less persuasive. In these laws and the debates that led to their passage, the US state and its representatives espoused virulently anti-Chinese rhetoric. In many ways, Bevis and Lucas's reductive analysis of this history reflects the very Orientalist beliefs regarding the supposed radical incommensurability of the East and West used to justify the exclusionary anti-Asian laws.

# 5

# The Student Question in the Era of Exclusion

## Exclusion, Race Science, and Chinese Labor

In 1882, the US Congress passed the Chinese Restriction Act, officially ending even the semblance of an open immigration policy between the United States and China by suspending the entrance of all Chinese laborers.[1] A year later, a *San Francisco Chronicle* editorial calling for an even stricter law redubbed it the Chinese Exclusion Law, more accurately capturing the aspirations of advocates for the complete foreclosure of Chinese migration.[2] As legal scholar Kitty Calavita argues, this law was predicated on the very racial science emerging from universities of the time, discussed in Chapter 3. Congress passed the law based "on the assumption that the Chinese were a distinct race with a biologically determined nature that was reflected in moral behavior, cultural preferences, and physiological traits."[3] Foreshadowing William W. Husband's 1921 concern about "American blood," senators and representatives drew explicit connections between the racialization of Chinese people and the question of labor as they urged their colleagues to "reject . . . the stagnant blood of Asiatic servitude."[4] In forwarding such arguments, senators acknowledged that theories of racial equity "may be right in theory" but that "in practice nobody pretends they are true." They clung to Social Darwinist ideas of race in part because, as they asserted, "[u]pon what other theory can we justify the almost complete extermination of the Indian, the original possessor of all these States."[5]

The 1882 Restriction Act was the first time the centralized administrative state of the post–Civil War era effectively used its power to structure the population via immigration policy. Eithne Luibhéid argues that it must be understood as more than a single expression of xenophobia and instead be taken as a reflection of the "changing ways the state apparatus categorizes and manages populations, identities, and resources in forms that are complexly inflected by race, class, and gender."[6] In other words, with the 1882 law, the US federal government concretized the tactical use of differentiating people to suit the desires of post–Civil War white power. Through its reliance on emergent categories of racial difference, the law effectively concretized racial logics as the "how" of state power. The exclusion law was so effective that the number of Chinese immigrants living in the United States dropped from 105,000 in 1880 to fewer than 62,000 in 1920.[7]

Even in its sweeping recrafting of immigration regulation, the 1882 law was, at least technically, constrained by the terms of the Angell Treaty, which, as discussed in Chapter 4, suspended "the coming of Chinese laborers to the United States" but also stipulated that "Chinese persons other than laborers" were exempt from such exclusion.[8] These exempt classes included "teachers, students, merchants or from curiosity, together with their body and household servants." Because of these exemptions, Paul Kramer and other scholars of immigration history and foreign relations argue, the immigration law functioned less as a wall and more as a "'filter' whose gaps were carefully calibrated and relentlessly policed."[9] By including specific categories of exceptionally desirable immigrants, the law undid the presumption that such categories were static and immutable. Kramer helpfully contends that the law "registered both absolutizing and civilizing distinctions, permitting the transit of civilized and civilizing elements within the Chinese population, while barring those larger populations whose lack of civilization was thought to pose a threat to the United States."[10] Students fit neatly into the civilizing category in their pursuit of their own civilization through an education in the United States and in their promise of extending the nation-states' civilizing reach upon their return to China. Madeline Hsu argues the law "laid the foundations for the legal, ideological, judicial, and institutional implementation of America's border regimes in all of its twenty-first-century contradictions, abuses, and ineffectiveness," not least of all in its designation of students as a special category of interest, one set in direct opposition to "the detested Chinese laborer."[11]

But the sieve through which even exempted student migrants traveled was "sharp-edged" and under continuous refinement.[12] The question of how to enforce the law plagued the border officials tasked with its implementation and, in more detrimental ways, the lives of the people trying to enter the country. As Calavita argues, rather than settling "the much vexed Chinese question," "the new law turned out to be 'full of vexatious and perplexing questions.'"[13] Between 1882 and the passage of the 1921 Emergency Quota Law discussed in

Part II's introduction, there were five distinct stages in the efforts to regulate student travel to the United States. Between 1882 and 1891, Chinese students and others trying to enter the country as members of exempt classes with the resources and connections to do so took recourse to the law in order to push back against the power of immigration officials who denied them entrance. After a series of US Supreme Court decisions between 1889 and 1895, this avenue of recourse narrowed and with it the definition of "student" under the oversight of increasingly restrictionist heads of immigration. Between 1895 and 1905, the regulation of student movement continued to tighten, eventually contributing to a powerful boycott of American goods in China. Between 1905 and 1908, collaborations between the US government, universities, and philanthropic and religious institutions underwrote a renaissance in educational projects between the United States and China, but this moment faded in the 1910s as calls to restrict immigration via quotas took hold, culminating in the brief removal of students from the list of persons exempted from exclusion in 1921.

## Students, Exemption, and Administrative Power

As per the terms of the 1882 act, Chinese persons traveling to the United States were to provide customs officials with evidence of their status as part of an exempt class of non-laborers in the form of a certificate issued by the Chinese government, written in English, that includes their "name, title or official rank, if any, the age, height, and all physical peculiarities, former and present occupation or profession, and place of residence in China."[14] Importantly, the Section also explains that these certificates are necessary in order to ensure the "faithful execution of articles 1 and 2" of the Angell Treaty, which clearly stipulate that members of exempt classes should be "allowed to go and come of their own free will and accord, and shall be accorded the rights, privileges, immunities, and exemptions which are accorded to the citizens and subjects of the most favored nation." Two years later, when Congress added amendments to the 1882 act to clarify and tighten its restrictions, they articulated that Chinese people of nonexempt classes were to be excluded regardless of their country of origin, that immigration officials were required to "record extensive identification for all Chinese immigrants," that the category "merchant" excluded "hucksters, peddlers, and fishmongers," and, most importantly for students, that a US consular visa had to be attached to Section 6 certificates.[15] Upon presenting themselves at the border, would-be students faced harassment, imprisonment, invasive medical exams, and more, often requiring advocacy from American supporters to navigate the legal terrain. As Erika Lee illustrates in her classic work on Chinese exclusion, from 1882 to 1905, California courts "heard over 9,600 Chinese habeas corpus cases," many from individuals who were detained despite presenting themselves as members of exempt classes, including students.[16] In his legal scholarship on the period, Christian Fritz shows that between 1882 and 1891, the California court heard over seven thousand writs of habeas corpus, with plaintiffs securing an over 80 percent success rate.[17]

The cases brought by Chinese immigrants frequently entailed challenges to "the legality of exclusion policies," with particular attention paid to whether Articles I and II of the Angell Treaty, providing for limited application of the law to laborers and the free travel of exempt classes, carried more weight than Section 6 of the 1882 Exclusion Law, requiring "every Chinese person other than a laborer" to obtain certification of their status. Applicants brought habeas corpus cases and charged that administrative procedures failed to respect their constitutional rights under the Fifth Amendment guarantee of "due process" to any "person" under US jurisdiction.[18] Through at least 1892, a legal precedent was established whereby Article II of the treaty held. In the 1882 Case of the Chinese Merchant, Justice Stephen Johnson Field, a Williams graduate, ruled that the Section 6 certificate is "designed to facilitate proof by Chinese other than laborers . . . that they are not within the prohibited class. It is not required as a means of restricting their coming."[19] The 1882 law was "framed in supposed conformity with the provisions" of the 1868 and 1880 treaties. To assert a requirement for such documentation would be to "impute to congress a purpose to disregard the stipulation of the second article of the new treaty, that they, meaning Chinese persons who are not laborers, should be 'allowed to go and come of their own free accord.'"[20] Field continues, reading Section 6 of the Exclusion Act through the congressional debates that preceded its passage in which it was agreed that to require certificates would be a violation of the Angell Treaty. At the same time, his ruling reaffirmed the state's important right to restrict immigration so as to "prevent the degradation of labor and preserve all the benefits of our society." So, while Field's ruling was helpful to would-be immigrants in the immediate sense, it also opened up a route for more expansive restrictions.

Over the next two decades, restrictionists grew emboldened, especially as scientific explanations of racial and civilization differences strengthened their grasp on both scholarly and more colloquial understandings, as discussed in Chapter 3. Between 1882 and 1902, the Exclusion Law was modified and expanded, often by requiring entrants to provide more and more elaborate forms of certification and inspection. The 1888 Scott Act shifted the terms of the law to more explicitly enact the intentions of US immigration officials to exclude "*all* Chinese except 'teachers, students, merchants, or travelers for pleasure or curiosity'" and prohibited the reentry of Chinese laborers, regardless of the duration of their prior residency.[21] Beth Lew-Williams argues that the more stringent terms of the 1888 act mark the actual beginning of the exclusion period fueled by the "unrelenting West Coast sinophobia and unanticipated enforcement problems" that flourished in the mid-1880s.[22] As the various amendments and enhancements to the 1882 act maintained student as an exempt status, "they did not protect students from scrutiny." Even when they presented a valid Section 6 certificate, students could still be denied at the border.[23] This is partly because none of the laws provided a definition for the category of "student," which "left it to individual inspectors to determine whom to admit."

More broadly, it was a result of what Calavita describes as the "law's indeterminacy" and an increasing reliance on "administrative discretion."[24] She looks to "frontline inspectors" delegated to actually enforce the law to argue that the "chaotic" enforcement of the law stemmed in part from the law itself and its linguistic "ambiguities" but also, and "more fundamentally," from "a series of contradictions and paradoxes associated with prevailing assumptions about race, class, and identity" that created openings for immigrant resistance.[25] At a basic level, the work of immigration officials was to determine if would-be entrants belonged to the class of desirable migrants presumed to be upper class or if they were laborers who should be excluded. But the categories themselves, that of merchant, student, and laborer, were inherently overlapping. Calavita is primarily focused on the duality of merchant versus laborer whereby upper-class merchants were held apart from the "Chinese race" on account of their class position. Whatever labor they performed was distinct from that of the laborer. In making this distinction, Calavita argues, "lawmakers were implicitly recognizing the social character of race despite their continual recourse to biological models through their references to blood and breeding stock."[26] Still, the inscrutability of the "merchant"/"laborer" duality was employed by immigration inspectors to allow for maximum exclusions.

For the first decade after the passage of the Exclusion Act, students, merchants, and other members of exempt classes continued to take their cases through the courts, especially after decisions like Field's in the Chinese merchant case. But Supreme Court decisions between 1889 and 1895 chipped away at the rights of noncitizens, limiting this avenue of recourse. In 1889's *Chae Chan Ping v. the United States*, Chae was denied entry into the country because as a laborer he was no longer allowed to reenter the country after the passage of the 1888 Scott Act. When he tried to challenge his denial, the court "used the occasion to announce a new theory underpinning the federal exclusion power."[27] They asserted Congress's plenary power to exclude noncitizens based on the nation-state's "vague and important and potentially limitless" sovereign capacity to exercise judgment on behalf of "the interests of the country."[28]

Possibly inspired by this decision, in 1891 Congress established the Office of the Superintendent of Immigration, a post intended to centralize immigration enforcement under the federal government. In so doing, they also granted the inspection officers working under the superintendent "power to administer oaths, and to take and consider testimony touching the right of any such aliens to enter the United States." Going still further, the law carved out a domain of administrative law wherein "all decisions made by the inspection officers or their assistant touching the right of the alien to land, when adverse to such a right, shall be final unless appeal be taken to the superintendent of immigration, whose action shall be subject to the review of the Secretary of Treasury."[29] The constitutionality of the law was affirmed a year later in *Nishimura Ekiu v. the United States*. The court rejected Ekiu's appeal of her denial to land in the United States by an immigration inspector on the grounds that "decisions of executive or administrative officers, acting within the powers expressly conferred by Congress, are due process of law."[30]

In 1892, Congress renewed the Chinese Exclusion Act as the Geary Act, extending exclusion for ten more years and instituting an internal registration system for Chinese laborers in the United States. Unsurprisingly, the Geary Act continued to tighten the knot of legal regulation constraining the movement of Chinese people across the border. Under its terms, Chinese laborers in the United States were required to carry a certificate of residence, what is now generally understood as the precursor to the green card, or be subject to detention and deportation. The act also allowed for arrests without warrants, narrowed the definition of "merchant," denied habeas corpus proceedings to Chinese immigrants stopped from landing, and more.[31] In other words, the regime of immigration management took shape.[32]

According to a 1908 publication by Ng Poon Chew, an advocate for Chinese rights in the United States, even though the Geary Act did not technically require members of exempt classes to obtain the certificate, immigration regulations required the arrest of any Chinese person in the country without one. Therefore, "any Chinese merchant, student or physician who was in this country at the time of registration and did not get a certificate is now liable to arrest and imprisonment."[33] The Chinese Consolidated Benevolent Association (CCBA or Chinese Six Companies) "ordered their ninety thousand or so members not to comply" with the registration order while they brought a legal challenge, which failed.[34] Afterward, it was widely accepted by all Chinese persons in the United States that it was necessary to comply with the registration order and acquire certificates of identity and the number of people traveling from China to the United States declined.

## Plenary Power and Administrative Sovereignty

Instead of being satisfied with the newly expansive powers granted to immigration enforcement, advocates for immigration restriction only increased the vigor of their work. In the context of Fredrick Jackson Turner's 1893 "closing of the frontier" speech and Woodrow Wilson's move to Princeton, Harvard graduates Charles Warren, Robert DeCourcy Ward, and Prescott Farnsworth Hall formed the Immigration Restriction League. During the 1894–1895 sessions, Congress established the Bureau of Immigration, granting it "broad Judicial and enforcement powers."[35] In 1897, President McKinley appointed Terrance Powderly, a restrictionist with deep connections to the labor movement, as Commissioner of Immigration. As Kramer summarizes, under Powderly's leadership and able to assume support from the courts, "officials whittled the 'exempt classes' down to nearly nothing, relentlessly scrutinizing Section 6 certificates with new rigor and suspicion, erring on the side of expulsion, and arresting and deporting migrants with little semblance of due process."[36] As Hsu explains, under Powderly and then his successor, Frank P. Sargent in 1902, port officials were instructed to "complete exclusion by assuming that even Chinese of the exempt classes were attempting fraudulent entry."[37]

One such case was *United States v. Chu Chee*. In 1896, "two Chinese boys," Chu How and Chu Chee, "aged, respectively 13 and 15 years," landed in Washington State, with documents from the Hong Kong Consulate attesting to their intention to join their father, who had been in the country for three years, and enroll in English schools.[38] Two years later, after Powderly's appointment, the district attorney of Oregon, where the Chus were attending school, charged them with unlawful presence and arrested them. The district court judge in Oregon ruled that the two could stay in the United States as long as they remained enrolled in school. But when the case was taken up to the US Supreme Court, this decision was overturned. Despite the fact that they were clearly students at the time of their arrest, their failure to adequately demonstrate this status under the specific and narrow terms of the Section 6 certificates upon their entry into the country rendered said entry unlawful, and they were subject to deportation.

In 1899, the same year as the Chu decision, the Bureau of Immigration turned its attention to refining the definition of "student" in its regulations. According to Krystyn Moon, when the Bureau released its first regulations curtailing membership in exempt classes, it enumerated that students "(1) must be under twenty-one years of age, (2) have previously attended school, and (3) must submit the name of the school they planned to attend in the US."[39] Just a year later, Moon continues, the Treasury Department, under which the Immigration Bureau was situated, released more regulations further refining the definition of "student":

> A person (1) who intends to pursue some of the higher branches of study, or who seeks to be fitted for some particular profession or occupation (2) for which facilities of study are not afforded in his own country; (3) for whose support and maintenance in this country, as a student, provision has been made, and (4) who, upon completion of his studies, expects to return to China.[40]

Moon explains that the implicit effect of these stipulations made it such that by the time of their implementation in 1900, "only students from wealthy families, pursuing a degree not offered in China, and planning to return home, could study in the US."[41]

## Chinese Nationalism and Educational Mobility

Before the distribution of these more stringent criteria for qualification as a student, the Qing government, its diplomatic representatives, and even the elite class of mobile Chinese more broadly had come to accept the terms under which US immigration procedures allowed for the transit of exempt and often elite Chinese subjects. After China's defeat in the 1894–1895 Sino-Japanese War, Qing officials were especially concerned with maintaining their diplomatic relations with the United States, whom they saw as a potential ally and a "lesser barbarian" who could aid them in their antagonisms with "the greater barbarians" such as Britain, Russia, and Japan.[42] Kramer describes how, at the turn of the century, "many Chinese officials had embraced exemption for the civilized not only as a necessity but as a virtue, emphasizing the restriction of migrant laborers (ideally by the Chinese state) and the protection of elite migration, which would both direct resources to the metropole and project the most civilized image abroad."[43] To support this argument, Kramer cites China's minister to the United States from 1896 to 1902, Wu Ting-Fang, writing in the *North American Review* in 1900. Wu asserts his belief that if Americans "think it desirable to keep out the objectionable class of Chinese, by all means let them do so."[44] However, he also implores his English-language audience to recognize two things. First, the advantage that American farmers and manufacturers would have much to gain from studying the "wants and habits of the Chinese."[45] And, second, the possibility that US immigration policy would be both less hostile and more effective were it to "exclude the illiterate and the degenerate of all nations."[46] As Kramer explains, "Wu sought to segregate—but not by race—the cosmopoli of the civilized and the unwashed."[47]

In subscribing to the civilizational thinking of the racial science of the time, Wu was in the mainstream of the Chinese elite where such modes of thinking had established a foothold in the 1890s.[48] Even as they were in opposition to each other, officials of the Manchu-led Qing government and the members of the rising nationalist movement both took up these logics to rationalize a broadly conceived Chinese empire. For anti-Manchu nationalists, racial logics contributed to the construction of a Han identity.[49] In her study of the emergence of the geopolitical age and the making of modern China, Shellen Xiao Wu briefly discusses how Qing officials "disgraced" by China's loss to British gunboats in the Opium Wars in the mid-nineteenth century "turned with great interest to science and technology from the West" and Japan.[50] Wu is primarily interested in the development of geographical knowledges and their uses for the constitution of the modern nation-state. As she explains, Chinese translators "recognized the racial hierarchy inherent in this new geography" and "its less-than-desirable implications for the place of Han Chinese within the Japanese spatial and racial hierarchies."[51] Still, they took up and reworked these frameworks as a way to assess different peoples' qualifications within a hierarchy of civilization, one in which China was relocated to the top.

In the 1890s, Yan Fu, who had received an education at the Royal Naval College in Greenwich, England from 1877 to 1879, translated several key works of Western thought into Chinese: Thomas Huxley's *Evolution and Ethics*, Adam Smith's *The Wealth of Nations*, John Stuart Mill's *On Liberty*, and Herbert Spencer's *Study of Sociology*. Sean Hsiang-Lin Lei argues that Yan's translation of *Evolution and Ethics* was no less than "THE most influential book in modern Chinese intellectual history," bringing Darwinian thought into Chinese intellectual culture.[52] Just after China's 1895 defeat and four years before undertaking his work as a translator, Yan penned an influential essay entitled "Definitive Treatise on Salvation." There, Yan argues that China must reform "or perish" and that the reforms must start with the Imperial civil service exam, which he argued should be replaced by "Western science."[53] Liang Qichao, another leading figure in the ingestion of Western racial scientific thought, aligned with Yan in his critique of the civil exams. When China lost the Sino-Japanese War, Liang was part of a group of young men who "began to call for dismantling the status quo and instituting changes to the Qing bureaucracy."[54]

In 1898, with a reform-minded young emperor in power and the Qing government weakened by its recent loss to Japan and new demands from European powers, Liang Qichao and others had an opportunity to enact their ideas. Their goals included abolishing the civil exam system, establishing a university in Peking for the study of the sciences and liberal arts as well as agricultural colleges, shifting to a constitutional monarchy, modernizing the military, and more. They pushed the Qing Dynasty to go beyond self-strengthening to more fully embrace fundamental changes. What the Emperor Guangxu proposed, however, was more of a "dynastic revitalization" project largely "consistent with what the Chinese throne had advocated . . . since the early 1860s."[55] Even so, the project and politics of its implementation proved unwieldy. On September 21, 1898, an arrest edict was issued for Kang Youwei, one of the reform movement leaders, and Empress Dowager Cixi staged a palace coup, displacing Guangxu and putting a stop to the reforms.

Yung Wing of the Chinese Educational Mission, discussed in Chapter 4, reemerges in this history as well. According to Edmund H. Worthy, "[l]iving in the protection of the foreign settlement in Shanghai, [Yung] created the 'Deliberative Association of China,' the purpose of which was 'to discuss the leading questions of the day, especially those of reform.'" When the reform movement failed, a price was put on Yung's head, and he fled to Hong Kong in 1900 and then on to the United States in 1902.[56] His return to the United States was complicated by the fact that the citizenship he had acquired while a student at Yale in 1852 had been revoked under the terms of the 1870 Naturalization Act and the Chinese Exclusion Act. Worthy writes that "how Yung managed to get into America is a mystery," but a *Hartford Times* article from June 18, 1902, reports that "he passed the inspector at the gangplank without a doubt of his right to land."[57]

Discontent continued within the Chinese population after the coup, directed both at the Qing and at the unrelenting incursions of missionaries and others from Britain, Japan, the United States, France, Germany, and other countries. After a number of environmental disasters struck the northern region of China, including Shandong, exacerbating existing tensions, a peasant army took form as the Righteous and Harmonious Fists. By the end of 1899, this army, dubbed "the Boxers" because the fighters were trained in martial arts or "Chinese boxing," began attacking Westerners, especially Christians, and Chinese people who had converted to Christianity "with the goal of purging China of foreign contamination."[58] After several successful battles, Empress Dowager Cixi came to see in the Boxers a chance to shift the power balance in China, ridding the empire of powerful foreign influences. She sent the Imperial Army to Beijing to support the Boxers, who had laid siege to the foreign legation starting in June of 1900. In response, in August, an international force from Japan, Russia, Britain, the United States, France, Austria-Hungary, and Italy captured Beijing, freeing the foreigners and Christians who had been held there for almost two months. In September, China and the other countries involved signed a protocol establishing the Boxer Indemnity Fund, providing reparations of over $300,000,000, which reduced China's uncommitted tax revenue by over a third, acting "as an incubus on China's program of reform and development."[59] Under the direction of Secretary of State John Hay, the United States made a claim for $25,000,000 of damages, an amount broadly seen by American representatives and others as radically out of proportion to the costs the country had incurred.

## Boycott, Educational Empire, and the Boxer Indemnity

In 1901, Chinese resentment continued unabated against the inflated reparations, Powderly's recently imposed restrictive definition of "student" and other policies, and much anticipation about the renewal of the 1882 Exclusion Law on the horizon. Wu wrote to Secretary of State Hay to protest the state of immigration enforcement, which, he alleged, excluded "a large class of Chinese of education, high rank, and business standing," a sweeping form of exclusion that equated to a "virtual nullification" of Chinese and American treaty agreements.[60] Concern also built among college administrators, who worried that Chinese students were choosing to travel to England rather than trying to navigate US immigration procedures. Edmund J. James, the president of the University of Illinois, collaborated with other administrators to advocate for an Open Door Policy for education, even writing directly to the Roosevelt administration in hopes of establishing university-based programs in China to increase the reputation of US higher education. Industrialists also worked to lobby the government toward anti-exclusionist ends. Fearing the harsh procedures Powderly might enact, the American Asiatic Association (AAA), a lobbying group for US exporters to China, sent its secretary, John Foord, and a cadre of industrialists and labor leaders to Washington, DC, in early 1902 to warn of the dangerous potential of even more robust Chinese exclusion for "the fortunes of U.S. commercial empire in China."[61] The free transit of students figured prominently in this advocacy. Kramer highlights Charles Hamlin of the Boston Merchants' Association, who warned that "the formalization of Powderly's rules would exclude forever 'every young student, and those are the classes who come here and learn American methods and return to China and obtain positions of power and influence.'"[62] But such efforts failed. In 1902, the Chinese Exclusion Act was made permanent, and all resident Chinese were required to procure a certificate attesting to their entitlement to remain in the United States.

Frank P. Sargent, Powderly's 1902 successor, continued the path toward full exclusion. After training as a photographer, Sargent served in the United States Cavalry in 1880 during the US war on the Apache, before working for the Southern Pacific Railroad, joining the Brotherhood of Locomotive Firemen, and, four years later, becoming the order's grand master.[63] Sargent's years of work with the railroad union likely shaped his staunch anti-immigration stance. His experience as a photographer may have contributed to his interest in technologies of visual evidence. In 1903, Sargent instituted a set of procedures for measuring immigrants to assess their application to enter called the Bertillon system, which had been developed by a French anthropologist and criminologist for the purpose of identifying criminals.[64] Calavita describes how the system used "physical indicators [as] routine markers of class," and thus to determine if an individual was a bona fide "holder of a section 6 certificate."[65] Calloused feet, sunburned legs, and other signs of having performed hard labor were used as evidence that an entrant was not in fact part of an exempt class. And harassment of Chinese immigrants also occurred beyond the ports. In October of 1903, immigration officials in Boston notoriously arrested 234 people in Chinatown.[66]

Between 1901 and 1904, a series of high-profile students attempting to enter the country faced issues at the border, further fueling agitation. In 1901, Luella Miner, a graduate of Oberlin College and missionary teacher in Tungchow, attempted to bring two students to study at her alma mater. The students were Fei Chi-Hao and Kong Xiangxi (H. H. Kung). Their cases were especially compelling because, as Miner documents in a 1902 article in the foreign affairs journal *The Outlook*, they had each aided American Christians in China during the Boxer Rebellion. Against what Miner describes as the "selfish interest" of the United States, "[t]echnicalities shut" the students "out of our land."[67] The technicalities in question were with the students' Section 6 certificates and took over a year to resolve.[68] Kong went on to graduate from Oberlin and Yale, where he received his master's in economics, and would eventually be a leading figure in China's nationalist government in the 1930s and 1940s.

In June of 1904, three years after Kong and Fei's arrival, Soong Ailing attempted to enter the country. Soong's father, Charles Jone Soong, studied at Trinity College, which became Duke University, and then received his theological certificate from Vanderbilt University in 1885. He helped found the Chinese YMCA and printed Bibles in Chinese. Soong Ailing, who would meet and marry Kong in 1914, also encountered what Ye describes as "humiliating treatment upon landing in America."[69] Due to issues with her paperwork, which might have been in part due to her powerful father's attempt to circumnavigate US immigration procedures, Soong was detained on a ship for over two weeks before her release was negotiated. Two months earlier, Sun Yat-Sen, a Chinese dissident and political exile educated in Hawai'i who would go on to be called the father of Chinese nationalism, also attempted to enter the United States. In an interesting reversal, however, to gain entry to the country, he asserted that he was actually an American citizen because he claimed to have been born in Hawai'i, which by 1904 had been annexed by the United States.[70] In so doing, he argued that the Section 6 certificate he'd used to enter the United States as a student in 1896 was not a renunciation of his status of Hawaiian. He prevailed in his case and was admitted to the country, despite the falsity of his claims.[71] The intimacy of these elite transnational circuits between the United States and China is further evidenced in that Soong Ailing went on to serve as Sun's secretary in 1911, and then her young sister Ching-Ling, who also attended Wesleyan College, married Sun in 1915.[72]

By the spring of 1905, the frustrations of the elite Chinese class, angered by the increasing repression at the US border, reached a tipping point. At the diplomatic level, Liang Ch'eng, a Chinese minister who had studied in the United States with the Chinese Education Mission (CEM) in the 1870s, worked to return US immigration policy to a more restrictionist perspective that would allow for the travel of exempt classes. But these efforts backfired, and in 1904 the United States insisted on making Chinese exclusion permanent, leading to China's withdrawal from the 1894 Gresham–Yang Treaty. US officials may also have been frustrated by Liang's efforts to persuade the United States to return some of the excess indemnity. By May of 1905, a boycott of US exports was set to begin in August.[73] Foord returned to Washington, DC, this time armed with a petition endorsed by twenty-nine corporate leaders expressing the deep investment of industrialists and exporters in an imperial, anti-exclusionist but pro-restrictionist position.

In the early summer of 1905, the popular news media were more taken by the story of four wealthy siblings detained at the port of Boston while seeking to travel through the United States on their return journey from London. The Kings had chosen to study in London instead of the United States in part because of concern about American immigration policies. After being assured by the London Embassy secretary that their status as students traveling to the United States as tourists meant that they were exempt from regulations requiring photographs and Section 6 certificates, the Kings traveled first class in late May, socializing with ease. In a June 2 article, the *Boston Daily Globe* reports that upon their arrival and despite presenting a letter of introduction from an ambassador, the Kings were subjected to "discrimination sufficient to disturb even their proverbial serenity."[74]

Adding to the insult, the King siblings were documented as "laborers" rather than "students." One of the siblings, Kungpah King, wrote about his experience for a Shanghai newspaper, providing a day-by-day rundown of their harassment and humiliation.[75] Emma J. Teng argues that these events "became a trigger incident" that "midwifed" a boycott of American goods in July of 1905. By June 21, 1905, *The New York Times* reported a meeting of six hundred Chinese students at Tien-Tsin organizing for "abstention" from the purchase of American goods and "the circulation of anti-American literature, the effort to stimulate home manufacturers, and a systematic recording of results."[76] The *Times* continues, "The immediate aim of this movement is to secure the repeal of the more oppressive provisions of our anti-Chinese laws." Importantly, however, the movement was not "directed to the general admission of all Chinese . . . only the admission under decent conditions of the student and merchant classes."[77] On July 20, the boycott began, led in no small part by students inspired by nationalist sentiments and the desire to foment the coming of a modern Chinese nation-state.

The response from the US government was swift. In fact, President Theodore Roosevelt attempted to stop the boycott before it even began. On June 24, just after *The New York Times* article, he issued Circular No. 81 to immigration officials instructing that exclusion laws should be enforced "without harshness" and "that exempt classes were to be treated with all courtesy."[78] Kramer describes this order as "the official end of the Powderly/Sargent exclusion policy."[79] Adam McKeown argues that the general assessment that the boycott failed to radically renovate US policy neglects the many meaningful changes that were implemented. For one, the boycott did create space for some meaningful development of Chinese production of flour and other goods.[80] On the immigration front, it also led to at least short-term shifts in the administration of policies. As Calavita demonstrates, immigration was thoroughly determined through its administration.

The real impact of the boycott can be seen in the appointments and procedures that occurred in its aftermath. Just a week after the boycott was announced, the commissioner general sent "a letter of caution" to all Chinese inspectors. Labeled "IMPORTANT," the letter issued "imperative instructions that . . . every possible endeavor shall be exercised to prevent the insurance of any just cause for complaint."[81] It particularly "emphasized the right of the exempt classes 'to come and go of their own free will and accord,'" halted their subjection to the Bertillon exam, and instructed inspectors "not to interrogate Chinese entering with Section 6 certificates."[82] In his December State of the

Union address, Roosevelt once again spoke in favor of a more attenuated immigration policy based in restriction but encouraging the travel of "Chinese students, business and professional men of all kinds" to the United States.[83] Efforts to stop the boycott failed, and protests continued through the end of 1905, only ending after the San Francisco earthquake in April 1906, which "dealt a paralyzing blow to the diasporic protest campaign."[84]

But the US display of support for Chinese students went well beyond changes to immigration policy. As Madeline Hsu discusses, the inflated Boxer Indemnity provided another vital point of negotiation and influence. In 1905, discussions were underway between William W. Rockhill, the minister-designate to China, and Liang, the Chinese minister, about the potential return of funds so long as they were used to finance education.[85] In June of 1905, William Howard Taft, Roosevelt's secretary of war, gave a speech calling for investments in the education of Chinese people as a "more subtle and strategic policy than using gunboats to open China to American influence and commerce."[86] In 1906, Edmund James, president of the University of Illinois, further advanced the plan in a proposal to Roosevelt where he explained that with China "upon the verge of revolution" it would behoove the United States to work to educate "the young Chinese of the present generation" in order to "reap the largest possible returns in *moral, intellectual, and commercial influence*."[87]

In his 1907 State of the Union address, Roosevelt officially requested congressional support to reform the indemnity agreement to remittance. He argued, in very direct terms, for the importance of educating Chinese students in the United States:

> This Nation should help in every practicable way in the education of the Chinese people, so that the vast and populous Empire of China may gradually adapt itself to modern conditions. One way of doing this is by promoting the coming of Chinese students to this country and making it attractive to them to take courses at our universities and higher educational institutions. Our educators should, so far as possible, take concerted action toward this end.[88]

This plan came to fruition with a December 31, 1908 executive order from Roosevelt enacting the remission. The first check arrived in January of 1909.[89] Some of the funds were used almost immediately to establish Tsinghua College, which was intended as a preparatory school for students to learn "in the American way, with American personnel and an American curriculum" before completing their education in the United States.[90] The Qing government reformed the CEM to facilitate the selection and administration of students, setting quotas for how many students should study specific fields such as engineering, mining, or agriculture.[91]

In the end, the remission of the Boxer Indemnity and the resulting funding for Boxer Indemnity Fund (BIF) students may have been the most significant outcome of the 1905 boycott. Many meaningful changes were made to immigration policy in 1906, not least of all dropping the Bertillon exam, reducing scrutiny of Section 6 certificates, broadening the definition of student and other exempt groups, and stopping arrests in the interior.[92] Ye argues that the new definition of student in the 1906 regulations facilitated the entrance of "a large number of Guangdong peasant boys entered the country as students but eventually settled to work as laborers," but its uneven administration meant that many students were still treated as suspect.[93]

Over the following years, enforcement gradually tightened. In 1908, an internal memo informally reinstated interior arrests. By 1911 "many of the modified policies put in place after the boycott had been reversed."[94] By then, however, the architecture of the BIF project was in place and students returned to the United States in larger numbers. In 1906, 300 Chinese students studied in the United States. By 1911 that number more than doubled to 650. By 1918, 1,200 Chinese students were in the United States, and between 1902 and 1929, 1,300 students received support from the BIF.[95] Most of the students came from families of relative wealth. Their reliance on government support was consistent but waned over time. Even before the BIF, over 60 percent of students relied on government funding in 1906. In 1910, that number declined to 32 percent, and then further still to 20 percent in 1925.[96]

The generation of students who traveled to the United States through the BIF were mostly born just before China's loss to Japan in the war of 1894–1895, when the Qing Dynasty's future appeared stable and Confucian learning was largely unchallenged. Through dramatic changes in China and in China's relationship to the world, fueled in part through Western incursions and Western knowledge, they came of age at a moment in which, as Ye describes, "nationalism was a central and definitive theme of modernity" and the very concept of China as a nation was under construction.[97] Ye provides an attenuated reading of Chinese modernization as the result of "the thoughtful people among this generation [who] consciously searched for ways to regenerate Chinese culture by a careful selection and digestion of Western knowledge."[98] As Ye describes, when the students traveled to the United States at the end of the first decade of the twentieth century, they "found themselves in a peculiar and precarious racial situation."[99] Their status as upper class meant they were often exempted from the most rigorous forms of harassment at the border and "as an intellectual elite seeking Western learning, they were in general kindly received by educated Americans" but they were still exposed to a social and cultural milieu in which Chinese people were understood and treated as an inferior race.

For the Chinese students studying in the United States in the early twentieth century, these contradictions became especially salient in their relationships with Chinese laborers. Ye explains that to some students, "the lower-class Chinese and their traditional way of life" were responsible "for the poor image of China held by the American public."[100] These students worked to distance themselves from laborers in an effort to cultivate "a new and westernized image."[101] As discussed earlier, students of this generation were embedded in a modern consciousness saturated by racial logics. While an awareness of the poor treatment of Chinese laborers might have "sharpened many students' nationalist sentiment," the development of their racial consciousness "did not lead most of them to challenge the premises of racial inequality." Instead, the students "largely accepted the racial hierarchy in the modern world and sought to improve China's position in it." Even their occasional work in support of Chinese laborers was, according to Ye, "ultimately to improve the image of China in America."[102]

Guided in many cases by elders who had themselves been part of the CEM in the 1870s, like Liang Cheng, discussed above, and Liang Tunyan, who became the Chinese minister of affairs in 1909, this younger generation took the mantle in agitating for a modern Chinese nation-state often informed by their experiences in the United States, which, for many, fostered a commitment to both nationalism and constitutional forms of government. In 1911, conditions in China changed dramatically when the Wuchang Uprising led to the anti-Qing Revolution and the establishment of the Republic of China, led by Sun Yat-Sen. Sun was born in Guangdong, China, in 1866, but traveled to Hawai'i to join his brother and attain an education. Sun attended missionary schools, including Iolani College, St. Louis College, and Oahu College.[103] Sun returned to China in 1883 but traveled to Hong Kong shortly after to train in the medical sciences. By the 1890s, he was fully ensconced in the movement to modernize China. By 1894, he had returned to Hawai'i to found the Revive China Society, which he would merge with the Furen Literary Society in Hong Kong a year later. During the Boxer Rebellion, he lobbied Li Hongzhang to transition China to a democratic republic. With this attempt rebuffed, Sun spent the next decade ensconced in the communities of people of Chinese descent in the United Kingdom, Japan, Singapore, Hong Kong, and Malaya, supporting various uprisings. In 1912, shortly after assuming leadership of the provisional government of the new Chinese republic, Sun wrote to Yung Wing, requesting his support in establishing the educational system for the new nation-state: "the establishment of a republic needs a great deal of talent. We have always heard of your name and talent. Now we sincerely hope that you will return and help establish a wholesome country so as to encourage our young republic."[104]

As Edmund James's proposal to Roosevelt in 1906 marks, there was a broad belief within US academic and industrial circles that a revolution in China could be an opportunity for US interests to exert and expand their sphere of influence and extraction. These interests set up a contradiction for immigration law: Since the initial creation of "exempt" classes in the 1880 Angell Act, US law was organized around an imagined divide between the student and the laborer. Students, and the very act of study they were supposed to undertake, were framed as being wholly distinct from labor. Yet, a major impetus for educating students from China, for bringing them to the United States to study, was to ensure their training on and in US-based technologies and knowledge systems in order to ensure their adoption in Chinese industry moving forward. In 1910, representatives from General Electric in Asia wrote to the State Department about the possibility of establishing a scholarship for Chinese students to study electrical engineering at US institutions. In response, the consul explained his understanding that "a Chinese student who has been trained on an American railway or in the shops of an American railway supply company will, in after years . . . give orders to American companies—the products of which he is intimately acquainted with."[105] As Qingjia Edward Wang explains in his reading of this letter, the scholarships did not take form, but the exchange demonstrates that the State Department grasped the importance of such a project. Also in 1910, a representative of the Department of Commerce and Labor wrote to the secretary of state about this conundrum. As the letter explains, "[o]ne of the principal reasons for the inclusion of students in the exempt classes was the belief that the commercial interests of the United States would benefit by having Chinese of that class become familiar with American institutions, civic and business, through having gained an education in our midst."[106]

The understanding that educating Chinese students in the United States would generate direct returns only sedimented over the next decade, as debates about the 1921 immigration law swelled. In 1920, an American consulate general in Shanghai wrote that "The reasons for securing these young men to pursue in the United State their technical education are apparent, because they are to be the future business men of China, and if the United States is fortunate enough in securing these students, the manufacturers in America will eventually profit by this condition."[107] But, as Wang continues, the issue of getting students practical training in US factories and shops proved to be a "thorny issue" since doing so required the students to work in such spaces.[108] Several months later, the consul in Shanghai wrote to the secretary of state making the case for changes to US immigration law to permit Chinese students "to study in manufacturing plants, accepting compensation for their work."[109] The letter acknowledges that such a practice "may be technically in violation of the Chinese Immigration Laws, but the benefits to be derived from such training are so great that many of these American firms and organizations have urged a modification."[110]

In 1921, the Chinese Merchants Association of the United States also submitted a proposal to receive a large group of Chinese students to train in practical skills in the United States. Other countries were also in the game. France, for instance, developed a program to recruit six thousand students to work in its shops and partake in technical training, and England had similar plans.[111] With these pressures in mind, the consul of Shanghai continued to advocate for changes in immigration law to allow for practical training into 1921, even after the passage of the Emergency Quota Act. While none of these efforts succeeded in carving out allowances for students to be compensated for practical training after graduation, they may have contributed to the broad pressure that reversed the initial removal of students from the exempt classes in the 1921 Emergency Quota law.

## The Foreign Student and the Immigration State

Passed in the isolationist shadow of World War I, the 1921 Emergency Quota Act was intended as a legislative stopgap rather than as a permanent solution to concerns immigration restrictionists extolled regarding the perils of open immigration. White "nativists" were not satisfied with the law's formula for the quotas, which were set in relation to the 1910 census. They argued, instead, that immigration restriction should be based on the 1890 census, which would ensure that the new immigration regime would properly shape the composition of the nation to fit their imagination of a white nation-state. When the act expired in 1922 it was extended until 1924, at which point Congress passed the 1924 Johnson–Reed Immigration Act. The Johnson–Reed Act dramatically decreased total migration to the United States to 155,000 annually and intensified the whitening effect of the quota restrictions by allotting every eligible "national origin" group a quota of only 2 percent of the number of members of that group tabulated in the 1890 census.[112] It also retained the exclusion of all immigrants ineligible to citizenship. An exemption for students was added, but, despite the sweepingly draconian effectiveness of the law, concern regarding it being "too-liberal" as applied to students persisted.

In the April 1924 congressional debate on the act's terms, Senator Samuel Shortridge from San Francisco argued that "the word 'study' is too indefinite. The word 'study' is too vague. It should be eliminated." Shortridge continued,

> We ought not to leave it so indefinite. I appeal to those familiar with words, who know that they be vague, ambiguous, uncertain, that we ought not to leave it to the Secretary to make those rules. We ought ourselves here to provide that those who come as students shall be bona fide students, not that they may come under the guise of students to study what we know not what, to continue as students we know not how long—to come for the vague purpose of "study" and speedily turn to become common laborers in competition with American labor.[113]

Here, Shortridge gives voice to a central concern that plagued efforts to regulate the travel of students to the United States since the first broad restrictions were placed on immigration in 1882: The matter of how to ensure that immigration procedures would effectively function as a filter that would exclude "undesirable" migrants while retaining the ability to selectively admit both immigrants and visitors whose travel through and time in the United States could serve the interests of the state and of capital. This issue has continued to vex capital's investment in training students in and on the tools of their trade to this day. Shortridge reiterated Stephen P. Duggan's suggestions from 1921 and successfully proposed an amendment that "those who come as students shall designate the school or the college or the university they desired to attend, and that that school or college or university shall be approved by our Secretary of Labor." Many of Duggan's other suggestions were incorporated as well, though the resulting law provoked as many questions and as much confusion.

In December of 1924, Chao Ying Shill, a 1924 graduate of the University of Minnesota and master's student in political science at the same institution who would go on to receive his JD in 1927 from Harvard, wrote a response to the 1924 Immigration Law for *Chinese Students Monthly*, the publication of the Chinese Students Association first published in 1906. "The Effect of the Immigration Bill of 1924 on Chinese Students" reviews the major facets of the law focusing on "where the bill pricks." Shill starts by discussing its exclusion of "all *aliens ineligible to citizenship*," which revolves around the question of "who and who are not *white persons*," a category from which Chinese people had been excluded through various Supreme Court cases starting in 1878 with *In re Ah Yup* and through to the 1922 *Ozawa v. United States*.[114] Shill then goes on to explain that despite the bar to immigration for nonwhite people, the law provides for two kinds of exempt classes. First, there are people whose travel is temporary enough to qualify them as "nonimmigrants," such as government officials, tourists, and people in transit through the country. Then there are "certain classes of people who are admitted in spite of their not being free white persons."[115] These include people previously admitted to the United States and "returning from a temporary visit for not more than a year abroad," immigrants who have been ministers or professors for the previous two years, and lastly, "students of at least 15 years of age" upon whom "the conditions imposed . . . are numerous."[116]

Shill's primary concern is that students must be admitted to a school accredited by the secretary of labor prior to their admission into the United States. To attain this accreditation, schools must agree to fulfill a set of new obligations stipulated by the law, most notably that it reports the termination of each student's attendance with the understanding that failing to do so will lead to the withdrawal of approval. Shill marks that the law "also makes it the duty of the students to see to it that their conditions are reported." If they fail to do so, "the student will be subject to deportation."[117] Shill joins the concerns discussed above about the capacity for students to attain technical training as part of their education because students are "not allowed to go into a factory for practice work for any length of time after graduation." Instead "the day he leaves college, he is to be shipped back."[118]

Shill closes his article with a discussion of "the danger of the law": its enforcement. Even by the time he published this piece, just seven months after the law first passed through Congress, he argues that law had already caused an "exasperating" amount of "embarrassment."[119] Many questions about how the law would be applied were still to be determined, but particular cases of concern were apparent. For instance, Shill describes a situation in which "an American citizen may derive advantages by having a Chinese rival who is no longer in college got rid of." Because of this, he continues, "Chinese students working for practical knowledge should, in the future, be more careful in the way they treat their fellow workers." The only hope Shill sees is "with the nonapplication of the letter of the law."[120]

In 1930, Ruth Crawford Mitchell, a sociology lecturer with a keen interest in international education at the University of Pittsburgh, prepared a report for the Institute for International Education (IIE) reviewing the material effects and broader implications of the 1924 Johnson–Reed Immigration Act for students and universities.[121] In her introduction to "Foreign Students and the Immigration Laws of the United States," Mitchell explains that "to many university officials the intricacies of the immigration regulations seem bewildering because in addition to not being thoroughly understood by either student or university they are not always immediately enforced by the Bureau of

Immigration."[122] And the terms of the regulations are indeed confounding. For one, while the number of noncitizen students in the United States increased almost 50 percent from 6,488 to 9,685 in the seven years before the report was published, only about half of those students were actually subject to the 1924 law; the other half were "definitely exempted from supervision by the terms of the same law" because they were not born in European, African, or Asian countries restricted by quota and were not excluded due to their racial ineligibility to citizenship.[123] In other words, students classified as white and traveling within the Western Hemisphere were free to enter the country for the purposes of study without any documentation. The law only provided guidance for how institutions were to administer the presence of the other half of noncitizen students—students from countries with quotas and anyone understood to be other than white. This is compounded by the fact that the Bureau of Immigration, tasked with regulating students, was, according to Mitchell, chronically understaffed and therefore often failed to prosecute evasions of the law. As a result, universities often neglected to follow the regulations.[124] But that is only the very beginning of what administrators had to unravel.

In a similar manner to Shill's review of the law, Mitchell explains that the 1924 Immigration Act categorizes "aliens" into two categories: "non-immigrant aliens" who only intend to visit the country temporarily and "immigrant aliens" who seek to come permanently. The category of "immigrant aliens" is further refined into two types: quota and non-quota. Mitchell continues, "With the single exception of *students* all aliens classified as *immigrant aliens* (quota or non-quota) are allowed to enter the United States for permanent residency. For some unexplained reason students are classified as the fifth type of non-quota immigrant aliens but their admission was expressly defined by law as *temporary*."[125] So, though it might seem as if Duggan's negotiated requirement that students "leave the country within a year" would place international students squarely in the nonimmigrant category, Mitchell illustrates that the murky workings of immigration law in the 1920s made it so that this was not the case: Students subject to the law were instead their own unique category and thus subject to both the higher vetting standards applied to immigrants and the temporal restrictions of nonimmigrants. The contradictions inherent to this classificatory system were clear at the time. After the passage of the law in 1924, but before its implementation in 1929, Secretary of Labor James Davis advocated the reclassification of students as nonimmigrants rather than non-quota immigrants, but to no avail.

A 1950 report on "The Immigration and Naturalization Systems of the United States" written for the Committee on the Judiciary under the direction of Pat McCarran sheds some light on the rationale behind the internally contradictory restrictions placed on noncitizen students. The report briefly references an explanation "advanced by an official of the Department of State" whereby

> Congress classified such students as nonquota immigrants so that they would be subject to all the immigration laws applicable to immigrants. It was his conclusion that originally the theory was that aliens who came to study for a period of years might settle down and acquire families, and because of their training, become desirable residents and potential citizens. Accordingly, if there existed any reason why they should not be eligible to remain permanently this should be determined at the time of admission and they were, therefore, subjected to all the requirements applicable to immigrants.[126]

Thus, students were admitted as non-quota immigrants who were required to leave the country after the conclusion of their study while simultaneously being imagined as potential or proximate immigrants who may very well want to stay in the country after their studies and who will be, as a result of their training "desirable residents and potential citizens." The immigration and visa systems were therefore tasked with evaluating students whose presence was "expressly defined by law as *temporary*" by the same standards as would-be immigrants because of what was proposed as a likely course of development.

The final language of section 4(e) of the 1924 immigration law describes a student eligible for a visa as follows:

> An immigrant who is a bona fide student at least 15 years of age and who seeks to enter the United States solely for the purpose of study at an accredited school, college, academy, seminary, or university, particularly designated by him and approved by the Secretary of Labor, which shall have agreed to report to the Secretary of Labor the termination of attendance of each immigrant student, and if such institution of learning fails to make such reports promptly the approval shall be withdrawn.

The law put into place a series of bureaucratic procedural checks on the veracity of a would-be student's status: First an institution must get approval from the secretary of labor; the student must gain admission to an accredited institution; the institution must verify the student's acceptance "by the issuance of three original Certificates of Admission signed by the University's officer of admission and stamped with the university seal"; copies of the certificate must be sent to the consul, attached to the visa and provided to the student. Next, the student must meet with the nearest American consul for an examination of documents certifying the student's passport, health, "army discharge, evidence of moral character, birth certificate and unmounted photographs." The consuls are also tasked with ascertaining if the "student has sufficient knowledge of English to pursue a regular course of study at the institution designated" and that the student has adequate financial resources. Upon arrival at the border, the student must then persuade each immigration official they encounter that they are "bona fide" and that students from most countries outside of Europe would receive a detailed health and immigration examination. Finally, throughout their stay, the institution in which a noncitizen student enrolls must regularly check and report upon the status of each student it enrolls under threat of losing its capacity to host any students in the future.[127] This stipulation also provided institutions with the means to force students whose presence was in any way undesirable to leave the institution and the country, should doing so seem advantageous, much as Shill worried about the possibility that a rival in the workplace could do the same. As Chapter 6 discusses, this would indeed come to be the scenario in several cases of prominent African students, including Barack Obama Sr.

It is notable that these procedures reflect Duggan's 1921 suggestions regarding the purpose, duration, and surveillance of noncitizen students in the United States and the responsibilities of educational institutions. They mirror closely the procedures still in place today. As Shill argues, one of the most concerning aspects of the law continued to emerge in its application since enforcement varied so widely depending on "the interpretation of the individual Consular office."[128] The act formalized procedures for administering the admission of noncitizen students as "nonquota immigrants" whose admission was "expressly defined as *temporary*" as well as the processes through which colleges and universities would be responsible for monitoring them and reporting their status to the federal government throughout their definitionally temporary stay in the country. The final form of the 1924 act would provide the basic framework for the admission and monitoring of noncitizen students in the United States that remains in place to this day. Yet, the significance of the 1921 act is frequently overlooked, downplayed, or entirely neglected in histories of noncitizen students in the United States despite or perhaps because of the fact that the Emergency Quota Act's racialist agenda of whitening the US nation-state was, until the very recent past, roundly reviled in public thought and discourse.[129] Part III and the conclusion tease out the implications of this history for the lives of students, the work of institutions of higher education, and the broader politics of race, incorporation, and empire-making in the mid-twentieth century.

# PART III

## *Education for a New Age of Empire*

On April 22, 1963, *Newsweek* magazine ran a cover story entitled "Foreign Students: Diplomas and Diplomacy."[1] The photograph accompanying the headline features ten students walking through an archway at Cornell Law School dressed in various states of "western" and/or otherwise ethnically specific attire (blazers and winter jackets, a sari, an Ankara cloth dress, a dashiki, a Baju Melayu).[2] The students are at once together and apart, nearly touching but not engaging with each other. Each appears almost like a paper doll layered onto the photo, abstract in their difference from the others, gazing away from and beyond the camera's lens. The May 6, 1963 issue printed a letter to the editor commenting on the "magnificent" cover, along with a wish that the issue had identified the students since "[a]ll of them are so unusual."[3] In response, the magazine provided a list of the students and their national affiliations as "Mohammed Sa'aid (Malaya), Nancy Chu (Hong Kong), Gayatri Chakravorty (India), Clara Ankrah (Ghana) . . . José Ochoa (Colombia), Kimon Valaskakis (Greece), Inge Schulthes (Germany), Edmund Jones (Trinidad) . . . Chibuzo Ajuka (Nigeria), Raymunda Urrich (Chile)."[4] Inside, the article features portraits of several of the students, including Sa'aid, Chu, and Chakravorty, from the cover as well as students identified as Aggrey Awori from Uganda, Viktor Ivanenko of the USSR, Ben Nzungu of Congo, Enrique Escudero of Peru, and Ipek Aksugur of Turkey. That Chakravorty—known now as Gayatri Chakravorty Spivak, distinguished professor of English and Comparative Literature at Columbia University—leads the students on the cover, smiling in a pink patterned sari and lavender coat, is of particular interest for scholars of postcolonial studies and cultural studies, not least of all given her field-defining scholarship on questions of coloniality, the

Figure 4. Cover of April 22, 1963 issue of *Newsweek* magazine featuring ten noncitizen students walking through an archway at Cornell University. @Newsweek (YouTube).

subaltern, personhood, and difference.[5] Here, like most of the other students, she smiles, but averts her eyes from the camera's gaze.

On the first page of the article, the authors, Mel Elfin and Constance Montague, provide a new title that fosters a more intimate and familiar relationship to one student in particular: "'Mo' is Sa'aid's Nickname at Cornell: 64,000 Foreign Students Ride the Diploma-Diplomacy Seesaw." True to its promise, the article opens with the story of Mohammed Sa'aid and what is presented as his remarkable acclamation to the Cornell campus and life in the United States. Since leaving his "native Malaya," Sa'aid

> has acquired a nickname, an interest in football, a collection of Playboy pin-ups, and most importantly, a new image of America. "Once," the peppery, 115-pound agricultural student says, "I thought most Americans were obnoxious, rich capitalists. Now I think only a few Americans are obnoxious, rich capitalists."

"Mo," as Sa'aid is casually referred to for the duration of the article, is figured as an idealized example of the prospects embodied by a US-educated global citizen. His ability to make light of his previous and even current opinion of "Americans" as "obnoxious, rich capitalists" suggests his independence of expression. At the same time, his acculturation to US naming practices, sports culture, and popular sexual openness and desires indicates the success of another, arguably more vital, affective adaptation process.

On the cover, Sa'aid wears a Malaysian Baju Melayu as he walks alongside the other students. Three pages into the article, a portrait depicts him sitting casually on a desk in what appears to be a dorm room, wearing a button-down shirt, sport coat, and shiny metal watch, smiling broadly with images of the *Playboy* bunny logo in the background. Tellingly, this photo is captioned, "Before coming here, foreign students see America as all black and all white, all good and all bad. We find there's much gray in between." Sa'aid's meaning is open to interpretation. He could certainly have been speaking in entirely abstract terms about the limits of wholly binaristic frames of thinking. Still, the language of "black and white" also opens questions of US racial politics during the charged moment of 1963. In not directly critiquing US racism, he models a version of the kind of potential political and corporate leaders hoped noncitizen students in the United States would embody. His perspective on race is especially useful in response to the Soviet critiques of US racism that increasingly drew attention in this period, and to which, as Part III illustrates, the recruitment of nonwhite students was a response. Such an articulation of the complications of race relations by a student who would be categorized within shifting US racial taxonomies as nonwhite and who hailed from a

Newsweek—Tony Rollo

**MALAYA. Mo Sa'aid, Cornell:** ***Before coming here, foreign students see America as all black or all white, all good or all bad. We find there's much gray in between.***

Figure 5. Mohammed Sa'aid, a student from Malaya studying at Cornell University, as photographed for *Newsweek* and featured on the third page of the April 22, 1963 article. @Newsweek (YouTube).

country and region hotly contested by the United States and the USSR, like Malaya, served to bolster racial liberalism's consolidating claims of inclusivity and progress.

Part III considers the political and social significance of the noncitizen student for the mid-century US university, and the mutually constitutive reconfiguration of US state and capitalist interests and their racial logics, with a particular attention to African students. To do so, I attend to the historical conditions that led to the recruitment of students marked as nonwhite within shifting US racial taxonomies and hailing from countries of various strategic importance to US foreign policy. As the *Newsweek* article illustrates, the figuration of students from particular regions and of specific racial identities is highly differentiated—some, like Sa'aid, are glowing with promise; others, like those of the African students, are markedly more ambiguous, flat, or even menacing. Part III provides a conjunctural reading of the *Newsweek* article as a prehistory of this moment of racial reconfiguration by asking how the desire for and presence of nonwhite noncitizen students prefigured both the 1965 shift away from overt racial exclusion in US immigration law and the 1966 emergence in sociological and popular discourse of what is now widely recognized as the model minority myth—two shifts frequently read as punctuating the post–World War II shift from a white supremacist United States to one organized through a nominally anti-racist racial liberalism.[6]

As I discuss further in the conclusion, from the mid-1960s onward, the model minority myth functioned as a central mechanism for the conditional inclusion of select nonwhite people in US power and politics, provided they demonstrated a commitment to the fundamental tenets of capitalist liberalism. Articulations from government and university officials in reports and publications such as *Newsweek* clearly illustrate that by the early 1960s, these students were recruited and desired *for*, rather than despite, their racial difference and the geopolitical opportunities they represented.[7] However, after a brief period during the 1950s when leaders in government and industry were especially interested in recruiting African students, by 1963 this tide had turned, and a resurgent anti-Blackness suffused both policy and popular media. When the *Newsweek* article was published, the state, capital, and the university had turned toward inclusion and incorporation of some forms of racial alterity over and against their prior strategy of education and export, but their commitment to African students had significantly waned. This shift, and the fear of African students and their potential for radical politics, underwrote the cultivation of a legal system for regulating students and the institutions that hosted them through the student visa. In the last instance, this system defers to executive power over foreign affairs and the protection of the nation-state's sovereignty through immigration policy, effectively rendering both students and the institutions that host them vulnerable to federal incursion.

As demonstrated in previous chapters, nonwhite noncitizen students were recruited to and attended institutions of higher education in what would become the United States throughout its existence. Frequently, various US-based institutions, primarily Christian missionary and often linked philanthropies, organized and funded their travels. It is telling, however, that by the mid-twentieth century, the US state came to play a central role in these processes as universities and colleges expanded their inclusion of such students, albeit temporarily and provisionally, even as barriers for nonwhite domestic students were being renovated or built anew. Even in 1963, many schools refused admission to nonwhite domestic students, and federal immigration law denied or severely restricted the entrance of nonwhite people into the country. The immigration policy that allowed the limited admission of nonwhite noncitizen students during this period built on the histories discussed in the previous chapters to negotiate a form of selective inclusion for nonwhite students, and specifically for Chinese students, from the 1875 Page Act through to the 1924 Johnson–Reed Immigration Act. As discussed in Chapter 6, "The State of the University and the University of the State After World War II," the 1952 Immigration and Nationality Act inaugurated the "F" student visa, which concretized the noncitizen student's relationship to the United States as temporary by shifting their categorization. The students, by way of this policy, transformed from "nonquota immigrants" to "non-immigrant visitors." These shifts were inflected by the emergent racial and geopolitical conditions of World War II and the Cold War—and thus reflected an internationalism suffused with white supremacist capitalism and liberal global ambition.

Acquiring an F visa posed a series of precedent-setting demands for student applicants at this time. First, it required the applicant to articulate a clear desire to come to the United States. Second, applicants needed to provide evidence of their ability to financially support themselves while in the country. Third, applicants would have to demonstrate "strong" economic and familial ties to their home country to reinforce the confidence that their stay in the country would be circumscribed by the length of their studies. The conditions of the visa provided limited exceptions allowing students to stay legally in the United States beyond their visa's termination date. To do so, students would have to continue their studies at higher and higher levels, secure employment with an entity approved by the US government to sponsor their visa under the new category of "H" (for highly skilled labor); or, in less frequent cases, marry a US citizen. This latter option was necessarily circumscribed for students who sought to marry across racial lines until 1967, when the Supreme Court legalized interracial marriages. Unless willing to navigate life in the United States without legal documentation, students would need to develop themselves into the kind of person the state deemed worthy of granting its continued hospitality or potential future citizenship. Doing so required incredible contortions under restrictive conditions—limited community support, cultural adjustment, legal scrutiny, flatly racist institutions and interlocutors, and often intense financial hardship. The assumption and intention, therefore, remained that students would return to their home countries after their studies. By the early 1960s, however, it was clear that many students would remain in the United States and that this could be useful for both the state and capital.

Read with this contextualization, it becomes clear that the *Newsweek* article is more than a simple collection of uplifting stories of individual students who traveled to the United States for their education. Instead, it can serve as a case study of the conjuncture of US higher education, immigration law, racial knowledges, and foreign policy at a pivotal point in the mid-twentieth century. Here, the desire for and presence of some nonwhite noncitizen students played a constitutive role in shaping the politics of universities, race, and difference with significant consequences, both domestically and internationally, in the formation and capacitation of an emergent mode of Cold War US empire. In what follows, I tease out the motivations, logics, programs, and policies through which this shift in the racial and geographic composition of the noncitizen student body at once expanded the domain of racial inclusion and possibility and cemented the strict conditions of inclusion sedimented by anti-Black, anti-radical, and anti-worker logics. At stake is the way that universities worked with and were raised by the state as a central demographic lever of US empire in its initial efforts to cultivate a heterogeneous and optimizable domestic population while facilitating the effort to globally distribute graduates trained in and ideally committed to US frameworks of political, economic, and cultural life. That is, as the "global agents of American universality" discussed in Chapter 2.[8]

# 6

# The State of the University and the University of the State After World War II

Mohammad Sa'aid, Gayatri Chakravorty, and the other students featured on the cover of *Newsweek* in April 1963, discussed in the introduction to Part III, were recruited to the United States as it solidified its self-proclaimed position as the leader of the "free world." As such, the story went, the United States was committed to a liberal democratic political system and a capitalist economy modified to suit this new role. The world in question was in flux. The post–World War II period, from 1945 into the 1960s, is often referred to as the "age of decolonization." A new global order emerged, with the proliferation of independent nation-states, the formal demotion of empires, and the establishment of international entities for governance and economic management including the World Bank (1944), the United Nations (1945), the North Atlantic Treaty Organization (1949), the Organization of the Petroleum Exporting Countries (1960), the Non-Aligned Movement (1961), and the Organization of African Unity (1963). During this period, Paul Kramer explains, "the nation emerged as an insurgent category, and ultimately as the only legitimate state form in the international order."[1] Both the diversity and specificity of the students featured in the *Newsweek* article bolster the United States' ambition as a leader in this world of nation-states. Each student hails from a country or territory amid political transformation, and of particular interest to the imperial vision of the US security state and corporate interests.

Reviewing the list of countries represented by the students in the *Newsweek* article paints a robust picture of the scale of world change underway during this period. In 1963, Ghana, Nigeria, Uganda, Malaysia, and Trinidad were in their first years of independence from British colonial rule. The postcolonial leaders of Ghana and Nigeria, Kwame Nkrumah and Nnamdi Azikiwe, had both been educated in the United States, while Trinidad's Eric Williams was educated in England. Hong Kong remained under British control, serving as a vital gateway for Western nations after the 1949 Chinese Revolution and the founding of the People's Republic of China. The Democratic Republic of Congo gained its independence from Belgium in 1960 but was in the midst of a series of civil wars and still reeling from the assassination of Patrice Lumumba, an act the United States was widely assumed to have contributed to. India, which had gained independence from Britain in 1947, was embroiled in ongoing border disputes with China and Tibet. In Germany, the Berlin Wall had just been constructed, and Greece was contending with the aftermath of its US-instigated civil war. Colombia and Chile were each the site of fierce conflict between US-backed pro-capitalist parties and democratic socialist politicians and guerrilla groups. Peru was under the control of a military junta installed after the coup d'état of 1962. Without exception, all of these fractious political states of being were keenly observed and often intervened upon by a United States government guided by a theory of containment first articulated by George F. Kennan, a foreign service officer, in the pages of *Foreign Affairs* in 1947. There, Kennan laid out a strategy by which Soviet power could be contained through "the adroit and vigilant application of counter-force at a series of constantly shifting geographical and political points."[2]

In September of 1961, a year and a half before the article was published, Yugoslav president Josip Broz Tito, working with Egyptian President Gamal Abdel Nasser and Indian Prime Minister Jawaharlal Nehru, convened a conference in Belgrade to create the Non-Aligned Movement (NAM). The conference built on conversations from the more widely historicized 1955 Bandung Conference, which gave form to a new collective of Afro-Asian Latin states within the United Nations, organizing "outside the East-West divide" as the "Third World."[3] In Belgrade, high-level representatives from twenty-two African, Asian, Latin American, and European states were in attendance, including Ghana's Kwame Nkrumah and Indonesia's Sukarno. While NAM's rhetoric of "peaceful co-existence" and refusal to ally with the USSR or the United States "exceeded the policies" it was able to enact, NAM's existence demonstrated the capacity of Third World countries to come together to denounce colonialism and racialism, articulate a refusal to serve as pawns in the Cold War, and make moves toward the democratization of the United Nations.[4] As discussed in further detail below, Nkrumah's participation was particularly disturbing for US officials as it was taken as evidence of the failure of a US education to secure the allegiance of graduates to the country or its interests. Indeed, the *Newsweek* article invokes Nkrumah as an example of what can happen when students leave the country with "an unfavorable impression" and, thus, also as evidence of the importance of the Central Intelligence Agency's effort to monitor the selection of students who study in the United States and their careers after they return to their home country.[5]

Despite the world-historical significance of all of these transformations, studies of US higher education during this period rarely attend to the stories or geopolitics surrounding noncitizen students, the programs that facilitated their presence on campuses, or the implications of these entanglements of universities and colleges and the state beyond the infusion of funds for military research and attendant fields of study.[6] Instead, this period is widely understood as the "golden era" of US higher education and the high point of the civil rights movement and global military Keynesianism, when both universities and America's democratic promise saw unparalleled expansion. This chapter provides a critical intervention into such histories. Its first section provides a review of the dominant frames for thinking the university and the state after World War II, with particular attention to the kinds of knowledges this relationship spawned. The second turns to the various policies, programs, and laws the state created to manage and make use of noncitizen students. The third and final section turns to the development and implementation of the 1952 McCarran–Walter Act, now commonly referred to as the Immigration and Nationality Act (INA), and serves as the primary basis for contemporary immigration law governing the lives and movement of noncitizen students. A key, but understudied, aspect of the act pertains to the shift of the student visa from governing students as "non-quota immigrants" to a wholly new category of persons: nonimmigrant aliens. As nonimmigrant aliens, under the McCarran–Walter Act, students on visas are placed in a uniquely liminal legal state, subject to pretravel processes and then extended governmental oversight while in the country. In the process, the institutions where they enroll are also drawn further into an auxiliary role within the state's immigration enforcement apparatus.

## The State of Knowledge

Just after World War II, a massive influx of public funds dramatically expanded college and university enrollments, underwritten in large part by funding for militarized research and a state-directed vision of citizen-making.[7] In his canonical study on postwar higher education, Roger Geiger explains the consensus view "that the GI Bill accelerated the educational advancement and deepened the intellectual capital of the country."[8] Political theorist Wendy Brown characterizes the growth of colleges and universities as "nothing short of a radical democratic event" in which "the masses would be educated for freedom."[9] Jeffrey Williams, a founding scholar in Critical University Studies, focuses on the material conditions that made this shift possible in his description of "welfare state universities" flooded with federal funding, a result of the dual fears of vast unemployment for returning service members, as was experienced after World War I, and the specter of the Soviet Union's technological prowess.[10] It is crucial to read both mainstream and progressive/leftist narratives of the expansion of US higher education during this period as definitionally connected to the instantiation of a new era of American imperialism organized in significant ways through the strategic deployment of the university as a tool in the fight against communism and for the cultivation of a citizenry equal to such a task.[11]

What President of the University of California Clark Kerr described in 1963 as the "'common-law marriage' between the federal government and leading universities" began to take shape in earnest in the 1940s, with decisive implications that went beyond the scale and funding for US higher education that conditioned the kind of knowledge produced, authorized, and disseminated on and from campuses.[12] Organized in the service of "national needs," Isaac Kamola discusses how this "new relationship . . . profoundly affected the production of academic knowledge."[13] This was especially the case as the nation-state itself came to serve as the nearly universal unit of political organization. Sociologists such as Harvard's Talcott Parsons took it as their charge to establish a functionalist approach to social scientific research, one that shifted the thrust of such work "away from social critique and toward the creation of a descriptive, omnidisciplinary theory of human action."[14] In so doing, they sought a basic framework for "social engineering."[15]

Guided by Parsons and supported with funding both private, from the Ford, Rockefeller, and Carnegie foundations, and public, via the emerging national security apparatus, in 1946 the Harvard Department of Social Relations (DSR) brought together scholars and students, including sociologist Edward Shils, anthropologist Clifford Geertz, psychologist Gordon Allport, and East Asianist Ezra Vogel, to develop this theory, applying it primarily to decolonizing spaces they deemed in need of modernization.[16] Harvard was not alone. They built on work in what was increasingly called the Behavioral Sciences at the University of Chicago with the founding of the Committee on the Behavioral Sciences in 1949.[17] Yale established its Institute of Human Relations in 1929, guided largely by the neo-behaviorist Clark Hull and his search for a "unified theory of social life."[18] By the late 1940s, they were embracing the label Department of Behavioral Sciences alongside Harvard's DSR. MIT's Center for International Studies, which followed similar theories, was founded in 1951. The Ford Foundation dubbed its social science unit the "Behavioral Sciences

Program" the same year, encouraging scholars to employ quantitative methods in their work.[19]

Suffused with technocratic optimism, discourses of development and modernization appeared to displace, but in most instances simply reworked, the pre–World War II framework of civilizing missions. As Frederick Cooper and Randall Packard argue, this new "problem of development gave rise to a veritable industry in the academic social sciences, with a complex and often ambiguous relationship to governmental, international, and private agencies."[20] A major goal of the development project was to influence future leaders of emerging states. In 1952, the US National Security Council (NSC) issued a report explaining that the "process of internal political change going on in these countries may lead to disorder" and create an opportunity for the Soviet Union to exert influence. "As a means of diminishing the threat posed by nationalist demands" the NSC suggested the United States "make the fullest practicable use of psychological and political programs . . . to influence the process of political change into channels that will effect the least compromise of Western interests."[21] A crucial aspect of such efforts was to "encourage the emergence of competent leaders, relatively well-disposed toward the West, through programs designed for this purpose, including, where possible, a conscious, though perhaps covert effort to cultivate such potential leaders."[22] The intensification of efforts to recruit students from decolonizing countries was a significant component of this strategy.

With the end of World War II, congressional, academic, and popular attention turned to the noncitizen student as a potential conduit for US political interests abroad and an active vector of communist ideas into the country. Under these conditions, African students were undoubtedly subject to an especially high degree of scrutiny as the federal government sought to extend its control over the recruitment and regulation of student movement. By 1948, George M. Atkinson, US vice consul in Accra, made clear the direct interest of the US state in noncitizen students and African students in particular. He was insistent that the education of Africans visiting the United States be controlled to prevent antagonism: "With the full realization that an international exchange of students can be an immense source of good will [*sic*] and propaganda, the consulate and the Gold Coast Government are now closely cooperating on all matters relating to students going to the United States."[23] As discussed in Chapter 7, with the direct entry of the US government into the field of the noncitizen student policy, the capacity of former African students to guide the project of African education was dramatically reduced, though not eliminated.

## International Education and the Security State

Atkinson's declaration regarding the importance of US government involvement in the selection and travel of students to the United States was part of a much broader shift in US political thought on what was then called "foreign student education." As Margarat O'Mara argues, after World War II, there was an "intensive effort by national policy makers to use international educational exchange as an instrument of diplomacy and propaganda, resulting in an upsurge in foreign student populations in the United States, particularly from former European colonies caught between the two poles of American and Soviet influence."[24] She describes the system that took shape between 1945 and the 1960s as "an infrastructure that used universities and philanthropies as agents of the state," instantiating "the parastatal nature of foreign student policy."[25] However, the expansion of the US government's direct involvement in international education was not uncontested. While presidents from Roosevelt through Kennedy publicly expressed strong endorsements of educational exchange as a form of diplomacy, congressional support was more challenging to muster due in part to opposition from anti-communist politicians who saw such programs as a back door through which political dissidents could enter the country, gain immigration status, and influence students. In their imaginations, noncitizen students and scholars were dangerous vectors through which foreign and anti-capitalist influence could pollute campuses and American society at large. The regulation structure that took shape between these two positions consolidated the paradoxical status of students as at once desirable and feared, recruited and regulated, venerable and vulnerable.

Practically synonymous with postwar international education, the Fulbright Program is broadly lauded as exemplary of postwar liberal internationalism in the popular lexicon. Teresa Bevis and Christopher Lucas posit that Arkansas Senator J. William Fulbright was inspired by "the horrors of World War II" to innovate "new ways to help thwart future conflicts through the sharing of knowledge and cultural understanding."[26] As such, the Fulbright Program could function both as a tool of containment, in offering what Christina Klein has described as "a heroic model of education . . . as a crusade against communism," and one of global integration, in its capacity to provide a "sentimental education" and "forge intellectual and emotional bonds" with the peoples of the world.[27] Fulbright himself was, as historian Sam Lebovic describes, a "nationalist globalist," forwarding a kind of postwar liberal internationalism that "presumed U.S. hegemony."[28] Falling in line, Lebovic continues, the people who administered the Fulbright Program had "an almost blind faith in the utility and strength of American culture."[29]

Fulbright's proposal for an international education program faced initial resistance but sailed through Congress to be signed by Harry Truman on August 1, 1946. This was possible in part because the bill was presented as relatively modest in scope and low in cost.[30] Supporters of the Fulbright Program frequently cited the precedent set by Theodore Roosevelt's Boxer Indemnity Fund in the early 1900s, when the United States required China to redirect its war debts to funding educational exchanges with the United States.[31] Using a similar model, Fulbright's 1945 bill proposed the use of funds from the sale of idle surplus military equipment left by the US military in foreign countries to fund the travel of US students and scholars abroad and international scholars to the United States. As a result of this arrangement, the bill did not require any federal appropriations.[32] While Fulbright funds supported US students and scholars abroad in countries that were indebted to the United States, they did not cover tuition or other costs of living for noncitizen students in the United States or extend funding to countries that did not have a surplus of US war materials.[33] Reducing the scope of the act allowed it to pass through Congress. It also limited its capacity to significantly impact the movement of students from most of the world to the United States.

Fulbright's funding solution is often framed rhetorically through a biblical reference to the Book of Isaiah as "literally [turning] swords into plowshares of the mind."[34] For instance, a 1956 report compiled by the Department of State on the first ten years of the program is titled "Swords into Plowshares, A New Venture in International Understanding."[35] According to Fulbright, international educational exchanges would expose the "people of the Free world" to American culture and were thus "one of the most effective weapons" in the "war of ideas."[36] In December of 1946, William Benton, an assistant secretary of state, wrote an article for *Ladies' Home Journal* titled "Our Best 'Weapon'—Exchange Students," in which he touted the loyalty of Chinese alumni to "the American universities where they had studied and to the country that had welcomed them."[37]

The same month, *The New York Times* also published a short article on international education titled "A Weapon of Peace," lauding the promise of the Fulbright project. This militarized language would seem to be at odds with Christian-pacifist antinuclear proliferation readings of "plowshares" as a shift from weaponry to peaceful civilian applications. Yet, a more literal interpretation calls attention to the actual function of the "plowshare" as the cutting blade of the plow. As such, a reference to the "plowshares of the mind" is at once much more ominous and perhaps also a more accurate description of the ideological work Congress intended these international education initiatives to perform. As Liping Bu discusses in her work on Cold War educational exchange and cultural diplomacy, such programs expedited "the cultural dominance of the United States," a process that included the promotion of US "ideas, values, ideologies, technologies, commerce, military defense, and ways of life—anything that boosted its favorable image and power."[38] By the fall of 1947, the Fulbright Program was active in twenty-five countries. While most of the countries were in Europe, including Austria, Belgium-Luxembourg, Denmark, France, Germany, Italy, the Netherlands, Norway, Sweden, and the United Kingdom, a few non-European countries were included as well, such as Burma (present-day Myanmar), Ceylon (present-day Sri Lanka), India, Iraq, and others. Notably absent are any countries in Africa other than Egypt and South Africa, which at the time was a sovereign nation-state within the British Empire. The stated purpose of the program was to build international understanding, but it was also intended to serve far greater pedagogic and even epistemological purposes.

Despite the Fulbright Program's continuing reputation as the iconic postwar educational exchange program, it was not immediately clear that the program was drawing enough students to be competitive with parallel recruitment efforts underway in the Soviet Union. In October 1947, for instance, Benjamin Fine reported for *The New York Times* that "International Students were Shifting to Russia." In the article, he cites a State Department official's claim that there had been a 40 percent decline in the number of students traveling to the United States in the year after the Fulbright Act's passage. According to Fine, the cause of this decline was manifold. But two primary concerns were the availability of funds for students to live in the United States, a concern the Fulbright bill did not address and, of particular distress to government and military officials, a dramatic increase in competition for students from the Soviets. The Department of State official stoked concern, arguing that the flow of students to the United States had "slackened" to the point where it "threatens to come to a virtual standstill."[39] While students had difficulty accessing American dollars at home or in the United States, the Soviet Union was offering students who otherwise were likely to have looked to the United States for their educations, scholarships, grants, and other inducements, including better food and housing than was provided to Russian students. As *The New York Times* reported, this situation created a "grave danger . . . that the United States will lose its leadership in the field of scholarship exchange."[40]

Contrary to this coverage, the Institute for International Education's (IIE) 1948–1949 annual report shows that the number of international students studying in the United States actually increased from just shy of 8,000 in 1945 to 11,000 in 1946 and then shot up again to over 16,000 in 1947. As such, it is important to read Fine's reporting and the State Department representative's comments regarding the declining number of noncitizen students in the United States in the specific context of the fall of 1947. Two particularly relevant coinciding events are the push for the passage of the Smith–Mundt US Information and Educational Act and a surge in the activities of the House Un-American Activities Committee in their hearings "regarding the community infiltration of the motion picture industry." As the Smith–Mundt Act made its way through Congress, many educators reiterated their commitment to separating "informational," i.e., state propaganda, programs and educational initiatives.[41] In 1946, Laurence Duggan, who had by this time taken over leadership of IIE from his father, Stephen Duggan, already feared the use of student exchange programs as propaganda tools, arguing that fellowships from the state "must not be a means whereby our government hopes to influence foreign students in the United States in favor of particular policies and programs."[42] IIE was joined by a chorus of educational organizations and associations, including the American Council of Learned Societies, the National Educational Association, and the American Council on Education, which also demanded a clear line between educational activities and government propaganda initiatives.

Over and against these protests, the 1948 Smith–Mundt Act stipulated that "a program of educational exchange shall become an essential part of the conduct of this nation's foreign affairs."[43] John Rankin, a Democratic congressman from Mississippi best known for his white supremacist, anti-communist, and pro-internment views, argued against the provision of federal support for educational exchange activities. "Communism," he contended, "is being spread in the educational institutions of America by those foreign immigrant professors."[44] Representative Clare Hoffman, a Republican from Michigan, supported Rankin and argued that it was absurd for the government to fight communism in Greece and Italy while simultaneously authorizing "the expenditure of millions to bring teachers of communism here." One of the most ubiquitous concerns from the opposition was that the bill would give "leftists" permanent legal status in the country. This concern echoed worries from the 1920s that, as discussed in Chapter 5, resulted in the exceptional categorization of students as non-quota immigrants granted only temporary status. This categorization rendered students subject to the same scrutiny as would-be immigrants, rather than the lower level of review for nonimmigrant visitors, due to the indefinite duration of "study" and because of the likelihood that, once educated in the United States, the students would become "desirable residents."[45]

Representative Karl Mundt responded to Rankin and Hoffman by asserting that any evidence of pro-communist beliefs would be grounds for deportation. In a statement to Congress, Dr. Karl T. Compton, a former president of the Massachusetts Institute of Technology and a member of the US Advisory Board on Educational Exchange, held, "Our people are prosperous and possess the highest standard of living of any in the world. We possess more freedoms than anyone else. Well then, let's bring the students over here and show them at first-hand just what democracy means."[46] Though efforts to pass the bill in June of 1947 failed, it eventually passed only after a joint congressional committee of five senators and seven representatives visited Bulgaria, Romania, Hungary, and Poland in the fall of 1947, just as Fine was reporting on the nonexistent decline in noncitizen students traveling to the United States. Having experienced a series of "successive nightmares" and witnessed the "incessant falsification of our country's motives" by communists, they filed a report that expressed "ever more strongly the conviction that enactment is urgent and vital." The bill was passed by late January 1948 with unanimous approval from the Senate.[47]

In allowing for the appropriation of funds for international educational exchange, Smith–Mundt introduced a new framing for the legal status of the subset of noncitizen students who participated in exchange programs supported by the federal government. The act also put in place the International Educational Exchange Program, the foundation for what would become the Exchange Visitor Program (EVP) in 1961 and the Student and Exchange Visitor Information System (SEVIS) in 2003. As discussed in Chapter 5, the 1924 Immigration Act placed students in an inherently contradictory position as non-quota immigrants subject to special temporal restrictions and oversight. Under Smith–Mundt, students participating in government sponsored exchange programs would be shifted out of the non-quota immigrant category to be categorized alongside visitors for business purposes as "non-immigrant visitors for business under clause 2 of section 3 of the Immigration Act of 1924 . . . for such a time and under such conditions as may be prescribed by regulations promulgated by the Secretary of State and the Attorney General." The law goes on to stipulate, a person admitted under this section who fails to depart from the United States at the expiration of the time for which he was admitted, or who engages in activities of a political nature detrimental to the interests of the United States, or in activities not consistent with the security of the United States, shall, upon warrant of the attorney general, be taken into custody and promptly deported. The use of language regarding "activities inconsistent with the security of the United States" reflects Cold War fears that were prevalent at the time and efforts by the bill's authors to assuage concerns voiced by the likes of Rankin and Hoffman. While reclassifying some students as nonimmigrant visitors rather than non-quota immigrants only affected a small portion of noncitizen students, it set an important precedent for future immigration laws and greatly expanded the power of the secretary of state and the attorney general over individual visa cases.

As early as January of 1949, just a year after the bill was passed, the plans laid by Smith–Mundt seemed to be paying off. *The New York Times* covered twenty-five thousand "future leaders" studying in the United States:

> They will be the teachers, the college presidents, the political leaders, the journalists, the scientists, the technicians. What better investment could this country make in good-will and in democracy than to make it possible for them to complete their education here? Here is a "Foreign Legion" that could be worth half a dozen battleships.[48]

Federal financial support for educational exchange was thus legitimated mainly because it was seen as a good investment for US security efforts and to ensure and even enhance the global dominance of capitalism. Smith–Mundt Act supporters believed that through international educational exchanges both the United States and capitalism would come to symbolize "abundance of material wealth, consumer culture, technological know-how, individual freedom, and political democracy."[49]

Despite this perception, the federal government continued to play a minor role in funding students after the act's passage, even as the need continued. As is illustrated in a chart from the 1950–1951 IIE *Open Doors Report*, two years after the act's passage, the US government was still only funding 5.4 percent of students to any degree, while a full 34.5 percent of students were completely self-supporting. Notably, at least a portion of the US government funds provided to students in 1950 were used to support Chinese students who were "stranded" in the United States after Mao Zedong led the Chinese Communist Party to state power in 1949 and the secretary of state enacted special provisions "for necessary expenses of tuition, subsistence, transportation, and emergency medical care for selected citizens of China for study or teaching in accredited colleges, universities, or other educational institutions in the United States."[50] As Daniel Rodgers has argued, many of these five thousand Chinese students were eventually able to get immigrant visas and naturalize making up "the first sizable increment of what came to be called the Asian 'brain drain.'"[51]

## The Nonimmigrant Student

While the actual fiscal impact of the 1948 Smith–Mundt Act may have been underwhelming, its effects upon US law and policy extended far beyond expanded federal appropriations for student funding. In many ways, the Smith–Mundt Act laid the groundwork for crucial aspects of the 1952 McCarran–Walter Act, which despite being amended many times over the last sixty years, continues to serve as the basis for contemporary US immigration law. As historian Jane Hong argues, the McCarran–Walter Act is "best known for its most draconian attributes: national security codes strengthening the power of the federal government to detain, denaturalize, and deport individuals suspected of holding subversive views."[52] McCarran–Walter's impact has been especially important for students, scholars, and laborers temporarily present in the United States. In 1950, the Committee on the Judiciary, under the leadership of Senator Pat McCarran, a staunchly anti-communist and anti-immigration Democrat from Nevada, commissioned a nine hundred-page report on "The Immigration and Naturalization Systems of the United States." As discussed briefly at the end of Chapter 5, one of the report's primary recommendations was "the narrowing of the classes of aliens who may qualify for nonquota status" by transferring groups of people granted short-term permission to reside in the country from classification as non-quota immigrants, including students, to nonimmigrants on temporary visas.[53]

In restructuring immigration law with an emphasis on temporary visas, the report referred directly to students, but the effects of the new system were more widespread. McCarran–Walter codified a new visa system that conditioned relationships between specific classes of workers and students—who were by definition not workers—and the state to allow for their temporary and conditional status in the country. However, the purpose of the visas extended to these two groups served quite different purposes. From workers, the visas enabled the state and capital to extract an immediate and exaggerated profit off the backs of an underpaid and almost rights-less population of workers. Students offered something quite different but no less valuable. Like visitors categorized officially as workers, the value of students was immediately available simply because, by being present in the United States, students aided governmental efforts to expose the domestic population to a more global world. But, government and corporate leaders understood the actual value of international education in a more speculative frame as the potential that students would serve as global ambassadors for American interests and the American way of life.

In its final form, McCarran–Walter largely preserved, consolidated, and codified the forms of nationalism, xenophobia, and racism embedded in previous immigration policies predicated on a vision of the United States as a predominantly white nation-state.[54] Bevis and Lucas's description of the act reveals the multiplicity and contradictions of its content, reception, and consequences. As they explain, "the new law imposed more rigid restrictions on entry quotas to the United States, codified the scattered provisions of several earlier legislative works . . . , tightened controls over aliens and immigrants, removed racial barriers, and made citizenship available to people of all origins for the first time."[55] The coexistence of more restrictive numerical limitations and the ostensible deracialization of naturalization requirements illustrates the unevenness of a law written at a time when the United States was attempting to remake its global image as more pluralistic but penned in part by McCarran, who was quite explicit regarding the nationalist undergirding of this law, which he described as necessary to preserve "the Nation, the last hope of Western Civilization." McCarran understood immigration law as a way to protect the nation, which he saw as an oasis on the verge of being "overrun, perverted, contaminated, or destroyed," and with it, "the light of humanity will be extinguished."[56] The contemporary system for evaluating and administering the student visa system took shape under the shadow of such intentions.

The 1952 INA was thus a major recasting of US immigration law saturated with strong xenophobic, anti-communist, and, as elaborated below, heteropatriarchal sentiments and goals. Bevis and Lucas are correct to contend that the law technically removed racial barriers; it included a sentence stating, "the right of a person to become a naturalized citizen of the United States shall not be denied or abridged because of race or sex," thus implementing "the general principle of color-blind citizenship," or in the legal lexicon appeared facially neutral.[57] But it also created the "Asia Pacific Triangle," which, according to Mae Ngai, "was a global race quota aimed at restricting Asian immigration to the United States": "[p]ersons of Asian descent born or residing anywhere in the world could immigrate only under the Asia-Pacific quotas of one hundred per country."[58] In doing so, the INA further sedimented the state's classification of Asian immigrant identities. As such, the 1952 INA reflected the United States' conflicted relationship to Asia in its effort to appear race-neutral even as it continued the exclusionary racist practices of past policies. McCarran–Walter's second amendment instated a "colonial quota" limiting immigration from "colonies and other dependent areas" to one hundred persons per year, which had dramatic effects on the movement of Black migrants from the Caribbean.[59] McCarran–Walter is thus emblematic of how the racial liberalism of the postwar moment, as theorized by Jodi Melamed, seeded immigration policy: Official state rhetoric extended racial logics under the guise of policy that appears race-neutral only in comparison to the explicit white supremacy of previous laws and policies even as the substance of the law made racial logics and the sweeping exclusion they made possible more rigid.[60] Despite the effort to appear racially progressive, the intention of the law was explicit enough for President Truman to veto it, calling the law "a slur on the patriotism, the capacity, and the decency of a large part of our citizenry."[61]

The INA mirrored and imposed upon immigrants and nonimmigrants alike the conservative securitizing impulses of the Smith–Mundt Act and earlier immigration laws from the 1920s by expanding its exclusion and expulsion provisions in ways that lay bare the consolidating white heteropatriarchal American culture of the postwar era. As Siobhan Somerville illustrates, the law's inclusion of the category of "constitutional psychopathic inferiority" was drawn from a stipulation in the 1917 immigration law to "keep out 'tainted blood,'" a clearly eugenicist conception motivated by a racialized imagination of national purity. As she argues, "while Congress removed overt references to race in the requirements for American citizenship, it maintained a logic of blood purification by invoking the sexualized figures of the adulterer and the homosexual."[62] In this way, the act illustrates the entangled processes of racialization and state regulation of sexuality by simultaneously removing the explicit language of race and introducing new provisions for exclusion covering adultery and homosexuality, coded as failure to exhibit "good moral character" and "physically and mentally defective individuals."[63]

The McCarran–Walter Act continued the restrictive logics of previous immigration laws, but the law's effects hardly stopped there. Its authors also introduced new selective principles for choosing which noncitizens, referred to in the act as "aliens," could travel to the United States under the temporally restrictive "visa." Effecting a stance that reflected the emerging speculative mode of capitalism of the postwar era, the act initiated a "preference" system for permanent and temporary immigrants by which the first 50 percent of the quota allotted for each country or, in the case of the Asia Pacific Triangle, each region would be given to immigrants based on "education, technical training, specialized experience, or exceptional ability of such immigrants and to be substantially beneficial prospectively to the national economy, cultural interests, or welfare of the United States" as well as their spouses and children.[64] The other 50 percent of immigration quotas were then reserved for the parents and children of US citizens. As Ngai explains, "the policy thus established a new set of norms of desirability based on educational level, skill, and familial ties to Americans."[65] This was a novel approach to immigration whereby "[t]he country could select the alien instead of the alien selecting the country."[66] Desire was thus doubly present in the 1952 INA since, as Somerville writes, the inclusion of preferential categories for migration belied how immigration is a relationship between a desiring immigrant and, just as importantly, a desiring nation-state that constitutes some potential immigrants and migrants as particularly "loveable."[67]

Though Bevis and Lucas neglect to critique the racist or heteropatriarchal aspects of the law, they do express a good deal of concern regarding the ways the INA "increased dramatically the extent of evaluation and documentation required [of students]."[68] Building directly on Smith–Mundt, McCarran–Walter recategorized all noncitizen students as a new special class of "nonimmigrant alien":

> (F) an alien having a residence in a foreign country which he has no intention of abandoning, who is a bona fide student qualified to pursue a full course of study and who seeks to enter the United States temporarily and solely for the purposes of pursuing such a course of study at an established institution of learning or other recognized place of study in the United States, particularly as designated by him and approved by the Attorney General after consultation with the Office of Education of the United States, which institution or place of study shall have agreed to report to the Attorney General the termination of attendance of each nonimmigrant student, and if such an institution of learning or place of study fails to make reports promptly the approval shall be withdrawn.

Here, the McCarran–Walter Act maintains several aspects of the 1924 Johnson–Reed Act, particularly the requirement that students retain a connection to a home country that they have "no intention of abandoning." Equally important, the act reaffirmed two powers for the federal government: One being the power of the government to determine individual students' worthiness of a visa, and another being the federal government's capacity to determine whether or not schools can host students at all, an approval that can be terminated upon an institution's failure to properly report on students. The act additionally imposed restrictions on students' ability to work while in the United States, a blow to students already struggling financially; installed new processes of screening potential students and visitors; and included provisions authorizing the attorney general to "prescribe special regulations, forms for the registration and fingerprinting" for some nonimmigrant visitors, including students.[69] A final aspect of the 1952 law cemented administrative power in the state and further rendered students vulnerable: Section 221(i) on the issuance of visas stipulates that "[a]fter the issuance of a visa or other documentation to any alien, the consular officer or the Secretary of State may at any time, in his discretion, revoke such visa or other documentation."[70] With this language, the law reserves an expansive right for the executive branch to unilaterally revoke a student's visa at will.

The new procedures were so onerous that they elicited pointed responses from some of the most powerful academic associations and scholars in the country. For instance, an October 1952 issue of the *Bulletin of Atomic Scientists* collected letters voicing concern about the law from Albert Einstein, Linus Pauling, Harold Urey, and James Frank; and a January 1953 issue of *The Scientific Monthly* featured a compilation of statements from the American Council of Learned Societies (ACLS), the American Association for the Advancement of Science (AAAS), and the National Science Foundation (NSF).[71] All of these statements and letters expressed shock and concern about the possible effects of what the ACLS described as "extensive and humiliating inquisitions and incredibly formidable questionnaires" that would-be visitors were subjected to.[72] The ACLS statement goes on to report that news "of these annoyances and delays spread rapidly, and the reputation of the United States is gravely injured."[73] AAAS warned that under the new immigration law, "American science faces the threat not merely of becoming provincial but also of becoming atrophied to the point where the national welfare and national security will suffer. Security and welfare are founded on knowledge, only part of which originates within the confines of the United States."[74] Edwards Shils, the editor of the *Bulletin of Atomic Scientists*, a professor of Social Sciences in the Committee on Social Thought at the University of Chicago, and key contributor to modernization theory, expressed the harshest criticisms of the law, writing that it was the product of "several unworthy, irrational prejudices which form constant counter-currents in American life and which at unhappy moments like the present seem to increase in strength. One of them is the fear and hatred of foreigners, which permeates both the Internal Security Act of 1950 and the Immigration and Nationality Act of 1952."[75]

## Visa Power and the Cold War University

The recategorization of students as "nonimmigrants" located them squarely between the legal structures of immigration control and the administrative procedures reserved for nonimmigrants as a special class. Students were thus subject to the documented legal stipulations applied to immigrants regarding excludability and the additions Somerville discusses regarding "good moral character" and physical and mental defects while also being subject to the specificities of visa law unique to nonimmigrant visitors. That is, while immigrants and nonimmigrants alike were subject to the 1952 INA, there is something unique about "aliens" who seek to enter the country temporarily that differs from the long-term commitment between a naturalized citizen and the state. The 1952 INA required nonimmigrants to convince their consular interviewer that they retained a "residence in a foreign country which he has no intention of abandoning."[76] As section 214(b) reads, "Every alien shall be presumed to be an immigrant until he establishes to the satisfaction of the consular officer, at the time of application for a visa, and the immigration officer, at the time of application for admission, that he is entitled to a nonimmigrant status under section 101 (a) (15)." Advocates of international education argued that the temporariness of the visa should mean that students and other nonimmigrants would be held to lower standards of scrutiny. For instance, the AAAS statement on the law argued along these lines, "the implications of visitation are so drastically different from those of immigration that the two merit not only separate considerations but distinctive procedural handling."[77] However, at a moment when restrictivist and protectionist logics were inflamed by McCarthyism, the dual affinities students were required to express to obtain visas simultaneously rendered them suspect.

Both students and the institutions they attended could be subject to significant punishment if they failed to fulfill the requirements for monitoring and reporting as laid out in the INA. For students, failure to comply made them immediately subject to deportation, if the state chose to pursue such a course of action. For institutions, failure to fulfill their duties would result in the removal of the institution's approval to sponsor students in the future. As a 1962 handbook for international student advisers published by The National Association of Foreign Student Advisers (NAFSA) explains, regulations are needed to "ensure that student status does not become a channel to immigration and to encourage the student to complete his studies promptly and to return home as soon as possible after his work is finished."[78] However, the regulations make it clear that the institutions and individual workers also operated under the threat of being denied the ability to host students in the future. The fact that noncitizen students and their host institutions were subject to administrative processes that exceed the terms of immigration makes it necessary to grapple with the particularity of students in their position as temporary visa holders, a category of nonimmigrants that the 1952 INA significantly expanded.

The experience of Mugo Gatheru, a Kenyan studying at Lincoln University, is one example of how fears of communist infiltration of the United States were operationalized through immigration law in support of a white supremacist project built on anti-Black racism and European colonialism. As historian James Meriwether documents, in September 1952, on the eve of the Mau Mau uprising against colonial forces in Kenya, Gatheru was "visited" and interrogated by an immigration official, presumably on campus.[79] Two months later, he received orders from the Immigration and Naturalization Service (INS) to leave the country or be deported, without explanation or a charge. According to a *New York Times* article from December 1952, however, the Department of Justice contended that Gatheru had obtained his visa under the false pretense that he had never been denied a visa in the past. They also asserted that they had "confidential information that makes him deportable under the Internal Security Act."[80] Gatheru argued against the charge of a fraudulent application, though he admitted that he had been denied a Certificate of Good Conduct, a necessary precursor to obtaining a visa, by the British colonial government in Kenya because of his work with the Kenya African Union paper. Gatheru was able to find support from a committee consisting of Lincoln University's president, Horace Mann Bond, faculty from Lincoln and Roosevelt University, and eventually the NAACP. They argued that the US government was acting under pressure from the British Colonial Office, which targeted Gatheru as a member of the Kikiyu tribe, a group associated with the anti-colonial Mau Mau guerrillas, also known as the Kenya Land and Freedom Party, a leading force in the Kenyan independence movement. Under such pressure, INS rescinded its deportation order in February of 1953, allowing Gatheru to remain in the country through the completion of his degree at Lincoln, and he was eventually able to overcome a second deportation order to remain in the country and complete his MA in Political Science. After moving to England to complete his JD, he eventually returned to the United States, spending the duration of his life teaching African and Middle Eastern history at California State University, Sacramento.[81]

# 7

# The Lure of America: The Management of Difference and the "African Student Problem"

Despite the title "'Mo' Is Sa'aid's Nickname at Cornell" emblazoned across the top of the 1963 *Newsweek* article analyzed in the introduction to Part III, its first page does not feature a portrait of Mohammed Sa'aid, the Malaysian student discussed in excited terms as exemplary of the promise of noncitizen student recruitment in its opening paragraphs. Instead, it includes, somewhat inexplicably, a photograph of three students shot from behind in silhouette, their identities obscured but their ethnic and racialized positions emphasized in their dress and skin tone and in the photo's caption. The students stare up at the large marble statue of Abraham Lincoln, only feet from the site where Martin Luther King Jr. would deliver his "I Have a Dream" speech just three months later. The students are shot in three-quarters, while Lincoln looms above them, filling nearly half the frame. The image is captioned: "African students at the Lincoln Memorial: America's lure," suggesting that the students are awed by the wonder of Lincoln's legacy, "lured," seemingly innately, to the promise of "American" equality and prosperity.

Though it seems innocuous, between two of the students at the very center of the image stands what appears to be a masculine white child, fully embodied, situated directly at Lincoln's feet. The inclusion of the white child suggests the possibility of a different reading, one in which the presence and the presumed desires of the African students are not the actual subjects of the image but are instead a necessary component in or accessory to the white child's position as primary at a historical moment and location when the politics of personhood, difference, and economy in the United States were threatened with reorganization and the displacement of whiteness. Aside from the cover image, every other picture in the article is a portrait of an individual student,

Figure 6. Image of three African students looking at the Lincoln Memorial as included in the *Newsweek* article and featured on the fourth page of the April 22, 1963 article. @Newsweek (YouTube).

**Kenyans sample catalogues: Harvard, Oxford, or Patrice Lumumba?**

Figure 7. Image of two students captioned, "Kenyans sample catalogues: Harvard, Oxford, or Patrice Lumumba?" @Newsweek (YouTube).

with the exception of this picture and two others, both of African students. One features Ben Nzungu of Congo playing soccer with a white student, James McQueen from North Carolina. The other, two unidentified students captioned "Kenyans sample catalogues: Harvard, Oxford, or Patrice Lumumba?" Here, Lumumba is a reference to Lumumba University, the recently opened Soviet University named for the Congolese independence leader and first prime minister who aligned with the Soviet Union before his assassination in 1961.

This chapter tracks geographic and demographic shifts in efforts to recruit noncitizen students to study in the United States, with a specific focus on the fluctuations in the US government's interest in recruiting and regulating African students between the late 1940s and the mid-1960s. As Chapter 2 illustrates, students from Africa traveled to the United States for higher education as early as the mid-1850s. Still, by the 1950s, the number of African students at US institutions of higher education in a given year was still under two thousand. But, as Chapter 6 demonstrates, the era of decolonization required new and more facially inclusive tactics of governance. Shaping the education of future national leaders was one key form of containment. The story here is told through the experiences of specific figures, including James Emman Kwegir Aggrey, Nnamdi Azikiwe, and Kwame Nkrumah, and the often short-lived organizations formed by either African students studying in the United States or by American philanthropic or governmental groups that sought to recruit such students and facilitate their experiences while in the country. As the chapter documents, the fates of these efforts were always conditioned by broader shifts in a domestic and international politics of race in which Blackness, especially when paired with critiques of capitalism, was broadly viewed as a threat to US empire requiring management, supervision, and, in many cases, expulsion.

## Demographic Shifts in the Decolonial Moment

While the *Newsweek* article frames the presence of "foreign students" as a relatively minor and recent phenomenon, noncitizen students had, as is argued throughout this project, played a constitutive role in the long history of higher education from the colonial period forward and its function as a technology for "accumulation by possession."[1] Still, the changes in this era were significant and multifold both by numerical measure and in their geographic specificity. Paul Kramer contends that the "explosive growth" in the number of students traveling to the United States in the postwar period can be measured along several axes: their growing numbers and expanding geographic diversity; the "proliferation of sponsoring programs," both governmental and nongovernmental; and the number of colleges and universities to which they traveled.[2] In other words, this "explosive growth" was the product of concerted efforts made by an array of US-based actors to cultivate and recruit a field of noncitizen students from specific geographic regions in the service of expanding American influence abroad.

In 1948, the Institute for International Education (IIE) published a report entitled "Education for One World," a telling title that gestures quite openly toward the ambitions of the US state and its educational arm in the immediate postwar era. The report includes data from the institute's first annual survey of "foreign students."[3] As discussed in the introduction to Part II, IIE was founded in 1919 by university faculty and administrators, as well as a former secretary of state, as the primary hub for international education in the United States, organizing directly with the government, universities, campus-based international student advisors, and students themselves. In the foreword to the 1948 report entitled "Windows on the World," IIE's vice president, Donald J. Shank, emphasizes the "special importance" of "personal contacts between the United States and other countries" and argues that with the travel of 26,759 students to the United States, "[e]ducationally, at least, 'one world' is today a reality, and there are no far-away places."[4] It is particularly telling that the foreword lists the types of geographic locations from which "academic visitors journeyed" in order, according to Shank, "to share in our American culture and customs."[5] The list included "151 countries" but also "colonies, dependencies, protectorates, absorbed states, and states a-borning," demonstrating the wide variety of political entities at play at this historical moment. The number of students traveling to study in the United States more than tripled between 1937 and 1949 from just under 7,000 to nearly 25,000. As the list of types of sending locations suggests, the geography of student travel also expanded with over eight thousand students traveling from "Asia" and the "Near East," and 378 students coming from "undesignated" locations because they were "not authorized to divulge" (3), the location was "unclear" (23) or "not given" (312), or they were refugees (10) or "stateless" (27).[6] The sheer variety of designations evidences the scale at which US institutions were working to manage this moment of global reordering.

While IIE took the lead, they were well supported, at least in advocacy, if not financially, by some within the government and especially the State Department, who saw great value in educational exchange programs. For instance, as Liping Bu documents, between 1946 and 1948, the State Department underwrote three national conferences to bring together university administrators and student advisors.[7] In a 1948 IIE news release, Assistant Secretary of State George Allen explained that the "impressions of the United States" the students "take back" to their home countries are "more significant than the technical knowledge and skills they acquire" because they "will return to positions of responsible leadership in their own countries."[8]

Despite this awareness, Congress was not forthcoming with funding, a gap that was filled in 1949 when the Ford Foundation shifted its interests toward educational exchange, providing more than two million dollars of support to the general functioning of IIE and two other organizations focused on international education between 1951 and 1956.[9] While Ford funded these programs, the federal government continued to exercise substantial influence on the projects, as evidenced by a 1953 statement from Melvin Fox, the foundation's exchange programs officer, stating that the "government program exercises a controlling influence over the exchange field and in a sense determines its character as well as its size and scope."[10] Bu reads this comment as making clear that "The Cold War created an environment where cultural expansion contributed to the 'empire-building' when military actions could not be used directly because of fear of total destruction."[11] In other words, working through Ford and IIE, the US government was able to use educational programs to expand its sphere of power.

By 1963, IIE's Open Doors Report trumpeted the "dramatic growth of exchange programs," with even more striking growth expected in the future.[12] Though the "significance of the exchange of men and women between nations" goes "beyond mere numbers," IIE tabulated that 78,000 "foreign citizens" were in the United States on "educational assignment," essentially tripling the number of students studying in the United States over just fifteen years.[13] Echoing much of the language and sentiment of the *Newsweek* article from the same year, as well as the modernization theory prevalent throughout universities discussed in Chapter 6, IIE president Kenneth Holland's foreword to the report explains that "[e]xchange programs have become a basic aspect of our foreign policy."[14] They "foster mutual understanding and do much to dispel misconceptions about the United States," and they play "a major role in the efforts of new and developing nations to educate and train the manpower they so urgently need if they are to fulfill their political, economic, and social aspirations."

As the charts below illustrate, the demographic makeup of the international student population also changed markedly between the early 1950s and the mid-1960s, with disproportionate growth from specific regions of interest for US foreign policy. Charts 1 and 9 show that the number of students traveling from the "Far East" grew from around 7,500 in 1952 to nearly 24,000 in 1963. This growth is especially remarkable in that the number of Chinese students coming to the United States after the 1949 Chinese Revolution dramatically decreased from 4,000 to effectively zero after the United States cut off diplomatic relationships with the newly established People's Republic in China.[15] Students from Taiwan and Hong Kong comprised a significant portion of this group.[16] The number of students from Africa, though still comparatively low, spiked rapidly between 1959, when less than 2,000 students traveled from the continent to the United States, to over 5,000 just four years later. These shifts were not coincidental. Rather, they were the result of concerted governmental, philanthropic, and corporatist efforts that worked to manage and optimize the recruitment of noncitizen students to convince decolonizing nations that the American-led global order presented a more viable path to development and modernization than did Soviet-aligned pathways and efforts to project an image of the United States as a non-racist country.

It is imperative that a reading of the *Newsweek* article and the conjunctural moment of noncitizen student recruitment, regulation, and education from which it emerged be attentive to the particular ways and historical moments at which differently racialized students and specifically Black students from

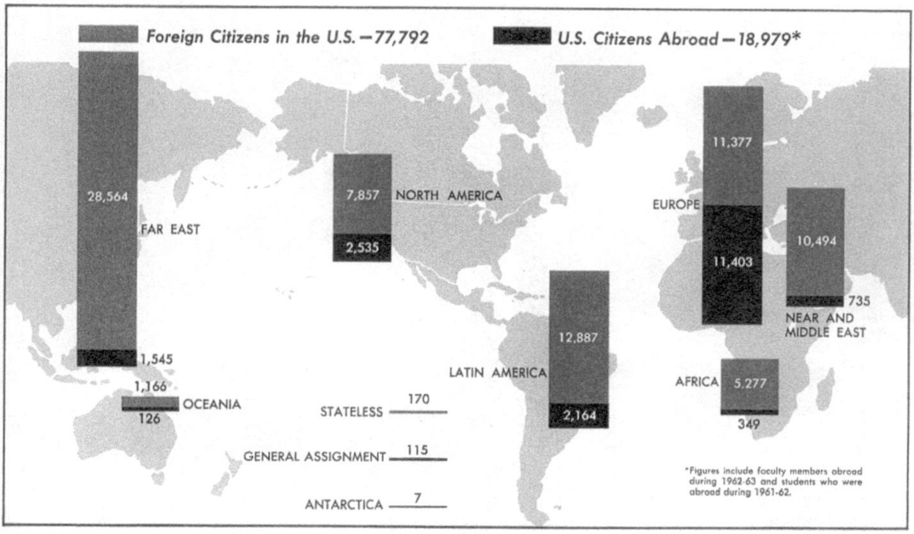


Figure 8. Chart 1 from the 1963 IIE Open Doors illustrating the number of noncitizens studying in the United States in 1963. The Institute of International Education (IIE). *Open Doors 1963 Report on International Educational Exchange* (1963, 5, 15).

Africa are incorporated into the idea of "America," or eschewed from it. As discussed in this book's conclusion, throughout the article, students from Asian countries are described in positively aspirational terms. Gayatri Chakravorty Spivak, for instance, is discussed through reference to her "90-plus average" and held up as evidence of just how truly exceptional some noncitizen students can be. But students from African countries are discussed by way of the involvement of the CIA in the selection of students sponsored by the US government, a point supported through a brief nod to Kwame Nkrumah, the Leninist Ghanaian independence leader who studied in the United States and then wrote a widely influential text critiquing what he termed Western neocolonialism. Unlike John F. Kennedy's speech welcoming Nkrumah to the United States just two years earlier in 1961 as a "distinguished citizen of a friendly country, and also a distinguished citizen of the world," the article does not attempt to appropriate Nkrumah's successes as a nationalist decolonial leader as a product of his American education.[17] Instead, he is invoked as a warning, an illustration that "not all foreign students leave with stars and stripes in their eyes."[18]

Mel Elfin and Constance Montague explain that Nkrumah "spent ten difficult years working his way through the University of Pennsylvania and nearby Lincoln University," eventually receiving four degrees but also, "some critics

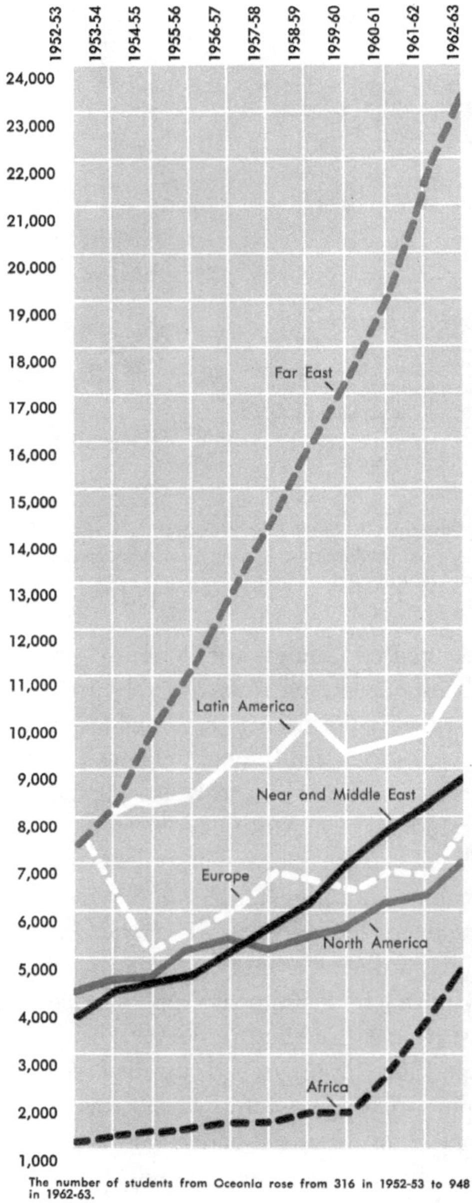


Figure 9. Chart 9 from the 1963 IIE Open Doors report illustrating the dramatic changes in the numbers of students traveling to the United States from the "Far East" and "Africa" between 1952 and 1963. The Institute of International Education (IIE). *Open Doors 1963 Report on International Educational Exchange* (1963).

say, an unfavorable impression that still influences his politics."[19] As such, the article contributes to a discourse of what Charisse Burden-Stelly describes as the "trifecta of foreignness, Blackness, and radicalism." In her deeply historicized theorization of what she terms Capitalist Racism and US governmentality, these three "mutually constituting forms of subversion and sedition" function to legitimate "extreme forms of violence and exclusion."[20] They constitute the negative and threatening figure of "the foreigner" who must be monitored and who is always available for deportation. They also, importantly, provided the rationale for the construction of a US immigration policy discussed in Chapter 6 that, in the final instance, cedes control of the management of noncitizens to the executive office of the government.

## Aggrey, Azikiwe, and the Politics of African Education

As discussed in Chapter 2, African students, mainly from Western and Southern Africa, traveled to study at US universities and colleges from the mid-nineteenth century forward, often in rather small numbers, concentrated at institutions designated for the education of Black students, and facilitated through missionary channels. James Emman Kwegyir Aggrey was one such student. His story grounds a genealogical thread of students through to Nkrumah and beyond. Born in 1875, a year after the British had formalized their colonization of the Gold Coast (historic Ghana), Aggrey's father sent him to be educated at the Wesleyan Methodist School at Cape Coast when he was seven. By fifteen, he was teaching classes. According to historian Sylvia Jacobs, it was there that he "absorbed the late nineteenth century view that it was the 'white man's burden' to 'civilize and Christianize' Africa."[21] "At the invitation of the Bishops of the American Methodist Episcopal Zion Church," he traveled from the Gold Coast to study at Livingston College in North Carolina in 1898, where he remained for ten years as a teacher after completing his BA, absorbing the leading ideas on education and specifically on the education of people of African descent of the time.[22] Between 1914 and 1922, he took classes at Columbia University, eventually completing his teaching diploma and master's degree as well as all of the coursework and comprehensive exams for a doctorate, though he never completed his dissertation.

He first returned to Africa in 1920 to complete research for his dissertation as part of a team organized by the Phelps–Stokes Education Fund "to study the educational needs of Africa, especially pertaining to the hygienic, economic, social, and religious condition of the Native people."[23] The fund, as historian Eric Yellin contends, was "a characteristically Progressive era" institution, nominally committed to a "universalistic belief in the value of all humans" but deeply entrenched in Christian civilizationism and a belief in "the cultural superiority of people of European descent."[24] The results of the study were published in 1922 as *Education in Africa: A Study of West, South, and Equatorial Africa By the African Education Commission, Under the Auspices of the Phelps-Stokes Fund and Foreign Mission Societies of North America and Europe*. The report's central finding encourages modes of education adapted to what it argues are the "actual needs" of African people and students. As the foreword explains, the report built on both Booker T. Washington and Samuel Armstrong, demonstrating "how the principles which originated in the Hawaiian mission field, and were developed to a high state of efficiency in the United States among the Negro peoples, may now best be applied to the educational work in Africa."[25] What this meant functionally was the transfer and adoption of models of education developed by Armstrong at the Hampton Institute in his work with the Freedmen's Bureau as "industrial education" under the new label of "adapted education." This approach was predicated on Armstrong's fundamental belief in nonwhite people's "deficiency in character." In this frame, as the studies' lead author Thomas Jesse Jones explains, education's central charge is turned to "drawing out the latent powers of the Negro, and fitting him for the hard task of living an upright, useful, and economically productive life."[26]

Aggrey returned to Africa in 1924, this time settling in Gold Coast and taking on the position of teacher and vice-principal at what was then called the Prince of Wales College, a newly established school organized around the principles espoused in the 1922 Phelps–Stokes report.[27] In 1927, the school was renamed Achimota College. As Gita Steiner-Khamsi and Hubert O. Quist illustrate, under the "adapted education" model Achimota College taught students "to accommodate to the limited opportunities of a racist environment" and that "they would only improve their social realities as blacks if they gradually worked their way up, cooperated with enlightened whites, and provided proof that they were deserving of being treated with dignity."[28] From primary through university level, the school's curriculum promoted agricultural and industrial education and an appreciation for manual labor.[29] By the time the Hampton/Tuskegee model was being implemented in British colonial spaces in the 1920s, it had fallen from popularity in the United States and was subject to robust critique. W. E. B. Du Bois, perhaps the leading Black American intellectual, had articulated his concerns about it in 1906, and by 1926, he was publishing what Steiner-Khamsi and Quist characterize as his "attack on adapted education" in the *Gold Coast Leader*.[30]

On his first trip in 1920, Aggrey met Nnamdi Azikiwe, then a sixteen-year-old student. Born in 1904 in Zungeru, Nigeria, while the country was also under British colonial rule, Azikiwe, who would go on to be a founder of the Nigerian nationalist movement, has been identified by scholars such as Jason Parker as "student zero" for African nationalists educated in the United States. According to his autobiography, *My Odyssey*, by the time he met Aggrey, Azikiwe had already encountered the writings of Marcus Garvey in "a badly mutilated copy" of *The Negro World* a classmate pulled from a wooden box. Azikiwe credits this brief encounter with Garvey's work as sparking his belief that Africans were "capable of appreciating the benefits of western civilization."[31] When he attempted to discuss these ideas with his father, he was warned that the colonial administration took Garvey's "teachings as seditious" and that being in possession of them could lead to arrest.

If reading Garvey was inspirational, meeting Aggrey was revelatory. Azikiwe describes his experience of hearing Aggrey give a sermon proclaiming "Nothing but the best is good enough for Africa," while "the scales fell from [his] eyes and [he] began to see a glorious future."[32] When Aggrey visited his school the following day, he gave Azikiwe a copy of *Negro Education: A Study of the Private and Higher Schools for Coloured People in the United States*, which would prove a vital resource in Azikiwe's pursuit of an education in America. As Azikiwe writes, the combination of Garvey's words and his encounter with Aggrey persuaded him that "not even death would stop me from reaching America in order to make my dreams come true."[33] He wrote to his father to plead for support, but was met with disappointment. Azikiwe spent several years "trapped in the vortex of economic insecurity" as a junior clerk in the colonial civil service. Through this experience, he came to question European rule and wonder about the "best way to offset the rapacious tendencies of economic man" under capitalism.[34]

Eventually, in 1925, the twenty-one-year-old Azikiwe traveled to Storer College in Harpers Ferry, Virginia. Unlike the vast majority of African students who had traveled to the United States before him, Azikiwe's journey and education were not sponsored by missionaries. Because of this, as Parker contends, his career provides the clearest marker of a "shift from the 'missionary' phase of the black Atlantic educational exchange to the 'political' one."[35] It also contributed to his experience of a great deal of economic and physical hardship. In his autobiography, he tells the story of finding campus work. Shortly after arriving at Storer, a professor instructed him that his experience as a civil clerk was useless and that the only campus work to help pay for his tuition would be serving as a fire stoker in the steam-heat plant. Reflecting the form of industrial education prevalent at the time, the professor told Azikiwe that "unless [he] was prepared to be re-educated, to use [his] hands as well [as his head], . . . coming to America would be futile."[36] After completing his first year of studies, he moved to Pittsburgh to earn money to continue his education. After failing to acquire the necessary funds to continue his studies, he worked in Pittsburgh for several months, the whole time evading the threat of deportation from immigration authorities.[37] In February of 1928, he enrolled at Howard University. There, he worked closely with Ralph Bunche, Alain Locke, for whom he worked as an assistant, and Leo Hansberry, who "opened a new world to" him in part through his "exposition of the concept of race," albeit through the theses of Johann Friedrich Blumenbach and Charles Darwin, and African history.[38] He found footing in his interest in African history. Halfway through his second year at Howard, he secured a scholarship from the Phelps–Stokes Fund. While at Howard, he also worked with a Trinidadian student, Malcolm Nurse, who would later become better known as George Padmore, to organize a protest of a visit from Sir Esme Howard, the British ambassador to the United States.[39] In the fall of 1929, he enrolled at Lincoln University, where he received his degree in 1930.[40]

With another scholarship from Phelps–Stokes, he began graduate studies in journalism at Columbia University in the summer of 1930. Once again without funds to continue his studies, he returned to Lincoln in the fall of 1930 as a graduate assistant with plans to work toward a master's degree at Lincoln and the University of Pennsylvania. By the summer of 1931, he had begun work toward a doctorate in political science, proposing a dissertation on "Mythology in Ontisha Society" inspired largely by the work of Bronislaw Malinowski and deeply engaged in African history. Upon his return to teaching at Lincoln in the fall of 1933, he was given the responsibility to teach several courses in history. However, his deep investment in the study and teaching of African history would lead to his eventual dismissal from Lincoln, where members of the administration and faculty "felt that the African had no history worthy of academic attention."[41]

In his detailed history of the institution, Lincoln's president from 1945 to 1957, Horace Mann Bond, describes how Azikiwe "argued strongly and persistently for the introduction of a course in Negro history," criticizing the "conventional ambitions of his fellow students and the apparent middle class aims of the institution."[42] As a result, the administration did not renew his position and thus effectively voided his visa to remain in the country, fueling his decision to return to Nigeria. Despite this experience, upon his return, Azikiwe "exhorted his fellows to go to black American colleges," writing in his 1969 manifesto, "Why should African youth depend on Oxford, Cambridge, Harvard, the Sorbonne . . . for intellectual growth? [An] African graduate of these universities . . . is nothing short of a . . . carbon copy of those [universities'] societies." For Azikiwe, forgoing an education in the colonial metropole to attend Black colleges in the United States instead was an explicitly political act for the formation of anti-colonial activists. As Olanipekun Laosebikan documents, "favorable views of 'America' would be widely disseminated through the newspaper empire he built upon his return to Africa in 1934. In this role, he functioned as a prolific recruiter for higher education, particularly black higher education in the United States."[43] One of his most famous recruits was none other than Kwame Nkrumah.

## Nkrumah and the Possibilities of Study

Nkrumah's interest in traveling to the United States for his education was sparked in the 1920s by his own brief encounter with Aggrey when he was a student at Achimota. The encounter was so meaningful that he writes in his 1957 autobiography, published the year Ghana achieved independence with Nkrumah as its leader, "It was because of my great admiration for Aggrey, both as a man and a scholar, that I formed the idea of furthering my studies in the United States of America."[44] It was also through Aggrey that Nkrumah's "nationalism was first aroused."[45] Various financial and logistical impediments stymied his efforts to travel to the United States, but, as he tells it, his nationalism and determination to go to America was revived in 1934 through his encounters with Azikiwe's writings in his "fiery nationalist" newspaper, the *African Morning Post*.[46] The two met briefly in Accra "some years earlier."[47] When Nkrumah experienced doubt after he boarded the vessel carrying him away from the Gold Coast (Ghana) and to Liverpool to secure his visa, he found a telegram from Azikiwe in his cabin. The telegram read "Goodbye. Remember to trust in God and in yourself" and provided Nkrumah with reassurance that the trip was "the beginning of all [he] had planned for."[48]

Traveling by way of London, where he acquired his visa, and New York, Nkrumah arrived at Lincoln in October of 1935, short on funds and behind on coursework. As his autobiography continues, he quickly made up the work and did well enough to secure an internal scholarship to cover a portion of his costs.[49] To make up for the rest, Nkrumah worked in the library and wrote papers for fellow students for pay.[50] On campus, he participated in speech contests and joined a fraternity. He spent summers in Harlem, where historian John Henrik Clarke describes him extending his "American education" by attending the "university of the Harlem streets," listening to oratory from street speakers.[51] Over the years, he was an active participant in African student groups where, according to Adom Getachew, he "sharpened his ideas about African unity." He also "connected with left-leaning political organizations and encountered the writings of Marcus Garvey," even joining a local branch of his University Negro Improvement Association.[52]

Nkrumah graduated from Lincoln in 1939 with majors in economics and sociology, and with outstanding debt to the institution, which meant his degree was withheld. He intended to start at the Columbia School of Journalism after graduation but held off for lack of funds. Instead, much like Azikiwe, he accepted an offer to return to Lincoln as a lecturer in philosophy because of "the nature of [his] passport as a student," which would not allow him to be out of school for several months.[53] Also following in Azikiwe's footsteps, he started at the Lincoln Seminary and the University of Pennsylvania, where he earned his master's in education and philosophy. Continuing as a student after his graduation allowed Nkrumah to extend his organizing alongside a group of fourteen other students Azikiwe recruited to travel to Lincoln for their education. This group, including the "eight Argonauts" who came in 1939, would go on to lead the political initiatives of African students in the United States during the Second World War. Virtually all its members later played significant roles in their respective countries' decolonization.[54]

As Laosebikan argues, the most prominent members of this group, which included Nkrumah as well as Kingsley Ozuomba Mbadiwe, Mbonu Ojike, Ako Adjei, and Nwafor Orizu, would shape US higher education both through their scholarship and in their collective activist work to promote "an awareness of African life and history to garner support for African independence" and "a space for the African student at the table of higher education in the United States."[55] In 1941, students, including Mbadiwe, Orizu, and Ojike met at Ohio State University to initiate an African Student's Association (ASA), which was then launched in New York later in the year.[56] Mbadiwe served as the organization's first president, and Nkrumah was its second starting in 1942. The ASA was unabashedly critical of colonialism, writing in its founding statement that the organization "condemns all nations that think of Africa only as a source of labor and raw materials, or merely as a market; and do emphatically demand that those who claim to be fighting for democracy implement their expressed ideals by considering Africa a sovereign land in all of its glorious heritage and history and in its potentiality as a full and equal member of the family of Nations-to-be."[57]

The ASA itself was short-lived, closing its doors in 1945. This was in part because many of its most prominent members, including Nkrumah, left the country in the mid-1940s, and in part because internal ideological differences about critiques of capitalism quickly surfaced between Nkrumah and Mbadiwe.[58] As Hollis R. Lynch surmises, "Nkrumah had already begun to espouse socialism while Mbadiwe remained uncritical of capitalism as a system."[59] In his autobiography, Nkrumah characterizes the schism as between Nigerian students who advocated for "colonial territories to struggle for themselves," and "Gold Coast students" who pushed for "territorial solidarity."[60] Nkrumah's thoughts on capitalism and imperialism during this period are reflected in a pamphlet he published in 1962, *Toward Colonial Freedom,* which he wrote mainly during his time as a student in the early 1940s. As he explains in his foreword, during this time, he was "so revolted by the ruthless colonial exploitation and political oppression of the people of Africa that [he] knew no peace."[61] He lays out his critique of colonialism, a process driven by the "struggle for raw materials" and "futile promises of 'preparing' colonial peoples for 'self-government,'" citing Vladimir Lenin's *Imperialism, the Highest Stage of Capitalism,* and concluding with a call for "Peoples of the colonies" to "UNITE," echoing Karl Marx and Fredrich Engels's *Communist Manifesto.*[62] With the end of World War II approaching, Nkrumah left New York for London in May of 1945, where he connected with George Padmore and stayed at the West African Students' Union Hostel.[63] Over the summer, he assisted Padmore and others in their preparation for the Fifth Pan-African Congress in October, chaired by W. E. B. Du Bois.[64] In 1947, he returned to the Gold Coast to build his nationalist movement in the Convention People's Party.

In Nkrumah's absence, Mbadiwe and Nwafor Orizu, a self-proclaimed Nigerian prince and another of the "eight Argonauts" who traveled to Lincoln in 1939 and a founding member of the ASA, took the lead in several projects intended to increase knowledge about Africa in the United States and access to the country for African students. According to Lynch, Mbadiwe had "no sympathy for socialism." This was, by Lynch's estimation, "doubtless due to the fact that [Mbadiwe] was born into one of the wealthiest Nigerian families" and, as such, "it suited his style to use wealth to gain power."[65] He believed in "philanthropic capitalism" as a way for "rich blacks [*sic*]" to "use their wealth to promote group interests.[66] When Mbadiwe split from the ASA in 1942, he shifted his focus to creating an organization highlighting Africa's cultural dimensions through drama, music, and dance. The African Academy of Arts Research (AAAR) opened in 1944. The AAAR gained the backing of national luminaries within the Black community, including Mary McLeod Bethune, "first lady among Afro-Americans," Elmer Carter of the Urban League, Walter White of the NAACP, and the first lady of the United States, Eleanor Roosevelt.[67] By 1947, the organization had raised enough funds to purchase a building in New York near City College on West 140th Street, which came to be called "Africa House." The space served as AAAR's headquarters and, as Laosebikan describes, "a social and cultural center for African students."[68]

Orizu founded the American Council on African Education (ACAE) in 1943 to secure "scholarships and maintenance for brilliant Africans in outstanding universities in this country."[69] A fundraising pamphlet the organization circulated from 1945 makes clear its commitment to the fundamentals of capitalism, emphasizing that "[u]neducated masses make neither good buyers nor good producers" and that the "role of the African peoples in supply of man power [*sic*], essential raw materials, and strategic bases for operation is well known."[70] A January 1, 1945 issue of *Time* magazine reports that Orizu and the ACAE had "secured 150 U.S. college scholarships."[71] In November 1945, Orizu was honored with a reception in Lagos that included an opening speech by Azikiwe in which he lauded Orizu as a "disciple." For his part, Orizu proclaimed his "dual purpose" for returning to Nigeria: "the education of Africans and to preach the gospel of the philosophy of Zikism."[72] According to Laosebikan, the ACAE would make good on plans to recruit and fund African students beginning in 1947, when twenty-five students traveled to the United States. Between 1947 and 1953, another ninety-six students would study in the United States through their efforts.

But throughout their existence, both ACAE and AAAR came under pressure and criticism from student participants, British colonial officials, and US immigration policy. Students and others accused Orizu of inadequately supporting the students whose travel he facilitated, a point of concern that gathered more attention in the Nigerian press after the death of Joseph Anisiobi, a student in Washington, DC, in February of 1948.[73] According to a 1949 *Survey of African Students in the United States* conducted by the Phelps–Stokes Fund, even by then, the ACAE appeared "to have grave weakness with an inadequate administrative organization."[74] These weaknesses included failures to pay student bills promptly and placing students at schools that were either unaccredited or failed to provide the appropriate course of study for the students' intended major. The *Survey* goes on to report that in June of 1949, members of the ACAE's executive committee worked to rectify some of these issues and "asked the Department of State to request American Consuls in Africa to withhold any further visas for students sponsored by the American Council."[75]

British colonial officials had significant concerns about students traveling from their colonial holdings to the United States, and especially to Black colleges and universities. As Jason Parker argues, they expressed concern "about the influence of black [*sic*] higher education in the United States," even going so far as to create institutions of higher education in Africa to combat their draw. For instance, in 1945, the British Protectorate government founded Makerere College in East Africa "with the intention of keeping colonial students at home and untouched by Pan-Africanism."[76] Their concern was for good reason. Ako Adjei, another of the eight argonauts, argued that "[f]or the African to stand on his own and face the white man on his own grounds, he must be educated in America. If you were educated in England, you couldn't do so, because we have so many English educated Africans already here who could do nothing. They thought they were English people in black skins."[77] European officials in Kenya, for instance, were reportedly especially concerned about "students who found their way to black colleges in America. These students, the authorities strongly believed, would import [the] 'virus' of self-assertion and nationalism that contaminated them in Tuskegee, Hampton, Howard and Lincoln."[78] One solution proposed by a British colonial official in 1947 was that "only the best students should be selected for American study."[79] By 1951, ACAE activity was a point of conversation for the British House of Commons, which appointed a West African student liaison to a posting in the United States. In this capacity, the official was able to gather complaints from students and use them to underwrite the withdrawal of the colonial government's support for ACAE's work and an investigation into its finances. In September of 1953, Orizu was sentenced to seven years in prison for fraud.[80]

The existing literature on the termination of ACAE and AAAR activity around student recruitment is less attentive to the impact of US immigration and visa policy on these programs and how they may have been impacted by shifts in the US government's involvement in international education, a significant oversight given the ratcheting up of immigration enforcement in the early years of the Cold War. Michael M. Ogbeidi briefly mentions that one issue for ACAE was the organization's subjection of the students whose travel it facilitated to "strict rules and regulations," such as staying in the United States for no more than four years and adherence to immigration laws, including avoiding membership in political organizations.[81] Congress would not renegotiate the terms of the student visa writ large until the 1952 McCarran–Walter Act, but from 1940 forward the anti-communist Red Scare was well underway and both noncitizens and Black people were in its crosshairs.[82] In 1940, Congress enacted the Alien Registration Act, which set out to "prohibit certain subversive activities," criminalized advocacy for overthrowing the US government, and instituted a registration program for all adult noncitizens, all with an eye toward easing the process for deportation.[83] The same year, Immigration and Naturalization Services was moved from the Department of Labor to the Department of Justice, concretizing a broader understanding of immigration as a matter of security. As Chapter 6 discusses in detail, with the passage of the McCarran–Walter Immigration and Nationality Act in 1952, the "foreigner" was officially codified as a threat to the nation-state, especially if and when such a person was Black and espoused anything akin to radical or anti-capitalist politics.

## Race and the International University

This period was also and relatedly a crucial turning point in US politics of race and difference on campus and beyond, and the new ways of making sense of racial formations attendant to them. Conventional renderings of US racial politics look to the 1950s to the 1960s as a period when civil rights were legally codified, and social justice movements realigned the meaning and material impact of race, effectively undercutting the fundamentally white supremacist organization of the country. For colleges and universities, this often meant a shift to racially integrated campuses. Many institutions did not admit Black students until the 1950s and 1960s.[84] The 1954 *Brown v. Board of Education* decision overturning *Plessy v. Ferguson*'s authorization of "separate but equal" did not directly apply to higher education, but it still had significant ramifications for the sector, especially in its international reverberations.[85] The efforts of the local community and the Arkansas governor to prevent the integration of Little Rock Central High School in 1957 are well-documented. Less well-known is the case of Autherine Lucy, whose registration to attend the University of Alabama in 1956 "provoked violent outbursts and marked the first clash between federal and state law enforcement agencies over the issue of school integration."[86]

As Azza Salama Layton argues, the Lucy case was also the first post-*Brown* case to garner international attention, overshadowing any positive press generated by the *Brown* decision with what the US Information Agency found to be "unfavorable impressions of the treatment of Negroes in the U.S."[87] As this statement evidences, the pressures for integration of campuses and the broader expansion of basic civil rights for nonwhite people did not only come from domestic sources. The NAACP and other groups may have "internationaliz[ed] the race issue," but the contradictions of fighting a war abroad "against racial and religious intolerance" with a segregated army and rampant segregation domestically were also ripe terrain for international critiques of the United States as early as 1942. With the burgeoning Cold War, the Soviet Union exploited US failures on racial equity.[88] By the end of the war, it was clear that the US state and US-based capital would need to manage and optimize their relationship to questions of race precisely because the rearrangements in the post–World War II global order required it. There was increasing pressure from abroad for the United States to live up to its stated ideals of "equality for all."[89]

Media coverage of nonwhite noncitizen students' experiences in the United States contributed to these narratives in important ways. While students were recruited with the explicit intention that they would export positive stories of America, the reality on the ground did not always lend itself to such an outcome. For instance, in 1947, *The New York Times* reported that, while international students "like" the United States "almost without exception," "visitors from Latin America, India, and other Eastern countries have occasionally encountered color discrimination."[90] One student identified as "from the Middle East" reported that he was unable to obtain a hotel room when he entered the United States at a southern port and was "compelled to ride in the car reserved for Negros" on the train ride to his college. After being refused service in Washington, DC, "he decided to don the turban he wears in his homeland. Now he is accepted as a 'foreigner.'" "It's not that I object to being mistaken for a Negro," he explained, "but I resent segregation as being a negation of all that is inspiring about Christian culture."[91]

The role of noncitizen students in the integration of campuses also frequently made it into newspapers. For instance, just two months before the *Newsweek* article, *The New York Times* noted that a Ghanaian student was accepted to the previously all-white Mercer University in Georgia—but only because his application was separated from the "issues of admitting Negro students . . . they are not one and the same."[92] Stories like this make it clear that noncitizen students, particularly students who were seen as Black, were not seamlessly folded into the campus cultures and that when they were included, it was distinctly not as Black but instead as "foreign" and "noncitizen." Still, from Mercer College to Harvard University, the racialized subjectivities of noncitizen students had to be accounted for and managed by university and college administrations.[93] And this was especially the case for Black African students who, like other nonwhite noncitizen students before them, were clearly understood as temporary visitors to rather than as potential members of the national community.

Read through this framework and with a broader understanding of the geopolitical significance of the countries from which students were recruited, as discussed in Chapter 6, it is apparent that the accomplishments of the civil rights era were indeed not solely about an overturning of the liberal order of things organized around a possessive investment in whiteness.[94] Instead, they were a recoding of the logics of race and possession required for the United States to extend and solidify its sphere of influence geographically and ideologically beyond the territorial boundaries of the nation-state. Or, more simply stated, during this period, race was recalibrated to meet the demands of the United States in a new age of empire. As demonstrated in previous chapters, on many campuses, both the process of racial integration and the work of exporting American ideas and ideals had long been underway through the recruitment and education of nonwhite noncitizen students. The postwar era saw an intensification of this process that worked to balance the established goals of exporting US-educated students in hopes that they would come to lead the political and economic lives of their home country with an emergent incorporative tactic that combined what was called the "brain drain" with the crafting of a US racial politics that was facially inclusive without unsettling the fundamentals of liberal, capitalist practices of exclusion predicated on assessments of independence, conditional inclusion, and discipline through the threat of deportation.[95] Looking to the 1950s and into the 1960s, these efforts are legible in the dramatic increase in the targeted recruitment of nonwhite noncitizen students accomplished through changes in immigration and visa law, the development of governmental and nongovernmental programs, and modifications in campus practices and policies.

## Recruiting Africa After 1952

After the McCarran–Walter Act passed over Truman's veto in 1952, international pressure on the United States to address its most overt practices of racism grew alongside a swell of decolonial movements across Africa, Asia, and the Caribbean.[96] In response, various governmental agencies articulated the ill effects of domestic racism on US foreign policy. For instance, as the *Brown v. the Board of Education* case wended its way through the courts, the Justice Department submitted an amicus brief in 1952 asserting that "the existence of discrimination against minority groups in the United States has an adverse effect upon our relations with other countries. Racial discrimination furnishes grist for the Communist propaganda mills, and it raises doubts even among friendly nations as to the intensity of our devotion to the democratic faith."[97] Informed by this concern, the 1950s witnessed a broadening belief in the strategic importance of the recruitment and education of noncitizen students for US diplomacy with specific attention to nonwhite students whose incorporation into the United States, even if only temporarily, could serve as evidence of the country's capacity for racial inclusion.

Despite this, the US government was wary of the potential costs of facilitating the education of African students. As James Meriwether asserts, Dwight D. Eisenhower, who served as US president from 1953 to 1961, saw the distribution of education and uplift as consistent with the paternalistic "civilizing mission" that burdened white governments.[98] But he and other members of his administration were of two minds when it came to the education of African students. On the one hand, they saw education as a way to help foster forms of independence that could align with American interests. But, on the other hand, they agreed with British colonial governments that there could be "risks" in the kind of independence education in the United States could foster.[99] Domestically, there was also "a latent fear that the presence of African students, coming from a continent with ambitions to overthrow white supremacy, might feed into and radicalize the civil rights struggle on American campuses."[100] As a result, the federal government held off on directly funding or supporting the recruitment and education of African students for much of the 1950s.

In 1953, philanthropic organizations, including Rockefeller and Carnegie, and individual donors took up the cause. Rockefeller and Carnegie supported the formation of the African American Institute (AAI) while a large number of individual supporters underwrote the founding of the American Committee on Africa (ACOA). AAI's founders were philanthropists, politicians, and business leaders who broadly supported increased public and private investment in Africa. They described their project as guided by an interest in "building friendly ties between the people of Africa and the Unites [*sic*] States . . . and assisting in the education and training related to the economic and social development of Africa."[101] In 1955, Horace Mann Bond, the president of Lincoln University, established AAI's International Advisory Council and persuaded former Lincoln students Azikiwe and Nkrumah, who had received an honorary doctorate from Lincoln in 1951, to join.[102] Anton Tarradellas illustrates that Azikiwe and Nkrumah's participation allowed AAI to present as a nongovernmental and nonpolitical organization, which in turn facilitated relationships with several African countries. Despite this appearance, Tarradellas asserts, "AAI was actually working for U.S. diplomatic and economic interests" and the organization made public statements to such an effect. For instance, in 1962, AAI's president Waldemar Nielsen baldly stated that the perception "that AAI is essentially a private organization is thus unrealistic, for we have many public obligations. The U.S. Government needs a well-qualified organization to carry out its affairs in Africa. AAI is and will remain primarily a government-contract organization."[103]

The ACOA was a nonprofit incorporated in New York State in September 1953, funded by individual donations and cochaired by A. Philip Randolph, president of the Brotherhood of Sleeping-Car Porters and a vice-president of the AFL-CIO, and Donald S. Harrington, minister of the Community Church of New York. Randolph and Harrington were supported by a seventy-five-member national committee consisting of leaders in education, politics, business, and the church. As a 1963 article by George M. Houser, a cofounder of the Congress of Racial Equity in 1942, staffer with the

Fellowship of Reconciliation in the 1940s and 1950s, one of ACOA's founders, and the organization's executive director from 1955 to 1981, stated, ACOA was primarily concerned with "those areas of Africa not yet independent or under white minority domination," with specific focus on South Africa.[104] While their work against white supremacy and colonialism is notable, especially as it laid the foundation for and extended into the anti-apartheid movement, it also entailed providing educational opportunities that, as historian Jim Harper explains, were intended to prepare African leaders as nation-builders in the model of capitalism and liberalism "before they fell 'victim' to the dictatorship of communism."[105] This often included organizing speaking tours for African leaders, which included special functions for Kwame Nkrumah and Ahmed Sékou Touré, who became the first president of independent Guinea in 1958. Crucially for the history centered here, the ACOA also facilitated a 1956 speaking tour for Tom Mboya, secretary-general of the Kenya Federation of Labor.[106]

In 1957, Nkrumah became the first head of state of an independent Ghana, an event celebrated by officials from sixty-nine countries and territories, including Vice President Richard Nixon, Martin Luther King Jr. and Coretta Scott King, A Philip Randolph, Ralph Bunch, and Congressman Adam Clayton Powell. In April 1958, he visited the United States and "palpable euphoria greeted him throughout black America."[107] Lester Granger of the National Urban League drew a line between the "hopes and aspirations of the black citizens in Arkansas in the Deep South and the triumph and expectations of the black men and women of Ghana."[108] At the time, Nkrumah had working relationships with both AAI and ACOA. Houser, of the ACOA, visited with him in Accra in 1954, and the organization staged events for him in the United States. Nkrumah was initially receptive to AAI's work as well. Just a year after he became head of state, for instance, AAI established an office in Accra and Nkrumah sent a statement of appreciation for "the good work your Institute aims to do for our two continents."[109] But 1957 also brought about several changes in other conditions. In October, the Soviet Union launched Sputnik. In March of 1958, the Central Committee of the Communist Party of the Soviet Union (CPSU), under the leadership of Nikita Khrushchev, distributed a plan to expand cultural relations, including educational projects, to provide scholarships to students from "colonial and dependent countries" to study in the USSR.[110] In February of 1960, Moscow announced plans to "bring thousands of African, Asian, and Latin American students to study" at the Peoples' Friendship University for the "Third World," putting increased pressure on the United States to respond with its own increases in recruitment.[111] The school opened its doors in September. US leaders in government, business, and education feared the Soviets' growing technological abilities and recruiting successes and looked to enhance their own efforts with new recruiting and education programs.

The most important programs in this effort were the African Scholarship Program of American Universities (ASPAU) and its direct predecessor, the Nigerian-American Scholarship Program (NASP), which took shape at Harvard in 1959, and an effort led by Tom Mboya of Kenya that became known as the African Airlifts. The African Airlifts, the most famous of which was the 1960 "Kennedy Airlift," began in 1957 when Mboya, a missionary- and British-educated Kenyan trade unionist, first visited the United States through the ACOA and secured eighty scholarships from colleges and universities for Kenyan students. He then worked with William Scheinman, a wealthy white member of the ACOA, who funded travel for thirty-six of the fifty-one students who came to the United States in 1957, with the remaining students pulling together funds from their families or communities.[112]

The following year, thirty-six more students came through the program, and then in 1959 Mboya, Scheinman, and other collaborators founded the African American Students Foundation (AASF) to facilitate funding for students. Notably, even when students had their primary costs of tuition and transport covered, they still had to meet the strict financial requirements of US immigration to attain a visa, which required demonstrating possession of at least $280. As Eric Burton argues, "even for East Africans in a salaried civil service position, it was virtually impossible to raise this amount individually, as it equaled several times the average U.S. $84 annual per-capita income of Africans in Kenya." As such, students had to rely on family and broader community, including their willingness to sell land and or take on debt.[113] In 1959, a student who would go on to be one of the Airlifts' most famous participants traveled from Kenya to study economics at the University of Hawai'i Manoa, becoming the first African student to enroll at the institution. His name was Barack Obama. While in Hawai'i, Obama married fellow student Stanley Ann Dunham when she was three months pregnant with their son. Obama would go on to leave Hawai'i, Dunham, and their soon-to-be son to travel to Harvard in pursuit of his PhD in economics. He received his MA in economics but, as his immigration records suggest, just before he could complete his doctorate the university administration collaborated with Immigration and Naturalization Services to have his visa revoked over concerns about his marital status and romantic life.[114]

It was only in 1960, however, that Mboya's Airlifts came to national prominence as a key point of the political theater in the presidential election between Nixon and John F. Kennedy. This was the case in large part because each candidate sought to signal support for civil rights and Black Americans without losing white Southern votes through their efforts to support the program.[115] Kennedy's advisors, in particular, were concerned that the Democratic hold on Southern states was at risk due to the pressures of the civil rights movement. As James Meriwether argues, both "campaigns needed ways to appeal to black voters without alienating the increasingly unsolid South" and both Nixon and Kennedy recognized that with the wave of decolonization "Africa seemed to be on the march," what others referred to as "the year of Africa."[116] They built on the final position of the Eisenhower administration, which understood the provision of educational assistance as being a double positive in that it could advance American interests and provide a counterpoint to the Soviet push into Africa "without overly challenging ideas of European rule."[117]

When Mboya needed financial support to enable the travel of 280 African students to the United States, he first turned to Nixon for assistance in securing the funds from the State Department in the early summer.[118] Especially after his trip to celebrate Ghana's independence in 1957, Nixon had centered US efforts in Africa in his work as vice president, leading one special assistant to the president for national security affairs to refer to him as the "'father' of a new African policy."[119] Mboya employed his relationship to Jackie Robinson to make his request. Robinson wrote Nixon a series of letters between June and July. There he communicates that funding the Airlift would make clear the State Department's investment in the "growth of democracy in Africa" but also serve as "*tangible evidence of [an] administration's dedication to civil rights since American Negros regard such a program as paramount issue.*"[120]

When appeals to Nixon proved fruitless, Mboya reached out, instead, to Kennedy, then serving as senator for Massachusetts, who had also taken up Africa, and especially the crisis in Algeria, as a mantel to display his investment in the "philosophy of freedom and independence for all peoples everywhere."[121] His campaign papers also extol the importance of educational exchange. Meriwether cites remarks Kennedy gave at a luncheon for the African Diplomatic Corps in June of 1960, where he advocated for a significant growth in "the number of African students—future African leaders—brought to this country for university training," a point he reiterated in future speeches as well.[122] Mboya technically met with Kennedy as a member of the Senate Foreign Relations Committee, but given that the State Department had already rejected a request for funding, Kennedy looked elsewhere for funding, turning to his family's foundation for $100,000 to support the students' travel.[123] Once word of the funding spread, Nixon and others urged the State Department to revise its decision, which it did. Mboya and the AASF, however, refused their funding since the Kennedy support was already in process.

Other events of the summer of 1960 also increased attention to African recruitment. As Mboya was soliciting support, a growing nationalist movement was gaining power in the mineral-rich Belgian colony of Congo, led by Patrice Lumumba. By June 30, the Republic of the Congo was independent, with Lumumba serving as the country's first prime minister. Just two weeks later, the province of Katanga seceded, throwing the region into chaos. Lumumba appealed to Soviet Premier Nikita Krushchev for support, which alarmed Washington since "the idea that an African leader could turn to the Soviets with little advance warning seemed quite plausible."[124] They saw Lumumba's relationship with the Soviets as a threat and searched for a way to remove him from leadership. On July 1, 1960, Nkrumah officially declared Ghana a republic with a new constitution and assumed the presidency. Of particular concern for the United States, the constitution included a clause that gave parliament "the power to provide for the surrender of the whole or any part of the sovereignty of Ghana once a United States of Africa was formed."[125] As Meriwether argues, the inclusion of this capacity marked Nkrumah's belief, shared with other anti-colonial nationalists, that the definition of the nation-state is not in fact static and, as Adom Getachew argues, "that nationalism was also a vehicle for demanding democracy and international equality" in ways that did not simply capitulate to American versions of these concepts.[126]

In August 1960, Lumumba traveled to Accra. He and Nkrumah signed a secret agreement aligning Ghana and Congo in a union of African states.[127] According to Ama Biney's biography, under these conditions, Nkrumah's formal policy of nonalignment was put under pressure as Lumumba connected with the Soviets. In his 1967 book *Challenge of the Congo*, Nkrumah makes clear that he saw the events in Congo as a "conspiracy . . . carried on under the banner of anti-communism."[128] The US government's desire to manage the threat it saw in Lumumba was accomplished when he was executed by US-aligned separatists in January 1961.[129] In response, Nkrumah took an increasingly revolutionary and socialist stance in his foreign policy, convinced of the necessity for a union of African countries, which he advocated for through the Casablanca Group. Shortly after, the Peoples' Friendship University for "Third World" students was renamed after Patrice Lumumba, cementing precisely the relationship the US government had tried to undo.[130] This context illuminates *Newsweek*'s decision to show Kenyan's students reading about Patrice Lumumba University in the image at the beginning of this chapter.

These events only further galvanized the United States' efforts in African student recruitment, at least in the short term. In addition to the public attention given to Mboya's efforts, David Henry, the director of admissions at Harvard University, also entered into the field of African student recruitment. He built on a project initiated in 1959 by Stephen O. Awokoya, the first minister of education in Western Nigeria, to bring Nigerian students to the United States. Henry was "aware of what was at stake with the upcoming independence of many African countries and concerned about Harvard's international stature."[131] Awokoya and Henry worked with AAI and the US government, specifically the US International Cooperation Administration (ICA), and procured support from the Ford Foundation, the Carnegie Corporation of New York, and the Rockefeller Brothers Fund to expand the Nigerian-American Scholarship Program to the rest of the continent through the ASPAU, which brought twenty-four students to the United States in the fall of 1960.[132] When approached about participating in ASPAU, Nkrumah refused due to his suspicion of the US government in the wake of Lumumba's assassination.[133] He was more interested in the Africanization of education and wanted to cultivate a "socialist-minded intelligentsia" toward such ends. In February 1961, he founded the Ideological Institute of Winneba, and in April, he signed an agreement to promote studies in the USSR.[134] Despite Nkrumah's resistance, the following year the Ghanaian government did eventually permit students to participate in ASPAU, though under specific conditions that limited participation to students in chemistry, physics, agronomy, and other applied sciences.

## The Limits of Racial Liberalism

But the US focus on recruiting and educating students from Africa was short-lived. By the time the *Newsweek* article was published in 1963, several historical shifts were at play. Domestically, the push toward the 1964 Civil Rights Act shifted attention away from managing critiques of US racial politics internationally and toward new laws that served to, at least facially, remake legal structures in the name of equality. As Mary Dudziak argues, in his first months in office, Lyndon Johnson employed his "particular skills" as a Texan and a legislator to move both the 1964 Civil Rights Act and the 1965 Immigration and Nationality Act through Congress. This was in part because he was encouraged to do so by international pressures, and "Africans and others paid close attention to American race relations."[135] Internationally, however, there was a concerted shift away from Africa and toward other parts of the world where US interests were seen as more at play, especially Vietnam and Southeast Asia more broadly. Dudziak also asserts that "the initial romantic enthusiasm for

African independence of many white American liberals" had subsided. Increasingly, African nationalists came to be read in parallel to Indigenous sovereignty movements in the United States, instead of as American revolutionaries. In more conservative assessments, this lined up neatly with the "rising militancy" of the civil rights movements and, in Johnson's estimation, Black people within and beyond the nation's borders "were getting harder to deal with."[136]

Efforts to educate noncitizen students in the United States, particularly those invested in the education of African students, bore the consequences of these changes. They increasingly confronted a deepening perception that "U.S. scholarship programs for undergraduate study in America create dissatisfied, misfit elites in many African countries," while, at the same time, a new image of "the alienated foreigner" was prevalent in America.[137] Reflecting these factors, the *Newsweek* article's discussion of African students is especially fraught. As discussed above, Nkrumah is figured as the primary example of noncitizen education gone awry, his failure to leave the United States with "stars and stripes" in his eyes discussed to justify CIA surveillance of students in America and upon their return to their home country.

Despite these concerns, at least in early 1963, Elfin, Montague, and the governmental officials they quote still saw great merit in the project of international education, especially in the competition with the USSR. As the authors explain, "in the academic struggle between East and West, the U.S. seems to have the clear, if not decisive, edge." Despite "reports that while 'American degrees' did not enjoy the same prestige as diplomas from Oxford or the Sorbonne, they are still more valuable abroad than a diploma from, say, Moscow's Patrice Lumumba University."[138] Furthermore, they continue, "Red recruiters, moreover, are handicapped by language (far more Asians and Africans speak English than Russian), by climate (the reputation of the bitter Moscow winter has spread to most secondary schools in tropical Africa), and by the theory that anyone susceptible to indoctrination deserves a college education. The Communists, not unexpectedly, often have a difficult time filling student quotas."

Still, the article also reflects concerns that the recruitment and education process is not without risks. On the final page, the article warns, "There is little question that the process could be tightened to prevent academic misfits from slipping through." To explain the consequences of not doing so, Elfin and Montague turn to an interview with Steven Muller, a Cornell government professor, who would go on to serve as president of Johns Hopkins from 1972–1990. According to Muller:

> "With an American student who can't make the grade, you tell him as gracefully as you can and hope he finds himself somewhere else," says

> Prof. Steven Muller of Cornell's government department. "However, a foreign student who doesn't earn a degree sometimes feels so ashamed he's almost incapable of going home. At Cornell we're not going to hand out watered-down degrees, but are we going to send foreign students home so embittered that they become lifelong enemies of the US?"[139]

Crucial to this configuration is that the imagined student would not remain in the United States—theirs was always a journey that required return.

# Conclusion

## *The University Double Bind: The Imperial Model Minority and the Records We Keep*

> [T]he putative center welcomes selective inhabitants of the margin in order to better exclude the margin. And it is the center that offers the official explanation; or, the center is defined and reproduced by the explanation that it can express.
>
> —GAYATRI CHAKRAVORTY SPIVAK

> Our circumscribed productivity cannot be dismissed as a mere keeping of records. We are part of the records we keep.
>
> –GAYATRI CHAKRAVORTY SPIVAK

> There is no document of civilization which is not at the same time a document of barbarism. And just as such a document is not free of barbarism, barbarism taints also the manner in which it is transmitted from one owner to another. A historical materialist therefore disassociates himself from it as far as possible. He regards it as his task to brush history against the grain.
>
> —WALTER BENJAMIN

This book argues that from the inception of institutions of higher education in what is now broadly recognized as the United States through to the early 1960s, efforts to recruit and educate noncitizen students—and especially students racialized as nonwhite and thus excluded by race-based immigration laws before 1965—were formulated with the intention that students would return to their home polities equipped with the knowledge and values to operate as agents of America's "empire of liberty" and its various permutations and developments. The April 1963 *Newsweek* article discussed in Part III, "Foreign Students: Diplomas and Diplomacy," illustrates how the post-1960 university repeats and extends this process, particularly in its warnings regarding the necessity for CIA supervision of Black students from Africa, like Kwame Nkrumah, a noncitizen student who studied in the United States and went on to become the first president of Ghana and strong advocate for a version of Pan-Africanism that troubled the presumptive power of the United States.[1]

Yet, other threads of the article also highlight the significant changes afoot during this period, as domestic and global concerns gave way to a reconfiguration of racial and national logics of belonging, and sought to utilize universities and noncitizen students in the process. This is especially apparent in the stories Mel Elfin and Constance Montague tell about students from Asia, such as Mohammed Sa'aid, which effectively demonstrate the efforts of the US state and popular publications to cultivate a vision of a more inclusive multiracial America, albeit one organized around anti-Blackness. Across the chapters, it becomes evident that the university, the state, and capital have long pursued agendas to manage the education and movement of students from outside their direct political jurisdiction—from Indigenous students in the British colonial period through to the present. Through the noncitizen student, this effort has attempted to expand, evolve, and resolve the contradictions of US universalism, liberty, and power in the service of what should properly be recognized as US empire, fundamentally shaping the form, function, and funding of institutions of higher education through to the present.

This endeavor has taken shape through the cultivated presence and performance of nonwhite noncitizen students on campuses and through their conditional and temporary inclusion in the university, capital, and the nation. Positioned as such, students came to play a vital role in the perpetually shifting articulations of racial and class logics, especially as they are inflected by questions of gender and sexuality, race, religion, and political affiliation. The writing of Gayatri Spivak, one of the students featured alongside Sa'aid by *Newsweek* who would go on to occupy the highest echelons of the US academy, is useful for such arguments, given her interest in the work and often violent effects of the US academy. As she wrote years after the *Newsweek* article was published, "[T]he putative center welcomes selective inhabitants of the margin in order to better exclude the margin. And it is the center that offers the official explanation; or, the center is defined and reproduced by the explanation that it can express."[2]

Spivak's analysis can be used to read the endgame of student recruitment and education: The *Newsweek* article and its afterlives serve as a trace of this stunted incorporative process in the period just before the new racial formations of the civil rights era concretized in the discourse of the model minority and newly inclusive immigration policy after 1965. Spivak's writing predicted how the inclusion of select noncitizen students, once and potentially future "inhabitants of the margin," within the universities of the metropole had the dual effect of enabling a better exclusion of the margin while simultaneously defining or redefining the center itself. Significantly, this was the very "center" that new policies regulating the movement of students during this period required students to both desire and, contradictorily, promise to leave—creating and revealing a series of double binds for students, institutions of higher education, and state and capital.[3]

As discussed in the introduction, Michel Foucault contends that knowledge predominantly functions by cutting. My interest here is in the knowledge the university validates and disseminates for the purposes of severing interconnections by defining and evaluating differences, people, resources, and more, often with an eye toward extractable value. In this way, universities are fundamentally conservative capitalist institutions in their work to produce and package products and people. Universities, as well as the institutional and personal debt they run on, are instruments of racial capitalism that seek to effectively capture and make individuals through a process of "differentiation and dominant comparative logics." As Jodi Melamed argues, these processes "create 'certainties' of discreteness, distinctness, and discontinuity—of discrete identities, distinct territorializations and sovereignties, and discontinuities between the political and the economic, the internal and the external, and the valued and the devalued."[4] However, as Melamed goes on to argue, that these institutions, racial capitalism in her theorization and the university in my extension of it, "need [. . .] to invalidate the terms of relationality . . . might reveal [their] weakness as much as [their] strength."[5] Melamed turns to the scholarly formation of ethnic studies, and specifically Cedric Robinson's *Black Marxism*, as an "apposite example" to the anti-relational impulse. Both disrupt anti-relational logics by making legible "the past, present, and future existence of the Black radical tradition."[6] *Degrees of Empire*, in turn, provides a way to think of the figure of the noncitizen student and the work of study in and of the university toward similarly disruptive ends in hopes of unsettling contemporary understandings of the purpose and constituency the university serves.

By way of conclusion, I turn here to the concept of the imperial minority and to Spivak's story and theorization of such a position. I do so not because she is somehow exemplary—her story is actually not at all "typical"—but because she is unique in the perspective she provides on the university and its perils and possibilities. As with the writings of noncitizen students cited throughout this project, I turn to her as a figure and a scholar, as a source of information and of insight that can help us grapple with the specific structures of law, knowledge, race, and the nation that shaped her educational experiences in the university, as well as her, and our, present conditions. Through her story and writing, I consider how the history of noncitizen students told here makes all the more apparent the constitutive role of the university and university-based scholars in producing both "the records we keep" and the conditions of the contemporary university. Despite the university's work to individualize and separate, the processes through which knowledge is continuously created, circulated, acquired, and reformulated are, or at least have been, collective ones in the classroom, meeting space, laboratory, office, picket line, dance floor, bedroom, on the quad, and across and beyond campuses.[7] These spaces of study and possibility disrupt efforts to program structures of knowledge, ways of relating, and even people themselves. As much as border policies seek to separate and regulate, the student visa also functions as a mechanism that conjoins the state, capital, and the university, structuring the effort to make borders and manage the movement of select students. The conditions of this relationship continue to shape the often-contradictory work of the university in the present and the double binds that institutions and people within them navigate.

## The Imperial Model Minority in, of, for, and against Empire

As discussed in Part III, efforts to recruit, educate, incorporate, and manage students from Asia, Africa, the Caribbean, and the Middle East on US campuses functioned as a pivotal and anticipatory component of the reconfiguration of US racial logics in the aftermath of World War II—a reconfiguration that at once expanded the bounds of whiteness and simultaneously sedimented narrow assessments of proper personhood and potential citizenship. I am not interested in suggesting that nonwhite noncitizen students were "like" the model minority or in some way analogous to US minority subjects who "make it" and thus supposedly prove the viability of the meritocratic promise of liberalism and capitalism. Their relationship to the university, the state, and capital is distinct from that of citizens racialized as outside of whiteness. It is helpful to turn to Madeline Hsu's exploration of the role of Chinese students in the transition of Chinese people in the United States, "from being racialized as an unwanted yellow peril to become welcomed model minorities within the space of one generation," to consider a broader geography and set of racial logics.[8] The figuration of some nonwhite noncitizen students as desirable, malleable, and temporary participants on campuses and within the nation-state, did, however, seem to function as a historical prefiguration of the model minority. This was possible precisely because the selection and management process for this group of students was created through immigration laws and policies that conditioned both their recruitment and their experiences in the United States. As a nascent and imperial form of the model minority, nonwhite noncitizen students had to negotiate the contradictions of expanding empire and the limits of liberal inclusion.

Victor Bascara argues that "[at] the heart of the model-minority myth is the notion that American culture can adapt to absorb persons and populations who had once been deemed explicitly, in the language of the Alien Land Laws, 'ineligible for citizenship' and, in the language of colonization, 'un-fit for self-government.'"[9] Bascara makes two important moves here. One is to link critiques of this new model of incorporating racialized individuals to the US states' imperial pursuits, both past and present. The second is to tie the model minority myth to a citizen-making project. Importantly, however, the legal conditions of their presence in the United States meant that noncitizen students could never fully embody this ideal trope; while the model minority was largely a matter of racial categorization, it also designated a specific relationship to the US nation-state: citizenship and its pursuit. As visa holders whose presence in the country is conditioned as necessarily temporary, the noncitizen student is not allowed to pursue citizenship. In many ways, however, it is precisely this constitutively ambivalent relationship to the state and the university that allowed the nonwhite noncitizen student to play such a crucial role in the remapping of US racial logics in the mid-century.

As "non-immigrant visitors," noncitizen students could never fulfill all the criteria of Americanness necessary to be "model minorities"; they are located, instead, somewhere between the model minority and the permanent immigrant. Lisa Lowe's essential work reminds us that in the dominant white American imaginary, the figure of the permanent immigrant is "at odds with the cultural, racial, and linguistic forms of the nation" and thus exists "in a site that defers and displaces the temporality of assimilation" necessary to embody the "model minority."[10] For individuals, this position can be quite precarious, yet, as Lauren Berlant argues, for the nation-state, such a figuration is quite ideal. As they theorize, in the imaginary relationship of the "immigrant" to the nation, the immigrant's desire for America constitutes the desirability of "America." As such, the problem of immigration for the nation-state is not that it is exclusionary but rather that once an immigrant becomes "American," there is a tendency toward being "complacent [and] unimaginative" because the driving force of the desire for America has been resolved.[11]

The noncitizen student's status as a temporary visitor—held in a particular kind of limbo and required by the terms of their visa to at once retain strong ties to another country while making clear their desire for the United States—creates a double bind that positions them as a proto-American global citizen, always in process and always desiring. If, as Bascara has argued, "the management of alterity is fundamentally the project and promise of imperialism," the indefinite duration of the noncitizen student's definitionally temporary status of conditional inclusion positions them as an ideal subject of the state and university.[12] In other words, the nonwhite noncitizen student is a crucial figure in the way it lays bare the global stakes of the model minority. The concept of the model minority emerged as part of a global project of state, capital, and the university. The student visa functions as a mechanism through which the state, capital, and university manage their contradictions, creating a complex space where noncitizen students can critique US imperialism while also furthering and benefiting from its agendas. Think, for instance, of Sa'aid's critique of Americans as "obnoxious rich capitalists" discussed in Chapter 7.

## Gayatri Spivak's Inhabitation of the University

In American Studies, postcolonial studies, and other fields and disciplines that ask critical questions of power, identity, and institutions, discussions of complicity frequently turn to Spivak's work, and particularly her argument that it is necessary to work through our relationships to "that *we* cannot not want," whether that be recognition, human rights, or inclusion.[13] While Spivak repeats this construction across several texts, at least twice she completes the clause by writing about "that *we* cannot not want to inhabit." This can be understood as a paradigmatic example of what Spivak discusses in her 2012 *An Aesthetic Education* as the "double bind of the postcolonial and the metropolitan migrant regarding the enlightenment," or, perhaps the university itself.[14] As she explains in the book's prologue, her work has often troubled audiences' expectations, leaving them "puzzled by the auto-critique of a member of the model minority," as they witness "metropolitan minority and postcolonial majority perspectives in a tug of war in the same subject."[15] Setting up the series of essays to follow, Spivak explains "that as a literary intellectual, [she] is here to use [her] imagination, not only to imagine the predicament of diaspora, exile, refuge, but also to deny resolutely that the manifest destiny of the United States is [to appear] to give asylum to the world."[16] Reading the collected essays retrospectively in the book's introduction, she describes the project as "productively undoing . . . [a] legacy of the European Enlightenment—the aesthetic."[17] To explain this approach of "productive undoing," Spivak frames the chapters as a collective effort to "[learn] the double bind," rather than to attempt to resolve it.[18] The double bind of inhabitation can also be taken up as a productive way to think the relationship of the noncitizen student to the university and, even more capaciously, a more general relationship of those of us who imagine a more just world to the contradictory histories and functions of these institutions.

In thinking about Spivak's inhabitation of the US university, now for over sixty years, it is worth taking seriously how the act of inhabiting a space, an institution, or a logic has co-constitutive effects. Several transformations in the university and the imperial nation-state have transpired since the 1960s, but all of them have been shaped, or constituted, at least in part, by the conditioned inclusion of nonwhite noncitizen students and governed by the basic framework of immigration and visa law this book tracks. Reading Spivak, her historical locations, and her theorization of questions of representation, incorporation, marginality, institutionality, and reproduction through the historical materialist approach of this project opens up crucial questions about the role of nonwhite noncitizen students as not only the objects of scholarly interest and institutional investment but also, clearly, as subjects of knowledge production themselves. It requires a consideration of how the "circumscribed productivity" of these former students "cannot be dismissed as a mere keeping of records." Instead, they "are part of the records we keep" and contribute to the record-making process.[19] And opening such questions of complicity, of the double bind, also reflects on the rest of us as occupants of and participants in this process too.

In their respective work on Spivak as a figure and a scholar, Sangeeta Ray (the author of a book-length study of Spivak's work), Mridula Nath Chakraborty, Jenny Sharpe, and others discuss the 1963 *Newsweek* article as a key component of the archive of Spivak's life—a rare moment of insight into the youth of the woman who has gone on to become one of the most highly regarded literary studies scholars of the later twentieth and early twenty-first centuries.[20] Describing Spivak in his foreword to the 1988 collection of her essays, *In Other Worlds: Essays in Cultural Politic*, Colin MacCabe homes in on her status as a former noncitizen student and thus as "the model product of an Indian undergraduate and an American graduate education—probably the most scholarly combination in the planet."[21] Both Ray and Chakraborty describe the *Newsweek* article as Spivak's first interview, thus placing significant importance on this moment given the prominence of the interview form throughout Spivak's career. To call the article Spivak's first interview might, however, be a bit overstated. The conversation for the piece only resulted in the inclusion of a single preternatural yet quintessential quote from Spivak. In a pullout box beneath a black and white portrait of Spivak wearing a cotton kurta and trousers with a draped dupatta, sitting, reading, pen in hand, finger on the page, staring furrow-browed at the camera, the caption reads: "INDIA. Gayatri Chakravorty, Cornell: *Why must Americans smile at people they haven't met? Still, I like my fellow students. We have our common traumas*."[22]

In a 1988 interview conducted by Angela Ingram and included in a collection of conversations with the scholar, Spivak references the *Newsweek* article as she discusses the particularities of race and class across the United States, India, and Britain. Reflecting on her interview with Elfin and Montague, whom she refers to simply as "these blokes," she tells Ingram:

> I had absolutely no compunction in producing this deathless line. I only know it because I got hate mail you wouldn't believe. I said—and I was being honest because I felt that I should say what I thought—"I don't understand why Americans who don't know you smile at you on the street. I've been traumatized." Can you imagine? Really. This was a very genuine kind of a thing. I now know that it was an astute thing to say. I was a luscious nineteen-year-old, and they smiled at me because, to an extent, they didn't really think. It's like women in *National Geographic* where they are allowed to have bare breasts. I was not someone with whom they had the same rules, the same sexual code of behavior.[23]

In response, Ray writes, "[r]eading this passage always makes me giddy. There is so much to unpack here" and goes on to observe that in her exchange with Elfin and Montague and in her reflection on the exchange with Ingram, Spivak manages to simultaneously invoke the politics of race, class, gender, caste, and I would add nationality and sexuality, to "challenge the notion of an essential foreigner captured in a seemingly unproblematic rendition of the Indian female student."[24] It is worth considering, however, how even as this "challenge" might trouble essentialist understandings of difference, it concomitantly contributed to emerging ideas about the malleability of race that bolstered and became productive for the emergent logics of racial liberalism. It is also significant that Spivak's recollection of the quote, in which she asserts her traumatization, deviates from what is quoted in the article, which invokes a kind of shared or "common" experience of trauma, seemingly creating a relationship of sameness rather than difference.

Chakraborty, on the other hand, reads in the 1963 comment "the germs of the ideas for Spivak's early feminist articles about the intersection between sex, gender, identity, origins and speech" but also gestures to the broader historical and geopolitical context of the article and its attention to the expanding recruitment of students from decolonizing global spaces caught up in what Elfin and Montague refer to as "the ideological struggle between West and

Newsweek—Tony Rollo

**INDIA. Gayatri Chakravorty, Cornell:** ***Why must Americans smile at people they haven't met? Still, I like my fellow students. We have our common traumas.***

Figure 10. Portrait of Gayatri Spivak, a student from India studying at Cornell University, as photographed for *Newsweek* and featured on the third page of the April 22, 1963 article. @Newsweek (YouTube).

East."[25] As she explains, the motivations for noncitizen student recruitment and education were always complicated by the fact that the students were a "much-needed presence" even as they were "continually challenged and looked upon with suspicion in the capitalist, multicultural nation."[26] That is, students were incorporated, but also held at bay, in ways that disparately impacted students from different places and of different races, genders, and religions. As Chapters 6 and 7 illustrate, this limited and varied inclusion of otherness invariably shaped noncitizen student experiences, the programs developed on campuses, and the institutions themselves. As Spivak argues in the epigraph included above, the inclusion of select "inhabitants of the margin" has the dual effect of enabling a better exclusion of the margin while simultaneously defining the center. What does this differential inclusion illuminate about the form and function of the US university in the mid-twentieth century and the foundations it produced for the university and nation-state of the present?

Like Chakraborty, Jenny Sharpe's more recent discussion of the *Newsweek* article in her review of Spivak's 2012 book *An Aesthetic Education in the Era of Globalization* locates the 1963 interview and Spivak herself in a broader history of the US university and the transnational movement of students after World War II.[27] It is significant that Spivak is, and even could have been, included as part of an article in a popular, liberal-leaning magazine such as *Newsweek* in the early 1960s. Spivak, as Sharpe points out, "belongs to a group of Asian and African intellectuals who came to the United States . . . as foreign students in a postwar effort to expand the subject-making project initiated in British India."[28] That is, she is part of a group of students who were exceptionally included in and even recruited to the United States during a period of time when individuals marked by their racial and ethnic difference from a then-consolidating form of American whiteness were, for the most part, formally legally excluded from becoming a part of the US nation-state and were only just beginning to be welcome on elite university campuses. As Sharpe discusses, Spivak did not follow the path prescribed for students at the time. "Instead of returning to India to train an elite cosmopolitan class of leaders," she remained in the United States, reaching the pinnacle of success in the academy, and "embarked on educating teachers for Indian village schools."

The "subject-making project" of colonial and neocolonial education is often understood as a unidirectional flow of logics and ideologies into colonial and neocolonial spaces from the metropole. Yet, as many scholars of transnational American Studies and postcolonial studies have argued, these processes also invariably, if unintentionally and unevenly, reverberate to shape the shifting logics and ideologies of the metropole as well; "the center is defined." In his reading of Spivak, Roderick Ferguson illustrates that the processes through which students are brought from the "margin" to the "metropole" enact a process of identification that makes "difference legible and admissible within institutional realms." Crucially, in doing so, institutions including the state and the university, "mediate the relationship between diasporic subjects and a new thing called 'marginality'" enacting a form of "[p]olitical emancipation" reduced to "the spirit of hegemonic institutionalization."[29] In this configuration, "modes of minority difference would be selectively incorporated, but not for the good of social redistribution."[30] Instead, the presence of difference could be instrumentalized toward any number of purposes, including eased labor extraction and the management of other forms of difference, as is the case with the logic of the model minority and its work to discipline minority subjects who fail to appropriately replicate white-adjacent ways of being. In that the university is uniquely positioned as a site of education, knowledge production, and individualization, it seems necessary to attend to the particular effects of the incorporation of students from elsewhere who embodied a marked form of difference from a whitewashed "American-ness" dominant on US university campuses.

Returning to Spivak's 2012 book is helpful on this point. Her broad object of analysis across the text is globalization and what she identifies as its twin modes of operation: capital and data, which combine to function as "information command." Her more narrow target, however, is the humanities and their diminishment by the university in its pursuit of a place of purpose within globalization. More sharply and directly, she writes, "the general terrain of the book is tertiary and post graduate education, the reproduction of citizens and teachers."[31] This project operates as a "legacy of the Enlightenment"—a liberal education that sets out to "privatize belief, rationalize the transcendent," a project that well suits capitalism. However, the fact that US universities have always required, at least in part, a kind of collectivizing—a worldly bringing together for the purposes of study—has also meant that they facilitate less-desirable forms of cosmopolitan connection. Take, for instance, Spivak's reflection on her exposure to the civil rights movement:

> the voice that still echoes from the Civil Rights/Black Power movement is from the Ocean Hill-Brownsville School District Struggle of 1968. I had received my Ph.D. the previous year. My experience in India, as it attempted to decolonize its school-system, was not far behind. This is why it is not the more famous struggles that I monumentalize but rather words retained by force of memory. I am not even sure who it was that said them. It may have been Reverend Galamaison: "This is a struggle against educational colonization." The other day I caught a voice on

> television of a little African-American girl who was then a student in that school district, now a mature woman who spoke of her experience and remarked: "We became third world. We became international."[32]

Here, Spivak illustrates a point made earlier in her chapter in stating her "conviction that we, the so-called oppositional discourses in the United States, must find a practical basis for unity in global contemporaneity, even if it nurtures false hope."[33] Key to this is the "persistent and shifting pursuit of the global history of the present," one that recognizes, looks to, and cultivates more internationalist and post-nationalist perspectives.[34] Such a perspective, as Lowe argues, requires surfacing "often obscured connections" across borders and disciplinary boundaries constructed by the "modern division of knowledge into academic disciplines, focused on discrete areas and objects of interest to the modern national university."[35]

One point of this "unity" that Spivak invokes seems, somewhat contradictorily, to be precisely her resistance to acquiring US citizenship. As she told Bulan Lahiri of *The Hindu* in a 2011 interview, Spivak is not "an American citizen," though her brother and mother both naturalized.[36] Instead, she occupies the position of resident alien, "a tax-paying non-citizen with a semi-permanent visa," a decidedly worldly figure who, despite a "tenaciously held territoriality," is "without significant civil rights" and thus "lacks access to the more salient abstractions of an everyday civility."[37] But it might be precisely this positionality and what she elsewhere describes as "the new immigrant intellectual's negotiable nationality" that can function as a vital intervention in the nationalistic thinking of and about the university in the present.[38] This is not to imagine the resident alien or the noncitizen student as a magical figure who somehow obliterates the double bind of the university/state/capital tether. Rather, it serves to illustrate the potential and possibility of another kind of inhabitation or being in and in relation to the university with an awareness of its violences, conservatism, and contradictions. It may also provide a way into thinking with a kind of educated hope, a way to maintain a relationship to the university that refuses narratives of the institution's benevolence.[39] A way of inhabiting the university and making use of its massive concentration of both material and temporal resources without allowing it to fully consume and possess one's most basic being.

## The University Double Bind

It is impossible to understand the work, the history, the function, or the future of the US university without reading it through its entanglements with the state and capital. Doing so requires disabusing oneself of the myth that the university is or ever has been bound by the borders of the nation-state, rather than animated in the service of creating such borders. Similarly, it is crucial to recognize that the enlightenment and progress professed as the university's guiding light is in the service of a civilizing mission that, as Walter Benjamin observed in 1940, has always been "at the same time" one of barbarism.[40] Much like Spivak's concern regarding the "records we keep," Benjamin draws attention to the documents of such processes as well as the manner of their transmission. Spivak's "we," which I read as college and university faculty, and the understanding "we're" trying to accomplish, are far better served by, as Spivak suggests, "learning the double bind." In part, this might mean contending with the ways we are necessarily in and of the university—educated in it, working in it, often even living in it. I hope we're also able to think about the ways many of us are, reluctantly or not, of this university—trained through it, existing in it, and sustained in our lives through our relationships to it.

But the university is in a double bind as well. In whatever small, temporary, or conditional sense, the university is of us too. Its being is constituted in part through our presence (or the withdrawal or rejection of our presence)—as well as the sprawling communities that extend from it—from the army of laborers around the world who generate the value that bloats some institution endowments to the people whose lives are enhanced or destroyed by the medicines, weapons, poetry, and analysis developed in campus labs, libraries, offices, and classrooms.[41] What responsibility do we have to act from our position in these institutions—from our places within this great concentration of resources, knowledge, and capacity? More pressingly, as I write this conclusion, Robin D. G. Kelley recently asked, "What is the responsibility of intellectuals committed to fighting fascism and genocide? How do we refuse and resist complicity when our own institutions are complicit? And what might we learn from earlier antifascist and anticolonial struggles?"[42] Kelley answers his question by rightly pressing the need to move beyond the university to "cast our lot with the insurgent class and enter the struggle" by joining movements fighting for tangible, life-making change in "tenants' rights, affordable housing, disability and reproductive justice, and trans rights; resisting ICE raids; joining the Debt Collective or the Poor People's Campaign in their fight for a livable future; supporting independent left think tanks such as the Hampton Institute, the People's Policy Project, the Institute for Policy Studies, or the Tricontinental Institute for Social Research; to building political capacity through groups like the Working Families Party." But I also concur with his caution against "abandoning the university."

The genealogy laid out in this book makes it clear that the university is a site of violence. It has functioned in core ways as a technology of power and expansion for the US state and as an empire. Full stop. And it has operated as a place and time of potential, especially as it has served as a space where people meet and dwell together, where the pursuit of "progress" is taken or goes awry because it cannot be determined in advance. Dwelling in this double bind feels necessary because in the space of the present, understandings of the past are remade in the service of a different present and new possibilities for the future. That palimpsest that is knowledge and knowledge making, the records themselves, are remade. The goal is certainly not to redeem the university or even those of us who exist in and through it, as if doing so is even possible. In the harshness of our present, as the state attempts to disappear and deport students and scholars for their work organizing against genocide, and as university leaders and boards all too often and all too readily collude with them, it is also necessary to see points of promise and of hope in the refusal of many to submit to efforts to divide, especially along lines of citizenship status.

# Acknowledgments

Like most academic books, and especially most scholars' first, this one is the culmination of many years spent in relation to and building relations through the university, which is also its primary object of study. I first began thinking critically about the university in my first years as an undergraduate student at Wesleyan University in the late 1990s. As I complete this project, I am back at the same institution, now as an assistant professor teaching in some of the same classrooms and alongside some of the same faculty with whom I studied twenty-five years ago. Throughout and in between, I've been fortunate to think with, work alongside, and learn from an array of scholars—some faculty, some students, and some with no formal relationship to the university at all. It is perhaps in part because of this recursive trajectory that I am reticent about attempts to bracket myself off from the university—to imagine who I would be, how I would think, or what I would know without coming up through and then remaining in relation to it. As I discuss in the conclusion, this is part of what I understand as the university double bind, a dynamic relationship that constitutes my being in a range of ways, but also, I contend, the university's.

This perspective is not shared by some of the people whose writing about the university I most appreciate and draw inspiration from. Fred Moten and Stefano Harney, for instance, quite famously advise "the subversive intellectual" to "be in but not of" the university. Roderick Ferguson and Robin D. G. Kelley echo this position. Still, my understanding of the university as a relation has been buoyed by my relationships organized through it and the debts I have accrued along the way. Here, I am again inspired by Moten and Harney and their theorization and valorization of debt as a queer relation, one in which debt functions as a mode of socialization, a way of relating that refuses the kind of cutting and differentiation at the core of so much knowledge production, as I also discuss in the conclusion of this book. This conceptualization of debt can be troubling—under finance capital, debt is the thing to be feared, avoided, paid down, or paid off. But, following Moten and Harney, I do not wish to void my debt. I have no aspiration of settling the ledger of kindness or support. I accept these debts and carry them forward with hope to proliferate them into the future. While I cannot take full credit, so to speak, for this project, I do accept responsibility for any errors or oversights, including those I may have failed to include in these acknowledgments.

My efforts to think the university with and through the figure of the noncitizen student initially took shape as a graduate student in the University of California, Davis's Graduate Group in Cultural Studies. There, I was fortunate to work closely with Caren Kaplan, who served as the chair of my dissertation and the chair of the graduate group. Along with her partner, Eric Smoodin, Caren fostered a deeply intellectual and convivial space that allowed students to pursue individual scholarly interests in innovative and creative ways while simultaneously encouraging us to find connections to each other and the world beyond academia—to refuse the negligence that professionalism and disciplinarity so often require. At Davis, I was also advised by Omnia El-Shakry and Beth Freeman, who each generously schooled me in their respective disciplines while also pushing me to use the insights of historiographic methods, close reading, and critical theorization to complicate and refine my analysis of the university. This project is immeasurably stronger and more capacious due to their guidance. In graduate classes, as a teaching assistant, and occasionally on a dance floor, I also benefited from the thoughtful guidance of Parama Roy, Julie Sze, Juana María Rodríguez, Robert Irwin, Joe Dumit, Kathleen Frederickson, and Cathy Kudlick.

The members of my cohort of cult studs, and those who came before and after, were also instrumental to my life and study in graduate school. Much of my thinking was shaped in conversations across classrooms, car rides, conference and protest organizing, and more with Tallie Ben-Daniel, Christina Owens, Cathy Hannabach, Terry Park, Magalí Rabasa, Sam Aranke, Sandy Gomez, Ingrid Lagos, Sara Bernstein, Xan Chacko, May Ee Wong, and especially with the "queers for public ed" collective, including Tristan Josephson, Toby Beauchamp, Benjamin D'Harlingue, Liz Montegary, and honorary cult stud, Cyn Degnan. I'm so grateful to count them as lifelong friends. All of this was enhanced as others joined the fold, including Yasmine Orangi, Kryst Muroya, Yael Kropsky, Lezlie Frye, and Nick Mitchell. With and from them, I came to understand so much about solidarity, clarity of vision, commitment, and how to throw a good party.

When I returned to Wesleyan in 2016, I joined an unusual sociology department, the only kind likely to see my work as belonging within its ranks, thanks in many ways to encouragement from Greg Goldberg, who I was fortunate to befriend at a Cultural Studies Association meeting, along with Craig Willse, who would go on to provide vital edits on an early version of this book and parts of what I hope will constitute the next. The rest of the department, then composed of Robyn Autry, Mary Ann Clawson, Jonathan Cutler, Kerwin Kaye, Basak Kus, Courtney Patterson-Faye, Rob Rosenthal, and now including Ben Haber, have provided a collegial academic home and ample latitude to explore ideas in writing and in the classroom. Thanks to this allowance, I've had the opportunity to work with several classes of Wesleyan students in courses organized around various spokes and iterations of this project—I extend my deep appreciation to the outstanding students in these classes and especially to fall 2025's Sociology 309, in which nine extraordinary students read and provided insightful feedback on the entirety of this book.

My return to Middletown also brought me back into relation with a community of scholars who helped shape my time as an undergraduate and just after. Christina Crosby and Natasha Korda, who advised my undergraduate thesis, welcomed me back to campus with open arms, minds, and homes. Christina and her partner, Janet Jakobson, who has supported my scholarship since the early 2000s as well, provided a warmth and depth of camaraderie and mentorship I could never have hoped for. I am so grateful for the years I had with Christina and her brilliance, though they were far too short, and thankful for the wisdom and kindness Janet continues to provide. Though I never ended up working with Janet at the Barnard Center for Research on Women, she kindly included me in numerous events and the BCRW community over the years, experiences that repeatedly reinvigorate my belief in the necessity of definitively feminist experiments in world-making. I also have a deep appreciation for other senior faculty members who have provided such valuable support and comradeship: Margot Weiss, Matt Garrett, Victoria Pitts-Taylor, Mary-Jane Rubenstein, Anthony Hatch, Indira Karmacheti, David Constantine, Justine Quijada, Jesse Torgenson, and Anu Sharma. And to the faculty with whom I've navigated the pre-tenure years, choosing solidarity and friendship over competition, including Ren Ellis Neyra, Mitali Thakor, Marina Bilbija, Roman Utkin, Lauren Silber, Heather Vermeulen, Valaria Lopez Fadul, Long Bui, Rachel Besharat-Mann, Alisha Butler, Sierra Eckert, and Roseann Lui.

I am especially indebted to J. Kēhaulani Kauanui, who has taught me so much as a friend and mentor and whose labor and deep commitment to Indigenous Studies fomented the founding of Wesleyan's Indigenous Studies

Research Network. Through ISRN, my own thinking about the structural extractive politics and practices of the university has sharpened, and my understanding of the relations of land and kin has come into focus. This is thanks to Kēhaulani and the group of scholars she cultivated, including Khalil Johnson, Joey Weiss, Roberto Saba, George Bajilia, Nina Griecci Woodsum, Lou Cornum, and Kristin Oberiano. My thanks, especially, to Khalil and Joey, who read significant portions of this manuscript and provided such smart, kind, and generative feedback.

One of the great pleasures of interdisciplinary scholarship is getting to learn from and with people with a broad range of interests and training. While the majority of my years have been split between Davis and Wesleyan, I'm also appreciative of the support I've received outside of these spaces. During my two-year stint in the Pioneer Valley at the University of Massachusetts, Amherst, Kiran Asher, Laura Briggs, Tanisha Ford, Millian Kang, Kristen Leng, Asha Nadkarni, Jordy Rosenberg, Britt Russert, Banu Subramaniam, Mecca Jamilah Sullivan, Angie Willey, Linda Hillenbrand, and Karen Lederer provided me an important space to land after graduate school. A special thanks to Annie Sollinger of UMass Special Collections and University Archives, who digitized the *Newsweek* images for Part III and the conclusion. I'm also especially grateful for the feedback I received during a book proposal workshop hosted by the Five College Women's Studies Research Consortium and for the opportunity to help coordinate speakers and conferences through which I developed or deepened my relationships with scholars whose work has shaped my own, including Amber Hollibaugh, Eithne Luibhéid, Chandan Reddy, Kadji Amin, and Lisa Lowe. Over the years, I've also had the good fortune to come into relation with a range of other scholars through conferences, reading groups, publication processes, or social circles whose writing and ways of navigating the academic world have inspired me. This includes Chandan Reddy, Jodi Melamed, Naomi Paik, Joan Scott, Jih-Fei Cheng, Dean Spade, Kevin Murphy, Jecca Nemakkal, Miranda Joseph, Nicole Rizzuto, Greta LaFleur, Evren Savci, Manijeh Moradian, Lisa Duggan, Debanuj DasGupta, Bench Ansfield, Lauren Berlant, Siobhan Somerville, Sandy Soto, Rachel Buff, Bec Young, Lazz Kinnamon, Aren Aizura, Cass Adair, Jina Kim, Maya Wind, Thea Quiray Tagle, Jason Wozniak, and Rana Barakat. A particular thanks is due to Grace Hong and Isaac Kamola, who served as reviewers for this book and, along with Janet, Kēhaulani, Dia Felix, and Sharon Stein, provided insightful notes that refined and strengthened its arguments in the final push to completion.

Over the last decade, I've had the incredible good fortune to collaborate, share concerns, and write with Eli Meyerhoff, Zach Schwartz-Weinstein, and Nick Mitchell as we've worked to think through an abolitionist approach to the study of the US university. The duration of this collaboration is a testament to our shared commitment to and care for the work, each other, and the possibility of a better world and, maybe, a better university. They have taught me so much and made this work so much better. This book would be far less interesting, abolitionist, and critical without them. I'm excited to see all that will come next in our work together and in other configurations. In the first years of our collaboration, we brought together a group of scholars for a conference to think about abolitionism and the study of higher education. Through this conference, our network extended, and I came to know, or know better, a collective of scholars who have also deeply shaped this work. This includes Dylan Rodríguez, Neha Vora, Vinetta Singh, Rana Jaleel, Davarian Baldwin, Sandy Grande, Morgan Adamson, Heather Steffen, Lucien Baskin, Conor Coco Tomás Reed, Curtis Marez, Bayley Marquez, Eli Thorkelson, Erin Dyke, Erica Meiners, Gillian Harkins, Jennifer Doyle, K. Wayne Yang, Laura Goldblatt, Max Haiven, Isaac Kamola, and Sheeva Sabati.

Thanks and appreciation are also due to my family and friends with less direct ties to academic work. My mom and dad, Dianne and Rod, along with their long-term partners, Pat and Taisie, my siblings, Erin, Amanda, and Nicholas, their partners, Mark, Chris, and Marlon, and children, Char, Sparrow, and Indigo, my aunts Debbie and Maggie, their daughter Francesca, and my partner's father Doug, their mother and stepfather Fran and Bob, and brother Sam have all been along for much of the ride toward the completion of this book, providing various forms of sustenance and at times enduring perhaps too-long discourses on the politics of US higher education and immigration along the way. Special appreciation is due to my brother Nicholas Boggs, without whose early encouragement to write, think, and pursue a life in the university, this book would certainly not exist. My thanks and love also to my dear friends, many of whom I've known since our teen years: Erin, Monica, SO, Lex, Dia, Brynn, Celeste, Hope, Jen, Mercer, Kate, Jess, Henry, Eliza, Katie, Tessa, Theo, Emily, Nora, Elia, Michael, Annemarie, Angie, Anuli, Pepper, Tin, D, Alli, Dom, and Elia. I learn so much from all of you.

My thanks also to everyone at Fordham University Press. Richard Morrison has gently and patiently guided this project over many years, allowing me and it the time required to come to this point. Though it took far longer than either of us imagined, working with him and the rest of the FUP team has made these last stages incredibly easy. This was due in large part to Lis Pearson's equally gentle but far more efficient copyediting and Kem Crimmins's ushering through the final production processes.

Liz Montegary and Benjamin D'Harlingue have known this project from its earliest inception in the mid-2000s through to its last stages. I'm pretty sure that if I hadn't finished it, one or both of them would have. Throughout graduate school and now well beyond, Liz has been a steadfast inspiration for how to do ethical work in, on, through, and often despite of the university, all with an eye toward making the university habitable for and supportive of genuinely good lives for her colleagues and students. Over the last two years, Ben has read every page of this manuscript, bringing his brilliance and erudition to bear on its arguments and historical framing. His edits, questions, and feedback sent me ferreting down some unexpected rabbit holes, much to the project's benefit.

Milo Thiesen has only known me as someone working on this book. They have patiently supported my early morning writing and the particular temporal flow of academic life, finding points of connection and important times to pull me away. Their love, humor, and insistence on taking time for art have carried through it all. It is also in large part thanks to Milo's love and support that Lola and Ben came into my life. In the last three years of writing this book, Ben has been my greatest distraction and motivation. I hope and imagine this will continue to be the case. In the end, this book is about the past, but it is for the present and the future.

## Appendix

*Timeline of Key Events in the History of Noncitizen Students and US Higher Education*

1619 — The Virginia colony allocates land at Henricus for the establishment of an "Indian college," linking early English higher education projects to Indigenous dispossession and conversion.

1636 — Harvard College is founded in the Massachusetts Bay Colony.

1649 — English Parliament passes "An Act for the Propagating of the Gospel," institutionalizing missionary education directed at Indigenous peoples.

1650 — Harvard's charter formally commits the college to the education of "English and Indian youth."

1661 — Caleb Cheeshateaumuck and Joel Iacoomes enroll at Harvard College.

1665 — Caleb Cheeshateaumuck graduates from Harvard, becoming the only known Native graduate of Harvard during the colonial era.

1693 — The College of William & Mary receives its royal charter.

1754 — Eleazer Wheelock establishes Moor's Indian Charity School, the precursor to Dartmouth College.

1765 — Samson Occom travels to Europe to raise funds for Wheelock's educational endeavors.

1769 — Dartmouth College is chartered.

1790 — The Naturalization Act restricts US citizenship to "free white persons."

1816 — The American Board of Commissioners of Foreign Missions (ABCFM) charters the Cornwall School for Foreign Mission Students in Connecticut.

1816 — The American Colonization Society (ACS) is founded to promote the migration of free Black Americans to Africa.

1822 — The ACS establishes Liberia.

1847 — Yung Wing travels to the United States to pursue an education.

1854 — The Ashmun Institute (later Lincoln University) is founded.

1854 — Yung Wing graduates from Yale College, becoming the first Chinese graduate of an American university.

1854 — Wilbur Fisk Burns travels from Liberia to Middletown, Connecticut, to study at a Wesleyan University.

1862 — Congress passes the Morrill Land Grant Act, the Homestead Act, and the Federal Anti-Coolie Act.

1868 — The Burlingame Treaty between the United States and China guarantees relatively free migration and educational access for Chinese students.

1870 — Ratification of the Fifteenth Amendment prohibits denying the right to vote on the basis of "race, color, or previous condition of servitude," while leaving intact the exclusion of Indigenous peoples, Asian immigrants, and women from full political participation in the United States.

1870 — The Naturalization Act extends citizenship eligibility to persons of African descent while continuing to exclude Asian immigrants.

1872 — The Chinese Educational Mission begins sending Chinese students to study in the United States.

1875 — Congress passes the Page Act, one of the first major federal immigration restriction laws targeting Chinese migrants.

1880–1881 — The Angell Treaty renegotiates the Burlingame framework and authorizes restrictions on Chinese labor immigration while exempting students, merchants, and teachers.

1881 — The Chinese Educational Mission is terminated.

1882 — Congress enacts the Chinese Restriction Act.

1888 — Congress passes the Scott Act, barring the reentry of Chinese laborers.

1889 — In *Chae Chan Ping v. United States*, the Supreme Court establishes the doctrine of plenary federal power over immigration.

1891 — The Office of the Superintendent of Immigration is established.

1892 — The Geary Act renews and expands Chinese exclusion policies.

1893 — Frederick Jackson Turner presents the "Frontier Thesis" at the World's Columbian Exposition in Chicago.

1898 — The United States annexes Hawaiʻi and acquires the Philippines, Guam, and Puerto Rico following the Spanish-American War.

1900 — The Boxer Rebellion and subsequent international intervention reshape US–China educational relations.

1903 — Congress passes the Philippine Pensionado Act, funding the education of Filipino students in the United States.

1905 — Chinese students, merchants, and officials organize a boycott of American goods in protest of exclusion laws and immigration practices.

1908 — The United States establishes the Boxer Indemnity scholarship program for Chinese students.

1919 — The Institute of International Education (IIE) is founded to coordinate and expand international educational exchange in support of US global influence.

1921 — Congress passes the Emergency Quota Act, removing the exception of students from immigration restrictions.

1922 — The IIE negotiates administrative exemptions permitting certain foreign students to enter outside quota restrictions.

1924 — Congress passes the Johnson–Reed Immigration Act, imposing strict quota restrictions on immigration and barring the immigration of persons ineligible for citizenship.

1935 — Kwame Nkrumah travels to the United States to pursue higher education, beginning a decade of study and political organizing at Lincoln University and the University of Pennsylvania.

1940 — Congress passes the Smith Act (Alien Registration Act), criminalizing advocacy of the violent overthrow of the US government and requiring the registration and fingerprinting of noncitizens, expanding federal surveillance powers that would later shape the monitoring of international students, migrants, and political dissidents during the Cold War.

1946 — Congress passes the Fulbright Act, creating the Fulbright Program for international educational exchange.

1948 — Congress passes the Smith–Mundt Act, institutionalizing educational exchange as an instrument of US foreign policy.

1952 — The McCarran–Walter Immigration and Nationality Act establishes the modern F student visa system and expands federal surveillance of noncitizen students.

1953 — The African American Institute (AAI) is founded to recruit and support African students in the United States.

1956 — Gayatri Chakravorty Spivak travels to the United States to begin graduate study at Cornell University.

1957 — Ghana achieves independence under Kwame Nkrumah.

1960 — The "Kennedy Airlift" expands African student recruitment to US universities.

1961 — Leaders including Kwame Nkrumah, Jawaharlal Nehru, Gamal Abdel Nasser, Josip Broz Tito, and Sukarno establish the Non-Aligned Movement (NAM), rejecting alignment with either the United States or the Soviet Union during the Cold War.

1963 — *Newsweek* publishes "Foreign Students: Diplomas and Diplomacy" (April 22), featuring Gayatri Chakravorty Spivak and other noncitizen students.

1965 — The Immigration and Nationality Act restructures US immigration policy and ends the national origins quota system.

1966 — Popular and sociological discourse surrounding the "model minority" emerges.

## Notes

### Preface. On Present Conditions: Trump's Promises and the Noncitizen Student

1. NPR Staff, "All the Executive Orders Trump has Signed After 1 Week in Office," *NPR*, January 28, 2025, https://www.npr.org/2025/01/28/nx-s1-5276293/trump-executive-orders.

2. Executive Order 14161 of January 20, 2025, "Protecting the United States from Foreign Terrorists and Other National Security and Public Safety Threats," The White House, https://www.whitehouse.gov/presidential-actions/2025/01/protecting-the-united-states-from-foreign-terrorists-and-othernational-security-and-public-safety-threats/.

3. As has now been widely reported, Kenneth Stern, director of the Study of Hate at Bard and one of the drafters of the IHRA definition, has since argued that the Trump administration is distorting the definition and using it to silence critics of Israel. Kaity Kline, "Weaponizing Antisemitism Makes Students 'Less Safe,' Says Drafter of Definition," *NPR*, March 20, 2025, https://www.npr.org/2025/03/20/nx-s1-5326047/kenneth-stern-antimsietim-executive-order-free-speech.

4. Jimmy Boegle, "A Fascinating Coincident Involving an Executive Order Number," *Coachella Valley Independent*, March 24, 2025, https://www.adl.org/resources/hate-symbol/1488.

5. President's Alliance on Higher Education and Immigration, "FAQs on Executive Order: Additional Measures to Combat Anti-Semitism," February 6, 2025, https://www.presidentsalliance.org/press/alliance-of-over-570-college-and-university-leaders-condemns-the-apprehension-and-detention-of-international-students-and-calls-on-the-administration-to-respect-constitutional-rights/.

6. The White House, "Additional Measures to Combat Anti-Semitism," January 29, 2025, https://www.whitehouse.gov/presidential-actions/2025/01/additional-measures-to-combat-anti-semitism/.

7. Nathan Layne and Tim Reid, "Trump Pledges to Expel Immigrants Who Support Hamas, Ban Muslims from the U.S.," Reuters, October 16, 2023, https://www.reuters.com/world/us/trump-pledges-expel-immigrants-who-support-hamas-ban-muslims-us-2023-10-16/.

8. "Palestine is Everywhere," last accessed February 3, 2025, https://web.archive.org/web/20250202003737/https://www.palestineiseverywhere.com/; Neil Bedi et al., "How Counterprotesters at U.C.L.A. Provoked Violence, Unchecked for Hours," *New York Times*, May 3, 2024, https://www.nytimes.com/interactive/2024/05/03/us/ucla-protests-encampment-violence.html.

9. "Police Enter Columbia University's Hamilton Hall Amid Pro-Palestinian Protests," *NPR*, April 20, 2024, https://www.npr.org/2024/04/30/1248012619/columbia-university-gaza-protests.

10. As university studies scholar and organizer Lucien Baskin relayed to me, the arrests at City College were more numerous and resulted in greater legal consequences than the actions at Columbia. That the arresting officers were campus police, rather than NYPD, complicates popular and often reformist narratives regarding the relative softness of university security forces.

11. Bedi et al., "How Counterprotesters at U.C.L.A. Provoked Violence."

12. Caroline Downey, "Trump Promises to 'Immediately Deport' Foreign Students Involved in Anti-Israel Protests," *National Review*, May 12, 2024, https://www.nationalreview.com/news/trump-promises-to-immediately-deport-foreign-students-involved-in-anti-israel-protests/.

13. Trump's statements and actions mirror a plank of "Project 2025," the conservative Heritage Foundation's vision for a radical restructure of the federal government that his campaign mendaciously worked to distance itself from throughout 2024. The platform includes a call to "prioritize national security in the Student and Exchange Visitor Program (SEVP)" by having Immigration and Customs Enforcement "end its cozy deference to educational institutions and remove security risks from the program." This would be accomplished in part by "working with the Department of State to eliminate or significantly reduce the number of visas issued to foreign students from enemy nations." Project 2025: Presidential Transition Project, Paul Dans and Steven Groves, eds, "Mandate for Leadership: The Conservative Promise," Heritage Foundation, 2023, 141, https://static.project2025.org/2025_MandateForLeadership_FULL.pdf.

14. Office of Senator Marco Rubio, "Rubio to Biden Admin: Revoke Visas of Pro-Hamas Protesters Now," May 9, 2024, senate.gov, https://web.archive.org/web/20250118185318/https://www.rubio.senate.gov/rubio-to-biden-admin-revoke-visas-of-pro-hamas-protesters-now/.

15. Rubio was not alone in making such calls. Two weeks earlier, *The Hill* reported on Tennessee senator Marsha Blackburn's statement that "for the students

who are out protesting, shouting 'Death to America' and 'Death to Israel' and . . . being Hamas sympathizers, if they're foreign students, I would pull their visa and deport them." Lauren Irwin, "GOP Senator Calls for Deporting Certain Foreign Student Protesters," *The Hill*, April 30, 2024, https://thehill.com/policy/international/4634492-gop-senator-calls-for-deporting-certain-foreign-student-protesters/. Importantly, Blackburn did not restrict her punitive vision to noncitizen students but also for the denial of loans to federal student loan recipients who participated in protests. In July, Congressman Nick Langworthy of New York, along with cosponsors from Texas and Florida, introduced the Veto Your Visa Act targeting noncitizen students who participate in Palestinian-solidarity protests. Office of Congressman Nick Langworthy, "Congressman Langworthy Introduces Legislation to Revoke Student Visas of Pro-Terrorist Protesters," July 25, 2024, https://langworthy.house.gov/media/press-releases/congressman-langworthy-introduces-legislation-revoke-student-visas-pro.

Just a day after Rubio's statement, the United Kingdom's Home Office withdrew a visa for Dana Abuqamar, a Palestinian law student at the University of Manchester, calling the nineteen-year-old who had lost fifteen family members in Israel's attacks on Gaza a "national security risk." Al Jazeera Staff, "UK Revokes Visa of Law Student who Addressed Pro-Palestine Protest," *Al Jazeera*, May 10, 2024, aljazeera.com.

16. Chris Cameron, "Trump Says He Would Give Green Cards to All Foreign College Students at Graduation," *New York Times*, June 20, 2024, https://www.nytimes.com/2024/06/20/us/politics/trump-green-cards-college-graduates.html.

17. Nick Robins-Early, "How Elon Musk Became Donald Trump's Shadow Vice-President," *The Guardian*, November 9, 2024, accessed September 8, 2025, https://www.theguardian.com/technology/2024/nov/09/elon-musk-trump-administration.

## Introduction. Noncitizen Students and US Higher Education: A Genealogy of Empire

1. In this effort to grapple with "the present conditions" I take inspiration from the introduction to the now canonical book *Policing the Crisis*, in which Stuart Hall and his collaborators describe their task of "struggling with the contradictions" that constitute such conditions in order to make "an intervention in the battleground of ideas." Stuart Hall et al., *Policing the Crisis: Mugging, the State and Law and Order* (Macmillan Press, 1978), x.

2. Roderick A. Ferguson, *The Reorder of Things: The University and Its Pedagogies of Minority Difference* (University of Minnesota Press, 2012), 5.

3. On "empire of liberty" see Ian Tyrrell, *Reforming the World: The Creation of America's Moral Empire* (Princeton University Press, 2010); Brandon Mills, *The World Colonization Made: The Racial Geography of Early American Empire* (University of Pennsylvania Press, 2020), 161. As is discussed further below, this

reading is inspired by David Kazanjian's exploration of Jefferson's thought in *The Colonizing Trick: National Culture and Imperial Citizenship in Early America* (University of Minnesota Press, 2003), 96.

4. On the import of specifying whiteness and settler together see Kevin Bruyneel's conclusion to *Settler Memory: The Disavowal of Indigeneity and the Politics of Race in the United States* (University of North Carolina Press, 2021).

5. There is also an important parallel discussion of undocumented students as noncitizen students. This status is not discussed in this book, in large part because discussions of this status did not emerge until after the historical period under consideration. See for instance, Rachel Ida Buff, "The Undergraduate Railroad," in *Immigrant Rights in the Shadows of Citizenship*, ed. Rachel Ida Buff (New York University Press, 2008); and The UndocuScholars Project, "In the Shadows of the Ivory Tower: Undocumented Undergraduates and the Liminal State of Immigration Reform," chrome-extension://efaidnbmnnnibpcajpcglclefindmkaj/https://www.undocuscholars.org/assets/undocuscholarsreport2015.pdf.

6. As Rachel Buff argues in *Against the Deportation Terror: Organizing for Immigrant Rights in the Twentieth Century*, "[b]eing foreign born meant being vulnerable to deportation and constant subjection to inspection, surveillance, and policing by federal immigration forces." Rachel Buff, *Against the Deportation Terror: Organizing for Immigrant Rights in the Twentieth Century* (Temple University Press, 2018); See also David Cole, "Are Foreign Nationals Entitled to the Same Constitutional Rights As Citizens?," *Jefferson Law Review* (2003): 367–88.

7. Mae M. Ngai, *Impossible Subjects: Illegal Aliens and the Making of Modern America* (Princeton University Press, 2004); David Cole, "Their Liberties, Our Security: Democracy and Double Standards," in Buff, ed., *Immigrant Rights*.

8. Buff, ed., *Immigrant Rights*; Lisa Lowe, *Immigrant Acts: On Asian American Cultural Politics* (Duke University Press, 1996); Naomi A. Paik, *Bans, Walls, Raids, Sanctuary: Understanding US Immigration for the Twenty-First Century* (University of California Press, 2020).

9. Paik, *Bans, Walls, Raids, Sanctuary*, 168.

10. Here, this project is in alignment with Eithne Luibhéid's work and her treatment of "'citizen' and 'noncitizen' not as natural or ontological categories but as status distinctions that have been created and contested within histories of power involving settler colonial, capitalist, cisheteronormative, and racist nation-state formation processes" (xi). As she continues, "Citizenship is commonly conceived in liberal thought as a universal status" but others "characterize nation-based citizenship as a strategy for population management that upholds systemic inequalities" (9). Eithne Luibhéid, *Abolitionist Intimacies: Queer and Trans Migrants Against the Deportation State* (Duke University Press, 2025).

11. As Hong writes, summarizing Lowe, "in the late nineteenth and early twentieth centuries, the US nation-state required a homogeneous citizenry, while US industrial capital required a heterogeneous workforce, differentiated by categories of race that were always articulated through gender and sexual

non-normativity." Grace Kyungwon Hong, *Death Beyond Disavowal: The Impossible Politics of Difference* (University of Minnesota Press, 2015), 66.

12. Evelyn Nakano Glenn, *Unequal Freedom: How Race and Gender Shaped American Citizenship and Labor* (Harvard University Press, 2002).

13. Hong, *Death Beyond Disavowal*, 66.

14. "Institute of International Education, "All Places of Origin," Open Doors, accessed May 11, 2026, opendoorsdata.org.

15. Hong, *Death Beyond Disavowal*, 70.

16. In 2006, Aihwa Ong argued that this shift in higher education from a "national to transnational space for producing knowledgeable subjects" has not only ruptured "the nation-state frame of educational strategies" with a shift to the global but has also contributed to the "flexible citizenship strategies of Asian elites," giving way to the neoliberal anthropos "primed for employment in knowledge-driven markets" (140). Aihwa Ong, *Neoliberalism as Exception: Mutations in Citizenship and Sovereignty* (Duke University Press, 2006); See for instance the United Kingdom's High Potential Individual Visa, which stipulates that the applicant "must have been awarded a qualification by an eligible university." "High Potential Individual (HPI) Visa: Eligibility," accessed May 11, 2026, https://www.gov.uk/high-potential-individual-visa/eligibility.

17. Other fields of intervention in the shape, size, and demographic makeup of the country are also crucial, most notably policies and politics of respectability, normality, and biological reproduction often referred to as population control or eugenics. Though beyond the scope of this project, it would be more than possible to write a thick thread of this book tracking the ways sexual politics are constitutive of the twinned histories of immigration and education. This story appears here, albeit insufficiently, for there is much else to say and to do. I hope to return to it in future writing in order to more substantially consider social reproduction theory as discussed by scholars including Cindy Katz, Lisa Duggan, Premilla Nadsen, Tithi Bhattacharya, and others. Nick Mitchell's forthcoming work will be especially crucial for bringing social reproduction theory to bear on the study of US higher education.

18. Christopher Loss, *Between Citizen and State: The Politics of Higher Education in the 20th Century* (Princeton University Press, 2012), 4.

19. Loss, *Between Citizen and State*, 10.

20. Craig Steven Wilder, *Ebony and Ivy: Race, Slavery, and the Troubled History of America's Universities* (Bloomsbury Press, 2013), 33.

21. Wilder's most fundamental and most overlooked argument is that universities materially and epistemologically provided the organizing logic for the nation-state as a project of domination over other nations, peoples, and lands and that this logic continues to govern university operations in the present.

22. Sandy Grande, "Refusing the University," in *Toward What Justice?: Describing Diverse Dreams of Justice in Education* (Routledge, 2018), 47.

23. W. Stitt Robinson Jr., "Indian Education and Missions in Colonial Virginia," *The Journal of Southern History* 18, no. 2 (1952): 154.

24. Patrick Wolfe, "Settler Colonialism and the Elimination of the Native," *Journal of Genocide Research* 8, no. 4 (2006); David Kazanjian, "'To See the Issue of His Exorbitant Practices': A Response to 'The Dispossessed Eighteenth Century,'" *The Eighteenth Century* 55, no. 2/3 (2014).

25. Abigail Boggs, "Educational Pasts, Enduring Colonial Presents: Indigenous Student Conscripts and the Foundation of the US University," *History of the Present* 12, no. 2, (2023).

26. Robert Lee and Tristan Ahtone, "Land-Grab Universities: Expropriated Indigenous Land is the Foundation of the Land-Grant University System." *High Country News*, 2020.

27. Madeline Y. Hsu, *The Good Immigrants: How the Yellow Peril Became the Model Minority* (Princeton University Press, 2015), 36.

28. Paul Kramer, "Is the World Our Campus? International Students and US Global Power in the Long Twentieth Century," *Diplomatic History* 33, no. 5 (2009): 781.

29. Penny M. Von Eschen, *Race Against Empire: Black Americans and Anticolonialism, 1937–1957* (Cornell University Press, 1997), 131; Liping Bu, "Educational Exchange and Cultural Diplomacy in the Cold War," *Journal of American Studies* 33 (1999).

30. Mel Elfin and Constance Montague, "Foreign Studies: Diplomas and Diplomacy," *Newsweek*, 1963, 59.

31. Edward Said, "Blind Imperial Arrogance," *Los Angeles Times*, July 20, 2003, https://www.latimes.com/archives/la-xpm-2003-jul-20-oe-said20-story.html. Just a year later, Karl Rove, who would soon become George W. Bush's deputy chief of staff, told *The New York Times Magazine*, "We're an empire now, and when we act, we create our own reality. And while you're studying that reality—judiciously, as you will—we'll act again, creating other new realities, which you can study too, and that's how things will sort out. We're history's actors . . . and you, all of you, will be left to just study what we do." Ron Suskind, "Faith, Certainty and the Presidency of George W. Bush," *New York Times Magazine*, October 17, 2004, https://www.nytimes.com/2004/10/17/magazine/faith-certainty-and-the-presidency-of-george-w-bush.html.

32. Bill Readings, *The University in Ruins* (Harvard University Press, 1996), 3.

33. Sheila Slaughter and Gary Rhoades, "Academic Capitalism, Managed Professionals, and Supply-Side Higher Education." *Social Text* 51 (Summer 1997): 9. http://www.jstor.org/stable/40342886.

34. Readings, *The University in Ruins*, 3.

35. Amy Kaplan, "'Left Alone with America': The Absence of Empire in the Study of American Culture," in *Cultures of United States Imperialism*, ed. Amy Kaplan and Donald E. Pease (Duke University Press, 1994).

36. Sunaina Maira and Piya Chatterjee, eds., *The Imperial University* (University of Minnesota Press, 2014), 11.

37. Moon-Ho Jung, *Menace to Empire: Anticolonial Solidarities and the Transpacific Origins of the US Security State* (University of California Press, 2022), 8–9.

38. Jung, *Menace to Empire*, 9.

39. Paul A. Kramer, *Blood of Government: Race, Empire, the United States, and the Philippines* (University of North Carolina Press, 2006).

40. Uday S. Mehta, "Liberal Strategies of Exclusion," in *Tensions of Empire: Colonial Cultures in a Bourgeois World*, ed. Frederick Cooper and Ann Laura Stoler (University of California Press, 1997), 59.

41. Mehta, "Liberal Strategies of Exclusion," 69.

42. Ong, for instance, argues "that education is a social technology—in the Weberian sense of appropriate means to an end—for constituting subjects in particular spaces of calculation." Ong, *Neoliberalism as Exception*, 139.

43. Maria P. Cantu, "Three Effective Strategies of Internationalization in American Universities," *Journal of International Education Leadership* 3, no. 3 (2013).

44. Phillip Altbach and H. de Wit, "The Challenge to Higher Education Internationalisation." *University World News*, February 23, 2018, https://www.universityworldnews.com/post.php?story=20180220091648602.

45. Sharon Stein, "Critical Internationalization Studies at an Impasse: Making Space for Complexity, Uncertainty, and Complicity in a Time of Global Challenges," *Studies in Higher Education* 46, no. 9 (2021): 1773.

46. Sharon Stein, "Confronting the Racial-Colonial Foundations of US Higher Education," *Journal for the Study of Postsecondary and Tertiary Education* 3 (2018): 78.

47. It is important to attenuate this point with an acknowledgment that once the United States took shape as a nation-state, the Constitution made an important and consequential distinction between "Indian tribes" and "foreign nations." As Maggie Blackhawk argues, "The 'law of nations,' rather than forming a distinctive body of international law separate from domestic constitutional law, included laws that many of the Founding generation presumed were relevant to the Constitution. With respect to 'Indians,' the text of the Constitution reflected hierarchies between 'civilized' and 'uncivilized' peoples in distinguishing between 'foreign nations' and 'Indian tribes.' The latter were accorded only partial sovereignty, restricted by the power of the United States." See Maggie Blackhawk, "The Constitution of American Colonialism," *Harvard Law Review* 137, no. 1 (2023): 29.

48. Adom Getachew, *Worldmaking After Empire* (Princeton University Press, 2020), 9; Manu Karuka, *Empire's Tracks: Indigenous Nations, Chinese Workers, and the Transcontinental Railroad* (University of California Press, 2019), 177.

49. Jung, *Menace to Empire*; Kaplan, "Left Alone With America"; Kramer, *Blood of Government*.

50. Lisa Lowe, *The Intimacies of Four Continents* (Duke University Press, 2015), 3.

51. "Family Visits Yale, New Haven in Honor of Man Who Inspired Christianity in Hawaii," *New Haven Register*, June 20, 2017, https://www.nhregister.com/colleges/article/Family-visits-Yale-New-Haven-in-honor-of-man-who-11311658.php.

52. Lowe, *Intimacies*, 47.

53. Michel Foucault, "The Will to Knowledge," in *Ethics: Subjectivity & Truth*, trans. Robert Hurley et al., ed. Paul Rabinow, *Essential Works of Foucault* 1954–1984 (The New Press, 1997), 12.

54. Michel Foucault, "Nietzsche, Genealogy, History," in Donald F. Bouchard's *Language, Counter-Memory, Practice* (Cornell University Press, 1977), 154.

55. Foucault, "Nietzsche, Genealogy, History," 139; Walter Benjamin, "Theses on the Philosophy of History," in *Illuminations*, ed. Hannah Arendt (Schocken Books, 1985); Michel Foucault, *Birth of the Clinic: An Archaeology of Medical Perception* (Tavistock, 1973). In *Birth of the Clinic*, Foucault explains this approach as "both historical and critical, in that it is concerned . . . with determining the conditions of possibility of medical experience in modern times" (ibid., 35). David Garland describes Foucault's genealogical method for conducting a history of the present as starting with a "present-day practice that is both taken for granted and yet, in certain respects, problematic or somehow unintelligible" and then working to "trace the power struggles that produced" it. David Garland, "What is a 'History of the Present'? On Foucault's Genealogies and Their Critical Preconditions," *Punishment & Society* 16, no. 4 (2014).

56. Foucault, "Nietzsche, Genealogy, History," 140.

57. This is complemented by Benjamin's description of history as "one single catastrophe which keeps piling wreckage" propelling the angel of history "irresistibly" "into the future."

58. Lawrence Grossberg, "Cultural Studies in Search of a Method, or Looking for Conjunctural Analysis," *New Formations* (2019).

59. Abigail Boggs et al., "Abolitionist University Studies: An Invitation." *Abolition Journal* (2019): 3.

60. Abigail Boggs and Nick Mitchell. "Critical University Studies and the Crisis Consensus," *Feminist Studies* 44, no. 2 (2018): 452.

61. US Congress, *Congressional Record*, 67th Cong., 1st sess., vol. LXI, pt. 1 (March 4–15; April 11–May 4, 1921), 556.

## Part I: Educate, Expropriate, and Export

1. "Native American Honored: Harvard Foundation Unveils Portrait of First Native American Grad," *The Harvard Gazette*, December 17, 2010, https://news.harvard.edu/gazette/story/2010/12/native-american-honored/.

2. K-Sue Park, "Money, Mortgages, and the Conquest of America," *Law & Social Inquiry* 41, no. 4 (2016): 1006–35.

3. Bobby Wright, "'For the Children of Infidels?': American Indians Education in the Colonial Colleges," *American Indian Culture and Research Journal* 12, no. 3

(1988): 73; See also Sharon Stein, "Confronting the Racial-Colonial Foundations of US Higher Education," *Journal for the Study of Postsecondary and Tertiary Education* 3 (2018): 77–96.

4. For an extended discussion of Indigenous engagements with the concept of sovereignty see J. Kēhaulani Kauanui, *Paradoxes of Hawaiian Sovereignty: Land, Sex, and the Colonial Politics of State Nationalism* (Duke University Press, 2018), 25–30; and Joanne Barker, *Native Acts: Law, Recognition, and Cultural Authenticity* (Duke University Press, 2011).

5. Manu Vimalassery. "Counter-Sovereignty," *J19: The Journal of Nineteenth-Century Americanists* 2, no. 1 (2014): 142.

6. While this book is concerned with the figure of the noncitizen student, in the period before the establishment of the United States, such students might better be termed nonsubjects in that they were not directly subject, in a formal sense, to the British Crown. Still, in tracing a genealogy of the noncitizen student it is crucial to recognize the continuities in the educational tactics and the uses of education for the broader project of settler colonialism and the enduring institutions at its foundation.

7. Bobby Wright, "The 'Untameable Savage Spirit': American Indians in Colonial Colleges." *The Review of Higher Education* 14, no. 4 (1991): 435.

8. On disavowal as settler practice see Kevin Bruyneel, *Settler Memory: The Disavowal of Indigeneity and the Politics of Race in the United States* (University of North Carolina Press, 2021).

9. Davarian Baldwin, "The Reparations Movement in Higher Education," *The Thinking Republic*, October 11, 2020, https://www.thethinkingrepublic.com/being-counted/the-reparations-movement-in-higher-education; See Ruth Simmon's letter on the purpose of the Brown University Steering Committee on Slavery and Justice from 2006 here: Slavery and Justice Report, http://brown.edu/Research/Slavery_Justice/about/report-letter.html. One of the programs sponsored by the steering committee brought together descendants of Native American captives transported from Rhode Island to Bermuda more than three hundred years ago with representatives of more than a dozen Native nations in the eastern United States and Canada; See also the University of Virginia's Universities Studying Slavery Consortium, https://slavery.virginia.edu/universities-studying-slavery; and Rutgers Scarlet and Black Project, *Scarlet and Black: Slavery and Dispossession in Rutgers History* (2016), https://scarletandblack.rutgers.edu/findings.

As Zach Schwartz-Weinstein shared with me, the Yale, Slavery and Abolition report (2001) follows a different trajectory, authorized and written not by the university but by a collaboration between the graduate student union and a local communist front organization as an explicit critique of the triumphalism surrounding the university's tricentennial. Yale administrators and senior faculty (especially David Briton Davis who is rumored to have attempted to get his student Diana Paton deported for her role in the 1995 grade strike six years earlier) dismissed the report, and a subsequent conference hosted by the university's

Gilder-Lehrman center on slavery and abolition largely ignored it. http://www.yaleslavery.org/Resources/about.html.

10. Vineeta Singh, "Universities Studying Slavery: Critical University Studies in Practice," *Remaking the University*, January 21, 2019, http://utotherescue.blogspot.com/2019/01/; See also, Vineeta Singh, "Slavery and the University: Histories and Legacies (Review)," *The Black Scholar* 51, no. 1 (2021): 75–78.

11. A key example of this is organizing at Yale University around the removal of John Calhoun's name from a college at Yale University that culminated in the college's renaming as Grace Hopper College in 2016, in part in response to an autonomous action by Corey Menafee, a Black dishwasher who worked in the dining hall. For more on this see Eli Meyerhoff's introduction to *Beyond Education: Radical Studying for Another World* (University of Minnesota Press, 2019), and his conversation with Zaina Alsous in *The New Inquiry*, "A Detrimental Education," April 16, 2020.

12. Dylan Rodríguez, "Racial/Colonial Genocide and the 'Neoliberal Academy': In Excess of a Problematic," *American Quarterly* 64, no. 4 (December 2012): 810.

13. Abigail Boggs and Nick Mitchell, "Critical University Studies and the Crisis Consensus," *Feminist Studies* 44, no. 2 (2018): 455.

14. Craig Steven Wilder, *Ebony and Ivy: Race, Slavery, and the Troubled History of America's Universities* (Bloomsbury Press, 2013), 33.

15. Wilder, *Ebony and Ivy*, 187.

16. On the idea of claim to "firsting," asserting that "non-Indians were the first people to erect proper institutions of social order worthy of notice" see Jean M. O'Brien, *Firsting and Lasting: Writing Indians Out of Existence in New England* (University of Minnesota Press, 2010), xii.

17. William & Mary, "History and Tradition," accessed September 3, 2025, https://www.wm.edu/about/history/.

18. W. Stitt Robinson Jr., "Indian Education and Missions in Colonial Virginia," *The Journal of Southern History* 18, no. 2 (1952): 154.

19. Robert Hunt Land, "Henrico and Its College," *William and Mary Quarterly*, 2nd ser., 18 (1898): 475, cited in Karen A. Stuart, "'So Good a Word': The Brafferton School, 1691–1777," (Master's Thesis, The College of William & Mary, 1984). Over the course of the 1610s, sparked in part by visits to England from Pocahontas and other members of the Powhatan Confederacy, a great deal of wealth was committed to the founding of such a school, backed by King James VI and I among others, and proposals were drawn for the institution's construction and management. In some accounting records, by 1620 collections in support of a college to educate Indigenous youth amounted to 2,043 pounds. See also, Wright "For the Children of Infidels?," 73.

20. Land, "Henrico and Its College," 475; and Danielle Moretti-Langholtz and Buck Woodard, eds., *Building the Brafferton: The Founding, Funding and Legacy of America's Indian School* (Muscarelle Museum of Art, 2019), 26, 41. According to the catalogue for "Building the Brafferton," that same year George Thorpe was

deputized by the Virginian general assembly to oversee college land and the establishment of a school. According to Moretti-Langholtz and Woodard, Thorpe developed a relationship with Opechancanough, the chief of the Powhatan Confederacy, through discussion of cosmology and religion and "provided the Pamunkey leader with an English timber-framed house." Sometime between 1620 and 1622 the College of Henricus, which was also known as "the East India School," materialized briefly. Even within the text of "Building the Brafferton," it is not entirely clear whether or not students actually enrolled. On one timeline the text specifies that "30 Indians were in attendance by 1621" but later the authors cite sources from 2002 and 1957 documenting Thorpe's encouraging "30 of the infidelles children to be reared and educated" at the school. Moretti-Langholtz and Woodard, *Building the Brafferton*, 26, 41.

21. Robinson, "Indian Education and Missions in Colonial Virginia," 159.

22. According to the website for the Lemon Project, the project's namesake was "Lemon," a man enslaved by the university in the early nineteenth century whose relationship to the university is described as "complex and ambiguous." The two-paragraph text acknowledges that "he owned neither his work nor his own person" but also highlights that that faculty gifted him a Christmas bonus one year, provided him with an allowance to purchase his own food, and, upon his death in 1817, "paid for the coffin in which Lemon was buried."

23. "The Lemon Project," accessed September 3, 2025, https://www.wm.edu/sites/lemonproject/index.php.

24. Robinson, "Indian Education and Missions in Colonial Virginia," 162, citing R. A. Brock, ed., *The Official Letters of Alexander Spotswood, Lieutenant Governor of the Colony of Virginia, 1710–1722*, 2 vols., Collections of the Virginia Historical Society, New Series (Virginia Historical Society, 1882–1885), I:124.

25. Buck Woodard, "Students at the Brafferton Indian School," in Moretti-Langholtz and Woodard, *Building the Brafferton*, 103. Woodard cites Alan Gallay, *The Indian Slave Trade: The Rise of the English Empire in the American South, 1670–1717* (Yale University Press, 2003).

26. Kristalyn Marie Shefveland, *Anglo-Native Virginia: Trade, Conversion, and Indian Slavery in the Old Dominion, 1646–1722* (University of Georgia Press, 2016), 3–4.

27. Justin Leroy, "Black History in Occupied Territory: On the Entanglements of Slavery and Settler Colonialism," *Theory & Event* 19, no. 4 (2016); As S. A. Smythe argues, discussions of the connection between racial capitalism and settler colonialism, which they define as "epistemological-material projects of genocide, super exploitation, and dispossession," must also grapple with how ideas about landedness or nonlandedness contribute to "the notion of Afro-descended people's nonbelonging." See S. A. Smythe, "Introduction: Unsettle the Struggle, Trouble the Grounds," *Postmodern Culture* 31, no. 1 and 2 (September 2020 and January 2021).

28. Dylan Duediger, "By Just Means to Acquire Some Children," in Moretti-Langholtz and Woodard, *Building the Brafferton*, 67.

29. Wilder, *Ebony and Ivy*, 44.

30. Dylan Duediger's discussion of the negotiations between Algonquian and European ways of understanding the meaning of tribute as a mode of political thought and relation provides a particularly nuanced reading of this history.

31. Moretti-Langholtz and Woodard, *Building the Brafferton*, 14–15.

32. Moretti-Langholtz and Woodard, *Building the Brafferton*, 219.

33. Woodard, "Students at the Brafferton Indian School," 102.

34. Woodard, "Students at the Brafferton Indian School," 118.

35. Moretti-Langholtz and Woodard, *Building the Brafferton*, 16. Moretti-Langholtz and Woodard write that they presented at NAISA twice, in 2007 and 2008, but based on the locations they identified it is more likely that they attended in 2007 and 2009.

36. M. Jean O'Brien and Robert Warrior, "Building a Professional Infrastructure for Critical Indigenous Studies: A(n Intellectual) History of and Prospectus for the Native American and Indigenous Studies Association," in *Critical Indigenous Studies: Engagement in First World Locations*, ed. Aileen Moreton-Robinson (University of Arizona Press, 2016), 38.

37. See for instance "Landback: Building a Movement for Collective Liberation," https://landback.org/.

38. As paraphrased by Sandy Grande in "Refusing the University," in *Toward What Justice?: Describing Diverse Dreams of Justice in Education* (Routledge, 2018): 54.

39. Kevin Bruyneel, "The American Liberal Tradition," *Settler Colonial Studies* (2013): 316.

40. On the politics and practice of land acknowledgments see Theresa Stewart-Ambo and K. Wayne Yang, "Beyond Land Acknowledgement in Settler Institutions," *Social Text* 39, no. 1 (March 2021): 21–46; and Chelsea Vowel, "Beyond Territorial Acknowledgments," Apihtawikosisan (September 2016), apihtawikosisan.com/2016/09/beyond-territorial-acknowledgments/.

41. K-Sue Park, "Money, Mortgages, and the Conquest of America," *Law & Social Inquiry* 41, no. 4 (2016): 1006–35.

42. Abigail Boggs et al., "Abolitionist University Studies: An Invitation," *Abolition Journal* (2019); and Robert Lee and Tristan Ahtone, "Land-Grab Universities: Expropriated Indigenous Land is the Foundation of the Land-Grant University System," *High Country News* (2020).

### 1. Native Students as "Foreign Students" and the Foundation of the US University

1. See, for instance, Sharon Stein, "A Colonial History of the Higher Education Present: Rethinking Land-Grant Institutions Through Processes of Accumulation and Relations of Conquest," *Critical Studies in Education* (2017).

2. Patrick Wolfe, "Settler Colonialism and the Elimination of the Native," *Journal of Genocide Research* 8, no. 4 (2006): 388; and Patrick Wolfe, *Settler Colonialism and the Transformation of Anthropology: The Politics and Poetics of an Ethnograph Event* (Casell, 1999).

3. Wolfe, "Settler Colonialism and the Elimination of the Native," 397.

4. Wolfe, "Settler Colonialism and the Elimination of the Native," 397.

5. Wolfe, "Settler Colonialism and the Elimination of the Native," 402.

6. Wolfe cites Richard H. Pratt, "The Advantages of Mingling Indians with Whites" (1892), selection in Francis P. Prucha, ed., *Americanizing the American Indians: Writings by the "Friends of the Indian," 1880–1900* (Harvard University Press, 1973), 260–71, 261, and points readers to Ward Churchill's *Kill the Indian, Save the Man: The Genocidal Impact of American Indian Residential Schools* (City Lights, 2004). For a further articulation of the shift in state tactics in the nineteenth century see Donald A. Grinde Jr., "Taking the Indian Out of the Indian: US Policies of Ethnocide Through Education," *Wicazo Sa Review* 19, no. 2 (2004): 25–32.

7. Wolfe, "Settler Colonialism and the Elimination of the Native." On this periodization see also Kevin Bruyneel, *The Third Space of Sovereignty: The Postcolonial Politics of US-Indigenous Relations*, Indigenous Americas Series (University of Minnesota Press, 2007).

8. Wolfe, "Settler Colonialism and the Elimination of the Native," 387.

9. Tristan Ahtone and Robert Lee, "Land-Grab Universities," *High Country News*, March 30, 2020, hcn.org.

10. J. Kēhaulani Kauanui and Patrick Wolfe, "Patrick Wolfe on Settler Colonialism," in *Speaking of Indigenous Politics: Conversations with Activists, Scholars, and Tribal Leaders*, edited by J. Kēhaulani Kauanui, with a foreword by Robert Warrior (University of Minnesota Press, 2018), 351.

11. David Kazanjian, "'To See the Issue of His Exorbitant Practices': A Response to 'the Dispossessed Eighteenth Century,'" *The Eighteenth Century* 55, no. 2/3 (2014): 277.

12. Haunani-Kay Trask, *From a Native Daughter: Colonialism and Sovereignty in Hawai'i* (University of Hawai'i Press, 1999), 18.

13. Saidiya V. Hartman, *Scenes of Subjection: Terror, Slavery, and Self-Making in Nineteenth-Century America* (Oxford University Press, 1997), 54.

14. Avery Gordon, *The Hawthorn Archive: Letters from the Utopian Margins* (Fordham University Press, 2018), 30.

15. Lisa Brooks, *Our Beloved Kin* (Yale University Press, 2018), 4.

16. Brooks, *Our Beloved Kin*, 6.

17. For a broad overview of Indigenous students and early US higher education see Bobby Wright, "The 'Untameable Savage Spirit': American Indians in Colonial Colleges," *The Review of Higher Education* 14, no. 4 (1991): 429–52.

18. Brooks, *Our Beloved Kin*, 73. For more on land settler expropriation of land through such agreements see K-Sue Park, "Money, Mortgages, and the Conquest of America," *Law & Social Inquiry* 41, no. 4 (2016): 1006–35.

19. On different interpretations of such agreements between settlers and Indigenous people see Patricia Seed, *American Pentimento* (University of Minnesota Press, 2001).

20. For an extensive study of slavery in the seventeenth- and eighteenth-century British colonies see Wendy Warren, *New England Bound: Slavery and Colonization in Early America* (W. W. Norton, 2016).

21. Craig Steven Wilder, *Ebony and Ivy: Race, Slavery, and the Troubled History of America's Universities* (Bloomsbury Press, 2013), 30.

22. Brooks, *Our Beloved Kin*, 80.

23. *New England's First Fruits: In Respect, First of the Conversion of some, Conviction of divers, Preparation of others of the Indians. 2. Of the progresse of Learning, in the Colledge at Cambridge in Massacusets Bay* (Printed by R.O. and G.D. (London) for Henry Overton, 1643).

24. Brooks, *Our Beloved Kin*, 80.

25. Brooks, *Our Beloved Kin*, 81.

26. Drew Lopenzina, *Red Ink: Native Americans Picking Up the Pen in the Colonial Period* (SUNY Press, 2012), 91. For more on the importance of education in the British colonial period see James Axtell, *The School Upon a Hill: Education and Society in Colonial New England* (Yale University Press, 1974); and Bernard Bailyn, *Education in the Forming of American Society: Needs and Opportunities for Study* (University of North Carolina Press, 1970).

27. Brooks, *Our Beloved Kin*, 82.

28. For further elaboration on this act and how it conditioned the actions of Henry Dunster, Harvard's first president, see Drew Lopenzina's *Red Ink*, in which he discusses Dunster's relationship to two Native youth in the 1640s. Lopenzina, *Red Ink*, 108.

29. Lopenzina, *Red Ink*, 107.

30. Brooks, *Our Beloved Kin*. To support this point, Brooks cites *An Act for Promoting and Propagating the Gospel of Jesus Christ in New England* (Printed for Edward Husband, Printer to the Parliament of England, 1649); Michael P. Clark, ed., *The Eliot Tracts: With Letters from John Eliot to Thomas Thorowgood and Richard Baxter* (Praeger, 2003), 223; *Charter of 1650* (May 31, 1650), Harvard University Archives, Cambridge, MA.

31. Brooks, *Our Beloved Kin*, 83.

32. Brooks writes "in early fall 1662 two young Wampanoag men arrived at Harvard Yard for commencement," but Lopenzina writes of their entrance in 1661. Brooks notes that in the 1650s John Sassamon, an orphaned Massachusett youth, attended Harvard before the founding of the Indian College. He did not graduate but went on to appear as "an interpreter on dubious deeds" for many Native leaders, including Metacom. In this capacity, Sassamon enabled the northern expansion of British claims of Dartmouth into Pocasset and Watuppa. These initial interactions with Harvard-educated Indians provided Native leaders with an early lesson in the need to be "cautious about colonial education." As Brooks contends, Sassamon's role

in these deeds and the "track record of deceptive documents" underscores that "these deeds themselves are *unstable* historical documents" thus undercutting the legality of broad swaths of British land claims. Brooks, *Our Beloved Kin*, 63–64, 79.

33. Brooks, *Our Beloved Kin*, 6.

34. Brooks marks that in the Western Abenaki language clock became known as "*papeezokewazki*, 'that thing which makes noise and does nothing useful.'" Brooks, *Our Beloved Kin*, 84.

35. For instance, Brooks further contends that Iacoomes and Cheeshateaumuck, like other Indians who embraced Christianity in the seventeenth century, were able to merge this white, European conceptualization of temporality with the "cyclical, spatialized conception of deep time, permeating all spaces and temporalities" that would have been far more familiar to them. Brooks, *Our Beloved Kin*, 84–85.

36. Wilder, *Ebony and Ivy*, 27; Wolfgang Hochbruck and Beatrix Dudensign-Reichel provide text from the 1665 Harvard College Laws to support "'Honoratissimi Benefactores': Native American Students and Two Seventeenth-Century Texts in the University Tradition," *Source: Studies in American Indian Literatures* 2, no. 4 (1992): 35–47.

37. Cited in Wilder, *Ebony and Ivy*, 28.

38. Hochbruck and Denudensign-Reichel, "Honoratissimi Benefactores," 38.

39. Lopenzina, *Red Ink*, 131.

40. Brooks, *Our Beloved Kin*, 97.

41. Brooks, *Our Beloved Kin*, 101.

42. John D. Burton, "Crimson Missionaries: The Robert Boyle Legacy and Harvard College," *The New England Quarterly* 67, no. 1 (1994): 132–40. Larnell was the last Native student to attend Harvard in the eighteenth century, supported by a scholarship from the Robert Boyle estate, which is discussed more below. According to John Burton, "Larnell had difficulties adjusting to Puritan culture; he had drinking problems at Harvard, as he had earlier at the Boston Latin School. He was expelled from Harvard once, and after returning to the college, he caught a fever and died in 1714" (ibid., 134). The Boyle fund did, however, cover his funeral costs.

43. Lopenzina, *Red Ink*, 125; Brooks, *Our Beloved Kin*, 102.

44. Hochbruck and Denudensign-Reichel, "Honoratissimi Benefactores," 46.

45. Brooks, *Our Beloved Kin*, 103.

46. Burton, "Crimson Missionaries," 132.

47. Wright, "The 'Untameable Savage Spirit,'" 433.

48. Robert Beverley Jr., *History and Present of State of Virginia* (Richmond, 1855), 91. "During that Gentleman's Presidency, which began *Anno* 1689, the Project of a College was first agreed upon."

49. W. Stitt Robinson Jr., "Indian Education and Missions in Colonial Virginia," *The Journal of Southern History* 18, no. 2 (1952): 162.

50. Wilder, *Ebony and Ivy*, 42.

51. Kristalyn Marie Shefveland, *Anglo-Native Virginia: Trade, Conversion, and Indian Slavery in the Old Dominion, 1646–1722* (University of Georgia Press, 2016),

91, citing H. R. McIlwaine, ed., *Executive Journals of the Council of Colonial Virginia*, vol. 1 (Virginia State Library, 1925), 311.

52. Burton, "Crimson Missionaries," 132.

53. Transcript of "Rules and Methods for Disposition of Rents and Profits," [1695], Box 3, Folder 1, Brafferton Estate Collection (UA 113), Special Collections Research Center, William & Mary Libraries, Williamsburg, VA.

54. Wilder, *Ebony and Ivy*, 44.

55. Shefveland, *Anglo-Native Virginia*, 8.

56. J. Kēhaulani Kauanui, "Tracing Historical Specificity: Race and the Colonial," *American Quarterly* 69, no. 2 (2017): 261; See also Kevin Bruyneel's chapter on Bacon's Rebellion in *Settler Memory: The Disavowal of Indigeneity and the Politics of Race in the United States* (University of North Carolina Press, 2021).

57. Shefveland, *Anglo-Native Virginia*, 61.

58. Shefveland, *Anglo-Native Virginia*, 62.

59. Robinson, "Indian Education and Missions in Colonial Virginia," 162, citing R. A. Brock, ed., *The Official Letters of Alexander Spotswood, Lieutenant Governor of the Colony of Virginia, 1710–1722*. 2 vols. Collections of the Virginia Historical Society, New Series (Virginia Historical Society, 1882–1885), I:124.

60. Owen Stanwood, "Captives and Slaves: Indian Labor, Cultural Conversion, and the Plantation Revolution in Virginia," *The Virginia Magazine of History and Biography* 114, no. 4 (2006): 456, citing Francis Nicholson to the archbishop of Canterbury, May 27, 1700, in William Stevens Perry, ed., *Historical Collections Relating to the American Colonial Church*, 5 vols. (Hartford, 1870), 1:121, 123–24; "Copy of part of a speech to the General Assembly of Virginia in Nov. 1711," Stevens Perry, *Historical Collections Relating to the American Colonial Church*, 1:129; Robert Beverley, *The History and Present State of Virginia* (Richmond, 1855), 216; See also "American Indian Education in Virginia," *Virginia Indian Archive*, accessed June 17, 2021, https://web.archive.org/web/20200811222341/http://www.virginiaindianarchive.org/exhibits/show/american-indian-education-in-v.

61. Buck Woodard, "Students at the Brafferton Indian School," in *Building the Brafferton: The Founding, Funding and Legacy of America's Indian School*, ed. Danielle Moretti-Langholtz and Buck Woodard (Muscarelle Museum of Art, 2019), 103. Woodard cites Alan Gallay, *The Indian Slave Trade: The Rise of the English Empire in the American South, 1670–1717* (Yale University Press, 2003).

62. I discuss William & Mary's August 2020 "Acknowledgement of Indigenous Peoples as the Historical Custodians of the Land at William & Mary" at length in Boggs, "Educational Pasts, Enduring Colonial Presents: Indigenous Student Conscripts and the Foundation of the US University," *History of the Present* 13 no. 2 (2023). When I researched, wrote, and had that article accepted for publication in 2022, the William & Mary website included no discussion of this history. In the interim, and to their credit, they have updated their page on "The Indian School at William and Mary" to address this history more directly. Yet, even as the updated page acknowledges that "first students at the Indian School (ca. 1702) were procured by Indian traders," in doing so they seem to want to redeem the school's

innocence, insisting that the young Indigenous people held captive on the campus were "not kept as slaves." Going a step further, the site then erases not just the memory of these people but the very idea that they had memories at all in relationship to their tribes, asserting by way of speculation that "having lost all memory and association with their natal communities it is likely they remained institutional wards at the Indian School for many years." See "Acknowledgement of Indigenous Peoples as the Historical Custodians of the Lands and Waterways of the Williamsburg Area," American Indian Resource Center, William & Mary, accessed July 23, 2026, https://www.wm.edu/as/anthropology/research/centers/airc/land-acknowledgement/; and "Brafferton House," *Williamsburg Ghost Tour*, accessed July 23, 2026, https://williamsburgghosttour.com/brafferton-house/.

63. Shefveland, *Anglo-Native Virginia*, 92.

64. Karen A. Stuart, "'So Good a Word': The Brafferton School, 1691–1777," (Master's Thesis, The College of William & Mary, 1984), 16; See also Shefveland, *Anglo-Native Virginia*, 83, 92.

65. Robinson, "Indian Education and Missions in Colonial Virginia," 163; See also Shefveland, *Anglo-Native Virginia*, 85–86; and Moretti-Langholtz and Woodard, *Building the Brafferton*, 104.

66. Wright, "The 'Untameable Savage Spirit,'" 432. Among the tribes Spotswood tried to entice to send students, the Tuscarora held out, continuing to war with the Virginians from 1711 to 1713. A primary sticking point in their negotiations was the Tuscarora's refusal to agree to the Virginian's demand that they "deliver children to secure the peace." An agreement was only met in 1714 after eventually conceding to a treaty after "Two leaders of the Tuscarora (Haweesaris / Basket and Naroniackkos / George) returned with Robert Hix and requested tributary status that would include a trade agreement with the Virginians and a promise to provide children." Many Tuscarora fled the area, traveling north to settle in Pennsylvania and New York, forming new alliances with the Onieda and then joining as the Sixth Nation of the Haudenosaunee Confederacy in 1722.

67. McIlwaine, *Executive Journals*, 1:290–91; Spotswood to Virginia Assembly, November 1711, Perry, Historical Collections, 129, cited in Stuart, "So Good a Word," 17.

68. Stuart, "So Good a Word," 80.

69. Stuart, "So Good a Word," 27.

70. Hugh Jones, *The Present State of Virginia: From Whence Is Inferred a Short View of Maryland and North Carolina*, ed. Richard L. Morton (University of North Carolina Press, 1956), cited in Stuart, "So Good a Word," 43; and Robinson, "Indian Education and Missions in Colonial Virginia," 166.

71. Jones, *The Present State of Virginia*, 12–13, 49–62, 99, cited in Stuart, "So Good a Word," 28.

72. Woodard, "Students at the Brafferton Indian School," 109.

73. Stuart, "So Good a Word," 56, citing *The Papers of Benjamin Franklin*, ed. Leonard W. Labaree et al. (Yale University Press, 1961) 4:482–83.

74. Woodard, "Students at the Brafferton Indian School," 109, 113.

75. Woodard, "Students at the Brafferton Indian School," 114, citing Robert Dinwiddie, *The Official Records of Robert Dinwiddie, Lieutenant-Governor of the Colony of Virginia, 1751–1758*, ed. R. A. Brock (Virginia Historical Society, 1883), 1:445–47.

76. Gregory D. Smithers, *The Cherokee Diaspora: An Indigenous History of Migration, Resettlement, and Identity* (Yale University Press, 2015).

77. Woodard, "Students at the Brafferton Indian School," 121.

78. Woodard, "Students at the Brafferton Indian School," 127.

79. Woodard, "Students at the Brafferton Indian School," 129.

80. Woodard, "Students at the Brafferton Indian School," 135.

81. Woodard, "Students at the Brafferton Indian School," 135.

82. Much as William & Mary and the Brafferton building have been the objects of study in both books and exhibitions, so too has scholarly and curatorial attention come to focus on Eleazar Wheelock's educative projects at Moor's Indian Charity School and Dartmouth College. In 2010, Colin Calloway published his study *The Indian History of an American Institution: Native Americans and Dartmouth* and then in 2013, Dartmouth's Rauner Special Collections library installed an exhibit, "'A Matter of Absolute Necessity' Eleazar Wheelock and Moor's Indian Charity School." James Axtell, "Mr. Wheelock's Little Red School," in *The European and the Indian: Essays in the Ethnohistory of Colonial North America* (Oxford University Press, 1981), 91; James Zug, "The Slaves of Dartmouth," *Dartmouth Alumni Magazine*, January/February 2007, accessed August 20, 2019, dartmouthalumnimagazine.com, retrieved August 20, 2019.

83. Axtell, "Mr. Wheelock's Little Red School," 91, citing Edwin Scott Gaustad, *The Great Awakening in New England* (Harper & Row, 1957), 74–75; James Dow McCallum, *Eleazar Wheelock, Founder of Dartmouth College, Dartmouth College Manuscript Series*, Number 4 (Hanover, NH, 1939), chapter 2.

84. Colin G. Calloway, *The Indian History of an American Institution: Native Americans and Dartmouth* (Dartmouth College Press, 2010), 4.

85. On Samson Occom's relationship to the racial logics of his era see Katy L. Chiles, "Becoming Colored in Occom and Wheatley's Early America," *PMLA* 123, no. 5 (2008): 1398–417.

86. Lisa Brooks, "On the Recovery of Native Space in the Northeast," in *Critical Indigenous Studies*, ed. J. Kēhaulani Kauanui (University of Minnesota Press, 2018), 33. "When you look at Samson Occom's life as a whole, rather than focusing on, say, his time, his association with Eleazar Wheelock; if you don't focus on, say, his Christianity, you see an incredibly rich and complex leader." What is often discussed as Occom's "autobiography" "wasn't an autobiography; it was simply a fragment of a letter that he wrote" (ibid., 33). Instead, this writing was actually "written as a result of the Mohegan land case" to establish his genealogy and to prove himself to "outsiders." As Linford Fisher writes, "one of his life's goals was to get Mohegans to see each other as one family, to ameliorate some of the

common conflicts that were tearing them apart." See Linford Fisher, *The Indian Great Awakening: Religion and the Shaping of Native Cultures* (Oxford University Press, 2012).

87. Calloway, *The Indian History of an American Institution*, 5.

88. Calloway, *The Indian History of an American Institution*, 5.

89. Calloway, *The Indian History of an American Institution*, 6.

90. Axtell, "Mr. Wheelock's Little Red School," 97.

91. Axtell, "Mr. Wheelock's Little Red School" cites the Papers of Eleazar Wheelock [1728–1770], Dartmouth College Library, Hanover, N.H. 762521.1, 764560.1.

92. Axtell, "Mr. Wheelock's Little Red School," 92.

93. Brooks, *Our Beloved Kin*, 87.

94. Brooks, *Our Beloved Kin*, 89–90.

95. Cited in Axtell, "Mr. Wheelock's Little Red School," 95.

96. Axtell, "Mr. Wheelock's Little Red School," 95. As Axtell explains in his endnote, he is citing "Papers of Eleazar Wheelock [1728–1779], Dartmouth College Library, Hanover, N.H.," and is followed by the calendar number as given in *A Guide to the Microfilm Edition of the Papers of Eleazar Wheelock* (Hanover, N.H.: Dartmouth College Library, 1971). The first three digits indicate the year of the manuscript: e.g., 760628 is 1760."

97. Calloway, *The Indian History of an American Institution*, 10.

98. Wright, "The 'Untameable Savage Spirit,'" 440, citing Wheelock Papers, 1772–79. Microfilm. Archives, Library, Dartmouth College, Hanover, New Hampshire, 764560.

99. Axtell, "Mr. Wheelock's Little Red School," citing Eleazar Wheelock, *Continuation of the Narrative* (1771), 5.

100. Axtell, "Mr. Wheelock's Little Red School," citing Wheelock, *A Plain and Faithful Narrative*, 15.

101. Calloway, *The Indian History of an American Institution*, 12; Wheelock to Oliver, December 17, 1762, MS 76267.2. The labor component of Wheelock's educational philosophy seems to have built on the model of the Irish Charter School in which student's manual labor was imagined to offset some of the costs of operating while simultaneously functioning as a kind of discipline and a mode of instilling Christian piety. I thank Khalil Johnson for this insight and the reference to Kenneth Milne's *The Irish Charter Schools, 1730–1830*.

102. Calloway, *The Indian History of an American Institution*, 10.

103. Calloway, *The Indian History of an American Institution*, 12.

104. Wright, "The 'Untameable Savage Spirit,'" 440.

105. Axtell, "Mr. Wheelock's Little Red School," citing McCallum, ed., *The Letters of Eleazar Wheelock's Indians*, 231.

106. Axtell, "Mr. Wheelock's Little Red School," citing McCallum, ed., *The Letters of Eleazar Wheelock's Indians*, 65.

107. Wilder, *Ebony and Ivy*, 162, citing Col. Henry Bouquet to Sir Jeffrey Amherst, June 25, 1763, July 13, 1763, July 26, 1773, August 27, 1763, and Sir Jeffrey Amherst to Col. Henry Bouquet, July 16, 1763, September 25, 1763, in Henry Bouquet, *The Papers of Col. Henry Bouquet*, ed. Sylvester K. Stevens and Donald H. Kent (Pennsylvania Historical Commission, 1940–1943), 203, 214–19, 250–51, 276–77.

108. Calloway, *The Indian History of an American Institution*, 16; David McClure and Elijah Parish, *Memoirs of the Rev. Eleazar Wheelock, D.D.* (Edward Little & Co., 1811), 223–24. See also James Tracy, *History of the American Board of Commissioners for Foreign Missions* (M.W. Dodd, 1842), 18.

109. Calloway, *The Indian History of an American Institution*, 18.

110. Calloway, *The Indian History of an American Institution*, 18; and Axtell, "Mr. Wheelock's Little Red School," 107.

111. "The Charter of Dartmouth College," December 13, 1769, Dartmouth Libraries Digital Collections, Dartmouth Libraries, accessed September 3, 2025, 1, https://www.library.dartmouth.edu/digital/digital-collections/dartmouth-college-charter.

112. Axtell, *The European and the Indian*, 90.

113. Wilder, *Ebony and Ivy*, 113.

114. Calloway, *The Indian History of an American Institution*, 23.

115. Wilder, *Ebony and Ivy*, 168.

116. Calloway, *The Indian History of an American Institution*, 23.

117. Axtell, "Mr. Wheelock's Little Red School," citing McCallum, *The Letters of Eleazar Wheelock's Indians*, 65.

118. Calloway, *The Indian History of an American Institution*, 29, citing Frederick Chase, *A History of Dartmouth College and the Town of Hanover, New Hampshire*, vol. 1, ed. John King Lord (John Wilson and Son, 1891), 309.

119. Calloway, *The Indian History of an American Institution*, 27, citing Wheelock to Occom, January 22, 1771, Ms. 771122; Occom to Wheelock, July 24, 1774, Ms. 771424; also in Samson Occom, *The Collected Writings of Samson Occom*, ed. Joanna Brooks (Oxford University Press, 2006), 98–100.

120. Axtell, "Mr. Wheelock's Little Red School," 89.

## 2. "Ridding America of these alien bodies" for the Empire of Liberty

1. David Kazanjian, *The Colonizing Trick: National Culture and Imperial Citizenship in Early America* (University of Minnesota Press, 2003), 96. Importantly, as Kazanjian and scholars including Samantha Seeley have detailed, both Black and white abolitionists of the era staunchly critiqued the ACS's project. As early as 1774 Phillis Wheatley expressed her objection to colonization in a letter to John Thornton. Just a year after the formation of the ACS, 3,000 Black Philadelphians roundly denounced the plan (Seeley, 94). Two of the most famous writings on the topic from the time are David Walker's 1829 *Appeal to the Coloured Citizens of the World* and William Lloyd Garrison's 1832 *Thoughts on African Colonization*.

Samantha Seeley, "Beyond the American Colonization Society," *History Compass* 14, no. 3 (2016): 93–104.

2. Thomas Jefferson, *Writings*, ed. Merrill D. Peterson (Library of America, 1984), 43–44, cited in Kazanjian, *The Colonizing Trick*, 116. Church ministers Samuel Hopkins and Ezra Stiles, who would go on to be the seventh president of Yale, first developed a plan to "link the emancipation of African slaves to the religious colonization of the African continent." The project never fully manifested due to a lack of funds and the advent of the Revolutionary War, but it did plant an important seed. In the late 1780s, Hopkins also proposed an African settlement for Black people from America specifically because it "would be beneficial to the expansion of Christianity and 'civilization.'" See Olanipekun Laosebikan, "From Student to Immigrant: The Diasporation of the African Student in the United States," (PhD diss., University of Illinois at Urbana Champaign, 2012), 26, 36.

3. Kazanjian, *The Colonizing Trick*, 31.

4. Kazanjian, *The Colonizing Trick*, 95.

5. On "empire of liberty" see Ian Tyrrell, *Reforming the World: The Creation of America's Moral Empire* (Princeton University Press, 2010); Brandon Mills, *The World Colonization Made: The Racial Geography of Early American Empire* (University of Pennsylvania Press, 2020), 161.

6. Matthew Simpson, ed., *Cyclopaedia of Methodism: Embracing Sketches of Its Rise, Progress, and Present Condition, with Biographical Notices and Numerous Illustrations*, rev. ed. (Louis H. Everts, 1880), s.v. "Burns, Francis," 114.

7. Sylvia Jacobs, "Nineteenth Century Black Methodist Missionary Bishops in Liberia," *Negro History Bulletin* 44, no. 4 (1981): 83. For an image of Burns, see John Chester Buttre, Rev. Francis Burns, Missionary Bishop of the M.E. Church in Western Africa [graphic], engraving after Mathew B. Brady, ca. 1858–1863, Library Company of Philadelphia, accessed September 3, 2025, librarycompany.org.

8. As is well documented in a 1986 Wesleyan senior thesis by Jeffrey Liss, Charles Ray was the first Black student to enroll at Wesleyan in 1832. He had previously been a student of Fisk's at the Wesleyan Academy. His tenure at Wesleyan was short-lived. As Liss describes, Ray's presence on campus caused "an uproar from the moment of his arrival," which resulted in a student resolution to remove Ray from "this Institution." For more on this see David Potts, *Wesleyan University, 1830–1910: Collegiate Enterprise in New England* (Wesleyan University Press, 1999), 55. Three students from Puerto Rico—Felipe Santiago De Mena, Ynocencio Geigel, and Ramon Gonzalez—enrolled in the 1841–1842 academic year but left before receiving degrees. Thus, when the Liberian student graduated in 1860, he was the first nonwhite student to obtain a Wesleyan degree.

9. Potts, *Wesleyan University, 1830–1910*, 55.

10. Mills, *The World Colonization Made*, 161.

11. *Wesleyan University, Alumni Record of Wesleyan University, Middletown, Conn, 3rd ed.* (Press of the Case, Lockwood & Brainard Company, 1883), 169; Frank Nicolson, *Alumni Record of Wesleyan University, Middletown Connecticut*, 4th ed. (Tuttle, Morehouse & Taylor, 1911).

12. See for instance, Christopher J. Lucas's seminal text *American Higher Education: A History* (Palgrave Macmillan, 2006), with forty pages on the period.

13. Teresa B. Bevis and Christopher J. Lucas, *International Students in American Colleges and Universities* (Palgrave Macmillan, 2007), 43. Yung Wing is discussed at great length in Chapter 3.

14. G. W. F. Hegel, *The Philosophy of History* (Colonial Press, 1899 [1837]), 86. Interestingly, the 1899 republication of the Hegel text includes an epigraph from W. V. Humboldt, often considered the founder of the modern research or "Humboldtian" university, "The History of the World is not intelligible apart from a Government of the World."

15. Benjamin Rush, "Thoughts Upon the Mode of Education Proper to a Republic," in *Essays on Education in the Early Republic* (1786), 9, cited in Kenneth Nivison, "'But a Step From College to the Judicial Bench': College and Curriculum in New England's 'Age of Improvement,'" *History of Education Quarterly* 50, no. 4 (2010): 460–87.

16. David L. Madsen, "The University of the United States: A Durable Dream," *The Journal of Higher Education* 33, no. 7 (October 1962): 354, citing *The Selected Writings of Benjamin Rush*, ed. Dagobert D. Runes (Philosophical Library, Inc., 1947), 87.

17. "From Thomas Jefferson to John Banister, Jr., 15 October 1785," Founders Online, National Archives, https://founders.archives.gov/documents/Jefferson/01-08-02-0499. [Original source: *The Papers of Thomas Jefferson*, vol. 8, 25 *February–31 October* 1785, ed. Julian P. Boyd (Princeton University Press, 1953), 635–38].

18. Lucas, *American Higher Education*, 117.

19. Lucas, *American Higher Education*, 121–22.

20. Meredith McCoy et al., "The Future of Land-Grab Universities," *Native American and Indigenous Studies* 8, no. 1 (Spring 2021): 171. The American Western University, which was eventually renamed Ohio University, was founded in 1802 as part of this process. See Richard Rees Price, *The Financial Support of State Universities: A Study of the Financial Resources of State Universities in the Light of the Experience of the Universities of the Old Northwest Territory, With a Suggested Policy for the Future* (Harvard University Press, 2014).

21. Lucas, *American Higher Education*, 117.

22. Steven Ambrose, *Duty, Honor, Country: A History of West Point* (Johns Hopkins University Press, 1966), 16.

23. David L. Blaney, *Political Economy as Theodicy: Progress, Suffering and Denial* (Routledge, 2024).

24. Jefferson's advocacy on such matters began with his 1778 bill for the Virginia legislature for the "More General Diffusion of Knowledge." Thomas Jefferson, "A Bill for the More General Diffusion of Knowledge," June 18, 1779, Founders Online, National Archives, archives.gov.

25. There were two efforts to revive the Indian School project in the 1780s but both were clearly designed for the purpose of securing new funding sources rather

than as part of an actual vision for education. When it became apparent that such funds were not forthcoming locally or through legal efforts to reinstate the Boyle support, they were dropped. As Woodard describes, "without the earmarked funding requirement 'to educate the Western Indians,'" the interest in procuring more Native youths ceased and no further students were educated at the 'Brafferton School.'" Danielle Moretti-Langholtz and Buck Woodard, eds. *Building the Brafferton: The Founding, Funding and Legacy of America's Indian School* (Muscarelle Museum of Art, 2019), 148, citing Brafferton Estate Collection, 1691–1935; Harrison to Madison 1/22/1784; J. E. Morpurgo, *Their Majesties' Royall Colledge: William & Mary in the Seventeenth and Eighteenth Centuries* (College of William & Mary, 1976), 212–13; Karen A. Stuart, "'So Good a Word': The Brafferton School, 1691–1777" (Master's Thesis, The College of William & Mary, 1984), 71–73.

26. Uday S. Mehta, "Liberal Strategies of Exclusion," in *Tensions of Empire: Colonial Cultures in a Bourgeois World*, ed. Frederick Cooper and Ann Laura Stoler (University of California Press, 1997).

27. Thomas Jefferson, "Bill for the More General Diffusion of Knowledge," (Dixon & Holt, 1784), no manuscript copy survives. Julian Bond, ed. *The Papers of Thomas Jefferson, Volume 2: January 1777 to June 1779* (Princeton University Press, 1950), 526–35. As Gregory Michael Dorr argues Jefferson's plan for education was in fact more democratic than others but it was "meritocracy in name only." Aside from the fact that it was only for white men, attaining schooling beyond three years in Jefferson's Virginia required the ability to pay. Gregory Michael Dorr, *Segregation's Science: Eugenics and Society in Virginia* (University of Virginia Press, 2008), 29.

28. *Autobiography of Thomas Jefferson 1743–1790*, ed. Paul Leicester Ford (G.P. Putnam's Sons, 1914).

29. Theodore J. Crackel, "The Military Academy in the Context of Jeffersonian Reform," in *Thomas Jefferson's Military Academy: Founding West Point*, ed. Robert McDonald (University of Virginia Press, 2004), 111–12. The politics, purpose, and curricular content of West Point continue to be sites of debate and dissension. In the early months of the second Trump administration, Secretary of Defense Pete Hegseth worked to undermine the civilian influence at the academy pledging, as *Politico* reports, to "'rip, root and branch the politics and divisive policies' out of service academies like West Point by ridding them of civilian faculty." See Jasper Craven, "Inside Pete Hegseth's Civilian Purge at West Point," *Politico*, August 29, 2025, https://www.politico.com/news/magazine/2025/08/28/pete-hegseth-civilians-west-point-00523613.

30. Ambrose, *Duty, Honor, Country*, 18.

31. Ambrose, *Duty, Honor, Country*, 18.

32. Jennings L. Wagoner and Christine Coalwell McDonald, "Mr. Jefferson's Academy: An Educational Interpretation," in McDonald, ed., *Thomas Jefferson's Military Academy*, 130; See also Theodore J. Crackel, "The Military Academy in the Context of Jeffersonian Reform," in McDonald, ed., *Thomas Jefferson's Military Academy*.

33. Ambrose, *Duty, Honor, Country*, 22.

34. Ambrose, *Duty, Honor, Country*, 25.

35. Ambrose, *Duty, Honor, Country*, 63.

36. Ambrose, *Duty, Honor, Country*, 64.

37. Ambrose, *Duty, Honor, Country*, 87, 89.

38. Ian Hacking, "Biopower and the Avalanche of Printed Numbers," *Humanities in Society* 5, no. 3/4 (Summer and Fall 1982): 281, 288; and Michel Foucault, *Security, Territory, Population* (Picador, 2007), 101.

39. Foucault, *Security, Territory, Population*, 101.

40. Linda Gordon, *Woman's Body, Woman's Right: Birth Control in America* (Penguin, 1976), 73.

41. Drew R. McCoy, "Jefferson and Madison on Malthus: Population Growth in Jeffersonian Political Economy," *The Virginia Magazine of History and Biography* 88, no. 3 (1980): 261.

42. Thomas Malthus, *An Essay on the Principle of Population* (Printed for J. Johnson, in St. Paul's Church-Yard, 1798), 4. There is much to be said about the broader implications of Malthus's theories, particularly his assertion that "human nature was to blame, in part because the passion for procreation was far more powerful than human reason and broke through the rational strains." As Gordon and McCoy discuss, this perspective fueled the elimination of poor relief in England in the early nineteenth century with significant implications up through the present. Meredith McCoy et al. "The Future of Land-Grab Universities," *Native American and Indigenous Studies* 8, no. 1 (2021): 263.

43. McCoy et al., "The Future of Land-Grab Universities," 265.

44. Cooper to Jefferson, February 16, 1804, Jefferson Papers, Library of Congress, cited in McCoy et al., "The Future of Land-Grab Universities," 266.

45. Graham Russell et al., eds., *The Book of Negroes: African Americans in Exile After the American Revolution* (Fordham University Press, 2021).

46. Charles I. Foster, "The Colonization of Free Negros, in Liberia, 1816–1835," *The Journal of Negro History* 38, no. 1 (1953): 43–44; and Horace Mann Bond, *Education for Freedom: A History of Lincoln University* (Lincoln University Press, 1976), 147.

47. David Kazanjian, *The Colonizing Trick: National Culture and Imperial Citizenship in Early America* (University of Minnesota Press, 2003), 31.

48. Kazanjian, *The Colonizing Trick*, 31.

49. Craig Steven Wilder, *Ebony and Ivy: Race, Slavery, and the Troubled History of America's Universities* (Bloomsbury Press, 2013), 248.

50. "Unauthorized Transformation," *African Repository and Colonial Journal*, Vol. XI, American Colonization Society: Washington, February 28, 1835 (Way & Gideon, Printers, 1835). Retrieved from the Atla Digital Library, https://commons.ptsem.edu/id/africanrepositor114amer_1, cited by Wilder, *Ebony and Ivy*, 256.

51. Wilder, *Ebony and Ivy*, 246.

52. Wilder, *Ebony and* Ivy.

53. M. Jean O'Brien, *Firsting and Lasting: Writing Indians Out of Existence in New England* (University of Minnesota Press, 2010), xvi. O'Brien builds on Ruth Wallis Herndon and Ella Wilcox Sekatau's work on officials in Revolutionary-era Rhode Island who classified Indigenous people as Black, in effect disappearing them from public records.

54. For more on the founding of ABCFM see David W. Kling, "The New Divinity and the Origins of the American Board of Commissioners for Foreign Missions," *Church History* 72, no. 4 (2003): 791–819. It is telling, however, that Kling's recounting of the founding of the organization makes no mention of any specific students, including ʻŌpūkahaʻia, an individual whose importance will become clear in the rest of the chapter.

55. Gardiner Spring, *Memoirs of the Rev. Samuel J. Mills: Late Missionary to the South Western Section of the United States, and Agent of the American Colonization Society Deputed to Explore the Coast of Africa* (Francis Westly, 1820), 24, quoted in John Demos, *The Heathen School: A Story of Hope and Betrayal in the Age of the Early Republic* (Knopf, 2014).

56. John Andrew, "Educating the Heathen: The Foreign Mission School Controversy and American Ideals," *Journal of American Studies* 12, no. 3 (1978): 332–33; See also Demos, *The Heathen School*. Coincidentally, on this same day, the Synod of New York and New Jersey announced plans "for an African School, for the purpose of educating young men of colour" to be located in Parsippany, New Jersey. For more on this school see Khalil Johnson who cites James Richards and Edward D. Griffin. Synods of New York and New Jersey, "African Seminary," *Christian Herald* 2 (November 1816): 102, 105.

57. "On Educating Heathen Youth in Our Own Country," *The Panopolist* 12 (1816): 297. Another articulation: "for the purpose of educating youths of Heathen nations, with a view to their being useful in their respective countries," Jedidiah Morse (1822), *A Report to the Secretary of War of the United States, on Indian Affairs*, S. Converse, 163, 264–66, https://archive.org/details/reporttosecreta01morsgoog.

58. Robert Hunt Land, "Henrico and its College," *William & Mary Quarterly*, 2nd ser., 18 (1898): 475, cited in Stuart, "So Good a Word"; and Karen Sánchez-Eppler, "Copying and Conversion: An 1824 Friendship Album 'from a Chinese Youth,'" *American Quarterly* 59, no. 2 (June 2007): 304.

59. An 1816 issue of *The Panoplist and Missionary Magazine* explains such an educational effort as strategically necessary because, "Most heathen nations . . . have contracted strong prejudices against their more enlightened brethren. . . . By employing natives, this great obstacle . . . would be removed." "On Educating Heathen Youth in Our Own Country," 298. Another articulation: Morse, "for the purpose of educating youths of Heathen nations," 163, 264–66, accessed September 3, 2025.

60. As Khalil Johnson argues, the missionaries believed "all humanity to be descended from a common Creator and chalked up distinctions among groups as a matter of habit, custom, and environment, not irreconcilable racial differences."

Despite this, the educational paradigm they initiated was distinctly aligned with apartheid. Khalil Johnson, "Red, Black & *Brown v. Board of Education*: African American Educators and Indian Country," (PhD diss., Yale University, 2018), 70.

61. Sánchez-Eppler, "Copying and Conversion," 304.

62. "On Educating Heathen Youth in Our Own Country," 297. Another articulation: Morse "for the purpose of educating youths of Heathen nations," 163, 264–66.

63. Edward C. Starr, *A History of Cornwall, Connecticut, a Typical New England Town* (Tuttle, Morehouse & Taylor, 1926), 136.

64. Demos, *The Heathen School*, 21.

65. See *A Narrative of Five Youth from the Sandwich Islands, Now Receiving an Education in This Country* (New York, 1816), 9. This story continues to circulate in various official publications from Yale. See for instance, Judith Ann Aschiff, "Aloha Blue," *Yale Alumni Magazine* (July 2004), http://archives.yalealumnimagazine.com/issues/2004_07/old_yale.html.

66. David A. Chang, *The World and All the Things Upon It* (University of Minnesota Press, 2016), 83.

67. Chang, *The World and All the Things Upon It*, 83.

68. Demos, *The Heathen School*, 22.

69. Demos, *The Heathen School*, 27.

70. Homi K. Bhabha, "Of Mimicry and Man: The Ambivalence of Colonial Discourse," *October* 28 (Spring 1984): 126. In the notes for this article, Bhabha thanks Gayatri Chakravorty Spivak for organizing the panel on which it was originally presented.

71. Demos, *The Heathen School*, 25.

72. Demos, *The Heathen School*, 26, citing Edwin Welles Dwight, *Memoirs of Henry Obookiah: A Native of the Sandwich Islands, Who Died At Cornwall, Connecticut, February 17, 1818, Aged 26* (Religious Intelligencer, 1818), 44.

73. James Tracy, *History of the American Board of Commissioners for Foreign Missions* (M.W. Dodd, 1842), 58, 57.

74. Demos, *The Heathen School*, 33.

75. Charles Prentise, James Harvey, and James Morris to the American Board Commissioners for Foreign Missions, August, 20, 1816, ABC 12.1, vol. 2, no, 8, cited in Demos, *The Heathen School*, 33.

76. Demos, *The Heathen School*, 34.

77. Tracy, *History of the American Board of Commissioners for Foreign Missions*, 58.

78. American Board of Commissioners for Foreign Missions, "*Minutes of the Seventh Annual Meeting*," *The Panoplist, and Missionary Magazine* 13 (January 1817): 80.

79. "*Report of the Committee of the Foreign Mission School*," *The Panoplist, and Missionary Magazine* 13 (January 1817): 17.

80. Demos, *The Heathen School*, 38.

81. *A Narrative of Five Youth from the Sandwich Islands*, 5.

82. *A Narrative of Five Youth from the Sandwich Islands*, 9.

83. Demos, *The Heathen School*, 39.

84. Demos, *The Heathen School*, 39, citing Edwin W. Dwight, *Memoirs of Henry Obookiah*, 1990 ed. (Woman's Board of Missions for the Pacific Islands and the Hawaiian Historical Society, 1990), 84, 80–81.

85. Demos, *The Heathen School*, 30.

86. Demos, *The Heathen School*, 70.

87. Starr, *A History of Cornwall, Connecticut, a Typical New England Town*, 155, cited in Demos, *The Heathen School*, 77.

88. Starr, *A History of Cornwall, Connecticut, a Typical New England Town*, 140.

89. Demos, *The Heathen School*, 82.

90. Chang, *The World and All the Things Upon It*, 84.

91. Demos, *The Heathen School*, 82–83.

92. Demos, *The Heathen School*, 83.

93. Cited in Demos, *The Heathen School*, 84.

94. Chang, *The World and All the Things Upon It*, 84.

95. Chang cites S. W. Papaula, "Helehelekalani" [More on Opukahaia], *Ka Nupepa Kuokoa* 4, no. 44 (November 4, 1865) and his argument that he was "he kanaka makua (a mature person)." Chang, *The World and All the Things Upon It*, 88.

96. Chang, *The World and All the Things Upon It*, 80.

97. J. Kēhaulani Kauanui, *Paradoxes of Hawaiian Sovereignty: Land, Sex, and the Colonial Politics of State Nationalism* (Duke University Press, 2018), 24.

98. Starr, *A History of Cornwall, Connecticut, a Typical New England Town*, 141.

99. Demos, *The Heathen School*, 100.

100. Gregory D. Smithers, *The Cherokee Diaspora: An Indigenous History of Migration, Resettlement, and Identity* (Yale University Press, 2015), 93.

101. Smithers, *The Cherokee Diaspora*, 75.

102. Cited in Demos, *The Heathen School*, 112.

103. Demos, *The Heathen School*, 114.

104. Demos, *The Heathen School*, 114–15.

105. Demos, *The Heathen School*, 115.

106. Demos, *The Heathen School*, 116.

107. Smithers, *The Cherokee Diaspora*, 71.

108. Demos, *The Heathen School*, 153.

109. Demos, *The Heathen School*, 154, italics in original.

110. Demos, *The Heathen School*, 156.

111. Demos, *The Heathen School*, 180, citing "Special Communication to the Public," in *Semi-Annual Report of the Foreign Mission School, for June 1825*, June 17, 1825, [n.p., n.d.], pamphlet, Torrington Public Library, Torrington, CT.

112. Demos, *The Heathen School*, 161.

113. "Quarterly Report of the Foreign Mission School," June 1, 1824, ABC 18.8, vol. 1, American Board of Commissioners for Foreign Missions records, Houghton Library, Harvard University, cited by Demos, *The Heathen School*, 162.

114. Demos, *The Heathen School*, 220, citing *American Board of Commissioners for Foreign Missions, Fifteenth Annual Report of the American Board of Commissioners for Foreign Missions* (Crocker and Brewster, 1824), 131; *American Board of Commissioners for Foreign Missions, Seventeenth Annual Report of the American Board of Commissioners for Foreign Missions* (Crocker and Brewster, 1826), 106.

115. Demos, *The Heathen School*, 220, citing Jeremiah Evarts to Rev. T. Stone, August 26, 1825, ABC 1.01, vol. 5, nos. 359061.

116. Demos, *The Heathen School*, 191.

117. The latter half of the 1820s also proved to be decisive for the future of the Cherokee Nation. While the melodrama of Ridge and Boudinot's romantic lives played out between Cornwall and the Cherokee Nation, radical changes were also taking shape in the federal government's attitude and actions in relationship to Native tribes. In 1819, Congress passed the Civilization Fund Act, which provided the federal basis for the formation of boarding schools toward the end of the nineteenth century as well as a small amount of the funds that flowed through Cornwall. See Francis Paul Prucha, "Documents of United States Indian Policy," Library of Congress Cataloging-in-Publication Data (2000), 33: "That for the purpose of guarding against the further decline and final extinction of the Indian tribes, adjoining the frontier settlements of the United States, are for introducing among them the habits and arts of civilization" annual sum/annuity is ten thousand dollars "and an account of the expenditure of the money, and proceedings in execution of the foregoing provisions, shall be laid annually before Congress." In 1824 Secretary of War John C. Calhoun created the Bureau of Indian Affairs (BIA), formally consolidating the otherwise disparate federal efforts to govern tribes within what was imagined to be the borders of the United States. The BIA functioned under the War Department to promote "civilization," often through schooling, and oversee and administer treaty negotiations. See Sharon O'Brien, "Bureau of Indian Affairs," *Encyclopedia of North American Indians* (Houghton Mifflin, 1996).

118. Demos, *The Heathen School*, 237.

119. Elias Boudinot, *An Address to the Whites: Delivered in the First Presbyterian Church, on the 26th May, 1826* (William F. Geddes, 1826), cited in Smithers, *The Cherokee Diaspora*, 85.

120. Smithers, *The Cherokee Diaspora*, 85. Here Smithers points his reader to Richard J. Perry, *From Time Immemorial: Indigenous Peoples and State Systems* (University of Texas Press, 1996), 32.

121. Smithers, *The Cherokee Diaspora*, 88.

122. Patrick Wolfe, "Settler Colonialism and the Elimination of the Native," *Journal of Genocide Research* 8, no. 4 (2006): 396.

123. Demos, *The Heathen School*, 244; Wilder, *Ebony and Ivy*, 250.

124. Smithers, *The Cherokee Diaspora*, 108.

125. Demos, *The Heathen School*, 245, 246.

126. Demos, *The Heathen School*, 246.

127. James Mooney, *Cherokee Legends and the Trail of Tears: From the Nineteenth Annual Report of the Bureau of American Ethnology* (S.B. Newman, 1956), 22, cited by Smithers, *The Cherokee Diaspora*, 113.

128. Johnson, "Red, Black & *Brown v. Board of Education*," 70, citing Synods of New York and New Jersey, "African Seminary," 88.

129. "African School," *African Repository and Colonial Journal* 1, no. 9 (November 1825): 276.

130. Vincent P. Franklin, "Education for Colonization: Attempts to Educate Free Blacks in the United States for Emigration to Africa, 1823–1833," *The Journal of Negro Education* 43, no. 1 (1974): 93.

131. Bond, *Education for Freedom*, 153.

132. Bond, *Education for Freedom*, 160.

133. Bond, *Education for Freedom*, 160.

134. Bond, *Education for Freedom*, 162–63.

135. Bond, *Education for Freedom*, 164.

136. Bond, *Education for Freedom*, 223.

137. Bond, *Education for Freedom*, 215. On the function of the concept of disability as a mode of disqualification from citizenship and equality see Douglas Baynton, "Disability and the Justification of Inequality in American History," in *The New Disability History: American Perspectives*, ed. Paul K Longmore and Lauri Umansky (New York University Press, 2001).

138. Oklahoma Historical Society, "Timeline of American Indian Removal," accessed May 10, 2026, okhistory.org.

139. Bond, *Education for Freedom*, 247.

140. Bond, *Education for Freedom*, 249–50.

141. *Dred Scott vs. Sandford* is now widely recognized as one of the worst decisions in the history of the US Supreme Court both in its utter failure to follow precedent, the Constitution, or historical reality regarding the legal and political status of people of African descent in the United States. In his majority decision, Chief Justice Taney argued, "A free negro of the African race, whose ancestors were brought to this country and sold as slaves, is not a 'citizen' within the meaning of the Constitution of the United States" and, because of this, "the special rights and immunities guaranteed to citizens do not apply to them." *Dred Scott v. Sandford*, 60 US 393 (1857).

142. Bond, *Education for Freedom*, 253.

143. Bond, *Education for Freedom*, 182.

144. Bond, *Education for Freedom*, 262.

145. Bond, *Education for Freedom*, 262.

146. Bond, *Education for Freedom*, 266.

147. Lincoln University, "Mission," accessed May 10, 2026, lincoln.edu.

148. Bond, *Education for Freedom*, 266. Another member of this new board was William E. Dodge, a businessman and philanthropist whose engagement with higher education extended beyond Lincoln. He was also on the founding Board of Trustees for the Syrian Protestant College which would be renamed the American University of Beirut.

149. Bond, *Education for Freedom*, 274.

150. Saidiya V. Hartman, *Scenes of Subjection: Terror, Slavery, and Self-Making in Nineteenth-Century America* (Oxford University Press, 1997), 115.

151. Hartman, *Scenes of Subjection*, 121.

152. Hartman, *Scenes of Subjection*, 127.

153. Hartman, *Scenes of Subjection*, 126.

154. Bayley Marquez, "The Black Model Minority: Slavery, Settlement, and the Genealogy of the Model Minority," *Du Bois Review* 19, no. 1 (2022): 130.

155. Pratt would go on to found the infamous Carlisle Indian Boarding School.

156. Samuel Armstrong, *The Journal of Christian Philosophy* (1884): 200–29, quoted in Robert Francis Engs, *Educating the Disfranchised and Disinherited: Samuel Chapman Armstrong and Hampton Institute: 1839–1893* (University of Tennessee Press, 1999).

157. Samuel C. Armstrong, "Lessons from the Hawaiian Islands," *The Journal of Christian Philosophy* 3 (January 1884), 200–229.

158. For more on the relationship of anti-Blackness to a longer genealogy of the concept of the model minority framework see Marquez, "The Black Model Minority."

159. Lucy E. Salyer, "Reconstructing the Immigrant: The Naturalization Act of 1870 in Global Perspective," *Journal of the Civil War Era* 11, no. 3 (2021): 382.

160. Salyer, "Reconstructing the Immigrant," 383; Moon-Ho Jung, *Coolies and Cane: Race, Labor, and Sugar in the Age of Emancipation* (Johns Hopkins University Press, 2006), 139.

161. Laosebikan, "From Student to Immigrant," 42; US Senate, Forty-first Congress, Naturalization Act of 1870, 5176.

162. *Congressional Globe*, 41st Congress, 2d session, Part VI, 5155. In Chapter 3 I contend with the implications of this narrowing.

163. Laosebikan, "From Student to Immigrant," 44.

164. Walter L. Williams, "Ethnic Relations of African Students in the United States, With Black Americans, 1870–1900." *The Journal of Negro History* 65, no. 3 (1980): 230.

165. Bond, *Education for Freedom*, 492.

166. Bond, *Education for Freedom*, 289.

167. Bond, *Education for Freedom*, 491.

168. Williams, "Ethnic Relations of African Students in the United States," 228.

169. Williams, "Ethnic Relations of African Students in the United States," 228.

170. Williams, "Ethnic Relations of African Students in the United States," 233.

171. Williams, "Ethnic Relations of African Students in the United States," 234.

172. Bond, *Education for Freedom*, 494. In 1847, Liberia declared independence from the ACS. Notably, even in this declaration the architects of Liberia's future in many ways fulfilled the colonizationist's vision in their identification with "the way of life in America" rather than with an ancestral connection to Africa. In the United States, news coverage of Liberia's independence privileged the role of American political values over any discussion of Black self-determination. Brandon Mills, *The World Colonization Made: The Racial Geography of Early American Empire* (University of Pennsylvania Press, 2020), 144. By 1850, plans were underway for a Liberia College, which historian Thomas Livingston argues made it the first proposed American collegiate institution with the specific purpose of educating Black students, albeit not in the United States. Livingston positions the college as "the West African outpost of the 'American College Movement.'" Thomas W. Livingston, "The Exportation of American Higher Education to Western Africa: Liberia College, 1850–1900," *The Journal of Nego Education* 45, no. 3 (1976): 251. In 1851 the college was chartered with significant financial support from a group called the Trustees of Donations for Education in Liberia and the New York Colonization Society, a state branch of the ACS. Responding to issues regarding denominationalism and institutional development in the United States, the missionary groups suggested that the college be national rather than sectarian and designed to "serve social rather than purely individual interests" (ibid., 252). The funders were especially invested in forming the college to avoid Liberian youth traveling to England for their education. Through their support of the college, the institution's American financiers maintained control over the selection of faculty, all of whom were Liberian but born in the United States or Caribbean, and provided a "set of rules and regulations for the administration of the College and course of studies, student regulations, and other matters" (ibid., 255). The curriculum they devised reproduced that of most US colleges of the time. After some delays, the college was inaugurated in Monrovia on January 28, 1862, making it the first "American degree-granting college to be established abroad" (ibid., 250). If the college opened before Burns left for the United States, perhaps he would have remained in Liberia for his studies. See Valentin-Yves Mudimbe, *The Invention of Africa: Gnosis, Philosophy, and the Order of Knowledge* (Indiana University Press, 1988). For facts about Blyden's life, see Moses N. Moore Jr., "Edward Wilmot Blyden: From Old School Presbyterian Missionary to 'Minister of Truth,'" *Journal of Presbyterian History* 75, no. 2 (Summer 1997): 103.

At the college's inaugural event Professor Edward Blyden, who would go on to be president of the institution from 1880–1884, remarked: "Perhaps this very day, one century ago, some of our forefathers were being dragged to the hold of some miserable slavery, to enter upon those horrible sufferings of the 'middle passage,' preliminary to their introduction into scenes and associations of deeper woe. Today, their descendants having escaped the fiery ordeal of oppression and slavery, and having returned to their ancestral home, are laying the foundation of intellectual empire, upon the very soil whence their fathers were torn, in their ignorance and degradation." "Proceedings at the Inauguration of Liberia College at Monrovia, January 28, 1862," *The African Repository*, xxxciii, no. 11 (November 1862), 24.

173. Quoted in Kenneth J. King, "African Students in Negro American Colleges: Notes on the Good African," *Phylon* 31, no. 1 (1970): 18.

174. King, "African Students in Negro American Colleges," 18.

175. W. E. B. Du Bois, *The Souls of Black Folk* (A. C. McClurg, 1903), 49. Later in this book, Du Bois remarks upon the increasing impossibility of an emigrationist strategy for Black Americans given US imperialist ventures, which he describes as "the recent course of the United States toward weaker and darker peoples in the West Indies, Hawaii, and the Philippines,—for where in the world may we go and be safe from lying and brute force" (ibid., 52).

176. On the double bind of freedom see Hartman, *Scenes of Subjection*, 115; Du Bois, *Souls*, 160–61. Washington would most famously articulate his position in his 1895 "Atlanta Compromise" speech, stating: "In all things purely social we can be as separate as the five fingers, and yet one as the hand in all things essential to mutual progress." This perspective cleared the way for the *Plessy vs. Ferguson* decision in 1896, which secured the legal sanctity of "separate but equal" in US law, and was similarly embraced by white Europeans who had "carved up" Africa in 1884 at the Berlin Conference. "Carve up" is language taken from Kwame Nkrumah's description of the Berlin Conference of 1884: "There are likely to be more coups and rebellions in Africa as long as imperialists and neo-colonialists are able to exploit your weaknesses. Unless we unite and deal with neo-colonialism on a Pan-African basis, they will continue to try to undermine our independence, and draw us again into sphere of influence comparable to the original carve-up of Africa arranged at the Berlin Conference of 1884." More of this history is discussed in Chapters 5, 6, and 7. Kwame Nkrumah, *Challenge of the Congo* (International Publishers, 1967), x.

177. Cited in King, "African Students in Negro American Colleges," 135.

178. Hollis R. Lynch, "K. O. Mbadiwe, 1939–1947: The American Years of a Nigerian Political Leader," *Journal of African Studies* 7, no. 4 (1980): 134. Washington would go on to have great sway over two other African students who studied in the United States in the later nineteenth century, John Langalibalele Dube from Natal and James Aggrey of the Gold Coast. Each would play major roles in shaping the educational landscape of Africa in the twentieth century. I discuss Aggrey in Chapter 7. Dube traveled to the United States in 1887 with a Christian missionary to South Africa who, by some accounts, had adopted him and, by others, agreed to facilitate his travel to the United States but only under the understanding that he would be required to support himself upon arrival. There is substantial scholarship on Dube. See for instance, Heather Hughes, "Doubly Elite: Exploring the Life of John Langalibalele Dube," *Journal of Southern African Studies* 27, no. 3 (2001): 445–58; R. Hunt Davis, "John L. Dube: A South African Exponent of Booker T. Washington," *Journal of African Studies* 2, no. 4 (1975): 497–528. Though,

like many of the figures discussed in this book, there are contradicting accounts of Dube's life, most seem to agree that he enrolled in the Oberlin Preparatory Academy in 1888, where he studied for two years. He left Oberlin without graduating and went on to have an illustrious career as a writer, educator, and politician. His first publication was a pamphlet, "A familiar talk upon my native land," written in 1891, in which Dube implores, "Christian minds of this enlightened land to the needs of those poor creatures who are stumbling and falling in a darkness worse than death." John Langalibalele Dube, "A Familiar Talk Upon My Native Land," 5, https://www.sahistory.org.za/archive/familiar-talk-upon-my-native-land-john-l-dube. He compares his people's "life of semi-barbarism" to their own "a life quickened by the beneficent impulse of the highest type of civilization." After providing his reader with insight into the life of the "the Zulu in his heathenisms and ignorance," Dube turns his attention to the "great work that the civilized world is carrying on to redeem this benighted land, to rescue it from bonds of ignorance and superstition" (ibid., 26). He concludes by emphasizing the importance of US-educated African missionaries and their ability to wield influence among their people other than white missionaries, whom the Zulus first look upon with suspicion as though they are coming to claim their land (ibid., 31).

But Dube's vision, or at his least articulation of a vision, for education shifted in the following years from this decidedly Christian perspective to a more complicated position that still sought the philanthropic support of white Americans but also advocated for the value of African thought and practice. After returning to South Africa in 1892 for four or five years, he returned to the United States and lived in New York. There he became acquainted with Booker T. Washington, first through his speeches and then in person. That Dube tracked down Washington is perhaps not a coincidence. R. Hunt Davis makes a compelling argument that Dube's thinking about education was already saturated with Washington's approach through his education through the American Board missionaries who taught in Natal, where he was raised.

After writing to Washington, Dube gave the 1897 commencement speeches at both the Hampton Institute and the Tuskegee Institute. In his speech, he extoled the virtues of industrial education as "the kind of work my people need." Davis, "John L. Dube," 506, citing John Dube, "Need of Industrial Education in Africa," *Southern Workman* 27, no. 7 (1897), 141–42. Dube returned to South Africa and founded the Zulu Christian Industrial School, which would eventually become the Ohlange Institution. The school was run almost entirely by instructors who had also studied in the United States, though almost exclusively at Black institutions. As an Oberlin College website details, Dube "was the founding president of the African National congress (1912), the political organization primarily responsible for overthrowing the Apartheid system" (https://www2.oberlin.edu/external/EOG/Dube/Dube.htm), and he also founded the first Zulu language newspaper and went on to be its editor. Years later, Dube referred to Washington as his "patron saint" and "guiding star." Cited in Davis, "John L. Dube," 497–98.

179. Bond, *Education for Freedom*, 488.

180. Reverend Robert Finely 1816, cited by Wilder, *Ebony and Ivy*, 247.

181. Reverend Robert Finely 1816, cited by Wilder, *Ebony and Ivy*, 247.

182. Jodi Byrd, *The Transit of Empire: Indigenous Critiques of Colonialism* (University of Minnesota Press, 2011), xxxvi. Byrd contends "we can see the complex dynamics of colonial discourses that exist horizontally among histories of oppression and inform continued complicities as historical narratives vie for ascendancy as the primary and originary oppression within lands shaped by competing histories of slavery colonialism, arrival, and Indigeneity."

183. Lowe, *The Intimacies of Four Continents*, 40.

## Part II: Empire's Educational Exemptions

1. Third Annual Report of the Director, *Institute of International Education*, New York, 1922, 7.

2. Mae Ngai, "Nationalism, Immigration Control, & the Ethnoracial Mapping of America in the 1920s," *OAH Magazine* (July 2007).

3. The debates establishing this expansion explicitly marked both Chinese and Indigenous people as ineligible for inclusion. Supreme Court cases in 1922 and 1923 solidified the legal status of people of Japanese and Indian descent as nonwhite. In the 1922 Ozawa case, the Supreme Court relied on scientific understandings of whiteness as "Caucasian" to deny Takao Ozawa's appeal for citizenship. Ozawa had lived in the United States for twenty years, attending Berkeley, California high school and the University of California for three years. Just a year later, in the 1923 Thind case, the same court overturned its own logic in finding that Bhagat Singh Thind was not eligible for citizenship despite meeting the racial standards they had used that classified people of Indian descent as "Aryan" or "Caucasian." According to the court, these racial standards did not matter since, in their opinion, Thind was clearly not "white" in the eyes of the "common man."

4. William Atherton Du Puy, "Will This Save the Human Races: W. W. Husband, Commissioner of Immigration, Says New Law Will Influence America's Future Generations," *Boston Daily Globe* (June 19, 1921).

5. US Congress, *Congressional Record*, 67th Cong., 1st sess., vol. LXI, pt. 1 (March 4–15; April 11–May 4, 1921), 556.

6. Butler is an important figure in broader histories of US higher education, especially the history of Columbia University. As Clyde Barrow documents, Butler was president of Columbia University from 1902 to 1945. In this role he helped shape the modern research university, especially in that he was widely seen as "an authoritarian president," memorably flexing his powers to remove Charles A. Beard and several other left-leaning and anti-war professors from the Columbia campus during World War I. He was especially critical of the concept of academic freedom and prescribed a narrow notion of "the *proper* freedom of speech of university professors," as one

constrained by "habits of self-control, self-direction, and self-ordering." He also, infamously, as Robin D. G. Kelley reports, "welcomed Nazi Germany's ambassador to the United States to speak on campus in December 1933." Clyde W Barrow, "God, Capitalism, and the State: The Cultural Counterrevolution in US Universities, 1980–1990," *New Political Science* 47, no. 1 (2025): 60; and Robin D. G. Kelley, "The Responsibility of Intellectuals in the Age of Fascism and Genocide," *The Boston Review* (Summer 2025), https://www.bostonreview.net/forum/the-responsibility-of-intellectuals-in-the-age-of-fascism-and-genocide/.

7. The Institute for International Education, "First Annual Report of the Director," Bulletin No. 1, New York, 1920, 1; See also Teresa B. Bevis and Christopher J. Lucas, *International Students in American Colleges and Universities* (Palgrave Macmillan, 2007), 97.

8. The Institute for International Education, "Fourth Annual Report of the Director," Bulletin No. 1, New York, February 10, 1923, 7.

9. The Institute for International Education, "Fourth Annual Report of the Director," 8.

10. Madeline Y. Hsu, *The Good Immigrants: How the Yellow Peril Became the Model Minority* (Princeton University Press, 2015), 25.

## 3. The Post-Emancipation University, Industry, Race, and International Politics

1. Importantly, the Morrill Land Grant Acts built on the established practice of allocating land for the purposes of higher education. See the discussion of the Northwest Ordinances of 1785 and 1787 in Chapter 2 and Meredith McCoy et al., "*The Future of Land-Grab Universities*," *Native American and Indigenous Studies* 8, no. 1 (Spring 2021): 171.

2. Robert Lee et al., "Land-Grab Universities," *High Country News*, March 30, 2020, retrieved April 21, 2020; Act of July 2, 1862 (Morrill Act), Public Law 37–108, July 2, 1862; Enrolled Acts and Resolutions of Congress, 1789–1996; Record Group 11; General Records of the United States Government; National Archives, Washington, DC, archives.gov.

3. R. C. Lewontin, "The Cold War and the Transformation of the Academy," in *The Cold War & the University: Toward an Intellectual History of The Postwar Years*, ed. Andre Schiffrin (The New Press, 1997), 11.

4. Abigail Boggs et al., "Abolitionist University Studies: An Invitation," *Abolition Journal* (2019): 13, 14.

5. Craig Steven Wilder, *Ebony and Ivy: Race, Slavery, and the Troubled History of America's Universities* (Bloomsbury Press, 2013), 286.

6. The founding of Rensselaer Polytechnical Institute occurred during the same period in which Sylvanus Thayer was formalizing West Point's curriculum and the same year as the formation of the Army Corp of Engineers, as discussed in Chapter 2.

7. Boggs, et al., "Abolitionist University Studies," 13; Christopher J. Lucas, *American Higher Education: A History* (Palgrave MacMillan, 2006), 178; Wilder, *Ebony and Ivy*, 286.

8. Christopher Newfield, *Ivy and Industry: Business and the Making of the American University, 1880–1980* (Duke University Press, 2003), 3.

9. Newfield, *Ivy and Industry*, 4.

10. Thomas Leonard, *Illiberal Reformers: Race, Eugenics, and American Economics in the Progressive Era* (Princeton University Press, 2016), 19.

11. Leonard, *Illiberal Reformers*, 20. For more on the history of the twentieth-century formation of economics as a field see Timothy Mitchell, "Economists and the Economy in the Twentieth Century," in *The Politics of Method in the Human Sciences: Positivism and Its Epistemological Others* (Duke University Press, 2005); and Timothy Mitchell, "The Work of Economics: How a Discipline Makes Its World," *European Journal of Sociology* 46, no. 2 (2005).

12. Clyde W. Barrow, "The Theory of Capitalist Regulation and the Development of American Higher Education," *Annual Meeting of the American Educational Association* (1991), 7.

13. James Lawrence Cabell, *The Testimony of Modern Science to the Unity of Mankind; Being a Summary of the Conclusions Announced By the Highest Authorities in the Several Departments of Physiology, Zoology and Comparative Philology in Favor of the Specific Unity and Common Origin of All the Varieties of Man* (Robert Carter and Brothers, 1859), cited in Gregory Michael Dorr, *Segregation's Science: Eugenics and Society in Virginia* (University of Virginia Press, 2008), 35.

14. Stephen Jay Gould, *The Mismeasure of Man* (W. W. Norton, 1981), 104.

15. Gould, *The Mismeasure of Man*, 106.

16. Gould, *The Mismeasure of Man*, 106.

17. Heather Remoff, "Malthus, Darwin, and the Descent of Economics," *American Journal of Economics and Sociology* 75, no. 4 (2016): 865.

18. In *Descent of Man*, published in 1871, Darwin does shift his attention to the human species, briefly arguing that "The break will then be rendered wider, for it will intervene between man in a more civilized state, as we may hope, than the Caucasian, and some ape as low as a baboon, instead of as at present between the negro or Australian and the gorilla." Charles Darwin, *The Descent of Man, and Selection in Relation to Sex* (John Murray, 1871), 201.

19. Rutledge M. Dennis, "Social Darwinism, Scientific Racism, and the Metaphysics of Race," *The Journal of Negro Education* 64, no. 3 (1995): 244. For more on Sumner, see Robert Green McCloskey, *American Conservatism in the Age of Enterprise: A Study of William Graham Sumner, Stephen J. Field, and Andrew Carnegie* (Harvard University Press, 1951).

20. On Social Darwinism see Richard Hoftstander, *Social Darwinism in American Thought* (Beacon Press, 1944).

21. See Francis Walker, "Immigration and Degradation," *The Forum* 11 (March–August 1891): 637. Notably, Walker also served as president of the American

Statistical Association in 1882 and the inaugural president of the American Economic Association in 1886.

22. Mae M. Ngai, *Impossible Subjects: Illegal Aliens and the Making of Modern America* (Princeton University Press, 2004), 31.

23. Leonard, *Illiberal Reformers*, 12.

24. Shellen Wu Xiao, *Birth of the Geopolitical Age: Global Frontiers and the Making of Modern China* (Stanford University Press, 2023), 111.

25. Frederick Jackson Turner, "The Significance of the Frontier in American History," in *The Frontier in American History* (Henry Holt and Company, 1920), 2, 11. As per a footnote in this publication, the basis of the paper was an article Turner published in a student publication at the University of Wisconsin in November of 1892 entitled "Problems in American History." There is more to be investigated in Turner's 1910 commencement speech for Indiana University, "Pioneer Ideals and the State University." There, Turner argues "the nation has no more promising agency than the State Universities, no more hopeful product than their graduates" (29). One exemplary quote: "The test tube and the microscope are needed rather than axe and rifle in this new ideal of conquest" (24).

26. Turner, "The Significance of the Frontier in American History," 23, 22. Importantly, and as is discussed at greater length, by 1893 the status of "immigrant" was definitionally restricted to whiteness.

27. Turner, "The Significance of the Frontier in American History," 4.

28. For more on this question of citizenship see Lauren Berlant's theorization of the "dead citizenship" of the citizen versus the live citizenship of the not-yet-citizen and their desire for America. Lauren Berlant, *The Queen of American Goes to Washington City: Essays on Sex and Citizenship* (Duke University Press, 1997).

29. Manu Karuka, *Empire's Tracks: Indigenous Nations, Chinese Workers, and the Transcontinental Railroad* (University of California Press, 2019), 171.

30. Kevin Bruyneel, *Settler Memory: The Disavowal of Indigeneity and the Politics of Race in the United States* (University of North Carolina Press, 2021). Bruyneel provides a related reading in this theorization of settler disavowal, which he describes as "an active form of deflection from the implications and obligations to attend to what one knows" (ibid., 3).

31. Karuka, *Empire's Tracks*, 168.

32. Robert Vitalis, *White World Order, Black Power Politics: The Birth of American International Relations* (Cornell University Press, 2015), 25. Vitalis points out that this assertion diverges from a general understanding of the field of International Relations as having emerged after World War I in think tanks including the Council on Foreign Relations and the Royal Institute of International Affairs (ibid., ix).

33. Vitalis, *White World Order, Black Power Politics*, 46–47.

34. Thomas Fallace, "Recapitulation Theory and the New Education: Race, Culture, Imperialism, and Pedagogy, 1894–1916," *Curriculum Inquiry* 42, no. 4 (2012): 512.

35. Gould, *The Mismeasure of Man*, 126.

36. Elizabeth Gagen, "Reflections of Primitivism: Development, Progress and Civilization in Imperial America, 1898–1914," *Children's Geographies* 5, no. 1–2 (2007); Jessica Blatt, "'To Bring Out the Best That is in Their Blood': Race, Reform, and Civilization in *the Journal of Race Development* (1910–1919)," *Ethnic and Racial Studies* 2004, no. 5 (2004).

37. Booker T. Washington, "Address by Booker T. Washington, Principal Tuskegee Normal and Industrial Institute, Tuskegee, Alabama, At Opening of Atlanta Exposition," (September 18, 1895), 304.

38. For more on Washington and Armstrong, see Chapter 2.

39. Aziz Rana, *The Two Faces of American Freedom* (Harvard University Press, 2010), 191–93.

40. Robert Vitalis, "The Noble American Science of Imperial Relations and Its Laws of Race Development," *Comparative Studies in Society and History* 52, no. 4 (2010): 922.

41. As Vitalis marks, Lowell "famously imposed a color bar in the new Harvard freshman dormitories in 1915." Vitalis, "The Noble American Science of Imperial Relations and Its Laws of Race Development," 922.

42. See Albert Lawrence Lowell, "The Colonial Expansion of the United States," *Atlantic Monthly* 83, no. 496 (January 1899): 145–54, cited in Vitalis, "The Noble American Science of Imperial Relations and Its Laws of Race Development," 923.

43. Victor Bascara, "New Empire, Same Old University? Education in the American Tropics After 1898," in *The Imperial University*, ed. Sunaina Maira Piya Chatterjee (University of Minnesota, 2014), 53–77. In a trajectory that aligns with efforts to colonize Liberia and the founding of a college there, the University of Puerto Rico was founded in 1903, the University of Hawai'i in 1907, and the University of the Philippines in 1908.

44. Bascara, "New Empire, Same Old University?," 60.

45. Malini Johar Schuller, "Celebrating Imperial Education: The 2001 Thomasite Centennial in the Philippines," *American Quarterly* 74, no. 4 (2022): 946.

46. W. Cameron Forbes, *The Philippine Islands*, vol. 1 (Houghton Mifflin, Riverside, 1928), 423; Patrick M. Kirkwood, "'Michigan Men' in the Philippines and the Limits of Self-Determination in the Progressive Era," *Michigan Historical Review* 40, no. 2 (2014): 66. Many Black Americans also participated in the US educational project in the Philippines. For instance, Carter G. Woodson, the founder of the Association for the Study of African American Life and *The Journal of Negro History*, taught in the Philippines from 1903–1906. Roland Sintos Coloma, "'Destiny Has Thrown the Negro and the Filipino Under the Tutelage of America': Race and Curriculum in the Age of Empire," *Curriculum Inquiry* 39, no. 4 (2009): 504.

47. Quoted in Coloma, "Destiny Has Thrown the Negro and the Filipino Under the Tutelage of America," 502–3.

48. Coloma, "Destiny Has Thrown the Negro and the Filipino Under the Tutelage of America," 507.

49. Alexander A. Calata, "The Role of Education in Americanizing Filipinos," in *Mixed Blessings: The Impact of the American Colonial Experience on Politics and Society in the Philippines*, ed. Hazel M. McFerson (Greenwood Press, 2002), 91–92.

50. "An Act Providing for the Education of Filipino Students in the United States and Appropriating for Such Purpose the Sum of Seventy-Two Thousand Dollars, in Money of the United States," Act No. 854 (August 26, 1903), *Official Gazette* 1, no. 52 (September 2, 1903): 645.

51. Teresa B. Bevis and Christopher J. Lucas, *International Students in American Colleges and Universities* (Palgrave Macmillan, 2007), 77. Bevis and Lucas write that the University of the Philippines was established in 1911, but other sources are in agreement with a 1908 founding.

52. Vitalis, *White World Order, Black Power Politics*, ix.

53. Vitalis, "The Noble American Science of Imperial Relations and Its Laws of Race Development," 910.

54. Ngai, *Impossible Subjects*, 11.

55. August Heckscher, *Woodrow Wilson* (Charles Scribner's Sons, 1991). 12.

56. Woodrow Wilson, "The Reconstruction of the Southern States," *The Atlantic Monthly* (January 1901), 6.

57. Ronald J. Pestritto, *Woodrow Wilson and the Roots of Modern Liberalism* (Rowman & Littlefield, 2005), 9.

58. Pestritto, *Woodrow Wilson and the Roots of Modern Liberalism*, 44.

59. Pestritto, *Woodrow Wilson and the Roots of Modern Liberalism*, 13.

60. Heckscher, *Woodrow Wilson*, 104.

61. Heckscher, *Woodrow Wilson*, 129.

62. Wilson's efforts were so successful that the first Black student would not graduate from Princeton until 1948. See Kenneth O'Reilly, "The Jim Crow Policies of Woodrow Wilson," *The Journal of Blacks in Higher Education* 17 (1997): 117.

63. Wilson, "The Reconstruction of the Southern States," 60.

64. A. Scott Berg, *Wilson* (Berkley, 2013), 307.

65. Nicholas Patler, *Jim Crow and the Wilson Administration* (University Press of Colorado, 2007), 3.

66. Patler, *Jim Crow and the Wilson Administration*, 73.

67. *The Crisis* (January 1915), 119–20, reprinted in William Loren Katz, *Eyewitness: The Negro in American History* (Pitman Publishing Corporation, 1967), 389–90.

68. D. W. Griffith, dir., *Birth of a Nation* (Triangle Film Corporation, 1915).

69. Erez Manela, *The Wilsonian Moment: Self-Determination and the International Origins of Anticolonial Nationalism* (Oxford University Press, 2007), 3.

70. Richard Seymour, "The Cold War, American Anticommunism and the Global 'Colour Line,'" in *Race and Racism in International Relations: Confronting the Global Colour Line*, ed. Alexander Anievas et al. (Routledge, 2015), 161.

71. Adom Getachew, *Worldmaking After Empire* (Princeton University Press, 2020), 40.

72. Getachew, *Worldmaking After Empire*, 40.

73. Getachew, *Worldmaking After Empire*, 41.

74. "Gov. Wilson Addresses Two Big Audiences: New Jersey Candidate Gets Warm Reception from Milwaukee People," News Report of three Addresses in Milwaukee, March 24, 1912, in Papers of Woodrow Wilson, 24: 260–61; Don Wolfensberger, "Woodrow Wilson, Congress and Anti-Immigrant Sentiment in America," Woodrow Wilson International Center for Scholars, United States of America (20070), retrieved from https://coilink.org/20.500.12592/3925m07 on April 17, 2026.

75. Steven G. Koven and Frank Götzke, *American Immigration Policy: Confronting the Nation's Challenges* (Springer, 2010), 130.

76. Henry Pratt Fairchild, "The Immigration Law of 1924," *The Quarterly Journal of Economics* 38, no. 4 (1924): 655. The federal government began to encroach upon state's rights to regulate immigration beginning with the Supreme Court's decision in the 1848 *Passenger Cases*, which reversed previous legal understandings and found that "states' head taxes on passengers were an unconstitutional infringement on the federal prerogative of regulating foreign commerce." See John Torpey, *The Invention of the Passport: Surveillance, Citizenship, and the State* (Cambridge University Press, 2000), 116.

77. Leonard, *Illiberal Reformers*, 142.

78. When Commerce and Labor separated, Labor was designated "to foster, promote, and develop the welfare of the wage earners of the United States, to improve their working conditions, and to advance their opportunities for profitable employment." See Jenny S. Breen, "Labor, Law Enforcement, and 'Normal Times': The Origins of Immigration's Home Within the Department of Justice and the Evolution of Attorney General Control Over Immigration Adjudications," *University of Hawaii Law Review* 42, no. 1 (2019): 4; Also Act of Mar. 4, 1913, Pub. L. No. 62–425, ch. 141, 37 Stat. 736 (1913) (creating the Department of Labor).

79. Erika Lee, *At America's Gates: Chinese Immigration During the Exclusion Era, 1882–1943* (University of North Carolina Press, 20), 30.

80. Kristofer Allerfeldt "'And We Got Here First': Albert Johnson, National Origins and Self-Interest in the Immigration Debate of the 1920s," *Journal of Contemporary History* 45, no. 1 (2010): 10.

## 4. Open Doors, Yung Wing, and Immigration Law Before Exclusion

1. For more on the role of US Christians during this era of international education see Liping Bu, *Making the World Like Us: Education, Cultural Expansion, and the American Century* (Praeger, 2003).

2. Despite being written in the 1920s, this text retains a great deal of significance within scholarship on noncitizen students in the United States today; this is apparent in its near verbatim reproduction in the most recent book to provide a thorough review of this history, Teresa Brawner Bevis and Christopher J. Lucas's

*International Students in American Colleges and Universities: A History* (Palgrave Macmillan, 2007).

3. Robert E. Speer, "Foreword," *The Foreign Student in America*, ed. W. Reginald Wheeler et al. (Association Press, 1925).

4. Michael H Hunt, *Frontier Defense and the Open Door: Manchuria in Chinese-American Relations, 1895–1911* (Yale University Press, 1973), ix.

5. For more on IIE see the introduction to Part II.

6. Chinese students started organizing on their own through the founding of the Chinese Students' Alliance (CSA) either in San Francisco in 1902 or in Berkeley in 1901. The initial West Coast organizing group of the CSA was focused on fomenting attachment to China in local, US-born Chinese youth, but the more formal Alliance of the Eastern States, which wrote its constitution in 1905, shifted CSA's focus toward students themselves. CSA was explicitly nationalist in a modern and civically engaged sense. As Hsu writes, CSA "hoped to foster nationalism over native-place ties and downplayed regional differences by adopting English as its official language." Madeline Y. Hsu, *The Good Immigrants: How the Yellow Peril Became the Model Minority* (Princeton University Press, 2015), 59. Several students who would go on to be significant players in Chinese politics were involved in the organization, including V. K. Wellington Koo, Hu Shi, and Yuan Shikai. See also Weili Ye, *Seeking Modernity in China's Name: Chinese Students in the United States 1900–1927* (Stanford University Press, 2001), 20. Ye argues that CSA was founded in 1902 in San Francisco, but Hsu says it was 1901 at UC Berkeley.

7. Liping Bu, "The Challenge of Race Relations: American Ecumenism and Foreign Student Nationalism, 1900–1940," *Journal of American Studies* 35, no. 2 (2001): 222.

8. John Mott to Andrew Carnegie, March 9, 1914, folder entitled "Correspondence 1908–1918," CFRFS box #10, YMCA Archives, cited in Bu, "The Challenge of Race Relations," 222.

9. John Mott to Andrew Carnegie, May 8, 1912, folder entitled "Correspondence 1908–1918," CFRFS box #10, YMCA Archives cited in Bu, "The Challenge of Race Relations," 223.

10. Bu, "The Challenge of Race Relations," 218.

11. Hsu, *The Good Immigrants*, 62.

12. See Tao Leigh Goffe, "Intimate Occupations: The Afterlife of the 'Coolie,'" *Transforming Anthropology* 22, no. 1 (2014): 53–61.

13. Speer, "Foreword," xvi. On the point of US higher education in spaces under US colonial rule in the early 1900s see Victor Bascara, "New Empire, Same Old University? Education in the American Tropics After 1898," in *The Imperial University*, ed. Sunaina Maira Piya Chatterjee (University of Minnesota, 2014).

14. Speer, "Foreword," 12.

15. It has been surprisingly difficult to track Wing's citizenship status. Various texts assert that he attained naturalized US citizenship at some point only to have it retracted after the passage of the 1870 Naturalization Act. Madeline Hsu addresses

this history briefly in her review of *Stepping Forth into the World: The Chinese Educational Mission to the United States, 1872–81*, by Edward J. M. Rhoads, *Journal of Asian American Studies* 15, no. 2 (2012): 230, and Martin B. Gold also briefly covers Wing's naturalization in *Forbidden Citizens: Chinese Exclusion and the U.S. Congress: A Legislative History* (TheCapitol.Net, 2012), 31.

16. According to Henry King, "Outline History of Student Migrations," in *The Foreign Student in America*, ed. W. Reginald Wheeler et al. (Association Press, 1925), 15, Wing acquired US citizenship in 1852 but was then refused from service in the Civil War illustrates some of the complications of US race and citizenship.

17. King, "Outline History of Student Migrations," 15.

18. Bevis and Lucas, *International Students in American Colleges and Universities*, xiv.

19. Bevis and Lucas are careful to document criticisms of both the United States and US higher education as they were recorded in 1831 by a Scottish novelist and in 1832 by an Irish clergyman. The novelist, Thomas Hamilton, provides an anecdotal account of the prejudice experienced by the son of a Haitian novelist whose "dreams of an American education and an enlightening experience in New York" were so severely damaged by his initial reception to the city that he abandoned them.

20. Bevis and Lucas, *International Students in American Colleges and Universities*, 52.

21. Bevis and Lucas, *International Students in American Colleges and Universities*, 44; See also Liel Leibovitz and Matthew Miller, *Fortunate Sons: The 120 Chinese Boys Who Came to America, Went to School, and Revolutionized an Ancient Civilization* (W. W. Norton, 2011).

22. Bevis and Lucas, *International Students in American Colleges and Universities*, 44.

23. Bevis and Lucas, *International Students in American Colleges and Universities*, 45.

24. Bevis and Lucas, *International Students in American Colleges and Universities*, 45. One must of course take into account that this is primarily, if not entirely, a symbolic commitment since in 1868, and even in the 2010s, the US government does not actually have jurisdiction over any educational institutions. Despite this, the gesture of educational exchange remains worthy of comment. Ming M. Zhu argues that the Burlingame treaty was a display of a certain kind of international benevolence by the United States. For "America" the treaty "was an opportunity to show the world that the Americans were more civil in their dealings with the Chinese and above the crude and distasteful acts of the British and their opium wars." Ming M. Zhu, "The Page Act of 1875: In the Name of Morality," *SSRN Electronic Journal* (2010), 5. Also see the text of the *Burlingame Treaty*, July 28, 1868, 16 Stat. 739, T.S. No. 48.

25. Zhu, "The Page Act of 1875," 49.

26. Bevis and Lucas, *International Students in American Colleges and Universities*, 53.

27. Hsu's work is especially effective in its more critical, theoretical, and transnational perspective on these histories. Her broader contextualization tells us a great deal about the relationship between efforts to educate noncitizen students and the development of liberal logics that make contemporary neoliberal policy and logics of personhood possible.

28. Lian Xi, "Returning to the Middle Kingdom: Yung Wing and the Recalled Students of the Chinese Educational Mission to the United States," *Modern Asian Studies* 49, no. 1 (2015): 152.

29. Edmund H. Worthy, "Yung Wing in America," *Pacific Historical Review* 34, no. 3 (1965): 270.

30. Leland Stanford, "Inaugural Address," January 10, 1862, https://governors.library.ca.gov/addresses/08-Stanford.html.

31. Manu Karuka, *Empire's Tracks: Indigenous Nations, Chinese Workers, and the Transcontinental Railroad* (University of California Press, 2019), 85.

32. US 37th Cong., Sess. Chs. 25, 27, 1862, 340–41.

33. Karuka, *Empire's Tracks*, 83.

34. Moon-Ho Jung, "Outlawing 'Coolies': Race, Nation, and Empire in the Age of Emancipation," *American Quarterly* 57, no. 3 (2005): 698. Efforts to intervene on "coolieism" also served as a rationale for US expansionism abroad in China, Cuba, and eventually in Hawai'i and the Philippines by the turn of the century.

35. Karuka, *Empire's Tracks*, 83.

36. Hsu, *The Good Immigrants*, 32. As Jung argues elsewhere, some pro-slavery Southerners were in fact "vocal critics of 'coolie' labor, animating a critique of the British turn from the use of enslaved African labor toward the 'coolie' system as a new form of slavery." Moon-Ho Jung, "What is the 'Coolie Question'?," *Labour History* 11 (2017).

37. Jung, "What is the 'Coolie Question'?," 6.

38. Jung, "What is the 'Coolie Question'?"

39. Lisa Lowe, *The Intimacies of Four Continents* (Duke University Press, 2015), 27.

40. Jung, "Outlawing 'Coolies,'" 698.

41. Jung, "Outlawing 'Coolies,'" 698.

42. Tao Leigh Goffe, "Intimate Occupations: The Afterlife of the 'Coolie,'" *Transforming Anthropology* 22, no. 1 (2014): 54.

43. Karuka, *Empire's Tracks*, 91.

44. Karuka, *Empire's Tracks*, 98.

45. Karuka, *Empire's Tracks*, 99.

46. Xi, "Returning to the Middle Kingdom," 158.

47. Hsu, *The Good Immigrants*, 29.

48. Zeng Guofan and Li Hongzhang, memorial to the Tongzhi Emperor, September 3, 1871 (nineteenth day of the 7th moon, the 10th year of Tongzhi), in Wen Qing et al., eds., *Chouhan yiwu shimo* (A Complete Account of the Management of Barbarian Affairs), *Tongshi juan* (The Volume for the Reign of the

Tongzhi Emperor) (Shanghai guji chubanshe, 2008), Chapter 82, 46–47, cited in Xi, "Returning to the Middle Kingdom," 158.

49. Yung Wing, *My Life in China and America* (Henry Holt and Company, 1909), 115.

50. Yung, *My Life*, 116.

51. Yung, *My Life*, 117.

52. Yung, *My Life*, 118.

53. Worthy, "Yung Wing in America," 265.

54. Yung, *My Life*, 125

55. Ye, *Seeking Modernity in China's Name*, 8.

56. Zhu, "The Page Act of 1875"; See also Nayan Shah, *Stranger Intimacy: Contesting Race, Sexuality and the Law in the North American West* (University of California Press, 2011).

57. Kerry Abrams, "Polygamy, Prostitution, and the Federalization of Immigration Law," *Columbia Law Review* 105 (2005): 641.

58. Leti Volpp, "Divesting Citizenship: On Asian American History and the Loss of Citizenship Through Marriage," *UCLA Law Review* 53 (2005): 405–83; Act of Mar. 3, 1875 (Page Law), ch. 141, 18 Stat., 477.

59. By 1877, articulations of logics of racial inferiority entered congressional discourse in a committee report that argued "There is not sufficient brain capacity in the Chinese race to furnish motive power for self-government." Kitty Calavita, "The Paradoxes of Race, Class, Identity, and 'Passing': Enforcing the Chinese Exclusion Acts, 1882–1910," *Law & Social Inquiry* 25, no. 1 (2000): 4.

60. "Additional Articles to the Treaty Between the United States of America and the Ta-Tsing Empire, of June 18, 1858," concluded at Washington, July 28, 1868.

61. Paul Kramer, "Imperial Openings: Civilization, Exemption, and the Geopolitics of Mobility in the History of Chinese Exclusion, 1868–1910," *The Journal of the Gilded Age and Progressive Era* 14, no. 3 (2015): 322.

62. Angell Treaty of 1880, signed November 17, 1880, *Treaties and Other International Agreements of the United States of America 1776–1949* (Bevans, Charles I), 6.

63. Thomas La Fargue, *China's First Hundred* (State College of Washington, 1942), 55.

64. La Fargue, *China's First Hundred*, 55–56.

65. Y. S. Tsao, "The Relation of the Returned Students to the Chinese Revolution," *The Journal of Race Development* 4, no. 1 (1913): 98.

## 5. The Student Question in the Era of Exclusion

1. "An Act to Execute Certain Treaty Stipulations Relating to Chinese," chapter 126, 22 STAT. 58 (1882) (repealed 1943). For a detailed history of this process see Shih-shan Henry Tsai, *China and the Overseas Chinese in the United States, 1868–1911* (University of Arkansas Press, 1983). Madeline Y. Hsu, *The Good Immigrants: How the Yellow Peril Became the Model Minority* (Princeton University Press, 2015), 13.

2. Hsu, *The Good Immigrants*, 1.

3. Kitty Calavita, "The Paradoxes of Race, Class, Identity, and 'Passing': Enforcing the Chinese Exclusion Acts, 1882-1910," *Law & Social Inquiry* 25, no.1: (2000): 11.

4. *Congressional Record: Proceedings and Debates of the 47th Congress*, 1st sess., vol. 13, pt. 2 (Washington, DC: Government Printing Office, 1882), 1977, https://babel.hathitrust.org/cgi/pt?id=hvd.32044109459537, cited in Calavita, "The Paradoxes of Race, Class, Identity, and 'Passing,'" 11.

5. *Congressional Record: Proceedings and Debates of the 47th Congress, 1st sess.*, vol. 13, pt. 2 (Washington, DC: Government Printing Office, 1882), 1487, https://babel.hathitrust.org/cgi/pt?id=hvd.32044109459537, cited in Calavita, "The Paradoxes of Race, Class, Identity, and 'Passing,'" 11.

6. Eithne Luibhéid, "Queer/migration: An Unruly Body of Scholarship," *GLQ* 14, no. 2–3 (2008): 503.

7. Ming M Zhu, "The Page Act of 1875: In the Name of Morality," *SSRN Electronic Journal* (2010): 6.

8. 1882 Chinese Exclusion Act as cited by Calavita, "Chinese Exclusion and the Open Door with China," 15.

9. Paul Kramer, "Imperial Openings: Civilization, Exemption, and the Geopolitics of Mobility in the History of Chinese Exclusion, 1868–1910," *The Journal of the Gilded Age and Progressive Era* 14, no. 3 (2015): 320.

10. Kramer, "Imperial Openings," 322. Kramer further elaborates on this argument in "Shades of Sovereignty: Racialized Power, the United States, and the World," in *Explaining the History of American Foreign Relations*, 3rd edition, ed. Frank Costigliola and Michael Hogan (Cambridge University Press, 2016), 251.

11. Hsu, *The Good Immigrants*, 7, 25.

12. Kramer, "Imperial Openings," 322.

13. Calavita, "Chinese Exclusion and the Open Door with China," 204.

14. Chinese Exclusion Act of 1882, Pub. L. No. 47-126, § 6, 22 Stat. 58, 60 (1882).

15. Erika Lee, *At America's Gates: Chinese Immigration During the Exclusion Era, 1882–1943* (University of North Carolina Press, 2003), 48; and Kramer, "Imperial Openings," 323.

16. Lee, *At America's Gates*, 47.

17. Christian Fritz, "Due Process, Treaty Rights, and Chinese Exclusion, 1882–1891," in *Entry Denied: Exclusion and the Chinese Community in America, 1882–1943*, ed. Sucheng Chan (Temple University Press, 1991), 29–30, cited in Adam McKeown, "Ritualization of Regulation: The Enforcement of Chinese Exclusion in the United States and China," *American Historical Review* (2003): 383; and Susan Sterett, "'Entitled to Have a Hearing': Due Process in the 1890s," *Social & Legal Studies* 3 (1994): 56.

18. As examples of particularly important decisions, see *United States v. Ju Toy*, 198 US 253 (1905); *United States v. Wong Kim Ark*, 169 US 229 (1896); *Wong Wing v. United States*, 163 US 228 (1896); *Fong Yue Ting v. United States*, 149 US 698 (1893); and *Chae Chan Ping v. United States*, 130 US 581 (1889). For other noteworthy

decisions, see *Ng Fung Ho v. White*, 259 US 276 (1922); *Low Wah Suey v. Backus*, 225 US 460 (1912); *Chin Yow v. United States*, 208 US 8 (1908); *Chin Bak Kan v. United States*, 186 US 193 (1902); *United States v. Sing Tuck*, 194 US 161 (1904); *Lem Moon Sing v. United States*, 158 US 538 (1895); and *Chew Heong v. United States*, 112 US 536.

19. For more on Judge Field see Robert Green McCloskey, *American Conservatism in the Age of Enterprise: A Study of William Graham Sumner, Stephen J. Field, and Andrew Carnegie* (Harvard University Press, 1951).

20. 13 F. 605 (D.Cal. 1882) CASE OF THE CHINESE MERCHANT. In re LOW YAM CHOW. United States Circuit Court, D. California. September 5, 1882. The judge continues, reading Section 6 of the 1882 law in through the congressional debates that preceded its passage: "In the debates in the senate on the original bill, which contained provisions nearly identical with those of section 6 in the bill which obtained the president's approval, it was strenuously urged that to exact a compliance with 'the cumbersome and burdensome provisions' with regard to certificates of identification, and which are required of the subjects of no other power, was a violation of the treaty which allows the permitted classes to go and come of their own free will and accord, and which guaranties to them all the rights, privileges, immunities, and exemptions accorded to the citizens and subjects of the most favored nation. To this it was replied that the provisions in the bill were merely for purposes of identification; that they were in the interest of the classes permitted to come; that it was no hardship to the permitted classes to leave it to the Chinese government to say who are merchants, traders, teachers, etc., and therefore not within the excluded class. But if the bill had declared, or had been supposed to declare, by necessary implication, that no Chinese person unprovided with a certificate should, under any circumstances, be allowed to land, and that its non-production should be conclusive evidence that the passenger was a Chinese laborer, while its production should only be prima facie evidence of the facts set forth therein, the bill might have encountered an opposition which would have endangered its passage."

21. Lee, *At America's Gates*, 48. California exclusionists went so far as to introduce legislation to bar all Chinese persons except diplomats, but it failed to pass.

22. Beth Lew-Williams, "Before Restriction Became Exclusion: America's Experiment in Diplomatic Immigration Control," *Pacific Historical Review* 83, no. 1 (2014): 26.

23. Krystyn R. Moon, "Immigration Restrictions and International Education: Early Tensions in the Pacific Northwest, 1890s–1910s." *History of Education Quarterly* 58, no. 2 (2018): 266.

24. Kitty Calavita, "The Paradoxes of Race, Class, Identity, and 'Passing': Enforcing the Chinese Exclusion Acts, 1882–1910," *Law & Social Inquiry* 25, no. 1 (2000): 2.

25. Calavita, "The Paradoxes of Race, Class, Identity, and 'Passing,'" 2. To make this argument, Calavita builds on as several theoretical traditions in legal studies to assert the indeterminacy of the law, the "role of administrative discretion in the 'lawmaking process,'" a literature that tends to look toward immigration policy in particular, studies of law, race, and intersectionality; and studies of the social construction of identity (ibid., 3).

26. Calavita, "The Paradoxes of Race, Class, Identity, and 'Passing,'" 14. It is telling, also, that the administrative responsibility for the law was delegated to customs officials, people generally responsible for managing the entrance of imported goods rather than people. Calavita argues that this "evocatively affirms the presumption that the Chinese would fit neatly into discrete categories and accepted or rejected like canned goods" (ibid., 15).

27. M. Kunal Parker, "The Rights of Noncitizens," *The Bill of Rights in Modern America*, ed. David J. Bodenhamer and James W. Ely Jr. (Indiana University Press, 2022), 241.

28. Parker, "The Rights of Noncitizens," 241, citing *Chae Chan Ping v. United States* (Chinese Exclusion Case), 130 US 581 (1889).

29. Immigration Act of 1891, ch. 551, 26 Stat. 1084 (1891), https://govtrackus.s3.amazonaws.com/legislink/pdf/stat/26/STATUTE-26-Pg1084a.pdf.

30. *Nishimura Ekiu v. United States*, 142 US 651 (1892)

31. Sue Fawn Chung, "Chinese Exclusion, the First Bureau of Immigration, and the 1905 Special Chinese Census: Registered, Counted, Arrested, Deported—1892–1906," in *Chinese America: History and Perspectives* (Chinese Historical Society, 2018), 22.

32. "Geary Act [An Act to Prohibit the Coming of Chinese Persons into the United States], ch. 60, 27 Stat. 25 (1892), https://loveman.sdsu.edu/docs/1892GearyAct.pdf. Under Section 4 "any Chinese person or person of Chinese descent convicted and adjudged to be not lawfully entitled to be or remain in the United States" was to be "imprisoned at hard labor afar a period of not exceeding one year" before being deported. This one component of the law was successfully challenged in *Wong Wing v. United States* in 1896 when the Supreme Court ruled that it "conflicts with the fifth and sixth amendments," showing that there was an outer limit to the capacities the court was willing to empower to immigration inspectors. https://supreme.justia.com/cases/federal/us/163/228/.

33. Ng Poon Chew, *The Treatment of the Exempt Classes of Chinese in the United States* (Chung Sai Yat Po, 1908).

34. Chew, *The Treatment of the Exempt Classes of Chinese in the United States.*

35. Chung, "Chinese Exclusion," 23.

36. Kramer, "Imperial Openings," 326.

37. Hsu, *The Good Immigrants*, 35.

38. Cited in Moon, "Immigration Restrictions," 268.

39. Moon, "Immigration Restrictions," 268.

40. Committee on Foreign Affairs, *Exclusion of Chinese Laborers*, S. Doc. No. 57–162 at 7 (1902), cited in Moon, "Immigration Restrictions."

41. Moon, "Immigration Restrictions," 268.

42. On Chinese perceptions of the United States in the nineteenth century Kramer cites R. David Arkush and Oufan Lee, *Land Without Ghosts: Chinese Impressions of American from the Mid-Nineteenth Century to the Present* (University of California Press, 1989); K. Scott Wong, "The Transformation of Culture: Views of America," *American Quarterly* 48 (June 1996): 201–32; Chang-Fang Chen, "Barbarian Paradise: Chinese Views of the United States, 1784–1911," (PhD diss., Indiana University, 1985); Merle Curti and John Stalker, "'The Flowery Flag Devils': The American Image in China, 1840–1900," *Proceedings American Philosophical Society* 96 (December 20, 1952): 663–90.

43. Kramer, "Imperial Openings," 325

44. Wu Ting-Fang, "Mutual Helpfulness Between China and the United States," *North American Review* (July 1900): 9, cited in Kramer, "Imperial Openings," 325.

45. Wu Ting-Fang, "Mutual Helpfulness," 5.

46. Wu Ting-Fang, "Mutual Helpfulness," 325.

47. Kramer, "Imperial Openings," 325.

48. See Marwa Elshakry, "When Science Became Western: Historiographical Reflections," *Isis* 101, no. 1 (2010): 98–109. Elshakry traces the introduction of "Western science" into Chinese culture by British Protestant missionaries (ibid., 102).

49. Peter Zarrow, "Liang Qichao and the Conceptualization of 'Race' in Late Qing China," *Bulletin of the Institute of Modern History*, Academia Sinica 52 (2006): 116.

50. Wu Ting-Fang, "Mutual Helpfulness," 104. One prominent player in this process was Zhang Zhidong, often described as the "founding father of modern Chinese military institutions" for his founding of the Guangdong Military Academy in 1887, who looked to Western learning as a source for Chinese self-strengthening. He did not "perceive his military reforms as westernization, but as learning from the foreigner's methods while distrusting the same foreigner's intentions." Adam Chang, "Reappraising Zhang Zhidong: Forgotten Continuities During China's Self-Strengthening, 1884–1901," *Journal of Chinese Military History* 6 (2017): 168.

51. Wu Ting-Fang, "Mutual Helpfulness," 105.

52. Sean Hsiang-Lin Lei, "The Dawn of Science as Cultural Authority in China: Tianyanlun (On Heavenly Evolution) in the Post-1895 Debate over the Engagement with Western Civilization," *East Asian Science, Technology and Society: An International Journal* 13, no. 3 (2022): 410.

53. Lei, "The Dawn of Science as Cultural Authority in China," 412.

54. Shellen Xiao Wu, *Birth of the Geopolitical Age: Global Frontiers and the Making of Modern China* (Stanford University Press, 2023), 107.

55. Luke S. K. Kwong, "Chinese Politics at the Crossroads: Reflections on the Hundred Days Reform of 1898," *Modern Asian Studies* 34, no. 3 (2000): 668.

56. Edmund H. Worthy, "Yung Wing in America," *Pacific Historical Review* 34, no. 3 (1965): 284.

57. Worthy, "Yung Wing in America," 285.

58. Hsu, *The Good Immigrants*, 39.

59. Michael Hunt, "The American Remission of the Boxer Indemnity: A Reappraisal," *The Journal of Asian Studies* 31, no. 3 (1972): 542.

60. "Mr. Wu to Mr. Hay," December 9, 1901, "Exclusion Laws—Complaints of Harsh and Unfair Enforcement," in *Papers Relating to the Foreign Relations of the United States with the Annual Message of the President Transmitted to Congress*, December 3, 1901, 72; "Mr. Wu to Mr. Hay," December 10, 1901, "Exclusion Laws—Representations against Reenactment as Affecting the United States and Territories, and Extension to the Philippine Islands," in *Papers Relating to the Foreign Relations of the United States with the Annual Message of the President Transmitted to Congress*, December 3, 1901, 75–97, cited in Emma J. Teng, "Chinese Elites and US Gatekeeping: Racial Discrimination and Class Privilege in Boston's 1905 King Incident," *Modern American History* 4 (2021): 8.

61. Kramer, "Imperial Openings," 332.

62. Charles Hamlin, *Journal of the American Asiatic Association*, February 8, 1902, 27, cited in Kramer, "Imperial Openings," 332.

63. "Life of F.P. Sargent, Grand Master," in *Souvenir of the 14th Annual Convention of the Brotherhood of Locomotive Firemen* (Brotherhood of Locomotive Firemen (Terre Haute, IN), 1888), 11, 13, 15, 17, https://archive.org/details/LifeOfFrankP.Sargent1888/page/n1/mode/2up.

64. Calavita, "The Paradoxes of Race, Class, Identity, and 'Passing,'" 22 n. 16.

65. Calavita, "The Paradoxes of Race, Class, Identity, and 'Passing,'" 25.

66. Teng, "Chinese Elites and US Gatekeeping," 2.

67. Luella Miner, "American Barbarism and Chinese Hospitality," *The Outlook* 72, no. 17 (1902): 984. This story received broad coverage including at least two stories in the *Washington Post*: "Passports Signed by Li Hung Chang," *Washington Post*, September 27, 1901, 3; and "Chinese Students Admitted," *Washington Post*, January 13, 1903, 4, cited in Moon, "Immigration Restrictions," 269.

68. Weili Ye, *Seeking Modernity in China's Name: Chinese Students in the United States, 1900–1927* (Stanford University Press, 2001), 89.

69. Ye, *Seeking Modernity in China's Name*, 89.

70. Tian Atlas Xu, "Immigration Attorneys and Chinese Exclusion Law Enforcement: The Case of San Francisco, 1882–1930," *Journal of American Ethnic History* 41, no. 1 (2021).

71. US Immigration and Naturalization Service, San Francisco District Office, "Photograph of Dr. Sun Yat Sen: 'hb Sun Yat Sen, 40, Xpl Korea 3-28-10, File No. 140-C,'" in *Contents of the File of Sun Yat Sen*, NARA Government Documents, https://www.archives.gov/publications/record/1998/05/sun-yat-sen.html.

72. The Soong sister's father, Charles Jone Soong, studied at Trinity College, which became Duke University, and then received his theological certificate from

Vanderbilt University in 1885. He helped found the Chinese YMCA and printed Bibles in Chinese.

73. Kramer, "Imperial Openings," 333.

74. "IVERNIA IN.: Cunarder Had Total of 1471 Passengers. Chinese Tourists Held by Immigration Officials. COl Billings Give His View on the Matter," *Boston Daily Globe*, June 2, 1905.

75. See Teng, "Chinese Elites and US Gatekeeping," 10.

76. "The Chinese Boycott," *New York Times*, June 21, 1905.

77. On the same day as *The New York Times* article was published, Julius Lay, American consul general in Canton, wrote to Assistant Secretary of State Francis Loomis asking for "instructions" regarding visa certification for students and travelers. He writes specifically about Au Tai Tum, an eighteen-year-old former mission school student, applying for "admission to enter the United States as a student." Lay explains that Au's brother, a commission agent in a New York firm, plans to select a school for him upon his arrival, but the arrangement fails to meet the requirements for providing a student entrance because the 1900 regulations required that students "designate the name of the school or college in which he intends to pursue his studies." He then explains the situation of a second would-be student who he had to deny a visa despite having clear qualifications for the same reason. Lay writes, "If a student must designate to me the school he proposes to attend, not one of the boys who are bona fide students would be able to obtain the visa of this office on their certificates, as it is impossible for them to state definitively what school or college they will matriculate for."

78. Adam M. McKeown, *Melancholy Order: Asian Migration and the Globalization of Borders* (Columbia University Press, 2008), 386–87.

79. Kramer, "Imperial Openings," 337.

80. Chung, "Chinese Exclusion," 30.

81. Calavita, "Chinese Exclusion and the Open Door with China," 216.

82. Calavita, "Chinese Exclusion and the Open Door with China," 216.

83. Cited in Kramer, "Imperial Openings," 337

84. Kramer, "Imperial Openings," 339.

85. Jane Leung Larson, "Articulating China's First Mass Movement: Kang Youwei, Liang Qichao, the Baohuanghui, and the 1905 Anti-American Boycott," *Twentieth-Century China* 33, no. 1 (2007): 8.

86. Stacey Bieler, *Patriots or Traitors: A History of American Educated Chinese Students* (Routledge, 2014), 44.

87. Cited in Bieler, *Patriots or Traitors*, 43. Before the end of the boycott, US college and university leaders organized their own effort to respond to the protestors' concerns. On February 24, 1906, *The Outlook* reports on a set of "definite and generous propositions" from the administrations at Harvard, Yale, and Wellesley to "[grant] privileges of instruction at those institutions" to ten, twelve, and three Chinese students respectively. "American Education for the Chinese," *Outlook* (1906), 387. The institutions would fund the program for the first four years after which some of the

students were to pay their own way while others were "to be nominated by the Chinese Government, and are to be sent to America at its expense." The brief article lauds the initiative as the completion of Yung Wing's program to promote friendship and provide "a guide and an inspiration to China's new civilization," stating that "nothing has yet been done in this country which will have a greater or more lasting effect in persuading the Chinese that Americans are friendly and not hostile to them than this action."

88. Theodore Roosevelt, "Seventh Annual Message," online by Gerhard Peters and John T. Woolley, The American Presidency Project, accessed September 4, 2025, https://www.presidency.ucsb.edu/node/206218.

89. Hongshan Li, *US-China Educational Exchange: State, Society, and Intercultural Relations*, 1905–1950 (Rutgers University Press, 2008), 60.

90. Y. C. Wang, *Chinese Intellectuals and the West, 1872–1949* (University of North Carolina Press, 2012), 71, cited in Hsu, *The Good Immigrants*, 47.

91. Hsu, *The Good Immigrants*, 47–48.

92. Calavita, "Chinese Exclusion and the Open Door with China," 216; and Kramer, "Imperial Openings," 339; "Chinese Law Revised: Committee Submits Report on Exclusion Rules," *Washington Post*, February 6, 1906.

93. Ye, *Seeking Modernity in China's Name*, 90.

94. Calavita, "Chinese Exclusion and the Open Door with China," 217.

95. Ye, *Seeking Modernity in China's Name*, 10.

96. See Ye, *Seeking Modernity in China's Name*, 233 n. 59.

97. Ye, *Seeking Modernity in China's Name*, 19.

98. Ye, *Seeking Modernity in China's Name*, 6. After the Boxer Rebellion, the Qing had also made concessions toward modernization, including the abolition of the imperial civil exam, which Liang Qichao had protested in the 1890s.

99. Ye, *Seeking Modernity in China's Name*, 82.

100. Ye, *Seeking Modernity in China's Name*, 83.

101. Ye, *Seeking Modernity in China's Name*, 83.

102. Ye, *Seeking Modernity in China's Name*, 83.

103. Irma Tam Soong, "Sun Yat-sen's Christian Schooling in Hawai'i," *The Hawaiian Journal of History* 31 (1997): 151–78.

104. Sun Yat-sen, *Kuo-fu Ch'ian-shu* (National Defense Research Institute, 1961), 517, cited in Worthy, "Yung Wing in America," 286. According to Worthy, Yung "strove for the benefit of China which bore him, while professing cultural and familial allegiance to American which educated him" (ibid., 287). He was "[a] Chinese patriot and an idealist—one who tried vainly to bring greater Western influence to bear on China" (ibid., 266).

105. Letter of American consulate general, September 5, 1910, RG 59,811.4, cited in Wang, *Chinese Intellectuals and the West, 1872–1949*, 61.

106. Letter of the Department of Commerce and Labor, October 28, 1910, RG 59, 811.42793, cited in Wang, *Chinese Intellectuals and the West, 1872–1949*, 68.

107. Letter of American consulate general, Shanghai, August 17, 1920, RG 59,811.42792/ 132, cited in Wang, *Chinese Intellectuals and the West, 1872–1949*, 63.

108. Wang, *Chinese Intellectuals and the West, 1872–1949*, 66.

109. Letter of the consul of Shanghai, April 1, 1920, RG 59,811.42793/109, cited in Wang, *Chinese Intellectuals and the West, 1872–1949*, 68–69.

110. Letter of the consul of Shanghai, April 1, 1920, RG 59,811.42793/109, cited in Wang, *Chinese Intellectuals and the West, 1872–1949*, 68–69.

111. Wang, *Chinese Intellectuals and the West, 1872–1949*, 69.

112. Ngai, *Impossible Subjects*, 23.

113. Samuel Shortridge, "Restriction of Immigration," *Congressional Record* 5793 (1924): 5808.

114. Chao-Yung Shill, "The Effects of the Immigration Bill of 1924 on Chinese Students," *Chinese Students Monthly* 20, no. 2 (1924): 16–19.

115. Shill, "The Effects of the Immigration Bill of 1924 on Chinese Students," 17.

116. Shill, "The Effects of the Immigration Bill of 1924 on Chinese Students," 17.

117. Shill, "The Effects of the Immigration Bill of 1924 on Chinese Students," 18.

118. Shill, "The Effects of the Immigration Bill of 1924 on Chinese Students," 18.

119. Shill, "The Effects of the Immigration Bill of 1924 on Chinese Students," 18.

120. Shill, "The Effects of the Immigration Bill of 1924 on Chinese Students," 18.

121. "Ruth Crawford Mitchell," *Vasser Encyclopedia*, accessed June 1, 2022.

122. Ruth Crawford Mitchell, *Foreign Students and the Immigration Laws of the United States* (Institute of International Education, 1930), 5.

123. Mitchell, *Foreign Students and the Immigration Laws of the United States*, 6.

124. Mitchell, *Foreign Students and the Immigration Laws of the United States*, 6.

125. Mitchell, *Foreign Students and the Immigration Laws of the United States*, 8.

126. US Congress, Senate, *The Immigration and Naturalization Systems of the United States*, 81st Cong., 2nd sess., 1950, S. Rep. 1515, 496.

127. Students from quota-exempt countries were also subject to some aspects of the new student immigration regime. They were required to apply for a visa at the consulate closest to their home and provide the consulate with "evidence of birthplace and race" and demonstrate that they meet the health requirements of the 1917 immigration law through certification from a physician. While they must also show that they have the financial means to make it to their final destination, they need not have evidence of their admission to an approved institution or their ability to speak English.

128. Mitchell, *Foreign Students and the Immigration Laws of the United States*, 12.

129. See, for instance Adam Serwer, "Jeff Sessions's Unqualified Praise for a 1924 Immigration Law," *The Atlantic*, January 10, 2017, https://www.theatlantic.com/politics/archive/2017/01/jeff-sessions-1924-immigration/512591/?utm_source=atlfb.

## Part III: Education for a New Age of Empire

1. Harrison E. Salisbury, "Washington Post Buys Newsweek," *New York Times*, March 10, 1961. While I do not discuss the particularity of *Newsweek* and the middlebrow imaginary of the world outside of the United States at length in this

chapter, Christina Klein's book-length study of this phenomenon offers a thorough study of publications, such as *Newsweek.* See Christina Klein, *Cold War Orientalism: Asia in the Middlebrow Imagination, 1945–1961* (University of California Press, 2003); Mel Elfin and Constance Montague, "'Mo' is Sa'aid's Nickname At Cornell," *Newsweek*, April 22, 1963, 59–62, 66.

2. As Nick Mitchell suggested in a conversation, it is not surprising that this story is sited at Cornell. In comparison to the other elite institutions with which it is aligned in the Ivy League, Cornell stands apart in a few ways, most clearly what Mitchell refers to as its "expansion capacity." This allowed it to "absorb *elite* student surpluses in a way that other campuses cannot, due to the fact that they are constrained by the dearth of available real estate in urban locations, and location-based enrollment limits with puritanical alcohol regulations (i.e., Dartmouth). Because it is so far from cities, Cornell accounts rarely have to deal with the kinds of glaring inequalities readily visible in other elite universities. In Ithaca, it is so much easier to make poverty, and even much of the working class, disappear." Personal correspondence.

3. Hugh Russell Fraser, "Letter to Editor," *Newsweek*, May 6, 1963, 2.

4. Response to Fraser, "Letter to Editor." With the notable exception of Spivak, it is difficult to track the lives and careers of the other students featured in this article. Chibuzo Ajuka graduated from Cornell with a BS in engineering in 1961. Given his inclusion here, it is likely that he stayed on for a graduate degree. A quote from someone with this name and identified as being from Nigeria appears in a "Report by African Students: The Terror in Angola" from the June 22, 1964 issue of *The Militant.* There, he is cited as tracking the origins of Pan-Africanist ideas to Marcus Garvey and W. E. B. Du Bois and tying this history to the May 1963 formation of the Organization of African Unity.

5. As discussed in this book's conclusion, in their respective work on Spivak as a figure and a scholar, Sangeeta Ray, Mridula Nath Chakraborty, Jenny Sharpe, and others consider this article as a key component of the archive of Spivak's life—a rare moment of insight into the youth of the woman who has gone on to become one of the most highly regarded literary studies scholars of the late twentieth and early twenty-first centuries. See Sangeeta Ray, *Gayatri Chakravorty Spivak: In Other Words* (Wiley-Blackwell, 2009); Mridula Nath Chakraborty, "Everybody's Afraid of Gayatri Chakravorty Spivak: Reading Interviews With the Public Intellectual and Postcolonial Critic," *Signs* 35, no. 3 (2010); Jenny Sharpe, "What Use Is the Imagination?," *PMLA* 129, no. 3 (2014).

6. Jodi Melamed, "The Spirit of Neoliberalism," *Social Text* (2006), 2. Because immigration law through to 1965 exempted the Western Hemisphere from the quota system instantiated by the 1924 Johnson–Reed INA, this chapter focuses on the movement of students from outside of this region, turning mostly to movement from Africa and Asia. During the period discussed, however, there were specific programs between the United States and Latin American countries, often funded at least in part by foundations such as Rockefeller and Carnegie. Under Roosevelt's "Good

Neighbor Policy," as Liping Bu argues, there were programs that "became a prelude to the government's total involvement in worldwide cultural exchange after 1945." Liping Bu, "Educational Exchange and Cultural Diplomacy in the Cold War," *Journal of American Studies* 33 (1999): 395. On the model minority myth's emergence see William Petersen, "Success Story, Japanese-American Style," *New York Times Magazine*, January 9, 1966; and Frank H. Wu, *Yellow: Race in America Beyond Black and White* (Basic Books, 2002), 62.

7. Mary Dudziak, *Cold War Civil Rights: Race and the Image of American Democracy* (Princeton University Press, 2000).

8. David Kazanjian, *The Colonizing Trick: National Culture and Imperial Citizenship in Early America* (University of Minnesota Press, 2003), 95.

## 6. The State of the University and the University of the State After World War II

1. Paul Kramer, "Power and Connection: Imperial Histories of the United States in the World," *American Historical Review* 116, no. 5 (2011): 1368.

2. George F. Kennan, "Resume of the World Situation," November 6, 1947, in *Foreign Relations of the United States, 1947, General; The United Nations*, vol. 1 (Government Printing Office, 1973), 770–77. Kennan's direct influence within the US government waned in the 1950s but the power of the basic logic of containment persisted. He served briefly as ambassador to the Soviet Union in 1952 and then returned to public service as the ambassador to Yugoslavia in 1961, just months before the Belgrade conference founding Non-Aligned Movement (NAM).

3. Vijay Prashad, *The Darker Nations: A People's History of the Third World* (The New Press, 2022), 15.

4. Prashad, *The Darker Nations*, 96.

5. Mel Elfin and Constance Montague, "'Mo' is Sa'aid's Nickname At Cornell: 64,000 Foreign Students Ride the Diploma-Diplomacy Seesaw," *Newsweek*, 1963, 59.

6. See for instance Ron Robin, *The Making of the Cold War Enemy: Culture and Politics in the Military-Intellectual Complex* (Princeton University Press, 2001).

7. Jeffrey J. Williams, "The Post-Welfare State University," *American Literary History* 24, no. 1 (2012): 190–216. There is a great deal to be said about the relationship of noncitizen students to the particularly militarized university of Cold War "America." While it is not the focus of the present project, this is an avenue of thinking I hope to engage later. Useful references include: Stuart W. Leslie, *The Cold War and American Science: The Military-Industrial-Academic Complex at MIT Stanford* (Columbia University Press, 1993); Robin, *The Making of the Cold War Enemy*; Andre Schiffrin, ed., *The Cold War & the University: Toward an Intellectual History of the Postwar Years* (The New Press, 1997); Herbert I. Schiller and Joseph D. Phillips, eds., *Super-State: Readings in the Military-Industrial Complex* (University of Illinois Press, 1972).

8. Roger L. Geiger, *American Higher Education Since World War II: A History* (Princeton University Press, 2019), 7.

9. Wendy Brown, *Undoing the Demos* (Zone Books, 2015), 185.

10. Williams, "The Post-Welfare State University," 194.

11. Isaac A. Kamola, *Making the World Global: US. Universities and the Production of the Global Imaginary* (Duke University Press, 2019), 11.

12. Kamola, *Making the World Global*, 31, citing Clark Kerr, *The Uses of the University*, 5th ed. (Harvard University Press, 2001), 37; See also David C. Engerman, "American Knowledge and Global Power," *Diplomatic History* 31, no. 4 (2007): 599–622.

13. Kamola, *Making the World Global*, 31.

14. Nils Gilman, *Mandarins of the Future: Modernization Theory in Cold War America* (Johns Hopkins University Press, 2004), 73.

15. Engerman, "American Knowledge and Global Power," 604.

16. Engerman, "American Knowledge and Global Power," 604.

17. Philippe Fontaine, "Walking the Tightrope: The Committee on the Behavioral Sciences and Academic Cultures at the University of Chicago, 1949–1955," *Journal of the History of the Behavioral Sciences* (2016): 335–56.

18. In 1929, Yale was led by its president James Rowland Angell, a functional psychologist and past president of the Carnegie Corporation who remained in office until 1937. Angell's central mission was to "recast Yale as a research university in the model of Chicago and Johns Hopkins." An initial success in this area was securing a Rockefeller award for $4.5 million to support an "Institute of Human Behavior" in 1929. Angell's father, James Burrill Angell, was president of the University of Michigan from 1871 to 1909. While serving in this position, he negotiated the 1880 Angell Treaty between the United States and China that has served as the foundation for the conditional and exceptional inclusion of noncitizen students in US immigration law, as discussed in Chapter 3. Jefferson D. Pooley, "A 'Not Particularly Felicitous' Phrase: A History of the 'Behavioral Sciences' Label," *Serendipities* (2016): 43; See also Jill Morawski, "Organizing Knowledge and Behavior at Yale's Institute of Human Relations," *Isis* 77, no. 2 (1986), 219–42.

19. There is much to be studied regarding the relationship of modernization theory to civilizing logics and shifts in race and socialization and I hope to engage this line of thought in future work. On the Ford Foundation's role in this history see Pooley, "A 'Not Particularly Felicitous' Phrase."

20. *International Development and the Social Sciences Essays on the History and Politics of Knowledge*, ed. Frederick Cooper and Randall M. Packard (University of California Press, 1998), 1.

21. US Department of State, "Statement of Policy Proposed by the NSC on 'United States Objectives and Policies with Respect to the Arab States and Israel,'" in *Foreign Relations of the United States, 1952–1954, Vol. IX, The Near and Middle East* (Government Printing Office, 1986), 4–5; Irene Gendzier, "Play it Again Sam,"

in *Universities and Empire: Money and Politics in the Social Sciences During the Cold War*, ed. Christopher Simpson (The New Press, 1998), 73.

22. Cited in Gendzier, *Universities and Empire*, 74.

23. Penny M. Von Eschen, *Race Against Empire: Black Americans and Anticolonialism, 1937–1957* (Cornell University Press, 1997), 131.

24. Margaret O'Mara, "The Uses of the Foreign Student," *Social Science History* 36, no. 4 (2012): 584.

25. O'Mara, "The Uses of the Foreign Student," 590.

26. Teresa B. Bevis and Christopher J. Lucas, *International Students in American Colleges and Universities: A History* (Palgrave Macmillan, 2007), 10, 103. Despite his internationalist bent, Fulbright was also very much a Southern Democrat who supported states' rights as a means toward maintaining segregation domestically. John Kyle Day, *Southern Manifesto: Massive Resistance and the Fight to Preserve Segregation* (University Press of Mississippi, 2014), 100.

27. Christina Klein, *Cold War Orientalism: Asia in the Middlebrow Imagination, 1945–1961* (University of California Press, 2003), 23.

28. Sam Lebovic, "From War Junk to Educational Exchange: The World War II Origins of the Fulbright Program and the Foundations of American Cultural Globalism, 1945–1950," *Diplomatic History* 37, no. 2 (2013).

29. Lebovic, "From War Junk to Educational Exchange," 283–84.

30. Ralph H. Vogel, "The Making of the Fulbright Program," *Annals, AAPSS* 491 (1987): 13. Even as a first term senator, Fulbright was highly active in his internationalist work. One of his first proposals was a resolution in 1943 calling for "the creation of appropriate international machinery with power adequate to maintain a just and lasting peace, among the nations of the world." Elizabeth Borgwardt, *A New Deal for the World: America's Vision for Human Rights* (Belknap Press of Harvard University Press, 2005), 162. The form of postwar global governance proposed in the UN Charter in 1945 was markedly more unilateral than Fulbright's 1943 proposal. In 1945 Fulbright protested the inclusion of the veto right for the "big powers" in the security council. "Fulbright, Hatch Now Hit Uno Veto: Arkansan Criticizes Truman's Program as Failing World Unity in Atomic Era," *New York Times*, November 25, 1945.

31. Lebovic, "From War Junk to Educational Exchange," 284. The Boxer Indemnity Fund is discussed in more length in Chapter 3.

32. Vogel, "The Making of the Fulbright Program," 12.

33. The federal government had in place some smaller-scale, specially arranged federal funding for students in the Western Hemisphere and with specific countries but nothing of the scale or scope required to support the numbers of students traveling to the United States from other countries and regions after the war. For instance, according to legal scholar Kit Johnson, some appropriations for exchanges with Latin America were made possible under a 1939 law that authorized the president to facilitate closer relationships "between the American republics" and in

1920 a special committee was set up to fund exchange with Belgium. Kit Johnson, "The Wonderful World of Disney Visas," *Florida Law Review* 63 (2011): 937–38; "Hoover Endorses Scholarship Plan," *New York Times*, February 17, 1946. According to *The New York Times*, Hoover's support for Fulbright's plan came largely from the successes of the Belgian Relief Commission, which was set up in 1920 to "educate Americans in Belgium, and to bring Belgian students to this country." Hoover testified to as much in support of Fulbright's bill. Funds to support students from Latin America were initiated as part of the State Department's Division for Cultural Affairs created in 1938. See Burton Paulu, "The Smith-Mundt Act: A Legislative History," *Journalism Quarterly* (1953): 300–314.

34. Richard T. Arndt and David Lee Rubin, eds., *The Fulbright Difference: 1948–1992* (Transaction Publishers, 1993), 14.

35. International Educational Exchange Service, *Swords Into Plowshares, a New Venture in International Understanding: The Story of the Educational Exchange Program Authorized By the Fulbright Act of 1946*, Vol. International Information and Cultural Series 48 (Department of State, 1956).

36. J. William Fulbright, "Open Doors, Not Iron Curtains," *New York Times*, August 5, 1951.

37. William Benton, "Our Best 'Weapon'—Exchange Students," *Ladies' Home Journal* 63, no. 12 (1946): 195.

38. Liping Bu, "Educational Exchange and Cultural Diplomacy in the Cold War," *Journal of American Studies* 33 (1999): 414. If, as Michel Foucault argues, power is "the implementation and deployment of a force relationship" then the Fulbright Program and other government-funded international education efforts of this era might best be understood, to continue the Foucauldian formulation, as a clear example wherein "politics is the continuation of war by other means." It can also be read as an example of the ways that knowledge cuts, as discussed in the introduction to this book. Michel Foucault, *"Society Must Be Defended": Lectures at the College De France 1975–76*, trans. David Macey, ed. Francois Ewald and Alessandro Fontana (Picador, 2003), 15.

In a 1967 statement to Congress, Fulbright would reflect on "the destructive effects of the war upon our domestic life," giving specific attention to the militarization of universities. It is ironic that a man who came to be so clearly concerned about the fact of universities becoming "appendage[s] to the government" was instrumental in laying the foundation for the movement of the government into the field of international education. See J. William Fulbright. "The War and Its Effects: The Military-Industrial-Academic Complex," in Schiller and Phillips, eds., *Super-State: Readings in the Military-Industrial Complex*, 173.

39. Benjamin Fine, "Foreign Students Shifting to Russia," *New York Times*, October 9, 1947.

40. Fine, "Foreign Students Shifting to Russia."

41. Bu, "Educational Exchange and Cultural Diplomacy in the Cold War," 409.

42. Stephen Mark Halpern, "The Institute of International Education: A History" (PhD diss., Columbia University, 1969), as cited by Bu, "Educational Exchange and Cultural Diplomacy in the Cold War," 411. There is much speculation about Laurence Duggan's life and 1948 death in relationship to allegations that he worked as an asset for the KGB. See for instance John Earl Haynes and Harvey Klehr, *Venona: Decoding Soviet Espionage in America* (Yale University Press, 1999).

43. *First Semiannual Report of United States Advisory Commission on Educational Exchange* (February 1949), 4, cited in Bu, "Educational Exchange and Cultural Diplomacy in the Cold War," 412.

44. Paulu, "The Smith-Mundt Act," 310.

45. Committee on the Judiciary, "The Immigration and Naturalization Systems of the United States," S. Res. 137, 80th Congress, 1st Session, as Amended, March 29, 1950, 497.

46. Benjamin Fine, "Advisory Commission Urges Open Door for Exchange Students from Communist Lands," *New York Times*, October 24, 1948.

47. Senate Report 855 (80th Cong., 2nd sess.), p. 2. The appendix is a 227-page report of the committee's observations, cited in Paulu, "The Smith-Mundt Act."

48. "To Spread Democracy," *New York Times*, January 18, 1949, 20.

49. Bu, "Educational Exchange and Cultural Diplomacy in the Cold War," 394.

50. Act of July 15, 1950, Pub. L. No. 81-744, Sec. 202, 64 Stat. 198, 198 (1950).

51. Roger Daniels, "United States Policy Towards Asian Immigrants: Contemporary Developments in Historical Perspective," *International Journal* 48, no. 2 (1993): 319.

52. Jane Hong, *Opening the Gates to Asia: A Transpacific History of How America Repealed Asian Exclusion* (University of North Carolina Press, 2019), 112.

53. Committee on the Judiciary, "The Immigration and Naturalization Systems of the United States," 510. In a "background" section on the classification of "races and peoples of the world" the authors somewhat inexplicably employ the 1775 writings of Blumenbach and his "fivefold classification of races," which they comment are "quite commonly used in studies dealing with the subject of races and peoples" (ibid., 7).

54. Marion T. Bennett, "The Immigration and Nationality (McCarran-Walter) Act of 1952, as Amended to 1965," *The Annals of the American Academy of Political and Social Science* 367 (1966): 130.

55. Bevis and Lucas, *International Students in American Colleges and Universities*, 133.

56. Immigration and Nationality Act of 1952. Pub. L. No. 82-414, 66 Stat. 163 (1952); Robert A. Divine, *American Immigration Policy, 1924–1952* (Indiana University Press, 1957), 179; Mae M. Ngai, *Impossible Subjects: Illegal Aliens and the Making of Modern America* (Princeton University Press, 2004), 342.

57. Immigration and Nationality Act § 311, 8 U.S.C. § 1422 (1952); Ngai, *Impossible Subjects*, 238.

58. Immigration and Nationality Act, Pub. L. No. 82-414, ch. 477, § 201, 66 Stat. 163, 175 (1952); Ngai, *Impossible Subjects*, 238.

59. Hong, *Opening the Gates to Asia*, 128.

60. Jodi Melamed, *Represent and Destroy: Rationalizing Violence in the New Racial Capitalism* (University of Minnesota Press, 2011), 53.

61. Harry S. Truman, "Veto of Bill to Revise the Laws Relating to Immigration, Naturalization, and Nationality," June 25, 1952, in *Public Papers of the Presidents of the United States: Harry S. Truman, 1952–53* (Government Printing Office, 1966), 441–47.

62. Siobhan Somerville, "Sexual Aliens and the Racialized State: A Queer Reading of the 1952 U.S. Immigration and Nationality Act," in *Queer Migrations: Sexuality, U.S., Border Crossings* (Minneapolis, London: University of Minnesota Press, 2005), 84.

63. Truman, "Veto of Bill to Review the Laws Relating to Immigration, Naturalization, and Nationality," 84.

64. Immigration and Nationality Act § 203(a)(1).

65. Ngai, *Impossible Subjects*, 238.

66. Ngai, *Impossible Subjects*.

67. Siobhan Somerville, "Notes Toward a Queer History of Naturalization," *American Quarterly* 57, no. 3 (2005): 661.

68. Bevis and Lucas, *International Students in American Colleges and Universities*, 134.

69. Immigration and Nationality Act § 263.

70. Immigration and Nationality Act of 1952, Pub. L. No. 82-414, § 221(i), 66 Stat. 163, 192 (1952). This aspect of the law was strengthened even further in 2004 with the addition of the following language: "There shall be no means of judicial review (including review pursuant to section 2241 of title 28 or any other habeas corpus provision [or provisions re mandamus or writs]) of a revocation under this subsection, except in the context of a removal proceeding if such revocation provides the sole ground for removal under section 1227(a)(1)(B) of this title." This reading derives from an email from Leti Volpp sent to the Sanctuary Campus Network in spring 2005 as faculty worked to make sense of and response to efforts to revoke the visas of hundreds of noncitizen students in the first weeks of Donald Trump's second administration.

71. Sidney Painter et al., "The Visa Problem," *The Scientific Monthly* 76, no. 1 (1953).

72. Painter et al., "The Visa Problem," 12.

73. Painter et al., "The Visa Problem."

74. Painter et al., "The Visa Problem," 15.

75. Edward A. Shils, "America's Paper Curtain," *Bulletin of Atomic Scientists* (1952): 213.

76. Immigration and Nationality Act § 168.

77. Painter et al., "The Visa Problem," 13.

78. Lenard H. Cooper et al., *Handbook for Foreign Student Advisers: Immigration Regulations*, 3rd rev. ed. (National Association of Foreign Student Advisers, 1962), pt. 5, sec. A., 2. NAFSA was formed in 1948 as a direct result of the Fulbright Act. For more on NAFSA's founding see Bevis and Lucas, *International Students in American Colleges and Universities*, 120–25.

79. James Meriwether, *Tears, Fire, and Blood: The United States and the Decolonization of Africa* (University of North Carolina Press, 2021), 76. Notably, after the Mau Mau uprising, one of the colonial government's first moves was to install Western-educated loyalists in positions of power from which they asserted that "black and white need each other in the task of building a prosperous and peaceful Kenya." Jim C. Harper, *Western-Educated Elites in Kenya, 1900–1963: The African American Factor* (Routledge, 2005), citing Bethwell Ogot, "The Decisive Years, 1956–63," in Bethwell Ogot and William Ochieng, eds., *Decolonization and Independence in Kenya* (Ohio University Press, 1999), 51–55.

80. "Student from Kenya Faces Ouster by US," *New York Times*, December 5, 1952, https://www.nytimes.com/1952/12/05/archives/student-from-kenya-faces-ouster-by-u-s.html.

81. Pam Oeltjen, "History Professor Caught Between Two Worlds," *State Hornet* 54, no. 54 (1996): 1.

## 7. The Lure of America: The Management of Difference and the "African Student Problem"

1. This concept theorized by David Kazanjian is discussed at more length in Chapter 1. David Kazanjian, "'To See the Issue of His Exorbitant Practices': A Response to 'the Dispossessed Eighteenth Century,'" *The Eighteenth Century* 55, no. 2/3 (2014): 277.

2. Paul Kramer, "Is the World Our Campus? International Students and US Global Power in the Long Twentieth Century," *Diplomatic History* 33, no. 5 (2009): 792.

3. Lawrence Duggan, *Institute for International Education: Twenty-Ninth Annual Report of the President* (Institute of International Education, 1948).

4. Donald J. Shank, "Windows on the World," *IIE Open Doors Report* (1948), 7.

5. Shank, "Windows on the World."

6. Shank, "Windows on the World," 14. Though she does not discuss students in particular, Linda K. Kerber, "Toward a History of Statelessness in America," *American Quarterly* 57, no. 3 (2005): 727–49.

7. Liping Bu, "Educational Exchange and Cultural Diplomacy in the Cold War," *Journal of American Studies* 33 (1999): 398.

8. Institute of International Education (IIE) news release May 4, 1948, box 10, file 9, NAFSA Records, University of Arkansas, cited in Bu 1999, 398.

9. Bu, "Educational Exchange and Cultural Diplomacy in the Cold War," 400–402.

10. Melvin Fox, "Report on Exchange of Persons Activities of the Ford Foundation," January 1953, 6. Ford Foundation Archives, Report 001567, cited in Bu, "Educational Exchange and Cultural Diplomacy in the Cold War," 414.

11. Bu, "Educational Exchange and Cultural Diplomacy in the Cold War," 414.

12. Kenneth Holland, "Open Doors Report 1963," *Institute for International Education* (1963), 2.

13. Holland, "Open Doors Report 1963."

14. Holland, "Open Doors Report 1963."

15. Committee on Educational Interchange Policy, *Chinese Students in the United States, 1948–1955: A Study in Government Policy* (Institute of International Education, 1956).

16. According to Bu, the expansion of student travel from Taiwan and Hong Kong in the 1950s can be tracked in part to a trip by Albert Sims, IIE's vice president, to Southeast Asia. According to minutes from a 1958 NAFSA-IIE Liaison Committee meeting, he descried that "Southeast Asia in general was exposed to a great abundance of scholarship offerings, mostly from Red China and the Soviet Union, where one could practically write his own ticket." As a result, "IIE set up more programs in Taiwan and Hongkong to strengthen US influence in the Far East, and American universities were called upon to play a creative role in helping the government meet the challenge." Bu, "Educational Exchange and Cultural Diplomacy in the Cold War," 407.

17. John F. Kennedy, "Remarks to President Nkrumah of Ghana at the Washington National Airport," The American Presidency Project, March 8, 1961, accessed September 5, 2025, https://www.presidency.ucsb.edu/documents/remarks-welcome-president-nkrumah-ghana-the-washington-national-airport. Notably, in this speech Kennedy invokes Thomas Jefferson's phrase that "the disease of liberty is catching," suggesting that Nkrumah's life's work is "to make sure that that disease of liberty spreads around the globe. He has fought for it in his own country. He fights for it in Africa–he fights for it in the world." "Liberty" here is defined in an American sense as individualism and market freedoms.

18. Mel Elfin and Constance Montague. "'Mo' is Sa'aid's Nickname At Cornell: 64,000 Foreign Students Ride the Diploma-Diplomacy Seesaw," *Newsweek* (1963), 60.

19. Elfin and Montague, "'Mo' is Sa'aid's Nickname At Cornell," 59.

20. Charise Burden-Stelly, *Black Scare/Red Scare: Theorizing Capitalist Racism in the United States* (University of Chicago Press, 2023); and Charise Burden-Stelly, "Constructing Deportable Subjectivity: Antiforeignness, Antiradicalism, and Antiblackness During the McCarthyist Structure of Feeling," *Souls* (2017).

21. Sylvia Jacobs, "James Emman Kwegyir Aggrey: An African Intellectual in the United States," *The Journal of Negro History* 81, no. 1/4 (1996): 49.

22. Thomas Jesse Jones, *Education in Africa: A Study of West, South, and Equatorial Africa By the African Education Commission, Under the Auspices of the*

*Phelps-Stokes Fund and Foreign Mission Societies of North America and Europe* (Phelps-Stokes Fund, 1922), xiv.

23. Founded in 1911 with funds bequeathed in the will of Caroline Phelps Stokes, the commission built on the Phelps Stokes familial involvement in the American Colonization Society. Historian Eric Yellin, for instance, cites documents from the Phelps-Stokes Fund papers that document that the "first Liberian flag had been made in the Phelps Stokes home." Olivia E. Phelps Stokes, "Biographical Sketch of Caroline Phelps Stokes from Educational Adaptations for Ten Years' Work of the Phelps-Stokes Fund, 1910–1920," Phelps-Stokes Fund Papers (SPFP), Box 1, Folder 1, Schomburg Center for Research in Black Culture, The New York Public Library, New York, 1–2; Jones, *Education in Africa*, xvi.

24. Eric S. Yellin, "The (White) Search for (Black) Order: The Phelps–Stokes Fund's First Twenty Years, 1911–1931," *The Historian* (2002): 319.

25. Jones, *Education in Africa*, xvii. Writing in 1970, historian and Africanist Kenneth J. King writes that the report also responded to concerns from colonial administrators about the potentially disruptive impact of US educations on African students, which had led the Colonial Office in Uganda to block all passports for students. The report suggested that Tuskegee should be exempt from such a ban since "Africans studying there would not be educated to agitate against colonial rule in Africa." See Kenneth J. King, "African Students in Negro American Colleges: Notes on the Good African," *Phylon* 31, no. 1 (1970): 18.

26. Samuel Armstrong, *The Journal of Christian Philosophy* (1884): 200–29, quoted in Robert Francis Engs, *Educating the Disfranchised and Disinherited: Samuel Chapman Armstrong and Hampton Institute: 1839–1893* (University of Tennessee Press, 1999); and Jones, *Education in Africa*, xxiii.

27. Jacobs, "James Emman Kwegyir Aggrey," 54.

28. Gita Steiner-Khamsi and Hubert O. Quist, "The Politics of Educational Borrowing: Reopening the Case of Achimota in British Ghana," *Comparative Education Review* 44, no. 3 (2000): 274.

29. Steiner-Khamsi and Quist, "The Politics of Educational Borrowing," 280.

30. Steiner-Khamsi and Quist, "The Politics of Educational Borrowing," 289.

31. Nnamdi Azikiwe, *My Odyssey: An Autobiography of Nnamdi Azikiwe* (C. Hurst & Company, 1970), 34. As Charisse Burden-Stelly discusses, from as early as 1918, US officials figured Garvey as an "undesirable alien," whose writings, organizing, and mere presence in the United States could "galvanize the Black masses with foreign ideas" and was thus "a key threat to US Capitalist Racist Society." Burden-Stelly, *Black Scare / Red Scare*, 63.

32. Azikiwe, *My Odyssey*, 38.

33. Azikiwe, *My Odyssey*, 40.

34. Azikiwe, *My Odyssey*, 44.

35. Jason C. Parker, "'Made-In-America?' The 'Black University' and the American Role in the Decolonization of the Black Atlantic," *The Journal of American History* 96, no. 3 (2009): 732.

36. Azikiwe, *My Odyssey*, 88.

37. Azikiwe, *My Odyssey*, 146.

38. Azikiwe, *My Odyssey*, 130, 118–19. In his speech marking his ascension to governor general of the new Republic of Nigeria Azikiwe included a tribute to Hansberry. Olanipekun Oladotun Laosebikan, "In Pursuit of the 'Golden Fleece': African Students and Higher Education in the United States, 1925–1959," *West Africa Review* 17 (2010): 32.

39. Azikiwe, *My Odyssey*, 132.

40. Azikiwe, *My Odyssey*, 142.

41. Azikiwe, *My Odyssey*, 157.

42. Horace Mann Bond, *Education for Freedom: A History of Lincoln University* (Lincoln University Press, 1976), 502.

43. Laosebikan, "In Pursuit of the 'Golden Fleece,'" 30.

44. Kwame Nkrumah, *Ghana: Autobiography of Kwame Nkrumah* (Echo Point Books & Media, 2023), 17.

45. Nkrumah, *Ghana*, 16.

46. Hollis R. Lynch, "K. O. Mbadiwe, 1939–1947: The American Years of a Nigerian Political Leader," *Journal of African Studies* 7, no. 4 (1980): 185.

47. Nkrumah, *Ghana*, 24.

48. Nkrumah, *Ghana*, 28.

49. Nkrumah, *Ghana*, 31.

50. Nkrumah, *Ghana*, 32.

51. John Henrick Clarke, "Kwame Nkrumah: His Years in America," *The Black Scholar* 6, no. 2 (1974): 11.

52. Burden-Stelly, *Black Scare/Red Scare*, 176, 110. Since his move from Jamaica to New York in 1916, Garvey, as Burden-Stelly explains, epitomized a figure most feared by the US government, a kind of West Indian Blackness transported to America as a source of alien subversion that combined race and class critiques with a push for the eradication of colonialism. Despite his eventual rightward shift, which included a "vehement anti-communist position," Garvey was deported in 1927 based on a series of charges of both subversion and fraud.

53. Nkrumah, *Ghana*, 33. Narratives of African students in the United States during this period illustrate how fear of encounter with immigration services structured their life decisions. As Laosebikan contends, "Faced with the prospect of deportation or worse, arrest if they delayed their stay beyond the completion of their studies, most African students during this period either left the United States for another foreign country or returned back to Africa." Olanipekun Laosebikan, "From Student to Immigrant: The Diasporation of the African Student in the United States" (PhD diss., University of Illinois at Urbana Champaign, 2012), 80.

54. Lynch, "K. O. Mbadiwe, 1939–1947," 185.

55. Laosebikan, "In Pursuit of the 'Golden Fleece,'" 27.

56. Laosebikan, "In Pursuit of the 'Golden Fleece,'" 34. Laosebikan discusses this organization as African Students Association (ASA), Nkrumah as the African

Students' Association of American and Canada, and Ama Biney as the Association of African students in the United States and Canada (AAS).

57. African Students Association, "Charter of Principles adopted at the Second Annual Conference-September 1942," *African Interpreter* 1, no. 2 (March 1943): 4, cited in Laosebikan, "In Pursuit of the 'Golden Fleece,'" 34.

58. Lynch, "K. O. Mbadiwe, 1939–1947," 190. In her extensive review of the scholarship on Nkrumah's life, Ama Biney argues that the rift was over whether or not to include African seamen in the association based on Nkrumah's contention that most of them traveled to the United States as students and were working to raise funds in order to return to school.

59. Lynch, "K. O. Mbadiwe, 1939–1947," 190.

60. Nkrumah, *Ghana*, 44.

61. Kwame Nkrumah, *Toward Colonial Freedom: Africa in the Struggle Against World Imperialism* (Heinemann, 1962) reprinted as Kwame Nkrumah, *Revolutionary Path* (Panaf Books, 1973), 13.

62. Nkrumah, *Revolutionary Path*, 15, 24, 41. In a 2016 article, Atta Britwum, a professor of French at the University of Cape Coast, Ghana, argues that despite his invocation of Marxian langue and texts, Nkrumah's theorization and political practice is fundamentally nationalist and privileges superstructural concerns, thus neglecting the economic base. Atta Britwum, "The Lure of the Image in the Mirror: A Reading of Kwame Nkrumah's *Toward Colonial Freedom*," *Legon Journal of the Humanities* 28, no. 1 (2017).

63. Nkrumah, *Ghana*, 50.

64. Nkrumah, *Ghana*, 53.

65. Lynch, "K. O. Mbadiwe, 1939–1947," 196.

66. Lynch, "K. O. Mbadiwe, 1939–1947."

67. Laosebikan, "In Pursuit of the 'Golden Fleece,'" 35. Roosevelt granted Mbadiwe a meeting in May of 1943 and then became a patron. Lynch, "K. O. Mbadiwe, 1939–1947," 191.

68. Laosebikan, "In Pursuit of the 'Golden Fleece,'" 35.

69. "Circular Letter from American Council on African Education, June 5, 1945," https://credo.library.umass.edu/view/full/mums312-b105-i039. ACAE was formally incorporated under New York State laws on April 12, 1944.

70. "American Council on African Education Pamphlet, 1945." *W. E. B. Du Bois Papers (MS312) Special Collections and Archives* (1945): https://credo.library.umass.edu/view/full/mums312-b105-i041.

71. "Education: Prince with a Purpose," *TIME* (1945).

72. "Mr. N. Orizu Says He Comes for African Education and Propagation of 'Zikism,'" *West African Pilot* (1945).

73. Michael M. Ogbeidi, "Non-Governmental Organisation and the Promotion of American Education in Nigeria, 1941–1954," *Nebula* 6, no. 4 (2009): 12.

74. Phelps-Stokes Fund, *A Survey of African Students Studying in the United States* (Phelps-Stokes Fund, 1949), 23.

75. Phelps-Stokes Fund, *A Survey of African Students Studying in the United States*, 23. The report also briefly discusses the Ebun Illuwa Foundation, which was only announced in March of 1949 and was intended to facilitate the travel of students to "receive vocational and industrial education."

76. Parker, "Made-In-America?," 738.

77. Cited in Parker, "Made-In-America?," 738.

78. Parker, "Made-In-America?," 730.

79. "African Students Seeking Help Here: British," *New York Times*, October 18, 1947.

80. Ogbeidi, "Non-Governmental Organisation and the Promotion of American Education in Nigeria," 17.

81. Ogbeidi, "Non-Governmental Organisation and the Promotion of American Education in Nigeria," 12.

82. Burden-Stelly, *Black Scare / Red Scare*.

83. Public Law 439, 76th Cong. 3d sess. (June 28, 1940).

84. Robert Bruce Slater, "The Black Who First Entered the World of White Higher Education," *The Journal of Blacks in Higher Education* 4 (1994): 47–56.

85. The Brown decision itself relied on social scientific research. See for instance Kenneth K. Wong and Anna C. Nicotera, "*Brown v. Board of Education* and the Coleman Report: Social Science Research and the Debate on Educational Equality," *Peabody Journal of Education* 79, no. 2 (2004).

86. Azza Salama Layton, "International Pressure and the US Government's Response to Little Rock," *The Arkansas Historical Quarterly* 56, no. 3 (1997): 260.

87. "Opinion About US Treatment of Negroes," report 38, July 24, 1956, Office of Research, Public Opinion Barometer Reports, 1955–1956, Records of the United States Information Agency, RG 30, cited in Layton, "International Pressure," 261.

88. Mary Dudziak, *Cold War Civil Rights: Race and the Image of American Democracy* (Princeton University Press, 2011), 12.

89. Dudziak, *Cold War Civil Rights*.

90. Benjamin Fine, "Global Campus," *New York Times*, October 5, 1947.

91. Fine, "Global Campus."

92. Warren Weaver Jr., "Theater Integration is Gained but Students Face Prosecution," *New York Times*, February 23, 1963.

93. This reference to Harvard is in regard to the university's practice in the 1940s of sending letters to would-be roommates to ask if they would be comfortable with a "dark-skinned" roommate. Ted Gup, "Life Lessons in Diversity," *The Chronicle of Higher Education* (October 2012).

94. George Lipsitz, "The Possessive Investment in Whiteness: Racialized Social Democracy and the 'White' Problem in American Studies," *American Quarterly* 47, no. 3 (1995).

95. For early work on the "brain drain" see Walter Adams, ed., *The Brain Drain* (The Macmillan Company, 1968); Carole Boyce Davies, "Deportable Subjects: US

Immigration Laws and the Criminalizing of Communism," *The South Atlantic Quarterly* (2001).

96. For an extended discussion of the McCarran–Walter Act's terms and impact on noncitizen students see Chapter 6.

97. Mary Dudziak, *Cold War Civil Rights: Race and the Image of American Democracy* (Princeton University Press, 2004), 34.

98. James Meriwether, *Tears, Fire, and Blood: The United States and the Decolonization of Africa* (University of North Carolina Press, 2021), 78.

99. Meriwether, *Tears, Fire, and Blood*, 78.

100. Meriwether, *Tears, Fire, and Blood*, 78.

101. AAIR, AAI 81202731, AAI, "The Metamorphosis of the African-American Institute Between 1953 and 1958," 1, cited in Anton Tarradellas, "Pan-African Networks, Cold War Politics, and Postcolonial Opportunities: The African Scholarship Program of American Universities, 1961–1975," *The Journal of African History* 63, no. 1 (2022): 79.

102. Tarradellas, "Pan-African Networks," 80

103. HMBP, Africa-America Institute, December 5, 1962, AAI, "Record of Staff Conference, Eagle Nest, November 9–12, 1962," 33, citation from Tarradellas, "Pan-African Networks," 80.

104. Ethan Vesely-Flad, "Today is George Houser's 99th Birthday!" *Fellowship of Reconciliation* (blog), June 2, 2015, https://web.archive.org/web/20150615044911/http://forusa.org/blogs/ethan-vesely-flad/today-george-housers-99th-birthday/13199.

105. Jim C. Harper, "Tom Mboya and the African Student Airlifts: Inclusion, Equity and Higher Education Among Kenyan Women and Men," *Africology: The Journal of Pan African Studies* 10, no. 9 (2017): 74.

106. Harper, "Tom Mboya and the African Student Airlifts," 74.

107. Meriwether, *Tears, Fire, and Blood*, 745.

108. Lester Granger, "Welcoming Remarks" (speech, July 29, 1958), box 39, series 1, part I, Records of the National Urban League, Manuscript Division, Library of Congress, Washington, DC, cited in Meriwether, *Tears, Fire, and Blood*, 745.

109. HMBP, Africa-America Institute, April 19, 1957–June 26, 1957, Kwame Nkrumah to Dr. Ross, May 28, 1957. See also Public Records and Archives Administration Department, Accra, Ghana (PRAAD), RG 3/5/1913, Secretary to the Prime Minister to Permanent Secretary, Ministry of Education, Ghana, 'Institute of African-American Relations,' March 11, 1957, cited in Tarradellas, "Pan-African Networks," 80.

110. See this decree of March 24, 1958 in Apollon Davidson and Sergej Mazov, eds., Rossija i Afrika. Dokumenty i materialy XVIII v.—1960g [Russia and Africa. Archival Documents and Material 18th century—1960s], v. 2 (IVI RAN, 1999), 158–59, cited in C. Katsakioris "Nkrumah's Elite: Ghanaian Students in the Soviet Union in the Cold War," *Paedagogica Historica* 57, no. 3 (2021): 2–3.

111. Meriwether, *Tears, Fire, and Blood*, 81.

112. Harper, "Tom Mboya and the African Student Airlifts."

113. Harper, "Tom Mboya and the African Student Airlifts," citing Airlift to America—the source is in the Airlift archives at, http://www.airlifttoamerica.org/pdfs/Statement%20on%20Program%20and%20Plans%20of%20AASF%20Jan%2014%201960.pdf.

114. Josh Gerstein, "Obama's Father Forced Out at Harvard," *Politico*, April 29, 2011, accessed September 4, 2025, https://www.politico.com/story/2011/04/obamas-father-forced-out-at-harvard-053968.

115. Meriwether, *Tears, Fire, and Blood*, 737.

116. Meriwether, *Tears, Fire, and Blood*, 737, 742.

117. Meriwether, *Tears, Fire, and Blood*, 80.

118. Meriwether documents Jackie Robinson's fascinating role as an interlocutor in this process.

119. Meriwether, *Tears, Fire, and Blood*, 743.

120. Robinson to Nixon, July 11, 1960, emphasis added, cited in Meriwether, *Tears, Fire, and Blood*, 752, italics in original.

121. John F. Kennedy, "The Challenge of Imperialism: Algeria," July 2, 1957, in *"Let the Word Go Forth": The Speeches, Statements, and Writings of John F. Kennedy*, ed. Theodore Sorensen (Delacorte Press, 1988), 331, 337, cited in Meriwether, *Tears, Fire, and Blood*, 744.

122. Meriwether, *Tears, Fire, and Blood*, 753.

123. Meriwether, *Tears, Fire, and Blood*, 755.

124. Meriwether, *Tears, Fire, and Blood*, 95.

125. Meriwether, *Tears, Fire, and Blood*, 16

126. Meriwether, *Tears, Fire, and Blood*, 15.

127. Ama Biney, *The Political and Social Thought of Kwame Nkrumah* (Palgrave Macmillan, 2011), 140.

128. According to Biney's note, "Nkrumah used these words in his letter to the UN secretary-general, Hammarskjold, on December 16, 1963"; see Kwame Nkrumah, *Challenge of the Congo* (International Publishers, 1967), 238.

129. Emmanuel Gerard and Bruce Kuklick, *Death in the Congo: Murdering Patrice Lumumba* (Harvard University Press, 2015).

130. Gerard and Kuklick, *Death in the Congo*.

131. Tarradellas, "Pan-African Networks," 79.

132. Tarradellas, "Pan-African Networks," 82.

133. Tarradellas, "Pan-African Networks," 86.

134. Tarradellas, "Pan-African Networks," 86.

135. Dudziak, *Cold War Civil Rights*, 179.

136. Dudziak, *Cold War Civil Rights*, 182.

137. Tarradellas, "Pan-African Networks," 88; and Margaret O'Mara, "The Uses of the Foreign Student," *Social Science History* 36, no. 4 (2012): 597.

138. Tarradellas, "Pan-African Networks," 60.

139. Elfin and Montague, "'Mo' is Sa'aid's Nickname At Cornell," 66.

## Conclusion. The University Double Bind: The Imperial Model Minority and the Records We Keep

1. Mel Elfin and Constance Montague, "'Mo' is Sa'aid's Nickname At Cornell: 64,000 Foreign Students Ride the Diploma-Diplomacy Seesaw," *Newsweek* (1963).

2. Gayatri Chakravorty Spivak, "Explanation and Culture: Marginalia," in *The Spivak Reader: Selected Works of Gayatri Chakravorty Spivak*, ed. Donna Landry and Gerald MacLean (Routledge, 1996), 107, 35.

3. In invoking the language of the double bind I'm thinking with Spivak, as is elaborated in this conclusion, but also with Karl Marx, Saidiya Hartman, and Michel Foucault. In Marxian thought, the double bind is often traced to "On the Jewish Question," where he writes, "The limits of political emancipation are evident at once from the fact that the state can free itself from a restriction without man being really free from this restriction, that the state can be a *free state* without man being a *free man*." The limit on this form of freedom is, as Marx goes on to explain, that in seeking freedom through the state, the political actor relies on the state as an intermediary between "man and man's freedom." Through reference to Marx, Hartman describes this as the condition of "being free to exchange one's labor and free of material resources." Running this fundamental Marxian conceit through Micheal Foucault's theories of power, she asks her reader to consider "the subjugation that rights instigate and the domination they efface." Karl Marx, "On the Jewish Question," in *The Marx-Engels Reader*, ed. Robert C. Tucker (W. W. Norton, 1978); Saidiya V. Hartman, *Scenes of Subjection: Terror, Slavery, and Self-Making in Nineteenth-Century America* (Oxford University Press, 1997), 115, 116.

4. Jodi Melamed, "Racial Capitalism," *Critical Ethnic Studies* 1, no. 1 (2015): 79.

5. Melamed, "Racial Capitalism," 79.

6. Melamed, "Racial Capitalism," 79. During his time at both the University of California, Berkeley as an undergraduate and Stanford as a doctoral student, Robinson was deeply immersed in a world of Black politics inhabited by noncitizen students from around the world, including Shymala Gopalan from India and Donald Harris from Jamaica, who would go on to be the parents of Kamala Harris.

7. On the individualizing impulses and effects of education and educational institutions see Eli Meyerhoff, *Beyond Education: Radical Studying for Another World* (University of Minnesota Press, 2019).

8. Madeline Y. Hsu, *The Good Immigrants: How the Yellow Peril Became the Model Minority* (Princeton University Press, 2015), 25.

9. Victor Bascara, *Model-Minority Imperialism* (University of Minnesota Press, 2006), 1.

10. Lisa Lowe, *Immigrant Acts: On Asian American Cultural Politics* (Duke University Press, 1996), 6.

11. Lauren Berlant, *The Queen of American Goes to Washington City: Essays on Sex and Citizenship* (Duke University Press, 1997), 199.

12. Bascara, *Model-Minority Imperialism*, xviii.

13. Gayatri Chakravorty Spivak, *Outside in the Teaching Machine* (Routledge, 1993), 45; and Gayatri Chakravorty Spivak, "'Bonding in Difference': Interview with Alfred Arteaga," in Landry and Maclean, eds., *The Spivak Reader: Selected Works of Gayatri Chakravorty Spivak*, 15–16.

14. Gayatri Chakravorty Spivak, *An Aesthetic Education in the Era of Globalization* (Harvard University Press, 2012), 4.

15. Spivak, *An Aesthetic Education*, x.

16. Spivak, *An Aesthetic Education*, xiv

17. Spivak, *An Aesthetic Education*, 1.

18. Spivak, *An Aesthetic Education*, 1.

19. Gayatri Chakravorty Spivak, *In Other Worlds: Essays in Cultural Politics* (Routledge, 1988), 105, 107.

20. Sangeeta Ray, *Gayatri Chakravorty Spivak: In Other Words* (Wiley-Blackwell, 2009), 4; and Mridula Nath Chakraborty, "Everybody's Afraid of Gayatri Chakraborty Spivak: Reading Interviews With the Public Intellectual and Postcolonial Critic," *Signs* 35, no. 3 (2010): 633.

21. Colin MacCabe, "Foreword," in *In Other Worlds: Essays in Cultural Politics* (Routledge, 1988), ix. In the next breath, he discusses the purported, or perhaps more accurately in his language "rumored," difficulty of Spivak's work and Spivak herself as "a difficult woman," a "difficult native."

22. Elfin and Montague, "'Mo' is Sa'aid's Nickname At Cornell," 61.

23. Angela Ingram, "Postmarked Calcutta, India," in *The Post-Colonial Critic: Interviews, Strategies, Dialogues* (Routledge, 1990), 85.

24. Ray, *Gayatri Chakravorty Spivak*, 4–5.

25. Chakraborty, "Everybody's Afraid of Gayatri Chakraborty Spivak," 634; Elfin and Montague, "'Mo' is Sa'aid's Nickname At Cornell," 59.

26. Chakraborty, "Everybody's Afraid of Gayatri Chakraborty Spivak," 635.

27. Jenny Sharpe, "What Use is the Imagination," *PMLA* 129, no. 3 (2014): 512–17.

28. Sharpe, "What Use is the Imagination," 513.

29. Roderick A. Ferguson, *The Reorder of Things: The University and Its Pedagogies of Minority Difference* (University of Minnesota Press, 2012), 174.

30. Ferguson, *The Reorder of Things*.

31. Spivak, *An Aesthetic Education*, 10.

32. Spivak, *An Aesthetic Education*, 146.

33. Spivak, *An Aesthetic Education*, 141.

34. Spivak, *An Aesthetic Education*, 141.

35. Lisa Lowe, *The Intimacies of Four Continents* (Duke University Press, 2015), 1.

36. Bulan Lahiri, "In Conversation: Speaking to Spivak," *The Hindu*, December 4, 2011, accessed September 4, 2025, https://www.thehindu.com/books/In-Conversation-Speaking-to-Spivak/article15130635.ece.

37. Spivak, *An Aesthetic Education*, 302.

38. Spivak, *An Aesthetic Education*, 154. This is not to suggest that such a diminishment of nationalist feelings happens for all or most students. Instead, as in

the case of Chinese students discussed in Chapter 3, the experience of studying in the United States has often had just the opposite effect. This has been observed more recently by Yige Dong in her 2017 article "How Chinese Students Become Nationalist: Their American Experience and Transpacific Futures," *American Quarterly* 69, no. 3 (2017).

39. Lisa Duggan and José Esteban Muñoz, "Hope and Hopelessness: A Dialogue," *Women and Performance: A Journal of Feminist Theory* 19, no. 2 (2009).

40. Walter Benjamin, "Theses on the Philosophy of History," in *Illuminations*, ed. Hannah Arendt (Schocken Books, 1985), 256.

41. I thank Zach Schwartz-Weinstein for this point on endowments.

42. Robin D. G. Kelley, "The Responsibility of Intellectuals in the Age of Fascism and Genocide," *The Boston Review* (Summer 2025), https://www.bostonreview.net/forum/the-responsibility-of-intellectuals-in-the-age-of-fascism-and-genocide/.

# Bibliography

Abrams, Kerry. "Polygamy, Prostitution, and the Federalization of Immigration Law." *Columbia Law Review* 105 (2005): 641–716. https://scholarship.law.duke.edu/faculty_scholarship/3826.

"Acknowledgement of Indigenous Peoples as the Historical Custodians of the Lands and Waterways of the Williamsburg Area," American Indian Resource Center, William & Mary, accessed July 23, 2026, https://www.wm.edu/as/anthropology/research/centers/airc/land-acknowledgement/.

Adams, Walter, ed. *The Brain Drain*. Macmillan, 1968.

African-American Institute. "The Metamorphosis of the African-American Institute Between 1953 and 1958." Unpublished report/Internal document.

African-American Institute, "Record of Staff Conference, Eagle Nest, November 9–12, 1962," December 5, 1962. Horace Mann Bond Papers. Special Collections and University Archives, University of Massachusetts Amherst Libraries.

"African School." *African Repository and Colonial Journal* 1, no. 9 (November 1825): 284–85.

"African Students Seeking Help Here: British." *New York Times*, October 18, 1947.

Ahtone, Tristan, and Robert Lee. "Land-Grab Universities." *High Country News*, March 30, 2020. http://www.hcn.org/issues/52-4/indigenous-affairs-education-land-grab-universities/.

Al Jazeera Staff. "UK Revokes Visa of Law Student Who Addressed Pro-Palestine Protest." *Al Jazeera*, May 10, 2024.

Alien Registration Act of 1940. Public Law 76-670. 54 Stat. 670 (1940).

Allerfeldt, Kristofer. "'And We Got Here First': Albert Johnson, National Origins and Self-Interest in the Immigration Debate of the 1920s." *Journal of Contemporary History* 45, no. 1 (2010): 7–26.

Alsous, Zaina. "A Detrimental Education." *The New Inquiry*, April 16, 2020. https://thenewinquiry.com/a-detrimental-education/.

Altbach, Philip G., and Hans de Wit. "The Challenge to Higher Education Internationalisation." *University World News*, February 23, 2018. universityworldnews.com.

Ambrose, Stephen E. *Duty, Honor, Country: A History of West Point*. Johns Hopkins University Press, 1966.

American Board of Commissioners for Foreign Missions. *A Narrative of Five Youth from the Sandwich Islands, Now Receiving an Education in This Country*. J. Seymour, 1816.

American Board of Commissioners for Foreign Missions. "Minutes of the Seventh Annual Meeting." *The Panoplist, and Missionary Magazine* 13 (January 1817): 80–92.

American Board of Commissioners for Foreign Missions. *Seventeenth Annual Report of the American Board of Commissioners for Foreign Missions*. Crocker and Brewster, 1826.

American Council on African Education, "Circular Letter, June 5, 1945," W. E. B. Du Bois Papers. Special Collections and University Archives, University of Massachusetts Amherst Libraries.

The Amistad Committee, Inc. "About the Yale, Slavery and Abolition Project." Accessed May 11, 2026. http://www.yaleslavery.org/Resources/about.html.

Andrew, John A. "Educating the Heathen: The Foreign Mission School Controversy and American Ideals." *Journal of American Studies* 12, no. 3 (1978): 331–42.

Angell Treaty (Burlingame Treaty). July 28, 1868. 16 Stat. 739.

Arkush, R. David, and Leo Outfan Lee. *Land Without Ghosts: Chinese Impressions of America from the Mid-Nineteenth Century to the Present*. University of California Press, 1993.

Armstrong, Samuel C. "Lessons from the Hawaiian Islands." *The Journal of Christian Philosophy* 3 (January 1884): 200–229.

Axtell, James. *The European and the Indian: Essays in the Ethnohistory of Colonial North America*. Oxford University Press, 1982.

Axtell, James. "Mr. Wheelock's Little Red School." In *The European and the Indian: Essays in the Ethnohistory of Colonial North America*. Oxford University Press, 1981.

Axtell, James. *The School Upon a Hill: Education and Society in Colonial New England*. Yale University Press, 1974.

Azikiwe, Nnamdi. *My Odyssey: An Autobiography of Nnamdi Azikiwe*. C. Hurst & Company, 1970.

Bailyn, Bernard. *Education in the Forming of American Society: Needs and Opportunities for Study*. University of North Carolina Press, 1970.

Baldwin, Davarian. "The Reparations Movement in Higher Education." *The Thinking Republic* (2021). https://www.thethinkingrepublic.com/being-counted/the-reparations-movement-in-higher-education.

Barker, Joanne. *Native Acts: Law, Recognition, and Cultural Authenticity.* Duke University Press, 2011.

Barrow, Clyde W. "God, Capitalism, and the State: The Cultural Counterrevolution in U.S. Universities, 1890–1990." *New Political Science* 47, no. 1 (2025): 60–78.

Barrow, Clyde W. "The Theory of Capitalist Regulation and the Development of American Higher Education." Paper presented at the Annual Meeting of the American Educational Research Association, 1991.

Bascara, Victor V. "New Empire, Same Old University? Education in the American Tropics After 1898." In *The Imperial University,* edited by Sunaina Maira and Piya Chatterjee, 53–77. University of Minnesota Press, 2014.

Bascara, Victor. *Model-Minority Imperialism.* University of Minnesota Press, 2006.

Baynton, Douglas C. "Disability and the Justification of Inequality in American History." In *The New Disability History: American Perspectives,* edited by Paul K. Longmore and Lauri Umansky, 33–57. New York University Press, 2001.

Bedi, Neil, Bora Erden, Marco Hernandez et al. "How Counterprotesters at U.C.L.A. Provoked Violence, Unchecked for Hours." *New York Times,* May 3, 2024.

Benjamin, Walter. "Theses on the Philosophy of History." In *Illuminations,* edited by Hannah Arendt, 256. Schocken Books, 1985.

Berg, A. Scott. *Wilson.* G. P. Putnam's Sons, 2013.

Berlant, Lauren. *The Queen of America Goes to Washington City: Essays on Sex and Citizenship.* Duke University Press, 1997.

Beverley, Robert, Jr. *The History and Present State of Virginia.* Richmond, 1855.

Bevis, Teresa B., and Christopher J. Lucas. *International Students in American Colleges and Universities.* Palgrave Macmillan, 2007.

Bhabha, Homi K. "Of Mimicry and Man: The Ambivalence of Colonial Discourse." *October* 28 (Spring 1984), 125–33.

Bieler, Stacey. *Patriots or Traitors: A History of American-Educated Chinese Students.* Routledge, 2004.

Biney, Ama. *The Political and Social Thought of Kwame Nkrumah.* Palgrave Macmillan, 2011.

Blackhawk, Maggie. "The Constitution of American Colonialism." *Harvard Law Review* 137, no. 1 (2023): 1–152.

Blaney, David L. *Political Economy as Theodicy: Progress, Suffering, and Denial.* Routledge, 2024.

Blatt, Jessica. "'To Bring Out the Best That is in Their Blood': Race, Reform, and Civilization in the *Journal of Race Development* (1910–1919)." *Ethnic and Racial Studies* 27, no. 5 (2004): 691–709.

Boegle, Jimmy. "A Fascinating Coincident Involving an Executive Order Number." *Coachella Valley Independent,* March 24, 2025.

Boggs, Abigail. "Educational Pasts, Enduring Colonial Presents: Indigenous Student Conscripts and the Foundation of the US University." *History of the Present* 13 no. 2 (2023) 141–65.

Boggs, Abigail, and Nick Mitchell. "Critical University Studies and the Crisis Consensus." *Feminist Studies* 44, no. 2 (2018): 455–73.

Boggs, Abigail, Eli Meyerhoff, Zach Schwartz-Weinstein, and Nick Mitchell. "Abolitionist University Studies: An Invitation." *Abolition Journal* (2019).

Bond, Horace Mann. *Education for Freedom: A History of Lincoln University.* Lincoln University Press, 1976.

Borgwardt, Elizabeth. *A New Deal for the World: America's Vision for Human Rights.* Belknap Press of Harvard University Press, 2005.

Boudinot, Elias. *An Address to the Whites: Delivered in the First Presbyterian Church, on the 26th May, 1826.* Philadelphia: William F. Geddes, 1826

Bouquet, Henry. *The Papers of Col. Henry Bouquet*, edited by Sylvester K. Stevens and Donald H. Kent. Pennsylvania Historical Commission, 1940–1943.

Boyce Davies, Carole. "Deportable Subjects: U.S. Immigration Laws and the Criminalizing of Communism." *South Atlantic Quarterly* 100, no. 4 (2001): 949–66.

"Brafferton House." *Williamsburg Ghost Tour.* Accessed July 23, 2026. https://williamsburgghosttour.com/brafferton-house/.

Breen, Jenny S. "Labor, Law Enforcement, and 'Normal Times': The Origins of Immigration's Home Within the Department of Justice and the Evolution of Attorney General Control Over Immigration Adjudications." *University of Hawai'i Law Review* 42, no. 1 (2019): 1–55.

Britwum, Atta. "The Lure of the Image in the Mirror: A Reading of Kwame Nkrumah's *Toward Colonial Freedom*." *Legon Journal of the Humanities* 28, no. 1 (2017): 1–17.

Brock, R. A., ed. *The Official Letters of Alexander Spotswood, Lieutenant Governor of the Colony of Virginia, 1710–1722.* 2 vols. Collections of the Virginia Historical Society, New Series, vols. 1–2. Virginia Historical Society, 1882–1885.

Brooks, Lisa. "On the Recovery of Native Space in the Northeast." In *Critical Indigenous Studies*, edited by J. Kēhaulani Kauanui, 21–34. University of Minnesota Press, 2018.

Brooks, Lisa. *Our Beloved Kin: A New History of King Philip's War.* Yale University Press, 2018.

Brotherhood of Locomotive Firemen (Terre Haute, IN). *Souvenir of the 14th Annual Convention of the Brotherhood of Locomotive Firemen.* Brotherhood of Locomotive Firemen, 1888.

Brown, Wendy. *Undoing the Demos: Neoliberalism's Stealth Revolution.* Zone Books, 2015.

Bruyneel, Kevin. "The American Liberal Tradition." *Settler Colonial Studies* 3, no. 3–4 (2013): 311–30.

Bruyneel, Kevin. *Settler Memory: The Disavowal of Indigeneity and the Politics of Race in the United States.* University of North Carolina Press, 2021.

Bruyneel, Kevin. *The Third Space of Sovereignty: The Postcolonial Politics of U.S.-Indigenous Relations*. University of Minnesota Press, 2007.
Bu, Liping. "The Challenge of Race Relations: American Ecumenism and Foreign Student Nationalism, 1990–1940." *Journal of American Studies* 35, no. 2 (2001): 217–38.
Bu, Liping. "Educational Exchange and Cultural Diplomacy in the Cold War." *Journal of American Studies* 33 (1999) 393–415.
Buff, Rachel Ida. *Against the Deportation Terror: Organizing for Immigrant Rights in the Twentieth Century*. Temple University Press, 2018.
Buff, Rachel Ida. "The Undergraduate Railroad." In *Immigrant Rights in the Shadows of Citizenship*, edited by Rachel Ida Buff, 301–14. New York University Press, 2008.
Buff, Rachel Ida, ed. *Immigrant Rights: In the Shadows of Citizenship*. New York University Press, 2008.
Burden-Stelly, Charise. *Black Scare/Red Scare: Theorizing Capitalist Racism in the United States*. University of Chicago Press, 2023.
Burden-Stelly, Charisse. "Constructing Deportable Subjectivity: Antiforeignness, Antiradicalism, and Antiblackness during the McCarthyist Structure of Feeling." *Souls* 19, no. 3 (2017): 342–58.
Burton, John D. "Crimson Missionaries: The Robert Boyle Legacy and Harvard College." *The New England Quarterly* 67, no. 1 (1994): 132–40.
Buttre, John Chester. *Rev. Francis Burns, Missionary Bishop of the M.E. Church in Western Africa [graphic]*. Engraving after a photograph by Mathew B. Brady, ca. 1858–1863. Library Company of Philadelphia. Accessed September 3, 2025. librarycompany.org.
Byrd, Jodi A. *The Transit of Empire: Indigenous Critiques of Colonialism*. University of Minnesota Press, 2011.
Cabell, James Lawrence. *The Testimony of Modern Science to the Unity of Mankind*. Robert Carter and Brothers, 1858.
Calata, Alexander A. "The Role of Education in Americanizing Filipinos." In *Mixed Blessings: The Impact of the American Colonial Experience on Politics and Society in the Philippines*, edited by Hazel M. McFerson, 89–98. Greenwood Press, 2002.
Calavita, Kitty. "Chinese Exclusion and the Open Door with China: Structural Contradictions and the 'Chaos' of Law, 1882–1910." *Social & Legal Studies* 10, no. 2 (2001): 203–26.
Calavita, Kitty. "The Paradoxes of Race, Class, Identity, and 'Passing': Enforcing the Chinese Exclusion Acts, 1882–1910." *Law & Social Inquiry* 25, no. 1 (2000): 1–40.
Calloway, Colin G. *The Indian History of an American Institution: Native Americans and Dartmouth*. Dartmouth College Press, 2010.
Cameron, Chris. "Trump Says He Would Give Green Cards to All Foreign College Students at Graduation." *New York Times*, June 20, 2024.
Cantu, Maria P. "Three Effective Strategies of Internationalization in American Universities." *Journal of International Education Leadership* 3, no. 3 (2013).

*Chae Chan Ping v. United States*. 130 US 581 (1889).

Chakraborty, Mridula Nath. "Everybody's Afraid of Gayatri Chakraborty Spivak: Reading Interviews with the Public Intellectual and Postcolonial Critic." *Signs* 35, no. 3 (2010): 633–35.

Chan, Sucheng, ed. *Entry Denied: Exclusion and the Chinese Community in America, 1882–1943*. Temple University Press, 1991.

Chang, Adam. "Reappraising Zhang Zhidong: Forgotten Continuities During China's Self-Strengthening, 1884–1901." *Journal of Chinese Military History* 6, no. 2 (2017): 157–92.

Chang, David A. *The World and All the Things Upon It: Native Hawaiian Geographies of Exploration*. University of Minnesota Press, 2016.

"The Charter of Dartmouth College." December 13, 1769. Dartmouth Libraries Digital Collections. Dartmouth College, Hanover, NH. Accessed September 3, 2025.

Chase, Frederick. *A History of Dartmouth College and the Town of Hanover, New Hampshire*. Vol. 1, edited by John King Lord. John Wilson and Son, 1891.

Chiles, Katy L. "Becoming Colored in Occom and Wheatley's Early America." *PMLA* 123, no. 5 (October 2008): 1398–1417.

Chinese Exclusion Act [An Act to Execute Certain Treaty Stipulations Relating to Chinese], ch. 126, 22 Stat. 58 (1882) (repealed 1943).

"Chinese Law Revised: Committee Submits Report on Exclusion Rules," *Washington Post*, February 6, 1906.

"Chinese Students Admitted." *Washington Post*, January 13, 1903.

Chung, Sue Fawn. "Chinese Exclusion, the First Bureau of Immigration, and the 1905 Special Chinese Census: Registered, Counted, Arrested, Deported—1892–1906." *Chinese America: History and Perspectives* (2018): 1–13.

Churchill, Ward. *Kill the Indian, Save the Man: The Genocidal Impact of American Indian Residential Schools*. City Lights, 2004.

Clarke, John Henrik. "Kwame Nkrumah: His Years in America." *The Black Scholar* 6, no. 2 (1974): 9–16.

Clark, Michael P., ed. *The Eliot Tracts: With Letters from John Eliot to Thomas Thorowgood and Richard Baxter*. Contributions in American History 199. Praeger, 2003.

Cole, David. "Are Foreign Nationals Entitled to the Same Constitutional Rights As Citizens?" *Jefferson Law Review* (2003): 367–88.

Cole, David. "Their Liberties, Our Security: Democracy and Double Standards." In *Immigrant Rights: In the Shadows of Citizenship*, edited by Rachel Ida Buff. New York University Press, 2008.

Coloma, Roland Sintos. "'Destiny Has Thrown the Negro and the Filipino Under the Tutelage of America': Race and Curriculum in the Age of Empire." *Curriculum Inquiry* 39, no. 4 (2009): 495–519.

Committee on Educational Interchange Policy. *Chinese Students in the United States, 1948–1955: A Study in Government Policy*. Institute of International Education, 1956.

Cooper, Frederick, and Randall M. Packard, eds. *International Development and the Social Sciences: Essays on the History and Politics of Knowledge*. University of California Press, 1998.

Cooper, Lenard H., et al. *Handbook for Foreign Student Advisers: Immigration Regulations*. 3rd rev. ed. National Association of Foreign Student Advisers, 1962.

Cooper, Thomas. "To Thomas Jefferson from Thomas Cooper, February 16, 1804." Founders Online, National Archives. archives.gov. [Original source: *The Papers of Thomas Jefferson*, vol. 42, *1 February–31 March 1804*, edited by James P. McClure, 458–60. Princeton University Press, 2016.]

Crackel, Theodore J. "The Military Academy in the Context of Jeffersonian Reform." In *Thomas Jefferson's Military Academy: Founding West Point*, edited by Robert M. S. McDonald, 103–26. University of Virginia Press, 2004.

Craven, Jasper. "Inside Pete Hegseth's Civilian Purge at West Point." *Politico*, August 29, 2025. https://www.politico.com/news/magazine/2025/08/28/pete-hegseth-civilians-west-point-00523613.

Dans, Paul, and Steven Groves, eds. *Mandate for Leadership: The Conservative Promise*. Heritage Foundation, 2023.

Darwin, Charles. *The Descent of Man, and Selection in Relation to Sex*. John Murray, 1871.

Davis, R. Hunt. "John L. Dube: A South African Exponent of Booker T. Washington." *Journal of African Studies* 2, no. 4 (1975): 497–528.

Demos, John. *The Heathen School: A Story of Hope and Betrayal in the Age of the Early Republic*. Knopf, 2014.

Dennis, Rutledge M. "Social Darwinism, Scientific Racism, and the Metaphysics of Race." *Journal of Negro Education* 64, no. 3 (1995): 243–52.

Dinwiddie, Robert. *The Official Records of Robert Dinwiddie, Lieutenant-Governor of the Colony of Virginia, 1751–1758*. 2 vols., edited by R. A. Brock. Virginia Historical Society, 1883–1884.

Divine, Robert A. *American Immigration Policy, 1924–1952*. Indiana University Press, 1957.

Dong, Yige. "How Chinese Students Become Nationalist: Their American Experience and Transpacific Futures." *American Quarterly* 69, no. 3 (2017): 559–67.

Dorr, Gregory Michael. *Segregation's Science: Eugenics and Society in Virginia*. University of Virginia Press, 2008.

Downey, Caroline. "Trump Promises to 'Immediately Deport' Foreign Students Involved in Anti-Israel Protests." *National Review*, May 12, 2024.

*Dred Scott v. Sandford*. 60 US 393 (1857).

Du Bois, W. E. B. *The Souls of Black Folk*. A. C. McClurg, 1903.

Du Puy, William Atherton. "Will This Save the Human Race? W. W. Husband, Commissioner of Immigration, Says New Law Will Influence America's Future Generations." *Boston Daily Globe*, June 19, 1921.

Dube, John. "Need of Industrial Education in Africa." *Southern Workman* 27, no. 7 (July 1897): 141–43.

Dudziak, Mary L. *Cold War Civil Rights: Race and the Image of American Democracy*. Princeton University Press, 2011.

Duediger, Dylan. "'By Just Means to Acquire Some Children.'" In *Building the Brafferton: The Founding, Funding and Legacy of America's Indian School*, edited by Danielle Moretti-Langholtz and Buck Woodard, 67–82. Muscarelle Museum of Art, 2019.

Duggan, Lawrence. *Twenty-Ninth Annual Report of the President*. Institute of International Education, 1948.

Duggan, Lisa, and José Esteban Muñoz. "Hope and Hopelessness: A Dialogue." *Women and Performance: A Journal of Feminist Theory* 19, no. 2 (2009): 275–83.

Dwight, Edwin W. *Memoirs of Henry Obookiah*. 1990 ed. Woman's Board of Missions for the Pacific Islands and the Hawaiian Historical Society, 1990.

"Education: Prince with a Purpose." *TIME*, January 1, 1945.

Elfin, Mel, and Constance Montague. "'Mo' is Sa'aid's Nickname At Cornell: 64,000 Foreign Students Ride the Diploma-Diplomacy Seesaw." *Newsweek*, 1963.

Elshakry, Marwa. "When Science Became Western: Historiographical Reflections." *Isis* 101, no. 1 (March 2010): 98–109.

England and Wales, Parliament. *An Act for Promoting and Propagating the Gospel of Jesus Christ in New England*. Printed for Edward Husband (London), 1649.

Engerman, David C. "American Knowledge and Global Power." *Diplomatic History* 31, no. 4 (2007): 599–622.

Engs, Robert Francis. *Educating the Disfranchised and Disinherited: Samuel Chapman Armstrong and Hampton Institute, 1839–1893*. University of Tennessee Press, 1999.

Fairchild, Henry Pratt. "The Immigration Law of 1924." *Quarterly Journal of Economics* 38, no. 4 (1924): 653–72.

Fallace, Thomas. "Recapitulation Theory and the New Education: Race, Culture, Imperialism, and Pedagogy, 1894–1916." *Curriculum Inquiry* 42, no. 4 (2012): 510–33.

"Family Visits Yale, New Haven in Honor of Man Who Inspired Christianity in Hawaii." *New Haven Register*, June 20, 2017.

Ferguson, Roderick A. *The Reorder of Things: The University and Its Pedagogies of Minority Difference*. University of Minnesota Press, 2012.

Fine, Benjamin. "Global Campus." *New York Times*, October 5, 1947.

Fisher, Linford D. *The Indian Great Awakening: Religion and the Shaping of Native Cultures in Early America*. Oxford University Press, 2012.

*Fong Yue Ting v. United States*. 149 US 698 (1893).
Fontaine, Philippe. "Walking the Tightrope: The Committee on the Behavioral Sciences and Academic Cultures at the University of Chicago, 1949–1955." *Journal of the History of the Behavioral Sciences* 52, no. 4 (2016): 335–56.
Forbes, W. Cameron. *The Philippine Islands*. Vol. 1. Houghton Mifflin, 1928.
Foster, Charles I. "The Colonization of Free Negroes in Liberia, 1816–1835." *Journal of Negro History* 38, no. 1 (1953): 41–66.
Foucault, Michel. *The Birth of the Clinic: An Archaeology of Medical Perception*. Translated by A. M. Sheridan Smith. Tavistock, 1973.
Foucault, Michel. "Nietzsche, Genealogy, History." In Donald F. Bouchard, *Language, Counter-Memory, Practice*. Cornell University Press, 1977.
Foucault, Michel. *Security, Territory, Population: Lectures at the Collège de France, 1977–1978*. Edited by Michel Senellart. Translated by Graham Burchell. Picador, 2007.
Foucault, Michel. "The Will to Knowledge." In *Ethics: Subjectivity & Truth*. Translated by Robert Hurley et al. Edited by Paul Rabinow. *Essential Works of Foucault* 1954–1984. The New Press, 1997.
Fox, Melvin. "Report on Exchange of Persons Activities of the Ford Foundation." Ford Foundation, January 1953.
Franklin, Vincent P. "Education for Colonization: Attempts to Educate Free Blacks in the United States for Emigration to Africa, 1823–1833." *Journal of Negro Education* 43, no. 1 (1974): 92–103.
Fraser, Hugh Russell. "Letter to Editor." *Newsweek*, May 6, 1963, 2.
Fritz, Christian G. "Due Process, Treaty Rights, and Chinese Exclusion, 1882–1891." In *Entry Denied: Exclusion and the Chinese Community in America, 1882–1943*, edited by Sucheng Chan, 25–56. Temple University Press, 1991.
"Fulbright, Hatch Now Hit Uno Veto: Arkansas Criticizes Truman's Program as Failing World Unity in Atomic Era." *New York Times*, November 25, 1945.
Gagen, Elizabeth. "Reflections of Primitivism: Development, Progress and Civilization in Imperial America, 1898–1914." *Children's Geographies* 5, no. 1–2 (2007): 15–28.
Gallay, Alan. *The Indian Slave Trade: The Rise of the English Empire in the American South, 1670–1717*. Yale University Press, 2003.
Garland, David. "What is a 'History of the Present'? On Foucault's Genealogies and Their Critical Preconditions." *Punishment & Society* 16, no. 4 (2014).
Garrison, William Lloyd. *Thoughts on African Colonization*. Garrison and Knapp, 1832.
Gaustad, Edwin Scott. *The Great Awakening in New England*. Harper & Row, 1957.
Geary Act [An Act to Prohibit the Coming of Chinese Persons into the United States]. ch. 60, 27 Stat. 25 (1892).

Geiger, Roger L. *American Higher Education Since World War II: A History.* Princeton University Press, 2019.

Gendzier, Irene. "Play it Again Sam: The Practice and Apology of Development." In *Universities and Empire: Money and Politics in the Social Sciences During the Cold War,* edited by Christopher Simpson, 157–188. The New Press, 1998.

Gerard, Emmanuel, and Bruce Kuklick. *Death in the Congo: Murdering Patrice Lumumba.* Harvard University Press, 2015.

Gerstein, Josh. "Obama's Father Forced Out at Harvard." *Politico,* April 29, 2011.

Getachew, Adom. *Worldmaking After Empire: The Rise and Fall of Self-Determination.* Princeton University Press, 2020.

Gilman, Nils. *Mandarins of the Future: Modernization Theory in Cold War America.* Johns Hopkins University Press, 2004.

Glenn, Evelyn Nakano. *Unequal Freedom: How Race and Gender Shaped American Citizenship and Labor.* Harvard University Press, 2002.

Goffe, Tao Leigh. "Intimate Occupations: The Afterlife of the 'Coolie.'" *Transforming Anthropology* 22, no. 1 (2014): 53–61.

Gold, Martin B. *Forbidden Citizens: Chinese Exclusion and the U.S. Congress: A Legislative History.* TheCapitol.net, 2012

Gordon, Avery. *The Hawthorn Archive: Letters from the Utopian Margins.* Fordham University Press, 2018.

Gordon, Linda. *Woman's Body, Woman's Right: Birth Control in America.* Penguin, 1976.

Gould, Stephen Jay. *The Mismeasure of Man.* W. W. Norton, 1981.

GOV.UK. "High Potential Individual (HPI) Visa: Eligibility." Accessed May 11, 2026. www.gov.uk.

Grande, Sandy. "Refusing the University." In *Toward What Justice?: Describing Diverse Dreams of Justice in Education,* edited by Eve Tuck and K. Wayne Yang, 47–65. Routledge, 2018.

Griffith, D. W., dir. *The Birth of a Nation.* Triangle Film Corporation, 1915.

Grinde, Donald A., Jr. "Taking the Indian Out of the Indian: U.S. Policies of Ethnocide Through Education." *Wicazo Sa Review* 19, no. 2 (2004): 25–32.

Grossberg, Lawrence. "Cultural Studies in Search of a Method, or Looking for Conjunctural Analysis." *New Formations* (2019): 38–68.

Gup, Ted. "Life Lessons in Diversity." *The Chronicle of Higher Education* (October 14, 2012).

Hacking, Ian. "Biopower and the Avalanche of Printed Numbers." *Humanities in Society* 5, no. 3/4 (Summer and Fall 1982): 279–95.

Hall, Stuart, Chas Critcher, Tony Jefferson, John Clarke, and Brian Roberts. *Policing the Crisis: Mugging, the State and Law and Order.* Macmillan Press, 1978.

Harper, Jim C. "Tom Mboya and the African Student Airlifts: Inclusion, Equity and Higher Education Among Kenyan Women and Men." *Africology: The Journal of Pan African Studies* 10, no. 9 (2017): 146–64.

Harper, Jim C. *Western-Educated Elites in Kenya, 1900–1963: The African American Factor.* Routledge, 2005.

Hartman, Saidiya V. *Scenes of Subjection: Terror, Slavery, and Self-Making in Nineteenth-Century America.* Oxford University Press, 1997.

Heckscher, August. *Woodrow Wilson.* Charles Scribner's Sons, 1991.

Hegel, G. W. F. *The Philosophy of History.* Colonial Press, 1899.

Hochbruck, Wolfgang, and Beatrix Dudensign-Reichel. "Native American Students and Two Seventeenth-Century Texts in the University Tradition." *Studies in American Indian Literatures* 2, no. 4 (1992): 35–47.

Hoftstadter, Richard. *Social Darwinism in American Thought.* Beacon Press, 1944.

Holland, Kenneth. "Open Doors Report 1963." Institute of International Education, 1963.

Hong, Grace Kyungwon. *Death Beyond Disavowal: The Impossible Politics of Difference.* University of Minnesota Press, 2015.

Hsu, Madeline Y. *The Good Immigrants: How the Yellow Peril Became the Model Minority.* Princeton University Press, 2015.

Hsu, Madeline Y. Review of *Stepping Forth into the World: The Chinese Educational Mission to the United States, 1872–81*, by Edward J. M. Rhoads. *Journal of Asian American Studies* 15, no. 2 (2012): 229–31.

Hughes, Heather. "Doubly Elite: Exploring the Life of John Langalibalele Dube." *Journal of Southern African Studies* 27, no. 3 (September 2001): 445–58.

Hunt, Michael H. "The American Remission of the Boxer Indemnity: A Reappraisal." *The Journal of Asian Studies* 31, no. 3 (May 1972): 539–59

Hunt, Michael H. *Frontier Defense and the Open Door: Manchuria in Chinese-American Relations, 1895–1911.* Yale University Press, 1973.

Immigration Act of 1891. Pub. L. No. 51-551, 26 Stat. 1084 (1891).

Immigration and Nationality Act of 1952. Pub. L. No. 82-414, 66 Stat. 163 (1952).

In re Low Yam Chow. 13 F. 605 (C.C.D. Cal. 1882).

Ingram, Angela. "Postmarked Calcutta, India." In *Gayatri Chakravorty Spivak, The Post-Colonial Critic: Interviews, Strategies, Dialogues*, edited by Sarah Harasym, 75–94. Routledge, 1990.

Institute of International Education, "All Places of Origin," Open Doors. Accessed May 11, 2026, opendoorsdata.org.

Institute of International Education. *First Annual Report of the Director.* Bulletin No. 1. Institute of International Education, 1920.

Institute of International Education. *Fourth Annual Report of the Director.* Bulletin No. 1. Institute of International Education, February 10, 1923.

Institute of International Education. *Third Annual Report of the Director.* Institute of International Education, 1922.

Irwin, Lauren. "GOP Senator Calls for Deporting Certain Foreign Student Protesters." *The Hill*, April 30, 2024.

"IVERNIA IN.: Cunarder Had Total of 1471 Passengers. Chinese Tourists Held by Immigration Officials. COI Billings Give His View on the Matter." *Boston Daily Globe*, June 2, 1905.

Jacobs, Sylvia M. "James Emman Kwegyir Aggrey: An African Intellectual in the United States." *The Journal of Negro History* 81, no. 1/4 (1996): 47–61.

Jacobs, Sylvia M. "Nineteenth-Century Black Methodist Missionary Bishops in Liberia." *Negro History Bulletin* 44, no. 4 (1981): 82–85.

Jefferson, Thomas. "A Bill for the More General Diffusion of Knowledge." June 18, 1779. Founders Online, National Archives. archives.gov. [Original source: *The Papers of Thomas Jefferson*, vol. 2, 1777–18 *June* 1779, edited by Julian P. Boyd, 526–35. Princeton University Press, 1950.]

Jefferson, Thomas. *Autobiography of Thomas Jefferson, 1743–1790*, edited by Paul Leicester Ford. G. P. Putnam's Sons, 1914.

Jefferson, Thomas. "From Thomas Jefferson to John Banister, Jr., 15 October 1785." In *The Papers of Thomas Jefferson, 25 February–31 October* 1785, vol. 8, edited by Julian P. Boyd, 635–37. Princeton University Press, 1953.

Jefferson, Thomas. *Writings*. Edited by Merrill D. Peterson. Library of America, 1984.

Johnson, Khalil Anthony, Jr. "Red, Black, & Brown: African American Educators in Indian Country." PhD dissertation, Yale University, 2018.

Jones, Hugh. *The Present State of Virginia*. Reprinted for Joseph Sabin, 1865.

Jones, Thomas Jesse. *Education in Africa: A Study of West, South, and Equatorial Africa By the African Education Commission, Under the Auspices of the Phelps-Stokes Fund and Foreign Mission Societies of North America and Europe*. Phelps-Stokes Fund, 1922.

Jung, Moon-Ho. *Menace to Empire: Anticolonial Solidarities and the Transpacific Origins of the US Security State*. University of California Press, 2022.

Jung, Moon-Ho. "Outlawing 'Coolies': Race, Nation, and Empire in the Age of Emancipation." *American Quarterly* 57, no. 3 (2005): 677–701.

Jung, Moon-Ho. "What is the 'Coolie Question'?" *Labour History* 113 (2017): 1–8.

Kamola, Isaac A. *Making the World Global: US Universities and the Production of the Global Imaginary*. Duke University Press, 2019.

Kaplan, Amy. "'Left Alone with America': The Absence of Empire in the Study of American Culture." In *Cultures of United States Imperialism*, edited by Amy Kaplan and Donald E. Pease, 3–21. Duke University Press, 1994.

Karuka, Manu. *Empire's Tracks: Indigenous Nations, Chinese Workers, and the Transcontinental Railroad*. University of California Press, 2019.

Katsakioris, Constantin. "Nkrumah's Elite: Ghanaian Students in the Soviet Union in the Cold War." *Paedagogica Historica* 57, no. 3 (2021): 272–91.

Katz, William Loren, ed. *Eyewitness: The Negro in American History*. Pitman Publishing Corporation, 1967.

Kauanui, J. Kēhaulani. *Paradoxes of Hawaiian Sovereignty: Land, Sex, and the Colonial Politics of State Nationalism*. Duke University Press, 2018.

Kauanui, J. Kēhaulani. "Tracing Historical Specificity: Race and the Colonial." *American Quarterly* 69, no. 2 (2017): 261–77.

Kauanui, J. Kēhaulani, and Patrick Wolfe. "Patrick Wolfe on Settler Colonialism." In *Speaking of Indigenous Politics: Conversations with Activists, Scholars, and Tribal Leaders*, edited by J. Kēhaulani Kauanui, with a foreword by Robert Warrior, 343–60. University of Minnesota Press, 2018.

Kazanjian, David. *The Colonizing Trick: National Culture and Imperial Citizenship in Early America*. University of Minnesota Press, 2003.

Kazanjian, David. "To See the Issue of His Exorbitant Practices: A Response to 'The Dispossessed Eighteenth Century.'" *The Eighteenth Century* 55, no. 2/3 (2014): 273–82.

Kennan, George F. "Resume of the World Situation." November 6, 1947. In *Foreign Relations of the United States, 1947, General; The United Nations*, vol. 1, 770–77. Government Printing Office, 1973.

Kelley, Robin D. G. "The Responsibility of Intellectuals in the Age of Fascism and Genocide." *The Boston Review*, Summer 2025. https://www.bostonreview.net/forum/the-responsibility-of-intellectuals-in-the-age-of-fascism-and-genocide/.

Kennedy, John F. "The Challenge of Imperialism: Algeria." July 2, 1957. In *"Let the Word Go Forth": The Speeches, Statements, and Writings of John F. Kennedy*, edited by Theodore Sorensen, 163–80. Delacorte Press, 1988.

Kennedy, John F. "Remarks of Welcome to President Nkrumah of Ghana at the Washington National Airport." March 8, 1961. Online by Gerhard Peters and John T. Woolley. *The American Presidency Project*. https://www.presidency.ucsb.edu/node/236126.

Kerr, Clark. *The Uses of the University*. 5th ed. Harvard University Press, 2001.

King, Kenneth J. "African Students in Negro American Colleges: Notes on the Good African." *Phylon* 31, no. 1 (1970): 16–30.

Kirkwood, Patrick M. "'Michigan Men' in the Philippines and the Limits of Self-Determination in the Progressive Era." *Michigan Historical Review* 40, no. 2 (2014): 47–73.

Klein, Christina. *Cold War Orientalism: Asia in the Middlebrow Imagination, 1945–1961*. University of California Press, 2003.

Kline, Kaity. "Weaponizing Antisemitism Makes Students 'Less Safe,' Says Drafter of Definition." *NPR*, March 20, 2025.

Kling, David W. "The New Divinity and the Origins of the American Board of Commissioners for Foreign Missions." *Church History* 72, no. 4 (2003): 791–819.

Koven, Steven G., and Frank Götzke. *American Immigration Policy: Confronting the Nation's Challenges*. Springer, 2010.

Kramer, Paul A. *Blood of Government: Race, Empire, the United States, and the Philippines*. University of North Carolina Press, 2006.

Kramer, Paul A. "Imperial Openings: Civilization, Exemption, and the Geopolitics of Mobility in the History of Chinese Exclusion, 1868–1910." *The Journal of the Gilded Age and Progressive Era* 14, no. 3 (2015): 322.

Kramer, Paul A. "Is the World Our Campus? International Students and U.S. Global Power in the Long Twentieth Century." *Diplomatic History* 33, no. 5 (2009): 775–806.

Kramer, Paul A. "Power and Connection: Imperial Histories of the United States in the World." *American Historical Review* 116, no. 5 (2011): 1348–91.

Kramer, Paul A. "Shades of Sovereignty: Racialized Power, the United States, and the World." In *Explaining the History of American Foreign Relations*, 3rd ed., edited by Frank Costigliola and Michael J. Hogan, 245–70. Cambridge University Press, 2016.

Kwong, Luke S. K. "Chinese Politics at the Crossroads: Reflections on the Hundred Days Reform of 1898." *Modern Asian Studies* 34, no. 3 (July 2000): 663–95.

La Fargue, Thomas E. *China's First Hundred.* State College of Washington, 1942.

Lahiri, Bulan. "In Conversation: Speaking to Spivak." *The Hindu*, December 4, 2011. Accessed September 4, 2025. https://www.thehindu.com/books/In-Conversation-Speaking-to-Spivak/article15130635.ece.

Land, Robert Hunt. "Henrico and Its College." *William and Mary Quarterly*, 2nd ser., 18, no. 4 (1938): 453–98.

Laosebikan, Olanipekun Oladotun. "From Student to Immigrant: The Diasporation of the African Student in the United States." PhD dissertation, University of Illinois at Urbana-Champaign, 2012.

Laosebikan, Olanipekun Oladotun. "In Pursuit of the 'Golden Fleece': African Students and Higher Education in the United States, 1925–1959." *West Africa Review* 17 (2010).

Larson, Jane Leung. "Articulating China's First Mass Movement: Kang Youwei, Liang Qichao, the Baohuanghui, and the 1905 Anti-American Boycott." *Twentieth-Century China* 33, no. 1 (November 2007): 3–26.

Layne, Nathan, and Tim Reid. "Trump Pledges to Expel Immigrants Who Support Hamas, Ban Muslims from the U.S." *Reuters*, October 16, 2023.

Layton, Azza Salama. "International Pressure and the US Government's Response to Little Rock." *The Arkansas Historical Quarterly* 56, no. 3 (1997): 257–72.

Lebovic, Sam. "From War Junk to Educational Exchange: The World War II Origins of the Fulbright Program and the Foundations of American Cultural Globalism, 1945–1950." *Diplomatic History* 37, no. 2 (April 2013): 280–312.

Lee, Erika. *At America's Gates: Chinese Immigration During the Exclusion Era, 1882–1943*. University of North Carolina Press, 2003.

Lee, Robert, and Tristan Ahtone. "Land-Grab Universities: Expropriated Indigenous Land is the Foundation of the Land-Grant University System." *High Country News*, 2020.

Lei, Sean Hsiang-lin. "The Dawn of Science as Cultural Authority in China: *Tianyanlun* (On Heavenly Evolution) in the Post-1895 Debate over the Engagement with Western Civilization." *East Asian Science, Technology and Society: An International Journal* 13, no. 3 (2019): 315–39.

Leibovitz, Liel, and Matthew Miller. *Fortunate Sons: The 120 Chinese Boys Who Came to America, Went to School, and Revolutionized an Ancient Civilization.* W. W. Norton, 2011.

Leonard, Thomas C. *Illiberal Reformers: Race, Eugenics, and American Economics in the Progressive Era.* Princeton University Press, 2016.

Leroy, Justin. "Black History in Occupied Territory: On the Entanglements of Slavery and Settler Colonialism." *Theory & Event* 19, no. 4 (2016).

Leslie, Stuart W. *The Cold War and American Science: The Military-Industrial-Academic Complex at MIT and Stanford.* Columbia University Press, 1993.

Lewontin, R. C. "The Cold War and the Transformation of the Academy." In *The Cold War & the University: Toward an Intellectual History of the Postwar Years,* edited by Andre Schiffrin, 1–34. The New Press, 1997.

Lew-Williams, Beth. "Before Restriction Became Exclusion: America's Experiment in Diplomatic Immigration Control." *Pacific Historical Review* 83, no. 1 (February 2014): 1–39.

Li, Hongshan. *U.S.-China Educational Exchange: State, Society, and Intercultural Relations, 1905–1950.* Rutgers University Press, 2008.

Lincoln University. "Mission." Accessed May 10, 2026. lincoln.edu.

Lipsitz, George. "The Possessive Investment in Whiteness: Racialized Social Democracy and the 'White' Problem in American Studies." *American Quarterly* 47, no. 3 (1995): 369–87.

Livingston, Thomas W. "The Exportation of American Higher Education to Western Africa: Liberia College, 1850–1900." *The Journal of Negro Education* 45, no. 3 (Summer 1976): 246–62.

Lopenzina, Drew. *Red Ink: Native Americans Picking Up the Pen in the Colonial Period.* SUNY Press, 2012.

Loss, Christopher. *Between Citizen and State: The Politics of Higher Education in the 20th Century.* Princeton University Press, 2012.

Lowe, Lisa. *Immigrant Acts: On Asian American Cultural Politics.* Duke University Press, 1996.

Lowe, Lisa. *The Intimacies of Four Continents.* Duke University Press, 2015.

Lowell, Albert Lawrence. "The Colonial Expansion of the United States." *Atlantic Monthly* 83 (January 1899): 145–54.

Lucas, Christopher J. *American Higher Education: A History.* Palgrave Macmillan, 2006.

Luibhéid, Eithne. *Abolitionist Intimacies: Queer and Trans Migrants Against the Deportation State.* Duke University Press, 2025.

Luibhéid, Eithne. "Queer/Migration: An Unruly Body of Scholarship." *GLQ: A Journal of Lesbian and Gay Studies* 14, no. 2–3 (2008): 169–90.

Lynch, Hollis R. "K. O. Mbadiwe, 1939–1947: The American Years of a Nigerian Political Leader." *Journal of African Studies* 7, no. 4 (1980): 184–203.

MacCabe, Colin. Foreword to *In Other Worlds: Essays in Cultural Politics,* by Gayatri Chakravorty Spivak. Routledge, 1988.

Madsen, David L. "The University of the United States: A Durable Dream." *The Journal of Higher Education* 33, no. 7 (October 1962): 353–60.

Maira, Sunaina, and Piya Chatterjee, eds. *The Imperial University*. University of Minnesota Press, 2014.

Malthus, Thomas. *An Essay on the Principle of Population*. J. Johnson, 1798.

Manela, Erez. *The Wilsonian Moment: Self-Determination and the International Origins of Anticolonial Nationalism*. Oxford University Press, 2007.

Marquez, Bayley J. "The Black Model Minority: Slavery, Settlement, and the Genealogy of the Model Minority." *Du Bois Review: Social Science Research on Race* 19, no. 1 (Spring 2022): 129–45. https://doi.org/10.1017/S1742058X21000345.

Marx, Karl. "On the Jewish Question." In *The Marx–Engels Reader*, edited by Robert C. Tucker. W. W. Norton, 1978.

Massachusetts Bay Colony. *Charter of 1650*. May 31, 1650. Harvard University Archives, Cambridge, MA.

McCallum, James Dow, ed. *The Letters of Eleazar Wheelock's Indians*. Dartmouth College Publications, 1932.

McCloskey, Robert Green. *American Conservatism in the Age of Enterprise*. Harvard University Press, 1951.

McClure, David, and Elijah Parish. *Memoirs of the Rev. Eleazar Wheelock, D. D.* Edward Little & Co., 1811.

McCoy, Drew R. "Jefferson and Madison on Malthus: Population Growth in Jeffersonian Political Economy." *The Virginia Magazine of History and Biography* 88, no. 3 (1980): 259–76.

McCoy, Meredith, Roopika Risam, and Jennifer Guiliano. "The Future of Land-Grab Universities." *Native American and Indigenous Studies* 8, no. 1 (2021): 169–75.

McIlwaine, H. R., ed. *Executive Journals of the Council of Colonial Virginia*. Vol. 1. Virginia State Library, 1925.

McKeown, Adam. *Melancholy Order: Asian Migration and the Globalization of Borders*. Columbia University Press, 2008.

McKeown, Adam. "Ritualization of Regulation: The Enforcement of Chinese Exclusion in the United States and China." *American Historical Review* 108, no. 2 (April 2003): 377–403.

Mehta, Uday S. "Liberal Strategies of Exclusion." In *Tensions of Empire: Colonial Cultures in a Bourgeois World*, edited by Frederick Cooper and Ann Laura Stoler, 59–86. University of California Press, 1997.

Melamed, Jodi. "Racial Capitalism." *Critical Ethnic Studies* 1, no. 1 (2015): 76–85.

Melamed, Jodi. *Represent and Destroy: Rationalizing Violence in the New Racial Capitalism*. University of Minnesota Press, 2011

Meriwether, James H. *Tears, Fire, and Blood: The United States and the Decolonization of Africa*. University of North Carolina Press, 2021.

Meyerhoff, Eli. *Beyond Education: Radical Studying for Another World*. University of Minnesota Press, 2019.

Mills, Brandon. *The World Colonization Made: The Racial Geography of Early American Empire*. University of Pennsylvania Press, 2020.

Miner, Luella. "American Barbarism and Chinese Hospitality." *The Outlook* 72, no. 17 (December 27, 1902): 984–88.

Mitchell, Ruth Crawford. *Foreign Students and the Immigration Laws of the United States*. Institute of International Education, 1930.

Mitchell, Timothy. "Economists and the Economy in the Twentieth Century." In *The Politics of Method in the Human Sciences*, edited by George Steinmetz, 126–41. Duke University Press, 2005.

Mitchell, Timothy. "The Work of Economics: How a Discipline Makes Its World." *European Journal of Sociology* 46, no. 2 (2005): 297–320.

Moon, Krystyn R. "Immigration Restrictions and International Education: Early Tensions in the Pacific Northwest, 1890s–1910s." *History of Education Quarterly* 58, no. 2 (May 2018): 261–94

Mooney, James. *Cherokee Legends and the Trail of Tears: From the Nineteenth Annual Report of the Bureau of American Ethnology*. S. B. Newman Printing Co., 1956.

Moore, Moses N., Jr. "Edward Wilmot Blyden: From Old School Presbyterian Missionary to 'Minister of Truth.'" *Journal of Presbyterian History* 75, no. 2 (Summer 1997): 103–18.

Morawski, Jill. "Organizing Knowledge and Behavior at Yale's Institute of Human Relations." *Isis* 77, no. 2 (1986): 219–42.

Morpurgo, J. E. *Their Majesties' Royall Colledge: William & Mary in the Seventeenth and Eighteenth Centuries*. College of William & Mary in Virginia, 1976.

Moretti-Langholtz, Danielle, and Buck Woodard, eds. *Building the Brafferton: The Founding, Funding and Legacy of America's Indian School*. Muscarelle Museum of Art, 2019.

Morse, Jedidiah. A *Report to the Secretary of War of the United States, on Indian Affairs, Comprising a Narrative of a Tour Performed in the Summer of 1820*. Converse, 1822.

"Mr. N. Orizu Says He Comes for African Education and Propagation of 'Zikism.'" *West African Pilot*, 1945.

Mudimbe, V. Y. *The Invention of Africa: Gnosis, Philosophy, and the Order of Knowledge*. Indiana University Press, 1988.

*New England's First Fruits: In Respect, First of the Conversion of some, Conviction of divers, Preparation of others of the Indians. 2. Of the progresse of Learning, in the Colledge at Cambridge in Massacusets Bay*. Printed by R. O. and G. D. for Henry Overton (London), 1643.

Newfield, Christopher. *Ivy and Industry: Business and the Making of the American University, 1880–1980*. Duke University Press, 2003.

Ng, Poon Chew. *The Treatment of the Exempt Classes of Chinese in the United States*. Chung Sai Yat Po, 1908.

Ngai, Mae M. *Impossible Subjects: Illegal Aliens and the Making of Modern America*. Princeton University Press, 2004.

Ngai, Mae M. "Nationalism, Immigration Control, & the Ethnoracial Mapping of America in the 1920s." *OAH Magazine of History* 21, no. 3 (July 2007): 11–15.

Nicolson, Frank W., ed. *Alumni Record of Wesleyan University, Middletown, Conn.* 4th ed. Tuttle, Morehouse & Taylor Company, 1911.

*Nishimura Ekiu v. United States*. 142 US 651 (1892).

Nivison, Kenneth. "'But a Step from College to the Judicial Bench': College and Curriculum in New England's 'Age of Improvement.'" *History of Education Quarterly* 50, no. 4 (2010): 461–87.

Nkrumah, Kwame. *Ghana: The Autobiography of Kwame Nkrumah* [1957]. Reprint, Echo Point Books & Media, 2023.

Nkrumah, Kwame. *Toward Colonial Freedom: Africa in the Struggle Against World Imperialism*. Heinemann, 1962.

NPR Staff. "All the Executive Orders Trump Has Signed After 1 Week in Office." *NPR*, January 28, 2025.

O'Brien, Jean M. *Firsting and Lasting: Writing Indians Out of Existence in New England*. University of Minnesota Press, 2010.

O'Brien, M. Jean, and Robert Warrior. "Building a Professional Infrastructure for Critical Indigenous Studies: A(n Intellectual) History of and Prospectus for the Native American and Indigenous Studies Association." In *Critical Indigenous Studies: Engagements in First World Locations*, edited by Aileen Moreton-Robinson, 33–48. University of Arizona Press, 2016.

O'Brien, Sharon. "Bureau of Indian Affairs." In *The Encyclopedia of North American Indians*, edited by Frederick E. Hoxie, 86–88. Houghton Mifflin, 1996

Occom, Samson. *The Collected Writings of Samson Occom*, edited by Joanna Brooks. Oxford University Press, 2006.

Oeltjen, Pam. "History Professor Caught Between Two Worlds." *State Hornet* 54, no. 54 (1996).

Office of Congressman Nick Langworthy. "Congressman Langworthy Introduces Legislation to Revoke Student Visas of Pro-Terrorist Protesters." July 25, 2024. https://langworthy.house.gov/media/press-releases/congressman-langworthy-introduces-legislation-revoke-student-visas-pro.

Office of Senator Marco Rubio, "Rubio to Biden Admin: Revoke Visas of Pro-Hamas Protesters Now," May 9, 2024.

Ogbeidi, Michael M. "Non-Governmental Organisation and the Promotion of American Education in Nigeria, 1941–1954." Nebula 6, no. 4 (2009): 79–103.

Ogot, Bethwell A., and William R. Ochieng', eds. *Decolonization and Independence in Kenya, 1940–93*. Ohio University Press, 1995.

Oklahoma Historical Society. "Timeline of American Indian Removal." Accessed May 10, 2026. okhistory.org.

O'Mara, Margaret. "The Uses of the Foreign Student." *Social Science History* 36, no. 4 (2012): 497–515.

"On Educating Heathen Youth in Our Own Country." *The Panoplist, and Missionary Magazine* 12, no. 7 (July 1816): 297–303.

Ong, Aihwa. *Neoliberalism as Exception: Mutations in Citizenship and Sovereignty.* Duke University Press, 2006.

O'Reilly, Kenneth. "The Jim Crow Policies of Woodrow Wilson." *Journal of Blacks in Higher Education* 17 (1997): 117–21.

"Opinion About US Treatment of Negroes," report 38, July 24, 1956. Office of Research, Public Opinion Barometer Reports, 1955–1956. Records of the United States Information Agency. Record Group 306. National Archives at College Park, MD.

Page Act of 1875, ch. 141, 18 Stat. 477 (1875).

Paik, Naomi A. *Bans, Walls, Raids, Sanctuary: Understanding U.S. Immigration for the Twenty-First Century.* University of California Press, 2020.

Painter, Sidney et al. "The Visa Problem." *The Scientific Monthly* 76, no. 1 (January 1953): 4–13.

"Palestine is Everywhere." Accessed February 3, 2025. archive.org.

Papaula, S. W. "Helehelekalani" [More on Opukahaia]. *Ka Nupepa Kuokoa* 4, no. 44 (November 4, 1865): 4. nupepa-hawaii.com.

Park, K-Sue. "Money, Mortgages, and the Conquest of America." *Law & Social Inquiry* 41, no. 4 (2016): 1006–35.

Parker, Jason C. "'Made-in-America?' The 'Black University' and the American Role in the Decolonization of the Black Atlantic." *The Journal of American History* 96, no. 3 (2009): 727–50.

Parker, Kunal M. "The Rights of Noncitizens." In *The Bill of Rights in Modern America*, edited by David J. Bodenhamer and James W. Ely Jr., 246–69. 3rd ed. Indiana University Press, 2022

"Passports Signed by Li Hung Chang." *Washington Post*, September 27, 1901.

Patler, Nicholas. *Jim Crow and the Wilson Administration: Protesting Federal Segregation in the Early Twentieth Century.* University Press of Colorado, 2007.

Pestritto, Ronald J. *Woodrow Wilson and the Roots of Modern Liberalism.* Rowman & Littlefield, 2005.

Perry, Richard J. *From Time Immemorial: Indigenous Peoples and State Systems.* University of Texas Press, 1996

Perry, William Stevens, ed. *Historical Collections Relating to the American Colonial Church.* Vol. 1, *Virginia.* Church Press, 1870.

Phelps-Stokes Fund. *A Survey of African Students Studying in the United States.* Phelps-Stokes Fund, 1949.

Philippine Commission. "An Act Providing for the Education of Filipino Students in the United States and Appropriating for Such Purpose the Sum of Seventy-Two Thousand Dollars, in Money of the United States." Act No. 854, August 26, 1903. *Official Gazette* 1, no. 52 (September 2, 1903): 645.

"Police Enter Columbia University's Hamilton Hall Amid Pro-Palestinian Protests." *NPR*, April 30, 2024.

Pooley, Jefferson D. "A 'Not Particularly Felicitous' Phrase: A History of the 'Behavioral Sciences' Label." *Serendipities* 1, no. 1 (2016): 38–81.

Potts, David B. *Wesleyan University, 1830–1910: Collegiate Enterprise in New England*. Wesleyan University Press, 1999.

Prashad, Vijay. *The Darker Nations: A People's History of the Third World*. The New Press, 2022.

Pratt, Richard H. "The Advantages of Mingling Indians with Whites." In *Americanizing the American Indians: Writings by the "Friends of the Indian," 1880–1900*, edited by Francis Paul Prucha, 260–71. Harvard University Press, 1973.

President's Alliance on Higher Education and Immigration. "FAQs on Executive Order: Additional Measures to Combat Anti-Semitism." February 6, 2025. presidentsalliance.org

Price, Richard Rees. *The Financial Support of State Universities: A Study of the Financial Resources of State Universities in the Light of the Experience of the Universities of the Old Northwest Territory, With a Suggested Policy for the Future*. Harvard University Press, 2014.

"Proceedings at the Inauguration of Liberia College at Monrovia, January 28, 1862." *The African Repository* 38, no. 11 (November 1862): 321–47.

Prucha, Francis Paul, ed. *Documents of United States Indian Policy*. 3rd ed. University of Nebraska Press, 2000.

"Quarterly Report of the Foreign Mission School," June 1, 1824. ABC 18.8, vol. 1. American Board of Commissioners for Foreign Missions Records. Houghton Library, Harvard University, Cambridge, MA.

Rana, Aziz. *The Two Faces of American Freedom*. Harvard University Press, 2010.

Ray, Sangeeta. *Gayatri Chakravorty Spivak: In Other Words*. Wiley-Blackwell, 2009.

Readings, Bill. *The University in Ruins*. Harvard University Press, 1996.

Records of the National Urban League. Manuscript Division, Library of Congress, Washington, DC.

Remoff, Heather. "Malthus, Darwin, and the Descent of Economics." *American Journal of Economics and Sociology* 75, no. 4 (2016): 865–89.

"Report of the Committee of the Foreign Mission School." *The Panoplist, and Missionary Magazine* 13 (January 1817): 17–20.

Richards, James, and Edward D. Griffin. "African Seminary." *The Christian Herald* 2, no. 9 (November 1816): 125–28. *Christian Herald*, 1816.

Robin, Ron. *The Making of the Cold War Enemy: Culture and Politics in the Military-Intellectual Complex*. Princeton University Press, 2001.

Robins-Early, Nick. "How Elon Musk Became Donald Trump's Shadow Vice-President." *The Guardian*, November 9, 2024. Accessed September 8, 2025.

Robinson, W. Stitt, Jr. "Indian Education and Missions in Colonial Virginia." *The Journal of Southern History* 18, no. 2 (1952): 152–70.

Rodríguez, Dylan. "Racial/Colonial Genocide and the Neoliberal Academy." *American Quarterly* 68, no. 4 (2016): 809–13.

Roosevelt, Theodore. "Seventh Annual Message." December 3, 1907. Online by Gerhard Peters and John T. Woolley. *The American Presidency Project*. Accessed September 4, 2025.

Rush, Benjamin. *The Selected Writings of Benjamin Rush*, edited by Dagobert D. Runes. Philosophical Library, 1947.

Rush, Benjamin. "Thoughts Upon the Mode of Education Proper to a Republic." In *Essays on Education in the Early Republic*, edited by Frederick Rudolph, 9–25. Harvard University Press, 1965.

Russell, Graham, Gao Hodges, and Alan Edward Brown, eds. *The Book of Negroes: African Americans in Exile after the American Revolution*. Fordham University Press, 2021.

"Ruth Crawford Mitchell." *Vassar Encyclopedia*. Vassar College. Accessed December 12, 2024. https://vcencyclopedia.vassar.edu/distinguished-alumni/ruth-crawford-mitchell/.

Said, Edward. "Blind Imperial Arrogance." *Los Angeles Times*, July 20, 2003.

Salisbury, Harrison E. "Washington Post Buys Newsweek." *New York Times*, March 10, 1961.

Salyer, Lucy E. "Reconstructing the Immigrant: The Naturalization Act of 1870 in Global Perspective." *Journal of the Civil War Era* 11, no. 3 (September 2021): 315–39.

Sánchez-Eppler, Karen. "Copying and Conversion: An 1824 Friendship Album 'from a Chinese Youth.'" *American Quarterly* 59, no. 2 (June 2007): 301–39.

Schiffrin, André, ed. *The Cold War & the University: Toward an Intellectual History of the Postwar Years*. The New Press, 1997.

Schiller, Herbert I., and Joseph D. Phillips, eds. *Super-State: Readings in the Military-Industrial Complex*. University of Illinois Press, 1972.

Schueller, Malini Johar. "Celebrating Imperial Education: The 2001 Thomasite Centennial in the Philippines." *American Quarterly* 74, no. 4 (2022): 945–68.

Schiff, Judith Ann. "Aloha Blue." *Yale Alumni Magazine* (July/August 2004).

Seed, Patricia. *American Pentimento: The Invention of Indians and the Pursuit of Riches*. University of Minnesota Press, 2001.

Seeley, Samantha. "Beyond the American Colonization Society." *History Compass* 14, no. 3 (2016): 93–104.

Serwer, Adam. "Jeff Sessions's Unqualified Praise for a 1924 Immigration Law." *The Atlantic*, January 10, 2017.

Seymour, Richard. "The Cold War, American Anticommunism, and the Global Colour Line." In *Race and Racism in International Relations*, edited by Alexander Anievas, Nivi Manchanda, and Robbie Shilliam, 157–74. Routledge, 2015.

Shah, Nayan. *Stranger Intimacy: Contesting Race, Sexuality, and the Law in the North American West*. University of California Press, 2011.

Shank, Donald J. "Windows on the World." In *IIE Open Doors Report*. Institute of International Education, 1948.

Sharpe, Jenny. "What Use is the Imagination?" *PMLA* 129, no. 3 (2014): 512–17.

Shefveland, Kristalyn Marie. *Anglo-Native Virginia: Trade, Conversion, and Indian Slavery in the Old Dominion, 1646–1722*. University of Georgia Press, 2016.

Shill, Chao-Yung. "The Effects of the Immigration Bill of 1924 on Chinese Students." *Chinese Students' Monthly* 20, no. 2 (December 1924): 20–25.

Shils, Edward A. "America's Paper Curtain." *Bulletin of the Atomic Scientists* 8, no. 7 (October 1952): 210–17.

Simpson, Matthew, ed. *Cyclopaedia of Methodism: Embracing Sketches of Its Rise, Progress, and Present Condition, with Biographical Notices and Numerous Illustrations*. Rev. ed. Louis H. Everts, 1880. s.v. "Burns, Francis."

Singh, Vineeta. "Slavery and the University: Histories and Legacies (Review)." *The Black Scholar* 51, no. 1 (2021): 76–78.

Singh, Vineeta. "Universities Studying Slavery: Critical University Studies in Practice." *Remaking the University* (2019).

Slater, Robert Bruce. "The Black Who First Entered the World of White Higher Education." *The Journal of Blacks in Higher Education*, no. 4 (1994): 47–56.

Slaughter, Sheila, and Gary Rhoades. "Academic Capitalism, Managed Professionals, and Supply-Side Higher Education." *Social Text* 51, (Summer (1997): 9–38. http://www.jstor.org/stable/40342886.

Smithers, Gregory D. *The Cherokee Diaspora*. Yale University Press, 2015.

Smythe, S. A. "Introduction: Unsettle the Struggle, Trouble the Grounds." *Postmodern Culture* 31, nos. 1–2 (September 2020/January 2021).

Somerville, Siobhan B. "Notes Toward a Queer History of Naturalization." *American Quarterly* 57, no. 3 (September 2005): 659–75.

Soong, Irma Tam. "Sun Yat-Sen's Christian Schooling in Hawai'i." *The Hawaiian Journal of History* 31 (1997): 151–78.

"Special Communication to the Public." In *Semi-Annual Report of the Foreign Mission School*, for June 1825, June 17, 1825. [N.p., n.d.]. Pamphlet. Torrington Public Library, Torrington, CT.

Speer, Robert E. Foreword to *The Foreign Student in America*, edited by W. Reginald Wheeler, Henry H. King, and Alexander B. Davidson, vii–xi. Association Press, 1925.

Spivak, Gayatri Chakravorty. *An Aesthetic Education in the Era of Globalization*. Harvard University Press, 2012.

Spivak, Gayatri Chakravorty. *In Other Worlds: Essays in Cultural Politics*. Routledge, 1988.

Spivak, Gayatri Chakravorty. *Outside in the Teaching Machine*. Routledge, 1993.

Spivak, Gayatri Chakravorty. *The Spivak Reader: Selected Works of Gayatri Chakravorty Spivak*, edited by Donna Landry and Gerald Maclean. Routledge, 1996.

Spring, Gardiner. *Memoirs of the Rev. Samuel J. Mills: Late Missionary to the South Western Section of the United States, and Agent of the American Colonization Society Deputed to Explore the Coast of Africa*. Francis Westly, 1820.

Stanford, Leland. "Inaugural Address." January 10, 1862.

Starr, Edward C. A *History of Cornwall, Connecticut, a Typical New England Town*. Tuttle, Morehouse & Taylor, 1926.

Stein, Sharon. "Confronting the Racial-Colonial Foundations of U.S. Higher Education." *Journal for the Study of Postsecondary and Tertiary Education* 3 (2018): 77–96.

Stein, Sharon. "Critical Internationalization Studies at an Impasse: Making Space for Complexity, Uncertainty, and Complicity in a Time of Global Challenges." *Studies in Higher Education* 46, no. 9 (2021): 1771–84.

Steiner-Khamsi, Gita, and Hubert O. Quist. "The Politics of Educational Borrowing: Reopening the Case of Achimota in British Ghana." *Comparative Education Review* 44, no. 3 (2000): 272–99.

Sterett, Susan. "'Entitled to Have a Hearing': Due Process in the 1890s." *Social & Legal Studies* 3, no. 1 (March 1994): 47–70.

Stewart-Ambo, Theresa, and K. Wayne Yang. "Beyond Land Acknowledgement in Settler Institutions." *Social Text* 39, no. 1 (March 2021): 21–46.

Stuart, Sarah Harrison. "'So Good a Word': The Brafferton School, 1691–1777." Master's thesis, The College of William & Mary, 1984.

"Student from Kenya Faces Ouster by US," *New York Times*, December 5, 1952. https://www.nytimes.com/1952/12/05/archives/student-from-kenya-faces-ouster-by-u-s.html.

Sun, Yat-sen. *Kuo-fu Ch'üan-chi* [Complete Works of the Father of the Nation]. National Defence Research Institute, 1961.

Suskind, Ron. "Faith, Certainty and the Presidency of George W. Bush." *New York Times Magazine*, October 17, 2004.

Synods of New York and New Jersey. "African Seminary." *The Christian Herald* 2, no. 6 (November 2, 1816): 88–92.

Tarradellas, Anton. "Pan-African Networks, Cold War Politics, and Postcolonial Opportunities: The African Scholarship Program of American Universities, 1961–1975." *The Journal of African History* 63, no. 1 (2022): 75–90.

Teng, Emma J. "Chinese Elites and US Gatekeeping: Racial Discrimination and Class Privilege in Boston's 1905 King Incident." *Modern American History* 4, no. 1 (March 2021): 1–24.

Torpey, John. *The Invention of the Passport: Surveillance, Citizenship, and the State*. Cambridge University Press, 2000.

Tracy, Joseph. *History of the American Board of Commissioners for Foreign Missions*. M. W. Dodd, 1842.

Transcript of "Rules and Methods for Disposition of Rents and Profits." [1695]. Box 3, Folder 1. Brafferton Estate Collection (UA 113). Special Collections Research Center, William & Mary Libraries, Williamsburg, Virginia.

Trask, Haunani-Kay. *From a Native Daughter: Colonialism and Sovereignty in Hawai'i*. University of Hawai'i Press, 1999.

Truman, Harry S. "Veto of Bill to Revise the Laws Relating to Immigration, Naturalization, and Nationality." June 25, 1952. In *Public Papers of the Presidents of the United States: Harry S. Truman, 1952–53*. Government Printing Office, 1966.

Tsai, Shih-shan Henry. *China and the Overseas Chinese in the United States, 1868–1911*. University of Arkansas Press, 1983.

Tsao, Y. S. "The Relation of the Returned Students to the Chinese Revolution." *The Journal of Race Development* 4, no. 1 (1913): 96–109.

Turner, Frederick Jackson. *The Frontier in American History*. Henry Holt and Company, 1920.

Tyrrell, Ian. *Reforming the World: The Creation of America's Moral Empire*. Princeton University Press, 2010.

"Unauthorized Transformation." *African Repository and Colonial Journal* 11, no. 2 (February 1835): 61.

*United States v. Ju Toy*, 198 US 253 (1905).

*United States v. Wong Kim Ark*. 169 US 649 (1898).

US Congress. *An Act to Create a Department of Labor*. Public Law 62-426. 37 Stat. 736. March 4, 1913.

US Congress. *Act of July 2, 1862 (Morrill Act), Public Law 37-108, which established land grant colleges*, July 2, 1862. Enrolled Acts and Resolutions of Congress, 1789–1996; General Records of the United States Government, Record Group 11. National Archives, Washington, DC. https://www.archives.gov/milestone-documents/morrill-act.

US Congress. *Additional Articles to the Treaty between the United States of America and the Ta-Tsing Empire, of June 18, 1858 [Burlingame Treaty]*. Concluded at Washington, July 28, 1868; ratified by the United States, August 16, 1868. 16 Stat. 739.

US Congress. *Congressional Globe*. 41st Cong., 2d sess., 1870.

US Congress. *Congressional Record*. 47th Congress, 1st sess. Vol. 13, pt. 2. Washington, DC: Government Printing Office, 1882.

US Congress. *Congressional Record*. 67th Cong., 1st sess., 1921. Vol. 61, pt. 1.

US Congress. *Congressional Record*. 68th Cong., 1st sess., 1924. Vol. 65, pt. 6.

US Congress. Senate. Committee on the Judiciary. *The Immigration and Naturalization Systems of the United States: Report of the Committee on the Judiciary Pursuant to S. Res. 137, 80th Cong., 1st Sess., as Amended, a Resolution to Make an Investigation of the Immigration System*. 81st Cong., 2d sess., 1950. S. Rep. 1515.

US Department of State. "Angell Treaty of 1880." Signed November 17, 1880. In *Treaties and Other International Agreements of the United States of America 1776–1949*, compiled by Charles I. Bevans, vol. 6. Government Printing Office, 1968–76.

US Department of State. "Mr. Wu to Mr. Hay," December 9, 1901. In *Papers Relating to the Foreign Relations of the United States, with the Annual Message of the President Transmitted to Congress, December 3, 1901*, 93–97. Government Printing Office, 1902.

US Department of State. "Statement of Policy Proposed by the NSC on 'United States Objectives and Policies with Respect to the Arab States and Israel.'" In *Foreign Relations of the United States, 1952–1954, Vol. IX, The Near and Middle East*. Government Printing Office, 1986.

US Immigration and Naturalization Service, San Francisco District Office. "Contents of the File of Sun Yat Sen." NARA Government Documents. National Archives and Records Administration. Accessed September 12, 2025.

US President. Executive Order 14161. "Protecting the United States from Foreign Terrorists and Other National Security and Public Safety Threats." *Federal Register* 90, no. 15 (January 24, 2025): 4983–4994.

United States. "An act in amendment to the various acts relative to immigration and the importation of aliens under contract or agreement to perform labor." *United States Statutes at Large* 26 (1891): 1084–1086. https://govtrackus.s3.amazonaws.com/legislink/pdf/stat/26/STATUTE-26-Pg1084a.pdf.

University of Virginia. "Universities Studying Slavery." Accessed May 11, 2026. https://slavery.virginia.edu/universities-studying-slavery/.

Vesely-Flad, Ethan. "Today is George Houser's 99th Birthday!" *Fellowship of Reconciliation* (blog). June 2, 2015. forusa.org.

Vimalassery, Manu. "Counter-Sovereignty." *J19: The Journal of Nineteenth-Century Americanists* 2, no. 1 (Spring 2014): 124–31.

Vitalis, Robert. "The Noble American Science of Imperial Relations and Its Laws of Race Development." *Comparative Studies in Society and History* 52, no. 4 (2010): 909–38.

Vitalis, Robert. *White World Order, Black Power Politics: The Birth of American International Relations*. Cornell University Press, 2015.

Volpp, Leti. "Divesting Citizenship: On Asian American History and the Loss of Citizenship Through Marriage." *UCLA Law Review* 53, no. 2 (2005): 405–83.

Von Eschen, Penny M. *Race Against Empire: Black Americans and Anticolonialism, 1937–1957*. Cornell University Press, 1997.

Wagoner, Jennings L., Jr., and Christine Coalwell McDonald. "Mr. Jefferson's Academy: An Educational Interpretation." In *Thomas Jefferson's Military Academy: Founding West Point*, edited by Robert M. S. McDonald, 118–53. University of Virginia Press, 2004.

Walker, David. *Appeal to the Coloured Citizens of the World*. Boston, 1829.

Walker, Francis A. "Immigration and Degradation." *The Forum* 11 (1891): 634–44.

Wang, Y. C. *Chinese Intellectuals and the West, 1872–1949*. University of North Carolina Press, 1966.

Warren, Wendy. *New England Bound: Slavery and Colonization in Early America*. W. W. Norton, 2016.

Washington, Booker T. "Address at the Opening of the Atlanta Exposition." September 18, 1895.
Weaver, Warren, Jr. "Theater Integration is Gained but Students Face Prosecution." *New York Times*, February 23, 1963.
Wesleyan University. *Alumni Record of Wesleyan University, Middletown, Conn.* 3rd ed. Press of the Case, Lockwood & Brainard Company, 1883.
The White House. "Additional Measures to Combat Anti-Semitism." January 29, 2025. whitehouse.gov.
Wilder, Craig Steven. *Ebony and Ivy: Race, Slavery, and the Troubled History of America's Universities*. Bloomsbury Press, 2013.
William & Mary. "History and Tradition." Accessed September 3, 2025.
William & Mary. "The Lemon Project." Accessed September 3, 2025.
Williams, Jeffrey J. "The Post-Welfare State University." *American Literary History* 24, no. 1 (2012): 118–35.
Williams, Walter L. "Ethnic Relations of African Students in the United States with Black Americans, 1870–1900." *The Journal of Negro History* 65, no. 3 (Summer 1980): 228–49.
Wilson, Woodrow. "Gov. Wilson Addresses Two Big Audiences: New Jersey Candidate Gets Warm Reception from Milwaukee People." News report, March 24, 1912. In *The Papers of Woodrow Wilson*, edited by Arthur S. Link, 24:252–54. Princeton University Press, 1977.
Wilson, Woodrow. "The Reconstruction of the Southern States." *Atlantic Monthly* (January 1901): 1–15.
Wolfe, Patrick. "Settler Colonialism and the Elimination of the Native." *Journal of Genocide Research* 8, no. 4 (2006).
Wolfe, Patrick. *Settler Colonialism and the Transformation of Anthropology*. Cassell, 1999.
Wolfensberger, Don. "Woodrow Wilson, Congress and Anti-Immigrant Sentiment in America." Woodrow Wilson International Center for Scholars, 2007.
Wong, Kenneth K., and Anna C. Nicotera. "*Brown V. Board of Education* and the Coleman Report: Social Science Research and the Debate on Educational Equality." *Peabody Journal of Education* 79, no. 2 (2004): 122–35.
*Wong Wing v. United States*. 163 US 228 (1896).
Worthy, Edmund H. "Yung Wing in America." *Pacific Historical Review* 34, no. 3 (August 1965): 265–87.
Wright, Bobby. "For the Children of Infidels?: American Indians Education in the Colonial Colleges." *American Indian Culture and Research Journal* 12, no. 3 (1988): 73–92.
Wright, Bobby. "The Untameable Savage Spirit: American Indians in Colonial Colleges." *The Review of Higher Education* 14, no. 4 (1991): 429–52.
Wu, Shellen Xiao. *Birth of the Geopolitical Age: Global Frontiers and the Making of Modern China*. Stanford University Press, 2023.

Wu, Ting-Fang. "Mutual Helpfulness Between China and the United States." *North American Review* 171, no. 524 (July 1900): 1–14.

Xi, Lian. "Returning to the Middle Kingdom: Yung Wing and the Recalled Students of the Chinese Educational Mission to the United States." *Modern Asian Studies* 49, no. 1 (2015): 150–76. https://doi.org/10.1017/s0026749x12000911.

Xu, Tian Atlas. "Immigration Attorneys and Chinese Exclusion Law Enforcement: The Case of San Francisco, 1882–1930." *Journal of American Ethnic History* 41, no. 1 (Fall 2021): 5–41.

Ye, Weili. *Seeking Modernity in China's Name: Chinese Students in the United States, 1900–1927*. Stanford University Press, 2001.

Yellin, Eric S. "The (White) Search for (Black) Order: The Phelps-Stokes Fund's First Twenty Years, 1911–1931." *The Historian* 65, no. 2 (2002): 319–52.

Zarrow, Peter. "Liang Qichao and the Conceptualization of 'Race' in Late Qing China." *Bulletin of the Institute of Modern History, Academia Sinica* 52 (June 2006): 113–63..

Zeng, Guofan, and Li Hongzhang. "Memorial to the Tongzhi Emperor, September 3, 1871 (nineteenth day of the 7th moon, the 10th year of Tongzhi)." In *Chouban yiwu shimo* (A Complete Account of the Management of Barbarian Affairs), *Tongzhi juan* (The Volume for the Reign of the Tongzhi Emperor), edited by Wen Qing et al. Shanghai guji chubanshe, 2008.

Zhu, Ming M. "The Page Act of 1875: In the Name of Morality." *SSRN Electronic Journal* (2010).

# Index

Note: Locators in *italics* indicate figures.

Abigail Boggs is Assistant Professor of Sociology and Education Studies and affiliated faculty in Feminist, Gender, and Sexuality Studies at Wesleyan University. Her writing has appeared in *American Quarterly*, *Feminist Studies*, *The Journal of Academic Freedom*, and other venues, and explores race, migration, higher education, and the politics of knowledge.

www.ingramcontent.com/pod-product-compliance
Lightning Source LLC
LaVergne TN
LVHW101716040926
847296LV00027B/173
* 9 7 8 1 5 3 1 5 1 4 5 6 3 *

DEGREES OF EMPIRE